Control of Canine Genetic Diseases

Control of Canine Genetic Diseases

George A. Padgett, DVM

Professor of Pathology

Michigan State University

Howell Book House

New York

Howell Book House
Published by Wiley Publishing, Inc., New York, NY

For general information on our other products and services, please contact our Customer Care Department within the U.S. at 800-762-2974, outside the U.S. at 317-572-3993 or fax 317-572-4002.

Wiley also publishes its books in a variety of electronic formats. Some content that appears in print may not be available in electronic books.

Cataloging-in-Publication Data is available upon request from the Library of Congress.
ISBN: 0-87605-004-6

Manufactured in the United States of America
5 4 3

Book design: A&D Howell Design
Cover design: Paul Costello

Table of Contents

The Author

Dr. George A. Padgett received his B.S. in 1959 and both his M.S. and D.V.M. degrees in 1961, all from Michigan State University. He went on to complete four years of postdoctoral work at Washington State University and spent a year as a guest investigator at Rockefeller University in New York City. He was on the faculty at Washington State University from 1965 to 1977 and on the faculty in Veterinary Pathology at Michigan State University from 1977 to the present.

Dr. Padgett has published more than 200 scientific papers and about the same number of papers in various lay publications. He has been the principal investigator or co-investigator on $15 million worth of research, training and construction grants funded by the National Institutes of Health, among other well-known organizations. Widely known in the dog fancy, he has presented seminars for ninety-three national breed clubs in the United States and Canada; he has also been a speaker on canine genetic diseases and for more than 100 other regional specialty and all-breed dog clubs.

He has been the principal author or co-author of several definitive publications that have established the mode of inheritance for thirty-two canine genetic diseases.

In 1997, Dr. Padgett was the recipient of the Eukanuba Canine Health Award for the best article on canine health as determined by the Dog Writers Association of America.

His major research interest is the subject of this book: the control of canine genetic diseases.

Dedication

To:
Debra Huggler, Kelly Watson, Patricia Thomas, the late Charlene Wellman, and Rebecca Ammon, all of whom helped me with the footwork or proofing of this book.

The ladies in the word processing center of the Veterinary Clinic, Kathy Winsky, Karen Schiffer, Martha Devlin, and Toni Tenlen, who produced this manuscript, especially Kathy, whose expertise accounted for most of the wonderful pedigrees in this book. They not only typed the book, they kept my grammar and sentence structure reasonably functional throughout the process.

My very special thanks to Kyle Walsh and her son Joshua, who turned the work into fun and without whose help I may not have completed the book in a timely fashion.

CHAPTER 1

Introduction

Genetic diseases in dogs have been with us for a long time. In fact, they probably started when dogs evolved many millennia ago. Because dogs are biologic mechanisms, as are people and all other living things, they are subject to mutations. As a general rule, mutations are negative; that is, they tend to alter some characteristics of the dog that make the animal less able to weather variations in the environment. Some mutations occur in various tissues of the body but do not involve the reproductive cells. We call these *somatic mutations.* They may do harm to the body—for instance, cause a cancer to develop—but are not passed to the next generation. We will not concern ourselves with mutations of this type.

In this book, we will concern ourselves with those traits that are passed to the offspring via the *gametes*—the sperm and the ovum. These are the traits that are a boon to the breeder if they are desirable and the bane of the breeder if they are detrimental. While in general, mutations are harmful, they are clearly not all harmful. Some mutations, we select for. While we do not know for certain what type of coat the original dog had, we now know there are many variations available genetically, such as wavy, curly, wiry, long, short and even no coat, as we see in the Chinese Crested (desirable) and in bald Beagles (undesirable). Some of these coat variations we use as a basis for a breed, such as German Wirehaired Pointers or Curly-Coated Retrievers, although they are not the only basis for these breeds. No matter what we think about coats in general, we know the original dogs could not have had all these variations. So over the years, mutations occurred in the coat genes causing the variations that we see. Breeders then selected for coat types they liked and stabilized them by inbreeding to form the more or less uniform coats we see on each breed today. The same things happened with eye color, ear type, coat color, height, weight and all the other characteristics that allow us to distinguish one breed from another and that distinguish each breed from the original dog, however the original dog may have looked. In other words, these are collections of beneficial mutations that breeders put together and stabilized to form the 400 or 500 distinct breeds known in the world today.

A given mutation may be highly prized in one breed and universally considered a horror in the next. Take, for example, the screw-tailed breeds like the Bulldog or the Boston Terrier. The screw tail is caused by an alteration in the vertebral body of the tail vertebra called *hemivertebra* that allows the tail to twist, and it is desirable in these instances. If a dog of one of these breeds had a straight tail, it would probably be laughed out of the show ring. On the other hand, if a dog of a straight-tailed breed like a Pointer or a Dachshund had a crook in its tail (and it didn't get stepped on or slammed in a screen door), it would most likely be due to the same trait—hemivertebra. In this case, the kinked tail is frowned upon but is really no detriment to the well-being of the dog; however, it has the potential to wreak havoc in the show ring. If the same trait, hemivertebra, occurs in the cervical, thoracic or lumbar spine, it can cause serious harm to the dog and may result in severe pain or posterior paralysis and may be severe enough to require euthanasia of the affected animal. The same trait can be good, so-so, or bad, depending on the breed and the circumstances. In each case, it is genetic, so how we view a trait is very important when we make a decision as to whether or not we are going to concern ourselves about it. This will be a thesis throughout this text; as you will see, you will have to make decisions about what to work on and what to put aside, at least for the moment.

The thrust of this book is the control of canine genetic diseases by breeders and breed clubs. But one of the first things a breeder asks when confronted with a defect that apparently appears suddenly among the progeny they produce is "Is this disorder genetic?"

Sometimes it is easy to tell whether a condition is genetic, but at other times, especially if there are only one or two cases, it is very difficult to determine whether it is or not, and in the final analysis, you may not be able to state with certainty that a trait is genetic in origin.

For traits that repeatedly occur within a breed, the first question to ask is "Is it familial?" While there are many situations in which a disorder occurs in multiple members of a litter, in most instances, the disorder will not recur in spaced litters unless it is genetic. Genetic traits must follow family lines, and they do occur in multiple, widely-spaced litters.

So if a defect occurs among the dogs in your kennel or in your breeding line, you must be sure the diagnosis is accurate. If it is, there are questions you can ask to determine whether a trait is likely to be inherited

a. In your breed

b. In other breeds

c. In other species

If the defect is inherited in dogs or in other species, then the chances that it is inherited in the affected dog(s) in your kennel are good. There are, of course, *phenocopies*—traits that are known to be genetic, but that can also be produced by something in the environment—that tend to confuse the situation. Cleft palate, a defect that occurs in nearly all breeds of dogs, is an example of a trait in which phenocopies occur. There are twenty-two compounds known to cause cleft palate in dogs. One of these is vitamin A. However, for vitamin A to cause cleft palate, a bitch would have to consume or receive 100,000 units of the vitamin on days 18 through 21 of her pregnancy (the critical period for cleft palate in dogs). That means the bitch would have to have access to the full-strength vitamin A additive or eat a couple of hundred pounds of dog food on days 18 to 21 of pregnancy. Neither of these things is likely to occur in the normal course of events. Other examples are the anti-inflammatory drugs like prednisone or prednisolone. If these drugs are given on days 18 through 21 or are carried over in the body from a slightly earlier treatment, they can cause cleft palate. The point here is that these compounds are not generally available in the environment. They have to be prescribed and given *exogenously* to the bitch. She cannot just pick them up on the street. The end result is that most cleft palates in dogs are inherited, despite the fact that phenocopies are known to occur.

My view is that a trait that is known to be inherited in your breed, in other breeds or in other species should be considered to be inherited in your dog unless proven otherwise. Ask yourself whether the mode of inheritance of the trait is known

a. In your breed
b. In other breeds
c. In other species

If the mode of inheritance of a trait that occurs in your kennel or line is known in your breed, your problem is straightforward. You may not like this simple fact, but if you follow the principles in this book, you can control the trait.

If the mode of inheritance of a trait is not known in your breed but is known in another breed, it is less straightforward. For the most part, the mode of inheritance of a trait in one breed is likely to be the same in another breed, even though there are good examples where that is not true. It is still the most reasonable course to follow in attempting to adjust to the situation. The best, of course, is to urge your breed club to determine the mode of inheritance of the trait in your breed.

If the mode of inheritance in dogs is not known, but it is known in other species, you are left even more uncertain of the way in which to proceed. Nevertheless, the mode of inheritance for a given trait is most often the same even between species. Here it is even more important that a breed club play a role in generating accurate information about the trait in dogs in general and in their breed in particular.

The most difficult situation to encounter is when a trait is not known to be inherited in any species. Even so, the first thing to do is the same as for a trait that is known to be inherited: MAKE SURE THE DIAGNOSIS IS ACCURATE.

If the diagnosis is accurate, the following factors must be considered:

1. Is it due to trauma?
2. Is it due to infection?
3. Is it due to diet?
4. Is it due to a teratogen?
5. Is it due to a toxin?
6. Is it due to a birth injury?
7. Is it due to a chromosomal aberration?

If you can prove that any these etiologies caused the trait, you are home free, because you do not have to consider the trait in regard to your breeding program, although you may very well have to worry about it in regard to kennel management.

When you cannot prove that any of the above etiologies caused the trait, problems begin to arise. Here is where a veterinarian's "famous" advice to breeders comes into play. "Don't worry about it; outcross, and even if it is genetic, it will go away." It is this "famous" advice that has messed up breeds of dogs from time immemorial. Instead of controlling a trait when there are one or two dogs or one or two families involved, we outcross the dogs and spread the trait throughout the breed. Many breed clubs also play a role here. They have guidelines, rules, suggestions or advice for their members that say you don't have to worry about a trait being genetic unless the dog or bitch produces at least two or three cases. In this situation, even the proverbial village idiot knows what to do—outcross the dogs. The breed club often gives this advice even if a trait is known to be genetic in other breeds, and of course, you end up spreading the disease. If the trait is new or very rare in a breed (one case per 5,000 dogs) and you outcross, you may breed that dog or bitch until their ears fall off, and they will never produce another case, because there are very few or no carriers of the trait in the general population of the breed. But you can be sure that you are spreading the gene(s) for the trait throughout the breed.

It is this "famous" advice that is currently causing breeders and owners of purebred dogs to spend $500 million annually to diagnose and correct genetic diseases in their breeds.

For situations in which you do not know the cause of a trait, and that trait has a severe detrimental effect on an animal, such as pain or permanent disability, you should determine that the trait is not genetic before you continue to mate dogs that produce it. Further, you should determine the cause of a trait if it is likely to cause severe monetary distress to any person who buys an affected puppy. This seems to me to be only good sense as well as fair play.

You should determine whether or not a severe trait is genetic before you proceed to spread it throughout a breed. This is discussed more fully in Chapter 8, "Test-Mating," but succinctly, you repeat the mating or, if possible, breed the affected dog back to the appropriate parent to determine whether the trait is genetic.

When all is said and done, if you want to find out whether a trait is genetic, you can. In my opinion, you should.

My intention is to make this a straightforward text, so we will not get into deep discussions about Mendel or the Lyon Hypothesis or intricate breeding schemes. Many who read this text will say that the author didn't discuss this or he didn't discuss that. They will clearly point out all the exceptions to the rule, and there will be some, I can assure you. To cover every contingency for every disease and to meet everyone's objections, I would need a book of several thousand pages, if not an encyclopedia, and I fear my hand would fall off before I was done compiling such a weighty tome.

For example, *mitochondrial* inheritance is important, but to my knowledge, it has not been clearly documented in any important way in dogs. Gene frequencies play a major role in the control of genetic disease, but with the exception of four breeds for which some data is available (Cairn and Scottish Terriers, Bichons Frises, and Newfoundlands), these frequencies are not well-established in dogs. Of equal importance are mutation rates, and these may well plague us even when DNA analysis allows us to identify specific genes in the various breeds. Since little information is available on these points, they will not be emphasized in this book.

My goal is to help prevent serious genetic diseases in dogs, both in breeds and in kennels. If you learn the material presented here, follow the guidelines, and apply this information to your breed or your kennel, you will reduce the frequency of disease, and it will not take you twenty-five years to do it.

You need three things to accomplish this task: knowledge, information, and honesty. All three are within your control.

CHAPTER 2

Background

Genetic disease in purebred dogs—what a fine state of affairs! *Time* magazine, the *Atlantic Monthly*, puppy buyers, lawyers, the daily papers, my co-owners and—especially, it seems—anyone I ever sold a show dog to are all yelling at me, wanting to sue me or won't even talk to me, because one of my dogs either developed or produced a genetic disease. "Why am I to blame?" asks the harried breeder. "All I wanted to do was produce good show dogs [or hunting, or obedience or guard dogs . . .]. My gosh, if Mary [or Alice, or John or Tom] had told me about this when I bought my bitch, I wouldn't be in all this trouble. It's not my fault. How did I know that puppy was going to develop progressive retinal atrophy [PRA, a progressive, inexorably blinding disease in many dog breeds]?"

How did it happen? Why is it like this?

The answer to both questions is easy, and it is the same answer in both cases. It happened and is like this because, over the years, almost no one has tried to do anything to control genetic disease in dogs. As a matter of fact, most of the things that they did inadvertently, not (I hope) intentionally, tended to foster genetic disease. There were no guidelines concerning the control of genetic disease, and for that matter, there are still no guidelines for that purpose. What is a breeder to do? What *should* a breeder do? What is ethical in regard to genetic disease? How long should a breeder be held liable if one of their dogs develops a genetic disease? These are all questions that need answers, and almost no one has tried to answer them. Not the American Kennel Club, not the parent breed clubs, not veterinarians and, for the most part, not the breeders themselves. Hopefully, when you have finished this book, you will have developed a philosophy that will allow you to answer these questions at least for yourself.

National breed clubs, the parent clubs, are the groups one would most naturally think would be most concerned about genetic disease in their dogs. They are the ones that control the standards for each breed, they hold the Specialty shows and matches and virtually all have voting rights with AKC. All of them somewhere in their constitution or bylaws or other such documents say words to the effect that at least one of their goals "is to improve the breed and bring its natural qualities to perfection." To me, that means you make every effort to produce healthy, winning dogs. Not just healthy dogs and not just winners—they must fit together *healthy, winning* dogs.

When you have finished this book, if you apply its principles, you should be able to do exactly that and so should your breed club.

National breed clubs just sort of grew up. They are collections of people who own the same breed. They hold shows to compare their dogs. If you attend a national Specialty, you will usually find a hospitality room where you can get a bite to eat and a drink and most especially run into friends from far-flung places, people you haven't seen for two or three years. You talk about the winners of yesterday, the new top stud and the Sweepstakes coming up on Saturday. Does my dog have a chance? Of course, you think so or you wouldn't be there. The Club holds a dinner honoring the people who have contributed to the breed and the winning dogs. An auction may be held to gather money for a charitable cause or to benefit some aspect of the breed. At some time during the Specialty, the governing board will meet to discuss and handle problems and to plan the next show. That's the way they are, that's the way they have always been. It's the fun of dogs, the sport of dogs, it's why people are in the show game. They enjoy it, and they *should* enjoy it. We shouldn't change it.

Historically, control of genetic disease was never part of the responsibilities of a breed club, so the vast majority has never done anything about genetic disease. About half the Specialty clubs have a genetic or health or breed improvement committee, but most of these committees haven't done a heck of a lot. About half of them have an education committee or its equivalent, and many of these committees plan and hold seminars. Most of the seminars are on movement or breeding a winning dog, or for judges to better understand conformation, or to achieve more effective training. A few are on behavior, and fewer yet are on genetic disease and its control.

If we wish to do anything about the control of genetic diseases on a breed-wide basis, we have to add a dimension to the role of breed clubs. We should not throw away what the clubs have been doing, and we shouldn't change what they are doing, at least not very much, because that's the fun of dogs. That's why we are breeders. That's why we travel tremendous distances—sometimes clear across the country to attend a Specialty show. But clubs can accept additional responsibilities if they sincerely wish to improve their breed and bring it to its greatest possible perfection.

Some of the things a breed club should do to enhance the ability of club members and other breeders to control genetic disease follow:

1. They should generate a list of genetic defects occurring in their breed by surveying members and owners. This list should be made available to members and breeders and the mode of inheritance of each trait should be listed if it is known.

2. They should form committees to assess the impact of each trait on the breed.

3. They should advocate the registration of dogs and bitches affected with genetic defects and those known to carry genes for these traits (dogs and bitches that produced the trait or that are offspring of affected dogs) in an open registry.

4. They should advocate the registration of dogs and bitches known to be free of the genes for various undesirable traits.
5. They should develop lists of dogs known to be affected with or that carry genes for a given trait that are available for test matings, and this list should be made freely available to breeders and members.
6. They should determine which defects should be attacked on a breed-wide basis.
7. They should develop a brochure discussing the diseases that occur in their breed, giving clinical signs, methods of diagnosis—including special equipment required, age of onset, mode of inheritance and potential treatments—and prognosis. This brochure should be made readily available to every club member, breeder and owner of dogs of the breed.
8. They should develop a brochure discussing the rationale of the various systems that can be used to control disease and how to handle carriers and potential carriers of the various traits.
9. They should strongly support those breeders and owners with the honesty, courage and foresight to openly register dogs affected with genetic disease, because there is no hope for control without knowledge. They should clearly state that the ethical course is to openly discuss dogs with defects or those that produce defects when selling a show dog, breeding prospect or stud service. All the peer pressure at their command should be used to support open registration if their goal as a breed club is to bring their dogs as close to perfection as possible as stated in the club's constitution.

A breeder generally becomes aware of genetic disease when one or more of the offspring that he/she produces develops a defect. Don't get me wrong—these breeders have heard of genetic disease before, but it didn't affect them or their dogs. They become truly aware of the situation when they, themselves, are in the middle of the soup. The defect may require the bitch to have a cesarean section (C-section) if it is a trait like anasarca (water puppies). The breeder may see the defect at or near birth—for example, a cleft palate. The breeder may see it as the puppy develops, such as a delay in or failure of the fontanelle to close or failure of one or both testicles to descend (monorchidism or cryptorchidism). More distressing are those traits that develop after the puppies are sold, such as craniomandibular osteopathy (CMO), Legg-Perthes, elbow dysplasia, or hip dysplasia. Now more people are involved, often children, veterinarians are involved, money is involved, people are angry, and sometimes lawsuits occur. Everybody is upset, including and probably most often the breeder, especially a new breeder. Breeders, particularly new breeders, ask themselves, "My goodness, how did that happen?" or "I'm going to find out about this." They call or rush over to the person they bought their bitch from and say, "One of my puppies developed CMO. Did you know about this?" That breeder promptly replies, "I have been breeding this line for 3,277 years and 6 months, and I have never seen

CMO! Sure I have heard about it. I think Sally's dog produced it, but they are out in California. "It has to be the stud!" Well, folks, you are now right smack in the middle of purebred dog breeding. Some people drop out of breeding at this point, since they are producing diseases they don't want to produce and don't know what to do about it. Their visions of producing their own Westminster winner are replaced by the harsh realities of genetics.

Some people persist and gradually work their way into the circle of breeders who kind of know what's going on in the breed. They get in on the gossip about whose dog produced what. Almost no one talks openly about genetic disease in purebred dogs. "Horrors!! What are you doing?? You are a bad person—unethical. I'm going to tell Mary you said that." Not openly, but in whispers. It's like when your seventeen-year-old daughter becomes pregnant and there's no husband in sight or when your husband gets thrown in the slammer for drunk driving. Nobody talks about it . . . openly! But everybody in the world gossips about it. Everybody! "Listen, don't tell anybody else, but DID YOU KNOW JOHN'S DOG PRODUCED . . . . *Shhh.*" That's the way it is right now. That's why genetic disease is common in purebred dogs; almost nobody talks about it openly.

Since nobody talks about genetic disease, it is difficult to get a reasonable idea of how much disease is around—how many dogs are involved. If we go to a dog show, we may see anywhere from a few hundred to several thousand dogs, and all of them are normal, pretty good specimens of their respective breeds. Only rarely do we see a dog with a defect, and these are usually brought to the show to help pad the point rating. We hear about all the dogs with *Orthopedic Foundation for Animals* (OFA) numbers or *Canine Eye Registration Foundation* (CERF) numbers, and all are normal. Nobody talks about dogs with defects. You don't see dogs with defects. It's not hard to pick up the idea that nearly all dogs are normal. Oh sure, there are a few with problems, but that's to be expected. The reality is that there are lots of dogs with genetic diseases of one kind or another, not all serious. But these are left at home, are sold or placed in pet homes or have been put down. You don't see them, and you don't hear about them. If you don't see that there is a problem or you don't know there is a problem, it is easy to think that there is not a problem. Under those circumstances, it is deceptively easy to think that all the talk about genetic diseases is just that—talk.

So what evidence is there that shows that genetic disease is a problem in purebred dogs? There is the general evidence—statements by veterinarians, breeders and purchasers of purebreds that genetic disease is common in their experience. About 500 genetic diseases have been reported in purebred dogs, and if our diagnostics were better, there would probably be more. Data from the OFA indicates that at least sixty breeds have a frequency of *hip dysplasia* (HD), ranging from 1 percent to 49 percent, and that all breeds from which they have received 100 radiographs have had dogs with this disease. Hip dysplasia has been reported in more than 170 breeds. CERF reports more than 119 breeds with *progressive retinal atrophy* (PRA), some with a frequency as high as 5 percent to 10 percent, and a similar number of breeds are reported to have cataracts, most of which are genetic in origin.

But the best information comes from dog clubs and surveys they have conducted. WATCH, a program started by several West Highland White Terrier breeders and endorsed by the national club surveyed members, breeders and owners of Westies to determine the *incidence* (the number of new cases occurring annually) of *craniomandibular osteopathy* (CMO), Legg-Perthes disease, and HD. They found the incidence to be 1.13 percent, 1.93 percent, and 0.56 percent, respectively. These three diseases alone account for 3.62 percent of all Westies produced annually, and we know there are thirty-five genetic diseases reported in this breed. The Cairn Terrier Club of America, the Bichon Frise Club of America, the Scottish Terrier Club of America and the Newfoundland Club of America have all had the courage to survey their breeders, members and owners in order to determine the frequency of genetic disease in their breeds. In Cairns, 40.3 percent; in Bichons, 29.8 percent; in Scotties, 33.5 percent; and in Newfies, 66.5 percent of the dogs reported had defects of one kind or another—again, not all serious problems. Traits such as undershot or overshot bites, umbilical and inguinal hernias, eye- and coat-color defects, tail abnormalities and mono- or cryptorchidism were included because they are genetic in origin, not because they harm the dog. From this data, we can calculate that each Cairn carries 5.03, each Newfie 4.52, each Scottie 4.7 and each Bichon 4.63 defective genes per dog. We know from the veterinary literature and these surveys that Newfoundlands have 46, Cairns have 52, Scotties have 58 and Bichons have 47 individual defects. About two-thirds of the Newfies and one-third of the Cairns, Scotties and Bichons have a defect, and by anyone's criteria, that is a serious problem. I would wager a large amount of money that this is not a unique situation in these four breeds. Instead, I believe it is a reflection of what is happening in most, if not all, purebred dog breeds.

Genetic disease is common in purebred dogs. If I, as a breeder, take you at your word and accept the fact that the great majority of, if not all, dogs carry four or five defective genes, what on earth can I do? That means that every time I sell or buy a dog, carriers become involved. Every time I pick a stud, I must accept as truth that he carries genes for four or five defects. Every time you buy, sell or breed a dog, you are involved with four or five defective genes, and of course, that is why genetic disease is common.

If most dogs carried no defective genes or only one defective gene, genetic disease would not be common. You could avoid it with ease. The problem in dogs that compounds the situation is that we also have *matadors*. Matadors are dogs that produce large numbers, perhaps hundreds or even thousands of offspring. These dogs spread their genes over an entire breed so that not only the number of defective genes carried is high (although no higher than in people), but the frequency of genes for a given set of traits is high (those traits carried by the matadors). As a result, with many traits in dogs (unlike in people), the risk of producing a given defect is just as high with an outcross as with inbreeding. (This point is discussed in depth later in this book.)

Take as an example Portuguese Water Dogs: between 1 percent and 4 percent of this breed is affected with PRA, a recessive trait. If we use the Hardy-Weinberg law on these numbers, we find that between 18 percent and 45 percent of all Porties carry this gene. So if a Portuguese Water Dog breeder outcrosses in about every two to five matings, this gene will emerge. If a dog also carries the gene for PRA, the breeder will produce dogs that go blind at two to five years of age with every third outcross on the average. The risk of producing a defective puppy due to a single defective gene with severe inbreeding (mother to son, father to daughter, brother to sister) is 12.5 percent per puppy. So, you would produce a defective puppy due to any one gene one time in eight on the average. In Portuguese Water Dogs, it is about as risky to outcross as it is to inbreed as far as PRA is concerned.

All right, if that is the situation regarding probable mathmatical incidence, let's say you are correct about it. What can I do about this as a breeder? To answer that question, of course, is why I am writing this book. But I want to briefly outline what I believe are the obligations of a breeder, as well as what you can do so you will understand what is required:

1. **Set goals for your dogs.** What do you want the dogs to do? This may be winning in conformation or Obedience Trials, hunting or working or just producing quality pets. What the goal is doesn't matter as much as whether you know what the goal is.

   I assume since you are reading this book that one of your goals is to produce healthy dogs and, more important, healthy, winning dogs. In order to accomplish your goal, you need to understand your breed, its temperament, its conformation, its working abilities and every other particular. This book will not and can not teach you that, because I don't know your breed and that is not the intent of this book. This involves the skill of the breeder. It is why breeding winning dogs is an art, not a science. Breeding at this stage involves the whole dog, 100,000 genes, and it is why you pick the whole dog first—because breeding for disease control only involves a few genes.

2. **Know which disorders occur in the dogs in your line.** If you don't know what diseases you have, how can you prevent them? This means you have to follow up on your puppies. You *need* to know what diseases develop in your puppies, so *you* must take the initiative to find out. You may be surprised to learn how many people appreciate your concern about the welfare of the puppies you place.

3. **Be honest about which disorders occur in your line.** You need to register affected dogs and proven carriers in an open registry. This is the hardest part for breeders: talking openly and letting people know that they have a dog that is affected with, or has produced one or more puppies with, a defect. It is essential that you know where disease occurs if you want to do anything about it, both for your own kennel and for the breed as a whole.

   Everyone must remember, especially breeders, that all dogs carry, on the average, four or five defective genes. So the question is not whether your dog carries a defect; it does—we know that. The important point is what defect it carries. If people tell you their dogs have never produced a defect, their dogs have probably produced only one litter, they don't follow up on their puppies or, what is most likely the case, they are being less than truthful. These individuals either don't know their own dogs, or they do know them and are prevaricating. In either case, stay away from them because they can not or will not provide the information you need to produce healthy, winning dogs.

4. **Develop a *hierarchy of disagreeability* for the various genetic diseases that occur in the breed as a whole and for those that occur in your own kennel.** We will spend a chapter on this subject later in the book. Briefly, developing a hierarchy means essentially evaluating the severity of various diseases and their impact on the dog itself and the people that purchase it. This hierarchy lets you decide what to work on, what to prevent and try to eliminate and what to put aside and not worry about, at least for the moment.

   If you produce a cryptorchid puppy, one with a blue eye when it should have dark eyes or a crook in its tail, isn't that better for the puppy, and its new owner, than a puppy that goes blind with PRA or cataracts, is a dwarf or is crippled with elbow dysplasia? No one wants to produce a cryptorchid puppy; that's not your goal. But there is clearly a difference in the severity of traits and the impact of these disorders on the dog itself and anyone purchasing it. There is a hierarchy of disagreeability, and breeders and breed clubs must develop one for themselves if they want to put order and sanity into disease control.

The last topic we must cover regarding background are the forces that have molded breeder and breed-club attitudes about what makes a breedable dog or defines what a breedable dog is. This is the crux of the problem of genetic disease in purebred dogs. Unfortunately, a discussion of this topic requires either generalizations or 3,000 pages, and I prefer the former. When you generalize, there are always exceptions; everyone can spot them and everyone is willing to point them out. I hope they are as willing to accept the thesis I am trying to present, albeit with some reservations.

Tradition says that breedable dogs do not produce puppies with genetic defects. Therefore, we do not like to discuss defects that the great dogs—the matadors—produce. We don't like to discuss these traits, because it tends to tarnish our dogs' images, to take the luster off them, to render these great dogs something less, in our opinion, than we consider they really are. We may discuss these traits privately, but not openly.

This tradition is reinforced by the registries that have developed over the years. The early registries, the OFA and CERF, are closed registries, discussing only normal dogs or the "good" dogs. I think we should try to understand how this came about. The OFA and CERF are not, and have not been, inimical to the health of dogs. They assess the phenotype of the dogs they examine, the clinical health of the dogs.

At the time they started 25 or 30 years ago, we could not have had an open registry, because breeders would not have accepted it. Breeders were not ready to openly discuss genetic disease in dogs, and many are still not ready to take this step today. Neither OFA nor CERF state that their clinical examination makes a dog breedable, because neither evaluates the genotype of the dog.

No matter what these two organizations state, however, breeders have come to accept an OFA or CERF number as meaning that a dog is breedable. Unfortunately, this attitude has been boosted again by the recent addition of OFA and CERF numbers to the "official" AKC pedigree. So here we are again trying to breed dogs for disease control based on phenotype when we know that carriers both for single-gene and polygenic traits are phenotypically normal. There is a little sense to it with polygenic traits, because we know mass selection (breeding based on a normal phenotype alone) works, although it is very, very slow. There is no sense to it with any of the single-gene traits except the dominant ones.

Again, we are presented with the "only talk about the good dog" philosophy by the actions of both of our major disease registries as well as by the AKC, the major dog registry in this country. We know this doesn't work. You cannot name one eye disease in any breed of dog in the United States in which the frequency of the disease has been reduced as a result of CERF. With only two exceptions, the Portuguese Water Dog and the Bernese Mountain Dog, the reduction in the frequency of hip dysplasia (not a percent change in frequency) has been almost nil for all other breeds over the last 30 years. Breeders have spent 30 million dollars on OFA radiographs with little or no results, because we cannot progeny test based on the data available from this organization. When are we going to learn that we need to know about the affected dogs if we want to control disease?

Tradition says that breedable dogs are dogs that win in the show ring (or in field or working trials, the obedience ring or any competitive format). In fact, AKC suggests that determining breeding worth is the major purpose of showing dogs. The implication is that dogs are brought closer to perfection by selecting the individual that wins the most shows, the most prestigious shows, or both and mating your bitch or dog to that winner.

For the sake of brevity, let's talk about conformation and remember that what I am saying also applies to all other methods of measuring dogs competitively.

I have a hard time thinking of a person trying to breed dogs for conformation using parents that cannot win in the show ring. But I have an even harder time thinking of a person using the winner at Westminster for breeding if that dog has Springer rage or produces puppies that develop portocaval shunts or other serious problems and then claiming that they are bringing their dogs (and breed) to perfection. In my opinion, that's just plain dumb. No, it's not dumb, *it's stupid!*

The purpose of a show should be to evaluate dogs competitively, matching them against the best animals in the breed to evaluate their potential value as breeding stock, and to have fun—to take part in the sport of dogs with or without the goal of breeding the winners. Showing dogs should be in and of itself fun; being involved in competition should be enjoyable, and there shouldn't have to be any other goal.

Certainly, selecting breeding stock based on phenotype alone is no better, because it is done by means of the show ring rather than through a radiograph. The important points to consider when selecting a dog for breeding follow:

1. What the grandparents and parents produced
2. What the parents' littermates are like
3. What the dog's littermates are like
4. What the dog has produced in terms of offspring

There are far more important factors than looking at the phenotype of the dog, whether you are breeding for disease control or conformation. The conformation of the dog involved is important, of course, but it is just one parameter. It is more difficult to hide defects in conformation than it is to hide an incipient case of PRA, but breeders do try to hide them, sometimes successfully. They try to hide conformation defects by grooming and/or handling and, on occasion, by more nefarious means. But the message here is the same: Hide the defects if you can, certainly don't talk about them, and if someone spots the defect, throw a rock at them.

If we want to make any impact in controlling genetic disease in dogs, we must agree that an ethical approach is based on fairness, openness, and honesty. While traditions are important to us and should remain important, they should be changed if they conflict with the exercise of our ethics as dog breeders.

C H A P T E R 3

The Development of Pedigrees

A pedigree is the time-honored method we use to illustrate inheritance. There are two types of pedigrees. One shows the linear inheritance of an individual and is the typical pedigree we see with purebred animals. It starts with the individual in question and goes back through the ancestors, listing the immediate forebears of each generation. The other is the typical pedigree we see when a genetic analysis of a trait or a family is undertaken. It contains the individual in question (propositus) and goes back through the ancestors in much the same way, but it also shows most of, if not all, the individuals related to the propositus, not only his direct lineage. I discuss the typical pedigree given to a buyer by the breeder in Chapter 6, "The Interpretation and Use of Pedigrees to Determine the Genetic Status of Given Dogs," which focuses on the geneticist's family pedigree.

This will seem tedious and a pain to some people, especially if a complicated pedigree is involved, but remember that if you draw your initial pedigree leaving it free of markings for any specific trait, you only have to draw it once. From then on, you work with copies, and you can make as many copies as you like without damaging the original. As your breeding program continues, you simply add to the original pedigree. The purpose of drawing your pedigree is that it allows you to visualize the traits and how they are passed among the family members. It can be a major help in determining the most likely mode of inheritance of a trait. It will allow you to determine the risk that various individuals within the family have for carrying the genes for various traits. It will be especially helpful in allowing you to select those animals least likely to carry a trait as well as to visualize those animals that have been testmated for the various traits found in your line. You will find if you draw the pedigree for your own stock, you will use it often in analyzing the risk of disease among the animals you produce. Pedigrees of this nature are used extensively throughout this book.

The following are the traditional symbols used in constructing a pedigree. It is not essential that you use these symbols, but if you do not use them, your pedigree will not be readily understood by anyone else reading it.

Males are illustrated by squares (see Figure 3.1). If the square is empty or blank, as this one is, it means the animal is phenotypically normal for the trait or traits depicted in the pedigree.

Females are illustrated by circles (see Figure 3.2). As with the male, if the circle is blank or empty, it means the female is phenotypically normal for the trait or traits depicted in the pedigree.

Fig. 3.1 ***Fig. 3.2***

If you know that a dog belongs in a family, but you do not know the sex, it is illustrated by a diamond (see Figure 3.3).

If an animal is phenotypically affected with the trait depicted by the square, circle or diamond, the shape is completely filled in, usually in black (see Figure 3.4).

Fig. 3.3 ***Fig. 3.4***

If the symbol has a dot in the middle or is half filled in (the latter is used more commonly), it means the animal is heterozygous or, as it is more commonly called, a defined or proven carrier for the trait depicted (see Figure 3.5). Indication of the carrier state with a dot in the middle is often reserved for a female carrier of a sex-linked trait.

If the symbol has a line through it or a cross below it, this indicates that the animal is dead (see Figure 3.6). Some use the cross below the symbol to indicate a stillbirth or perinatal death (within the first 10 days of life). They use the symbol with the line through it to indicate death after 10 days of age. The line must extend through the symbol, or it will not be visible if the animal is affected with the trait depicted.

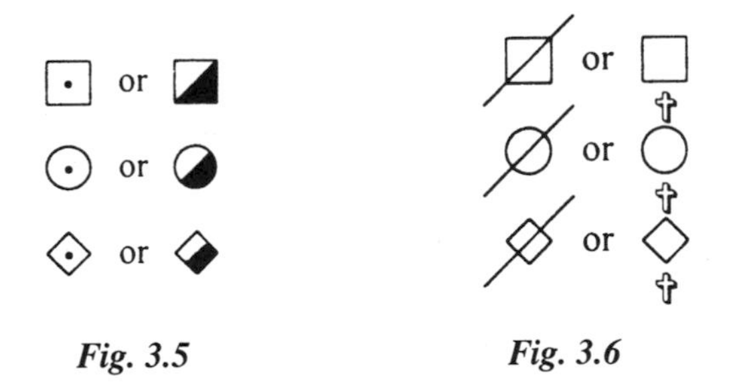

Fig. 3.5 ***Fig. 3.6***

A symbol with a question mark inside it indicates that you have no other knowledge or information about that dog, or it may indicate that the dog was not examined for the trait depicted in the pedigree (see Figure 3.7).

Fig. 3.7

A small, filled-in square in the corner of the symbol (or various combinations of this type of marking) means whatever you want it to mean and allows you to show multiple traits on the same pedigree (see Figure 3.8). All four corners could be used with various types of marks. If you want someone else to be able to read your pedigree, you must explain this type of marking on the pedigree.

If the symbol has a line under it or an arrow pointed at it, it means that this animal is the propositus (see Figure 3.9). Other names for the propositus are *index case* and *proband.* The propositus, index case, or proband is the first individual in the pedigree to be identified with or diagnosed with the disease depicted by the pedigree. In a research situation (where the pedigree is not already drawn), the pedigree is built up or built around this case.

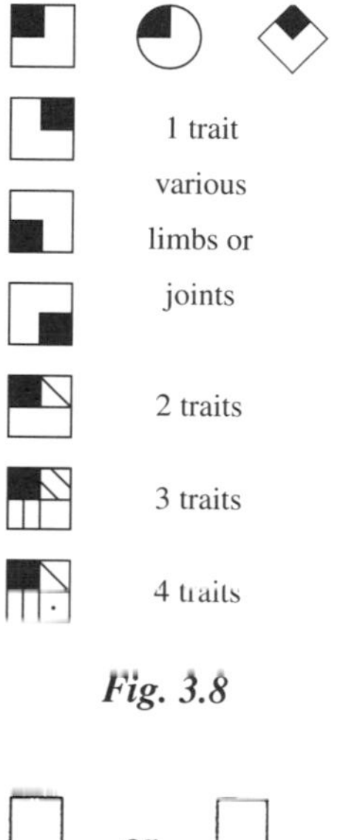

Fig. 3.8

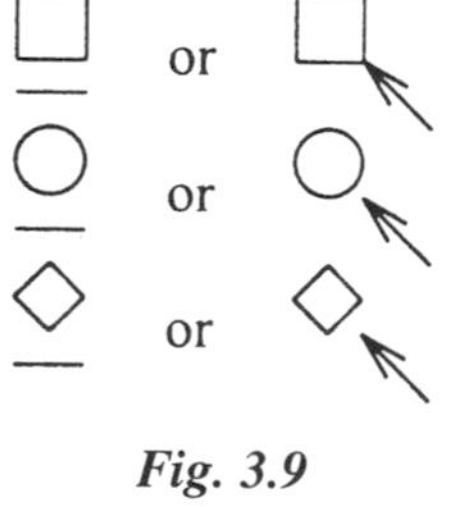

Fig. 3.9

A horizontal line indicates a mating (see Figure 3.10).

Figure 3.11 indicates a mating between a given dam and sire. The sire is generally placed on the right, and the dam on the left. In more complicated pedigrees (as are most for dogs), it may be more propitious to put the dam or sire in the middle or wherever it works out best to facilitate the next set of matings.

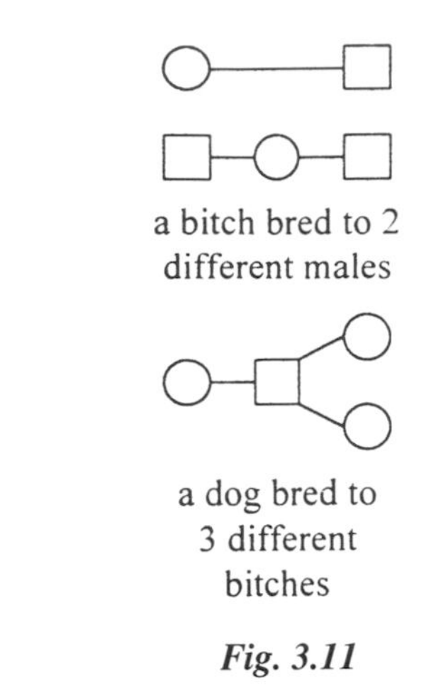

Fig. 3.10

Fig. 3.11

A vertical line indicates offspring (see Figure 3.12).

Figure 3.13 indicates a dam and sire with four offspring.

Figure 3.14 illustrates the method of numbering individual dogs in the pedigree. You may want to number only those individuals used for breeding or that are defined carriers or are affected with a specific trait.

Figure 3.15 illustrates the method of showing the birth year of the litter. This information is especially important with late-onset diseases.

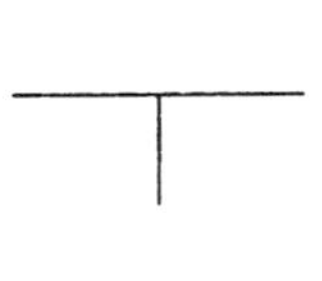

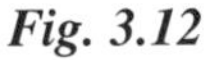

Fig. 3.12

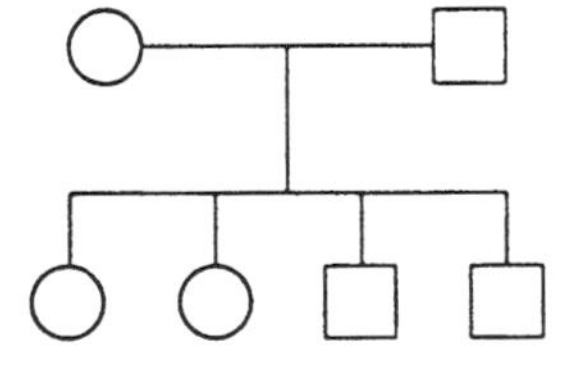

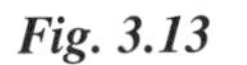

Fig. 3.13

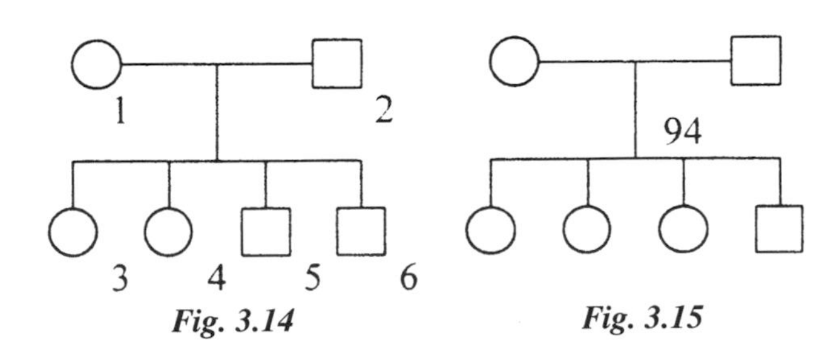

Fig. 3.14

Fig. 3.15

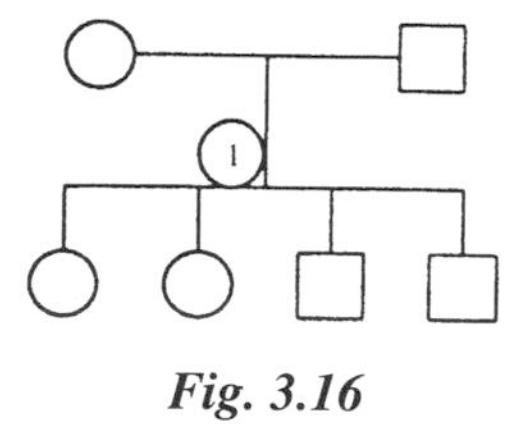

Fig. 3.16

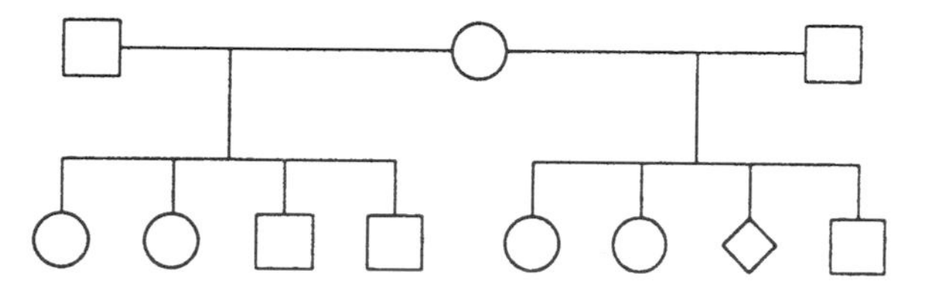

Fig. 3.17

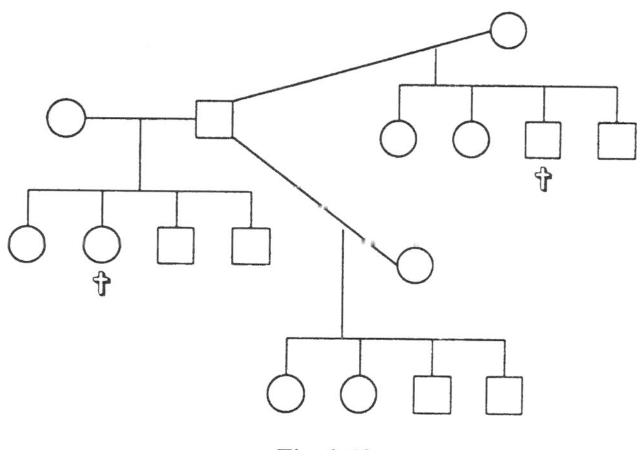

Fig. 3.18

The method of numbering litters may be useful in allowing you to relate the litter to other data you have (see Figure 3.16).

Figure 3.17 shows a dam bred to two different males, producing four offspring with each sire. The sex of one puppy is unknown.

Figure 3.18 shows a sire bred to three different females, producing four offspring with each dam. Two puppies were dead at or near birth.

Figure 3.19 shows a sire bred to nine females, with varying numbers of puppies in each litter. Four puppies have the trait depicted. Four bitches and the sire carry the gene for this simple recessive trait. Two males are shown as dead.

A loop indicates that you are skipping the line—that the lines do not intersect (see Figure 3.20).

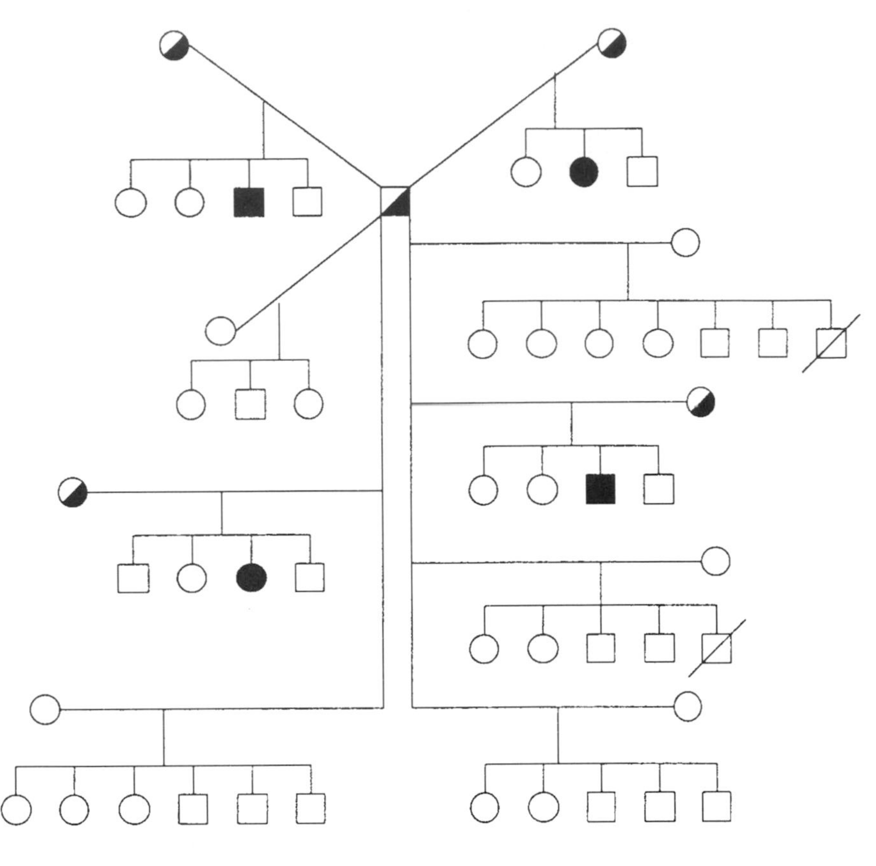

Fig. 3.19

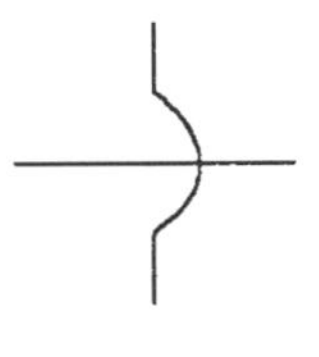

Fig. 3.20

Figure 3.21 shows a pedigree using the symbols described above. The written description of this family is more difficult to understand and visualize, even though it presents the same information. The trait depicted is most likely to be an autosomal recessive.

A sire (dog #2) was bred to two females. With the first dam (bitch #1), he produced a seven-puppy litter (litter #1, four males, three females) in 1990 that contained two affected offspring (one male, one female). This sire and dam are proven carriers of this trait. The daughter (bitch #4) was the propositus, developing the

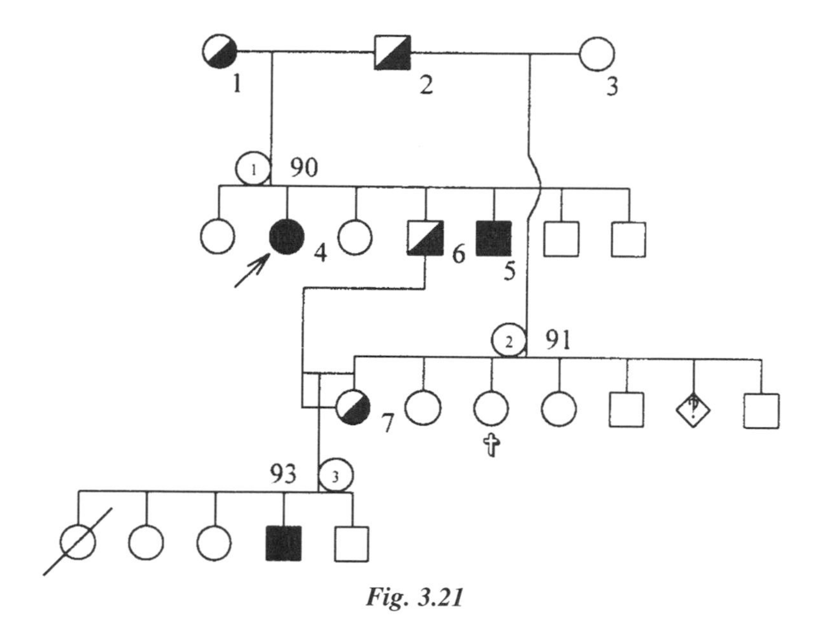

Fig. 3.21

disease at five months of age. Her brother (dog #5) developed the disease at ten months of age.

The second litter produced by sire #2 resulted from a mating to bitch #3 (litter #2). It also contained seven puppies (two male, four female, one sex unknown) born in 1991. One female puppy was dead at birth. Another puppy was sold at ten weeks of age, and the breeder forgot to record the sex. This puppy was not examined for the presence of this trait. The five remaining puppies were phenotypically normal for this trait at fourteen months of age.

Dog #6 was bred to bitch #7 (litter #3), producing five puppies (two males and three females) in 1993. One female in this litter died of undetermined cause at six months of age. There was one affected male in this litter, making his sire (#6) and dam (#7) proven carriers of this trait.

Placement of the various animals as you build a pedigree can make it easier to draw and to read. There is no specific place in which a given animal should be drawn in a pedigree, but if an animal is to be used in a subsequent mating, it should be placed in a convenient location. This helps keep the pedigree clean-looking and allows you to avoid crossing too many lines. You may want to make one or two rough drafts, moving the animals used in matings around to help you avoid putting too many matings in one area. You need to give plenty of space to sires that are used extensively in order to avoid crossing lines and so that you can add matings as they occur.

If your pedigree is too large or grows too large to fit on a reasonably sized sheet of paper, add a second sheet of paper, marking where the two pedigrees (sheets) join or attach to each other (see Figure 3.22).

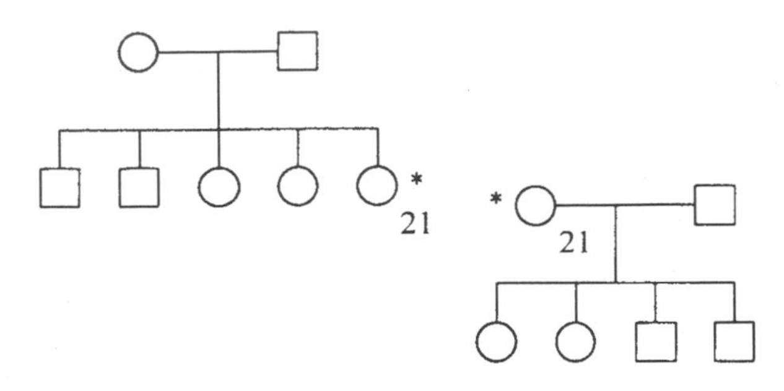

Fig. 3.22 **Indicates the pedigrees join or interlock through bitch #21.*

Questions on Chapter 3

1. Draw the following pedigree:

   A litter (litter #1) born in 1989 contained 5 puppies (2 females, 2 males, 1 sex unknown). All puppies were phenotypically normal. The parents were both phenotypically normal. The dam died in 1990.

2. Draw the following pedigree, numbering the significant dogs described:

   A litter of 4 Scottish Terriers (2 males, 2 females) was born in 1990 (litter #1). The parents were phenotypically normal. The litter contained 1 male (the propositus), which developed *craniomandibular osteopathy* (CMO) at 5 months of age. This trait is autosomal recessive, which means that both parents are proven carriers. The phenotypically normal male puppy was bred to an unrelated female in 1992, producing a litter of 3 puppies (litter #2, 2 females, 1 male). All 3 were phenotypically normal at 1 year of age.

3. Draw the following pedigree using all of the appropriate symbols:

   A Labrador male was bred to 9 different bitches, producing the following litters:

   #1 – 5 puppies (3 male, 2 female)

   #2 – 6 puppies (2 male, 4 female)

   #3 – 7 puppies (4 male, 3 female)

   #4 – 3 puppies (3 female)

   #5 – 7 puppies (5 male, 1 female, 1 sex unknown)

   #6 – 4 puppies (2 male, 2 female)

   #7 – 6 puppies (3 male, 3 female)

#8 – 1 puppy (1 male)

#9 – 8 puppies (4 male, 4 female)

The first 3 litters were produced in 1988. Litters #4 and #5 were produced in 1989, and the other 4 were produced in 1990. The bitch producing litter #2 was rebred in 1990 to the same stud (litter #10), producing a litter of 5 (3 males, 2 females). The bitch producing litter #7 was bred to an unrelated stud in 1992 (litter #11) and had a litter of 4 (2 males, 2 females). One of these male puppies was dead at birth. The bitch producing litter #1 was killed by an automobile in 1991 when she escaped from her leash. The original male was bred to an unrelated female in 1990 (litter #12), producing a litter of 5 (3 males, 2 females). All of the matings in this pedigree are now complete. (If this were your own pedigree, you would now copy the original and work with the copy so that you could reuse the original to make a copy for the next trait.)

In 1991, a bitch puppy (the propositus) in litter #3 produced by sire #1 and dam #4 developed *progressive retinal atrophy* (PRA), an autosomal recessive trait. Three months later, her brother came down with the same disease. Mark the proven carriers. In 1993, a male in litter #7 produced by sire #1 and dam #8 developed PRA. Mark the proven carrier.

Answers to Questions on Chapter 3

1.

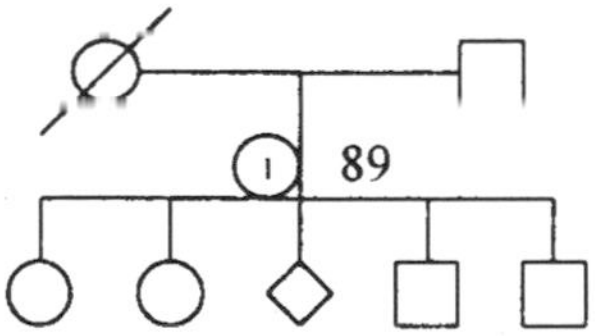

1 89

Fig. 3.23

2.

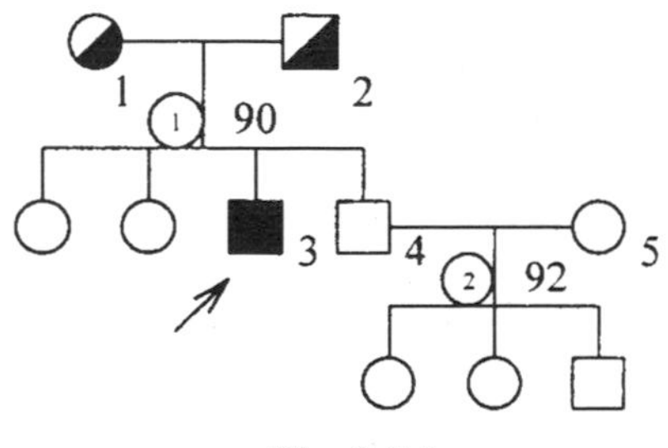

Fig. 3.24

3. In this pedigree, we show that bitch #3 was bred twice by sire #1 by giving two separate circles the same number (indicating that it is the same bitch), as shown in Figure 3.25. Figure 3.26 shows an alternative way that works just as well.

   Remember as you check your work against these answers that it does not matter whether you mark the exact same symbol (a circle or square) that I marked when we added the information about PRA to the pedigree (except for the proven carriers, sire #1, dam #3, and dam #8), because I did not state that a specific dog was involved—just that it was a male or female. Also, keep in mind that your dog's pedigree does not have to look exactly like this one. You could have put the various matings in different places. What is important is that the lines going to the various males and females are correct and that the sex and number of the offspring are correct.

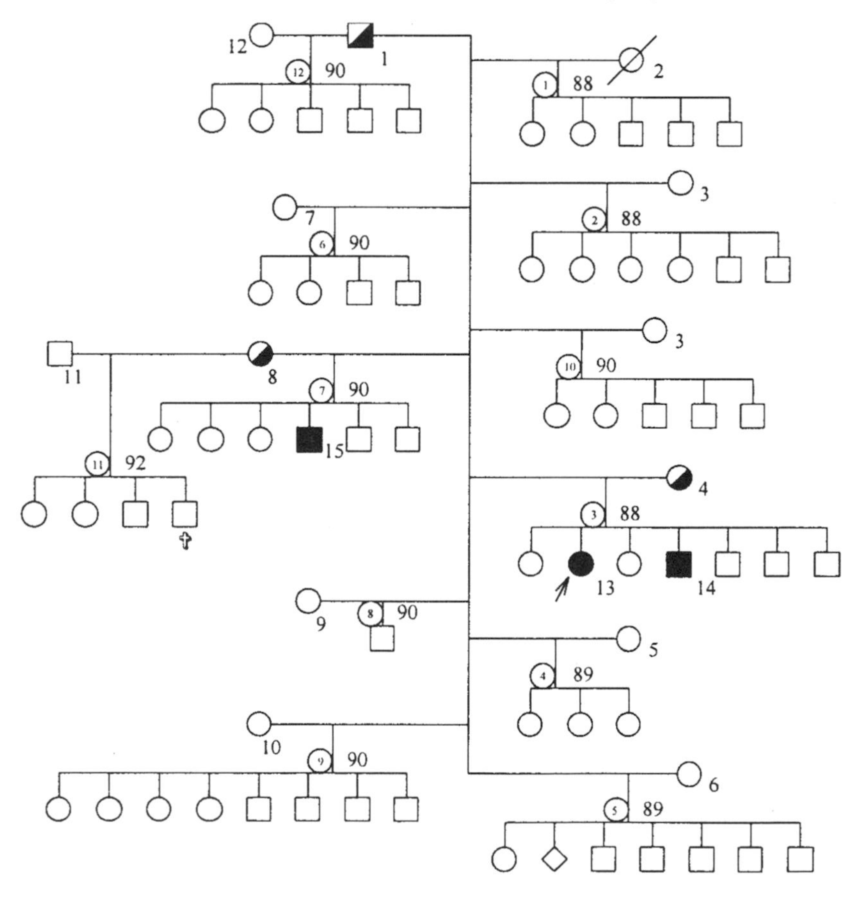

Fig. 3.25

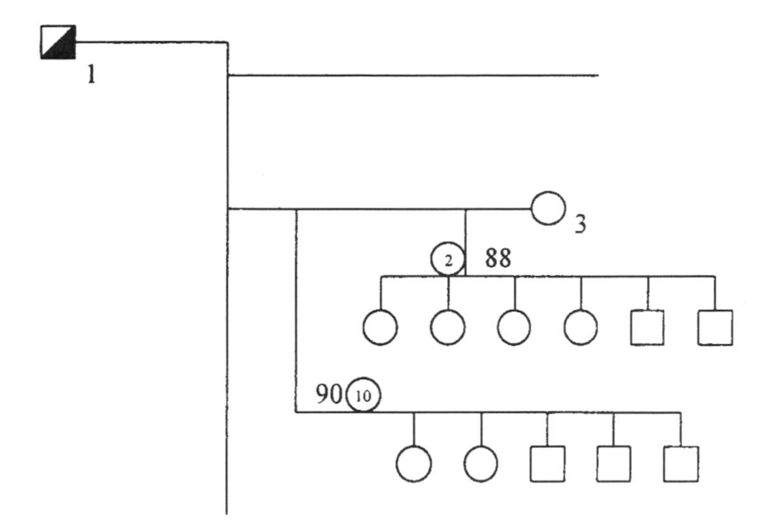

Fig. 3.26

CHAPTER 4

Modes of Inheritance

Knowing the mode of inheritance of a trait (the type of Mendelian inheritance) is essential to the control of genetic disease. This chapter discusses the various methods by which traits are inherited. There is no attempt here to describe DNA, chromosomes, miosis (how reproductive cells divide) or fertilization to form the zygote, except as they directly relate to the inheritance of specific traits. For explanations of these phenomena, I refer you to Willis,[1] Nicholas,[2] Hutt,[3] Robinson[4] and many others who cover these topics fully. Suffice it to say that the genes are located in the chromosomes, and the way chromosomes divide during miosis creates the random character of inheritance, allowing us to statistically predict traits. It is this predictability that allows us to control traits.

There are many facets to the way traits are inherited and in the way they are presented to us as various kinds of defects. But the approach used in this book is straightforward; I don't worry about all the ifs, ands, buts, exceptions and possible differences that occur in genetics. I fully expect to be roundly criticized for my temerity in writing for the breeder rather than the geneticist. My experience in talking with numerous breeders and presenting seminars to them for more than twenty years has brought me the understanding that there are relatively few of them with Ph.D.s and fewer yet who are rocket scientists and brain surgeons. So I believe that while getting into all of the technical aspects of genetics would please geneticists, it would not be of much practical help to breeders. My goal here is to present a methodology that will allow breeders and the veterinarians who advise them to use genetic principles to control genetic disease in kennels and in breed populations. You will find few formulas in this book that will let you calculate the various risks a dog has to develop or carry a specific trait, but you will find numerous tables that will allow you, within reasonable limits, to do the same thing. I hope they suffice.

There are four major modes of inheritance in dogs that cause most of the defects we see in this species: autosomal recessive or simple recessive, autosomal dominant, sex-linked recessive, and polygenic. These four modes of inheritance are considered

(1) Willis, M. B. *Genetics of the Dog.* New York: Howell Book House, 1989.
(2) Nicholas, F. W. *Veterinary Genetics.* Oxford: Clarendon Press, 1987.
(3) Hutt, R. B. *Genetics for Dog Breeders.* San Francisco: W. H. Freeman Co., 1979.
(4) Robinson, R. *Genetics for Dog Breeders.* Oxford: Pergamon Press, 1982.

in depth and are the focus of this book. When clear-cut exceptions to this approach occur that apply to common traits that are present in dogs, they also are discussed.

We will begin the discussion on modes of inheritance with a brief introduction to the units of inheritance: the genes.

Genes form the physical hereditary link between generations. Inheritance is particulate, because any given gene or set of genes that determines or modifies a body characteristic is acquired by the offspring in an *all or none* fashion. Each individual has two genes for a certain trait, because each autosome (non-sex chromosome) is present in duplicate, one maternal and one paternal chromosome being passed to the offspring. The genes are arranged in a linear fashion along the chromosomes and are part of the DNA structure that makes up the chromosomes. Two genes situated at the same position or site on homologous (paired or matched) chromosomes are called *alleles*. Alleles are alternative forms of the same gene. If an individual possesses two identical genes for a specific trait, he is said to be *homozygous* for that particular gene. If the two genes at the same position are unlike in action, the individual is *heterozygous* or a carrier for that particular gene. In addition to the autosomal or non-sex chromosomes, each animal has two sex chromosomes. Dogs have thirty-nine pairs of chromosomes, thirty-eight pairs of autosomal chromosomes and one pair of sex chromosomes. Any organism, whether a single cell or a dog, a cat or a person, is the product of its genes, or *genotype*, acting in a specific environment.

The *phenotype* is the external manifestation of an organism—what you can see or measure—and is an expression of both the genotype and the environment. The phenotype could be eye color, hair length, a straight front or something that can be measured, such as blood sugar or hormone levels. Differences between individuals are considered to be a result of interplay between both hereditary and environmental factors, or nature and nurture. As E. C. MacDowell says, "Heredity sets limits while environment decides the exact position within these limits."

In some conditions, heredity appears to play a major role, such as in blood-group antigens. In other disorders, such as diabetes mellitus in Keeshonds, there is an interaction between environment and heredity. In diabetes, the lack of insulin or the inability of cells to react to insulin causes a severe rise in blood sugar (glucose). The increased amount of sugar cannot be properly metabolized and produces severe clinical disease. If a dog is maintained on a low-sugar diet and is regularly given exogenous insulin, many of the serious effects of diabetes can be prevented. So we have modified a genetic disease and, in this case, improved the phenotype by controlling the environment. Of course, we could also do the opposite; we could make the disease more severe by increasing the sugar (glucose) in the diet and not giving insulin to the affected dog. Sometimes it is easier than that; for example, if a dog has inherited luxated patellas (slipped kneecaps), and it is kept it in a crate or small cage, it may never show that trait. Traits can be modified by the environment, made more or less severe, and in many cases, it is not due to the intervention of people.

Genetic traits cannot be caused by the environment, but you may be able to modify or alter a dog in a way that causes a disorder that mimics an inherited trait. For example, if you remove the pancreas surgically or give a dog alloxan, which damages the islets of Langerhans, the dog will not be able to produce insulin and will develop diabetes. A dog modified in this way will respond to insulin therapy and low-sugar diets in the same manner as a Keeshond with inherited diabetes. Such a condition is called a *phenocopy*. It is not inherited and never will be. If you breed a diabetic dog to a bitch that is diabetic because it was treated with alloxan, all the puppies will be normal as far as diabetes is concerned. You could repeat the matings 100 times, and the puppies would always be normal. Phenocopies do not have to be manmade—they also occur in nature. There are viruses like encephalomyocarditis that can cause phenocopies of diabetes in people and in mice. Like surgically-induced diabetic dogs, offspring from individuals with diabetes caused by viruses are also phenotypically normal in regard to diabetes. Phenocopies, although they mimic inherited traits, are not inherited themselves.

Simple Mendelian traits can be separated into dominant and recessive modes of inheritance. If a trait can be manifested phenotypically by the sole effect of one gene of a gene pair, it is said to be *dominant*. A dominant gene is illustrated by a capital or uppercase letter, such as *A*. If both genes in the pair are required to manifest the trait, it is said to be *recessive*. A recessive gene is illustrated by a lowercase letter, such as *a*.

Usually, it is easy to predict what will occur in offspring that is the product of a "single-gene" disease (one that has a single-gene mode of inheritance). Generally, you can determine the pattern of inheritance by studying the pedigree (performing a retrospective analysis) or by performing selected breedings to determine the exact mode of inheritance.

However, it should be pointed out that many genetic diseases probably do not have a discernible simple mode of inheritance but instead have a polygenic or multifactorial mode of inheritance. That is, the inheritance of an observed character is determined by the combined action of more than one gene pair. It may be as few as two pairs, or it may be an undetermined number of pairs for complex structures such as the head or the hips.

Autosomal Recessive Inheritance

An autosomal recessive trait is a characteristic that results when a matched pair of alleles (genes) is present on the autosomes (one from each parent). An autosome can be any of the thirty-eight non-sex chromosomes. When a matched pair of genes (alleles) occurs on a pair of chromosomes, they are said to be *homozygous*. Such a trait is not necessarily detrimental; for example, blue eyes in people are recessive. Our purpose here, however, is to discuss detrimental traits. While we realize that many recessive traits are not harmful, those that we consider here will be so. Whether or not the trait is harmful, what we say here applies regardless.

With an autosomal recessive trait, dogs that are heterozygous (possess one recessive gene for the trait) for the defect are generally phenotypically normal. There are a few exceptions to this generality, and with some traits, the heterozygous or carrier state can be detected. Examples are some of the enzyme defects, such as globoid cell leukodystrophy (β-galactosidase deficiency, occurring in West Highland White and Cairn Terriers, Beagles, Miniature Poodles, Blue Tick and Basset Hounds, and Pomeranians), and the Portuguese Water Dog storage disease (Gm 1 gangliosidosis). These traits can be detected in the carrier state by some clinical pathology biochemical tests that have been used as the basis for control of these disorders in some breeds. At the moment, the carrier status for one trait—PRA—in one breed—Irish Setters—can be determined by molecular genetic techniques. Hopefully, more of these will become available in the future.

So, with a few exceptions, the generality holds true that carriers of recessive traits cannot be detected except by the production of affected offspring. The production of affected puppies reveals the genotype of phenotypically normal parents and thus is the basis for control of these disorders. Since an affected dog gets one gene for each pair of genes from the sire and the other from the dam, both parents must be carriers. There is no escape for either parent. Such parents are called *proven carriers* (or obligate carriers), since they proved they were heterozygous (had one gene for the trait) by producing an affected offspring even though they themselves were phenotypically normal.

The general characteristics of an autosomal or simple recessive trait follow:

1. The gene is located on any one of the thirty-eight pairs of autosomes.
2. To be expressed (to show the trait) the gene must be present in the homozygous state (both genes must be identical).
3. The trait tends to occur in one generation and then skips one or two generations until carrier descendants are again mated, allowing the genes to be expressed.
4. Each of the parents of an affected puppy is a proven carrier (heterozygote) of the abnormal gene but generally shows no phenotypic manifestation of the trait.
5. If a given trait is rare in a breed (one affected among 2,000 or 3,000 normal dogs) there may be increased inbreeding among the parents (increased consanguinity) of affected dogs.
6. Matings between heterozygotes (carriers), on the average, produce 25 percent affected (homozygous recessive), 50 percent carriers (heterozygous) and 25 percent that do not have the mutant gene (homozygous dominant or wild type).
7. On the average, males and females are affected equally.

Using a Punnett Square, we can readily demonstrate how genes are distributed through crosses between heterozygotes. This applies to any single-gene autosomal recessive trait. Examples of such traits are cyclic neutropenia (gray Collie syndrome) in Collies, generalized *progressive retinal atrophy* (PRA) in many breeds and *craniomandibular osteopathy* (CMO) in Scotties, Westies and Cairns.

Figure 4.1 shows the results of crossing the genes from the sire and the dam:

1 *AA*	Homozygous dominant that is phenotypically and genetically normal
2 *Aa*	Phenotypically normal and genetically heterozygous (carriers)
1 *aa*	Homozygous recessive that is affected with the trait

Sire / Dam	A	a
A	AA	Aa
a	Aa	aa

Fig. 4.1

This type of mating, which is typically observed with an autosomal recessive trait, can be illustrated in another way.

Both ways of showing how genes distribute when carriers of a recessive trait are bred together result in the expected 3:1 Mendelian ratio (see Figure 4.2). We have an average of three phenotypically normal dogs and one affected dog for this type of cross. Therefore, the risk that a phenotypically normal puppy is a carrier from a mating such as this (in which both parents are carriers) is 66.66 percent.

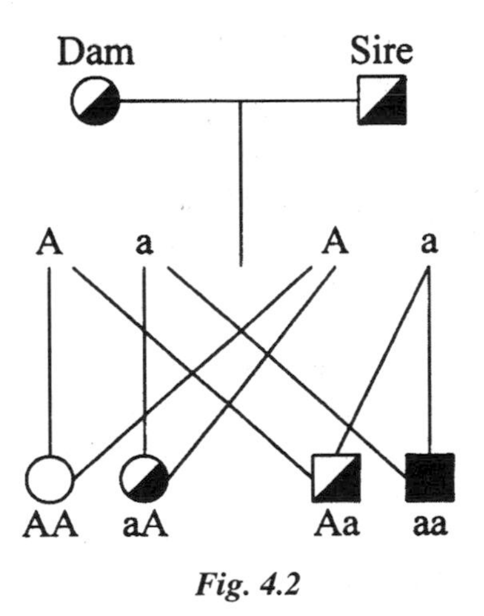

Fig. 4.2

Now let's use a Punnett Square to illustrate a mating between a dog affected with a recessive trait and a bitch that is a carrier (see Figure 4.3).

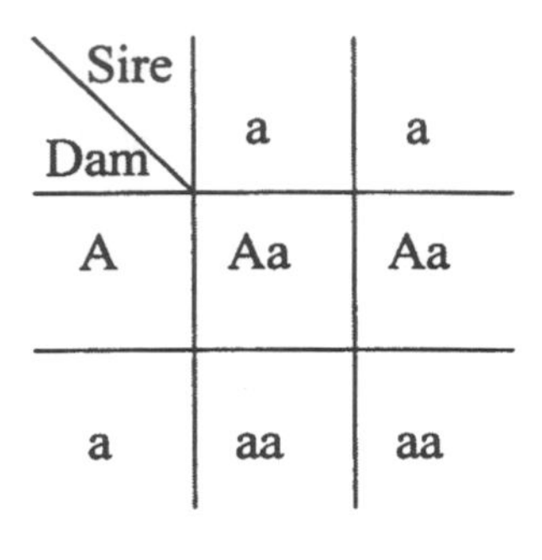

Dam \ Sire	a	a
A	Aa	Aa
a	aa	aa

Fig. 4.3

Cross the genes from the sire and the dam, and you get the following:

2 *Aa*	Heterozygous (carrier) dogs that are phenotypically normal
2 *aa*	Homozygous recessive dogs that are phenotypically affected with the trait in question

This type of mating produces a 1:1 Mendelian ratio. We have two phenotypically normal dogs, but both are carriers, and two phenotypically affected dogs. As we will see, this 1:1 ratio is also produced when a carrier of a dominant trait is bred to a phenotypically and genetically normal dog. Therefore, the results of a single mating generally will not allow us to determine the mode of inheritance of a trait occurring in a kennel or a line.

The distributions of genotypes and phenotypes for the various kinds of recessive matings are illustrated on the following pages. These examples use an average distribution in a family of four.

Figure 4.4 shows a situation in which the sire and dam are genotypically and phenotypically normal. All four offspring are genotypically and phenotypically normal as well.

Figure 4.5 shows a case in which the dam is phenotypically and genetically normal; the sire is phenotypically normal and genetically a carrier. Two offspring are phenotypically normal carriers. Two offspring are phenotypically and genetically normal. The results are the same if the dam is the carrier and the sire is normal.

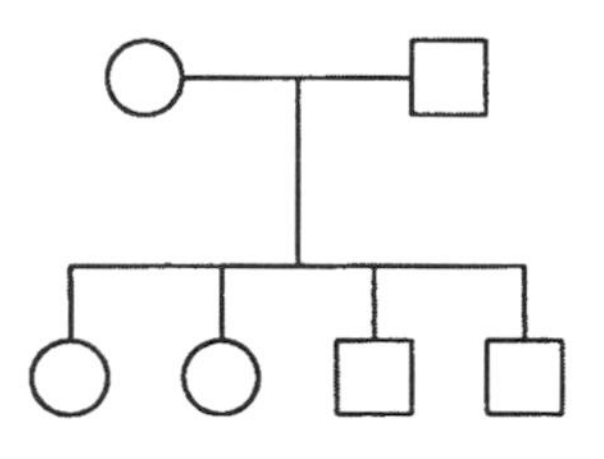

Fig. 4.4

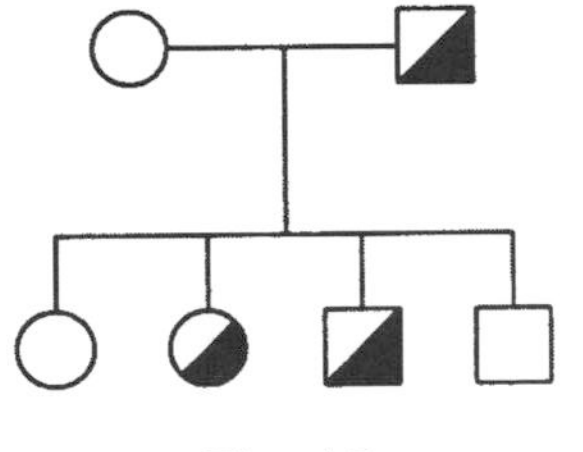

Fig. 4.5

In Figure 4.6, both the sire and dam are phenotypically normal but genetically carriers. We have a 3:1 phenotypic ratio (three normal, one affected). One puppy is phenotypically and genetically normal, and two puppies are phenotypically normal but genetically carriers; one puppy is phenotypically affected and homozygous recessive.

In Figure 4.7, the dam is affected and the sire is phenotypically and genetically normal. All four puppies are phenotypically normal and are defined carriers, because one parent is affected. The results are the same if the sire is affected and the dam is normal.

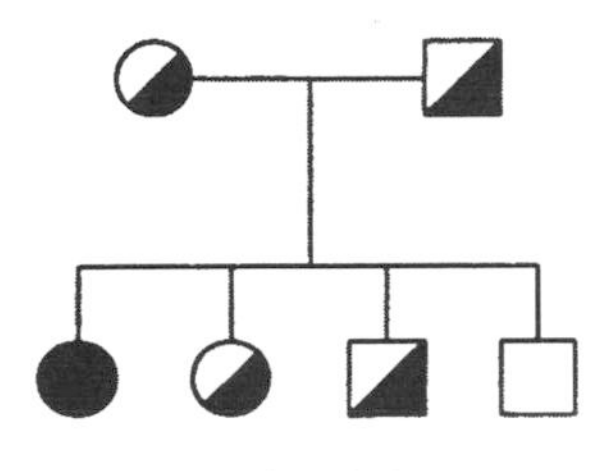

Fig. 4.6

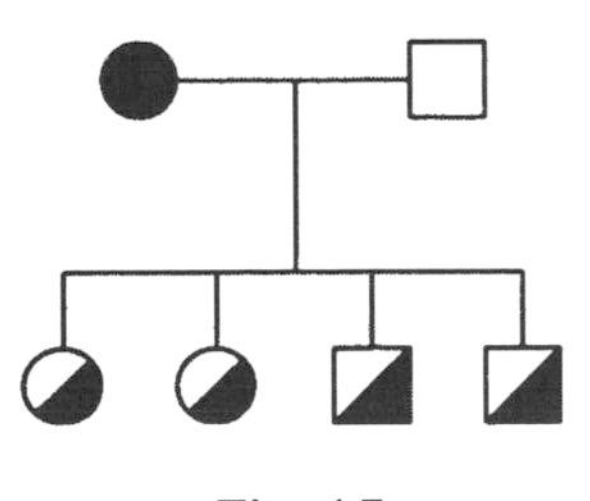

Fig. 4.7

Figure 4.8 shows the results when the sire is affected and the dam is a phenotypically normal carrier. Two puppies are affected with the trait. Two puppies are phenotypically normal defined carriers of the trait. The results are the same if the genetic makeup of the dam and sire are reversed.

Now take a look at Figure 4.9: Both the sire and dam are affected with the trait. All four puppies are affected with the trait. Since both parents are affected, all four puppies must be affected. This is the crucial mating to differentiate a recessive and a polygenic trait.

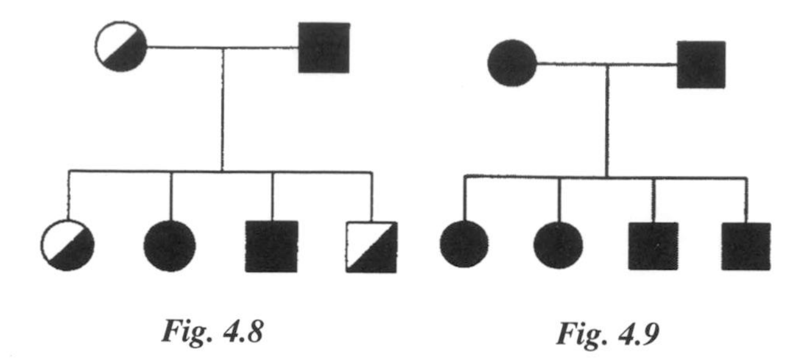

Fig. 4.8 *Fig. 4.9*

Suppose that you have a dog and a bitch that carry separate autosomal recessive traits. What happens when you breed them together? Again, using the Punnett Square, we can determine the average distribution of the traits in the progeny. As examples, let's take *cyclic neutropenia* (CN, or gray Collie syndrome) with the genes illustrated as *B* dominant and *b* recessive, and PRA with the genes illustrated as *C* dominant and *c* recessive. With both parents carriers for both traits, there are four possible gene combinations from each parent and thus sixteen possible combinations among the offspring, as shown in Table 4.1.

Table 4.1

Possible offspring produced by two carriers of both CN and PRA.

Dam Bb, Cc
BC, Bc, bC, bc

Sire Bb, Cc
BC, Bc, bC, bc

Sire / Dam	BC	Bc	bC	bc
BC	BBCC	BBCc	BbCC	BbCc
Bc	BBCc	BBcc	BbCc	Bbcc
bC	BbCC	BbCc	bbCC	bbCc
bc	BbCc	Bbcc	bbCc	bbcc

Gene Combination	*Description*
1 *BBCC*	A dog that is homozygous dominant for both traits and is thus phenotypically and genetically normal.
2 *BBCc*	Two dogs that are homozygous dominant for CN, so they are phenotypically and genetically normal for this trait. Both are phenotypically normal for PRA but are carriers for this trait.
2 *BbCC*	Two dogs that are homozygous dominant for PRA, so they are phenotypically and genetically normal for this trait. Both are phenotypically normal for CN but are carriers for this trait.
1 *BBcc*	A dog that is homozygous dominant for CN so is phenotypically and genetically normal for this trait. It is homozygous recessive for PRA and will develop this disease.
4 *BbCc*	Four dogs that are carriers for both traits, as were their parents.
2 *Bbcc*	Two dogs that are phenotypically normal but are carriers for CN; they are homozygous recessive for PRA and will develop this disease.
1 *bbCC*	A dog that is homozygous dominant for PRA so is phenotypically and genetically normal for this trait; it is homozygous recessive for CN and will develop this trait.
2 *bbCc*	Two dogs that are homozygous recessive for CN, so they will develop this trait. They are both phenotypically normal for PRA but carry genes for this trait.
1 *bbcc*	A dog that is homozygous recessive for both traits and will develop both diseases.

With two traits involved, sixteen genotypic combinations are possible. Now let's count them by phenotype alone. Nine dogs are phenotypically normal for both traits. Three dogs are phenotypically normal for CN but are affected with PRA. Three dogs are phenotypically normal for PRA but are affected with CN. One dog has both traits. This gives us a 9:3:3:1 Mendelian distribution, but does it coincide with the 3:1 Mendelian ratio of normal to affected that we expect for an autosomal recessive trait? Yes, it does. Four dogs are affected with PRA, and four dogs are affected with CN (remember, one dog has both diseases). Eight dogs are carriers for PRA, and eight dogs are carriers for CN (remember, four dogs are carriers for both traits). Four dogs are homozygous dominant for PRA, and four dogs are homozygous dominant for CN (remember that one dog is homozygous dominant for both traits). The 3:1 Mendelian ratio holds true for any recessive trait in any combination, but this illustration points out the difficulty when dealing with two traits at one time. Only one dog out of the sixteen potential genotypes allows the breeder to escape genetically from both diseases. It is for this reason that we suggest you work with one trait at a time.

Autosomal Dominant Inheritance

An autosomal dominant trait is a disorder that results when a trait is shown or expressed, even though the pair of alleles (genes) causing the trait are not matched (homozygous). Dominant traits are expressed in the heterozygous (*Aa*) state, and therefore both parents do not have to have a gene for the disorder to cause the trait to occur. However, since the trait is expressed in the heterozygous state, one parent must show the trait in order for it to occur among the offspring. There are a few exceptions to this rule, which will be discussed later. At the present time, we are not sure how or why a dominant gene masks or hides the recessive alleles, and it may be that the concept of dominance is operational and may not reflect any intrinsic property of the gene. Nevertheless, the fact that dominant traits are expressed in certain ratios can be easily demonstrated.

The general characteristics of an autosomal or simple dominant trait follow:

1. The gene is located on any one of the thirty-eight pairs of autosomes.
2. The gene is generally present in the heterozygous state.
3. At least one parent of an affected offspring must show the trait, unless a new mutation is involved.
4. The trait occurs in successive generations (no skipping).
5. About 50 percent of the offspring of an affected dam or sire will also be affected.
6. On the average, males and females are equally affected.
7. Dogs that are phenotypically normal are also genotypically normal.

Using a Punnett Square, we can demonstrate how the genes and phenotype are distributed through crosses between heterozygotes. This applies to any single-gene dominant trait. Examples of such traits are Ehlers-Dandos syndrome (cutaneous asthenia) in English Springer Spaniels, as well as deafness due to the dominant merle gene in Collies, Dachshunds, and the twelve or fifteen other breeds that may exhibit the merle color pattern.

Figure 4.10 shows the results of crossing the genes from a sire and dam that both show the trait because they are heterozygous:

1 *AA*	A homogenous dominant dog that is phenotypically and genetically abnormal
2 *Aa*	Dogs that are phenotypically affected and are genetically carriers
1 *aa*	A homozygous recessive dog that is phenotypically and genetically normal

Sire / Dam	A	a
A	AA	Aa
a	Aa	aa

Fig. 4.10

Again, we get a 3:1 ratio, but in this case, three dogs are affected and the phenotypically normal dog is also genotypically normal.

The distribution of genotypes and phenotypes for the various kinds of dominant matings are illustrated on the following pages using an average distribution in a family of four. Remember, since with a dominant trait, a heterozygous individual displays the affected phenotype, you cannot always determine whether an animal is heterozygous or homozygous for the trait just because a dog is affected. As a general rule, most animals displaying a dominant trait are heterozygous, but you determine the actual genotype by assessing a number of matings. I will discuss this point more fully after we look at typical pedigrees.

Figure 4.11 shows a situation in which the sire and dam are genotypically and phenotypically normal. With autosomal dominant traits, we have no hidden carriers as we do with a recessive trait, so one would not expect to see this type of pedigree.

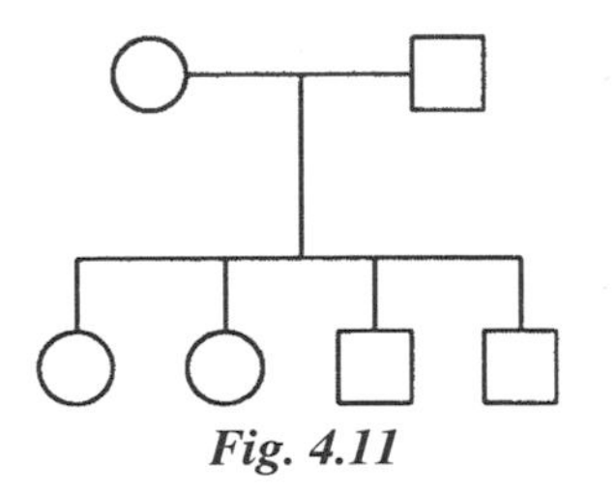

Fig. 4.11

For purposes of clarity, we will illustrate the genotype under each symbol, since a completely blackened symbol does not tell us the genotype as it does with a recessive trait.

In Figure 4.12, the dam is a carrier of a dominant trait, and the sire is phenotypically and genotypically normal. The results are the same if the sire is a carrier and the dam is normal. Two offspring are heterozygous and affected, and two are phenotypically and genetically normal.

Figure 4.13 shows the results of a dam and sire that are both carriers. We have a 3:1 phenotypic ratio (three affected, one normal). One puppy is homozygous dominant and affected, two puppies are heterozygous and affected, and one puppy is homozygous recessive and phenotypically and genetically normal.

Figure 4.14 shows the results of a dam that is homozygous and a sire that is heterozygous. The whole family is affected, with two of the offspring being heterozygous and two homozygous. The results are the same if the genotype of the dam and sire are reversed.

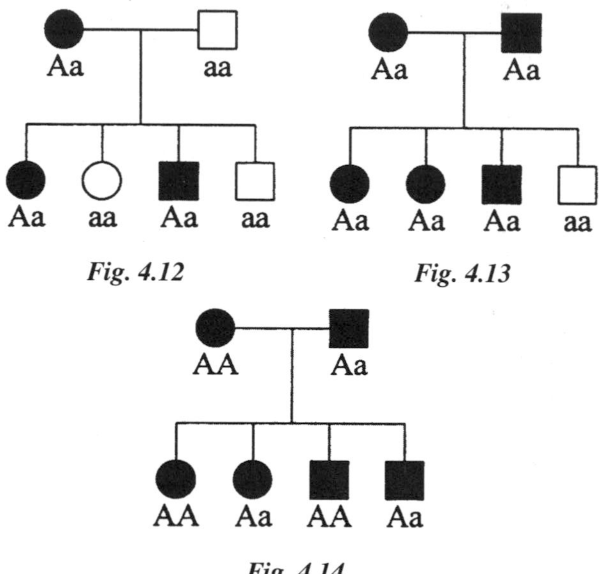

Fig. 4.12

Fig. 4.13

Fig. 4.14

In Figure 4.15, the dam is homozygous dominant and affected, and the sire is genotypically and phenotypically normal. All four offspring are affected and heterozygous. The results are the same if the genotype of the dam and sire is reversed.

Figure 4.16 shows a dam and sire that are both homozygous and affected, as are all four offspring.

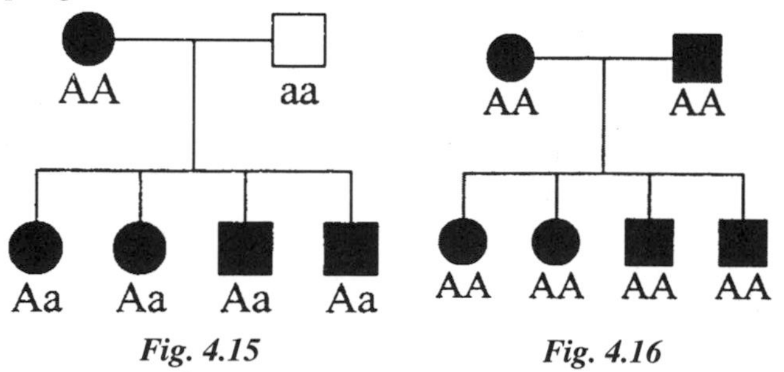

Fig. 4.15

Fig. 4.16

As you can see from the five pedigrees illustrated above, anytime either the bitch or dog is homozygous dominant, all of the puppies are affected. However, as you can see even in the pedigrees when the sire or dam or both are heterozygous, we expect one-half or three-fourths of the offspring to be affected. In this situation, you will often get litters in which all of the puppies are affected due to the random statistical distribution of the gene(s) of concern. Therefore, a larger number of litters (or offspring) is needed to be sure of the genotype of the affected parent(s). In Chapter 5, "Tables and Probabilities," you will be able to observe numerically how the genes distribute randomly.

Dominant traits may express themselves differently if they are homozygous (*AA*) rather than heterozygous (*Aa*). The two examples presented for dominant traits—the Ehlers-Dandos syndrome and dominant merle deafness—illustrate this point. Data suggests that the Ehlers-Dandos syndrome in English Springer Spaniels is lethal in the homozygous dominant state. There appears to be about a 25 percent reduction in litter size when heterozygotes are mated. The dominant hairlessness in Chinese Cresteds and the Pelger-Huet anomaly in American Foxhounds are other examples of homozygous dominant lethals. That the homozygous dominant state is not always lethal is clear, since there are numerous examples where it is not, and the dog with that genotype displays the same trait as the heterozygote. The dominant gene that causes merling in Collies and the dappled color phase in Dachshunds in the heterozygous state is not generally considered to be lethal in the homozygous condition, but these animals are often deaf and/or blind as well as nearly all white.

Dominant traits are sometimes said to have *incomplete penetrance* or *variable expressivity.* This means that the gene is present, but the affected phenotype is not displayed or expressed. The most common example of this characteristic of some dominant genes (also a few recessives) is von Willebrand's disease, which is seen in multiple breeds. The presence of a dominant gene in the absence of the phenotype that should be displayed, of course, plays havoc with control procedures. As a rule, dominant traits are not much of a problem in dogs, because the standard procedure that most breeders use in selecting breeding stock—"do not breed affected dogs"—tends to eliminate them or to greatly reduce the frequency of a trait in a kennel or breed. Von Willebrand's disease seems to be an exception to this rule and is discussed more fully in Chapter 9, "Registries and Prioritizing Genetic Diseases."

Sex-Linked Traits

Sex-linked genes, like genes on autosomal chromosomes, can be either dominant or recessive. They are nearly always on the X-chromosome. I don't know of a single defect in dogs in which the gene is part of the Y-chromosome. The distinctions we have between autosomal dominant and recessive traits also apply to sex-linked traits. That is, the dominant gene masks or hides the recessive gene in the female, since the female has two X-chromosomes, just as she has two of each of the autosomes. In the male, since he has only one X-chromosome, the single recessive gene that is part of that chromosome expresses itself and causes the same trait that seems to require two genes in the female. Mary Lyon put forth the concept in 1961 that only one X-chromosome was active (Lyon hypothesis, single active X hypothesis) in any given cell, which seems to explain this apparent dilemma. A more detailed explanation of this hypothesis can be found in Nikolas.[5] The term *hemizygous* is used with a sex-linked trait in a male, since he has only one gene causing the defect.

The general characteristics of a sex-linked recessive trait follow:

1. On the average, half the male offspring of a carrier dam are affected with the trait.
2. On the average, half the female offspring of a carrier dam also are carriers.
3. The trait may skip generations.
4. The pattern of transmission is often called *oblique,* because the gene goes from phenotypically normal dams, to affected sons, and then to phenotypically normal carrier daughters.
5. Affected males transmit the gene to all of their daughters and to none of their sons, because the sons receive the Y- and not the X-chromosome.
6. If both parents are affected with the trait, all offspring are affected.
7. For an affected female offspring to emerge, the dam must be at least a carrier, and the sire must be affected with the trait.
8. Most affected offspring in a typical pedigree are male.
9. There may be related affected males on the maternal side of the pedigree, but only rarely (if ever) on the paternal side.
10. All male offspring of an affected female are affected with the trait when the sire is normal, and all daughters are phenotypically normal carriers.

The distributions of phenotypes and genotypes in typical sex-linked recessive pedigrees are shown in the following figures. X-chromosomes that carry the gene of concern are illustrated by the symbol $\overline{X}$.

In Figure 4.17, the dam is a phenotypically normal carrier of the trait, and the sire is phenotypically and genetically normal. Both female offspring are phenotypically normal: One is genetically normal, and the other is a carrier. One son is affected with the trait and is hemizygous (his X-chromosome has the gene in question). The other son is phenotypically and genetically normal.

Figure 4.18 shows an example in which the dam is homozygous recessive for the trait, and the sire is phenotypically and genetically normal. Both daughters are phenotypically normal carriers, and both sons are affected and are hemizygous.

(5) Nicholas, F. W. *Veterinary Genetics.* Oxford: Clarendon Press, 1987.

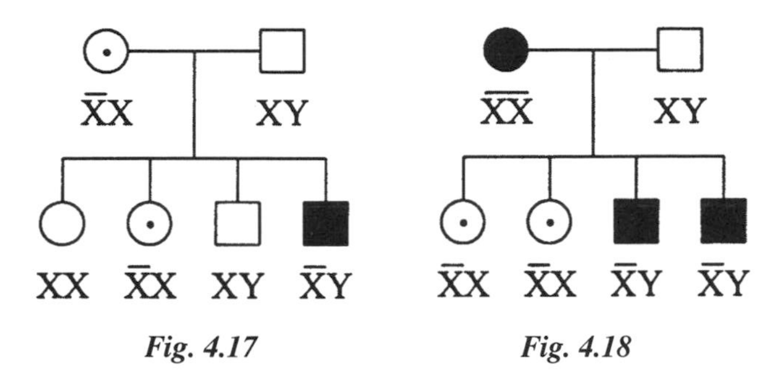

Fig. 4.17 *Fig. 4.18*

In Figure 4.19, the sire is affected, and the dam is phenotypically and genetically normal. Both daughters are carriers, and both sons are phenotypically and genetically normal.

Figure 4.20 shows the results of a sire that is affected and a dam that is a carrier. One daughter is affected, the other a carrier. One son is affected, the other normal.

Finally, look at Figure 4.21. Both the sire and dam are affected, as are all of their offspring. Both daughters are homozygous, and both sons are hemizygous.

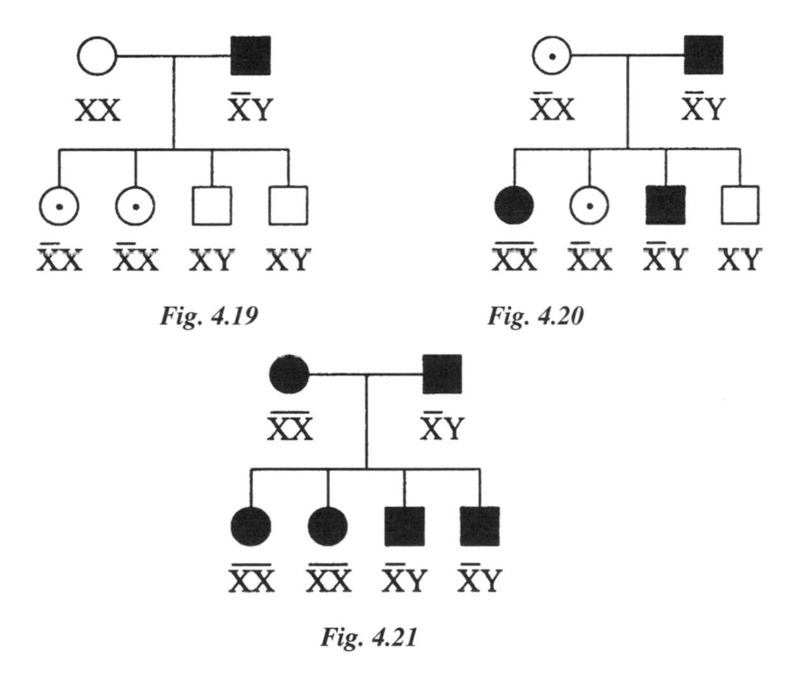

Fig. 4.19 *Fig. 4.20*

Fig. 4.21

As you can see from these pedigrees, you usually cannot distinguish a sex-linked and autosomal recessive pedigree based on a single mating. They can be separated, but multiple matings and families are required, as you will discover in Chapter 6, "The Interpretation and Use of Pedigrees to Determine the Genetic Status of Given Dogs."

The general characteristics of a sex-linked dominant trait follow:

1. As with autosomal dominant traits, sex-linked dominant traits are passed from generation to generation and do not usually skip generations.
2. Affected males pass the defect to all of their female offspring and to none of their male offspring when mated to normal dams, because the male puppies receive the Y-, not the X-, chromosome.
3. As with autosomal dominant traits, every affected dog must have at least one affected parent, unless a new mutation is involved.
4. Like autosomal dominant traits, where the affected animal is generally heterozygous, in sex-linked dominant traits, the affected dam is also generally heterozygous; therefore, she transmits the trait to half her daughters and half her sons.

The following figures show the distributions of phenotypes and genotypes in typical sex-linked dominant pedigrees in families of four. The X-chromosome that carries the gene of concern is illustrated by the symbol $\bar{X}$.

In Figure 4.22, the dam is heterozygous and the sire is normal. One son and one daughter are affected, with the daughter being heterozygous and the son hemizygous. The other son and daughter are normal.

The example in Figure 4.23 looks at a sire that is affected and a dam that is normal. Both daughters are affected and heterozygous, and both sons are normal.

Figure 4.24 shows a situation in which the sire is affected, and the dam is affected and heterozygous. Both daughters are affected; one is heterozygous and the other homozygous. One son is affected and hemizygous, the other son is normal.

In Figure 4.25, the dam is affected and homozygous, and the sire is normal. All offspring are affected; both daughters are heterozygous, while the sons are hemizygous.

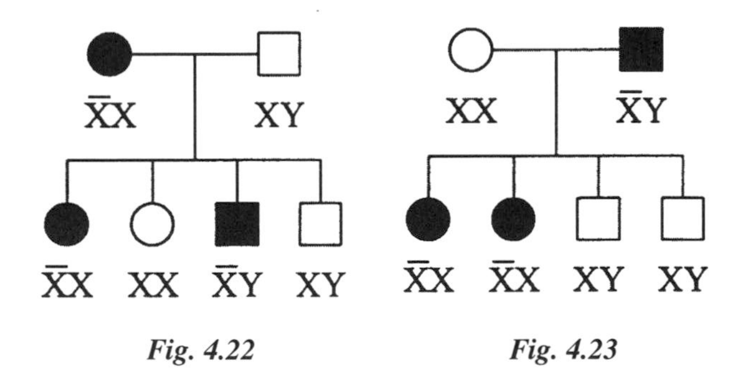

Fig. 4.22 *Fig. 4.23*

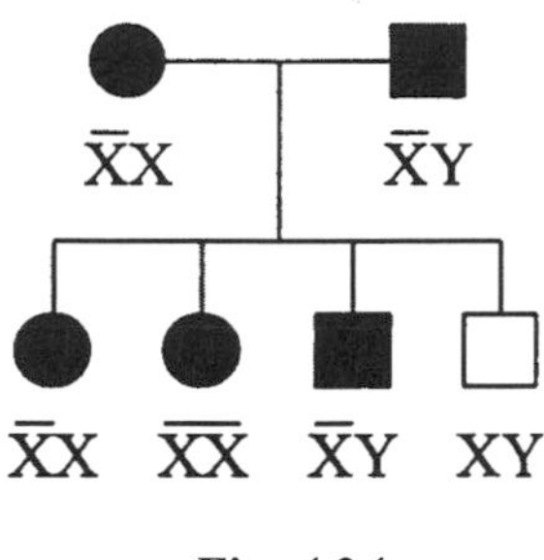

Fig. 4.24

In Figure 4.26, both the sire and dam are affected, and the dam is homozygous. All offspring are affected; the daughters are homozygous, while the sons are hemizygous.

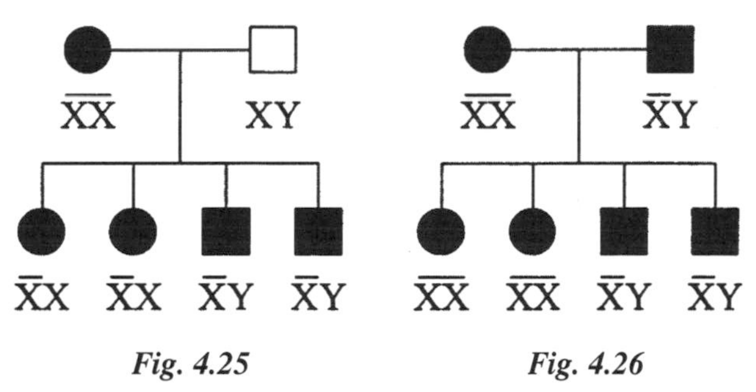

Fig. 4.25 *Fig. 4.26*

Polygenic or Multifactorial Traits

Up to now in this chapter, we have considered modes of inheritance for single-gene traits. These are referred to as *simple Mendelian traits*, because the distribution of the genes and the resultant phenotypes can be predicted relatively easily. This is true even if there are two or three separate traits in one individual, because each trait segregates independently and follows the general rules we have set down for recessive, dominant, and sex-linked modes of inheritance.

Unfortunately, not all traits are simple. Numerous traits are controlled by a number of genes, each of which adds in increments to the total phenotype. These are termed *complex Mendelian traits,* because multiple genes are involved and therefore distribution of specific phenotypes cannot be predicted. Many, if not most, traits that breeders are interested in have complex modes of inheritance. A dog's topline, or its front, or ear placements and tailsets, are examples of traits requiring many genes to cause the specific phenotype involved.

In fact, the whole dog, which is estimated to be composed of 100,000 or so genes, might be considered to be a very complex polygenic trait. Despite the fact that a very large number of genes are involved, we know it is possible to control them, to bend them to our will, to make them do, within reason, whatever we want them to do. If we could not manipulate a large number of genes, we would not have 400 or 500 distinct dog breeds in the world as is clearly the case today. Breeders know they can control traits like the depth of the stop, the height, the gait and the appearance of the head, because they have done it and these all involve numerous genes. However, for some reason, they have difficulty believing they can control complex genetic defects.

We call these complex defects *polygenic traits,* indicating that more than one gene is involved in producing the phenotype. They have also been termed *multifactorial, quantitative* and *metric traits,* indicating that they are in some way measurable or that factors in addition to genes may play a role in determining the exact phenotype. This is indeed the case. Just as we discussed environmental factors that influence single-gene traits, such factors also play a role in producing the final phenotype with polygenic traits.

The environmental factors may be much more subtle than the examples discussed earlier, but they are there just the same. Such factors as the uterine environment, nutrition and exercise can be involved, but the exact sequence, order or method by which this takes place is not well understood. We know, for example, that behavior, an inherited characteristic, can be readily modified by socialization, or the lack thereof, and by training; hence the whole field of Obedience.

The breeds of the Sporting Group inherit the instinct to hunt and, given the opportunity, will do so independent of any special effort on the part of the owner. But few will disagree with the fact that their natural ability to hunt can be enhanced given a little training. So the environment clearly plays a role with polygenic traits, as it can with single-gene traits, but the environment cannot cause genetic traits (except through mutation).

The environment can make hip dysplasia more or less detrimental to the phenotype, but a dog will not develop hip dysplasia if it does not have the complement of genes necessary to produce that trait. Breeders tend to get very confused on this point, due to the plethora of papers and presentations by veterinarians and geneticists that discuss the environmental factors that influence polygenic traits, such as hip dysplasia, elbow dysplasia, osteochondritis dissecans, and luxated patellas. But an operator of one kennel or the entire fancy of a breed will not get rid of or reduce the frequency of a disorder like luxated patellas by keeping all of their dogs in cages. Whether the supporting environment is maintained or withdrawn does not matter if a dog or bitch has the genetic composition for luxated patellas; the gene will be passed on to their offspring, and luxated patellas will appear among the offspring or their descendants.

Just as the environment can modify polygenic traits, so can the genetic makeup of the individual. The term *polygenic,* of course, means many or multiple genes, rather than one pair of alleles. We do not know the exact number of genes involved in the production of any polygenic trait in dogs. Most geneticists believe that a number of genes are involved in these traits, some of which modify the normal structure and others that cause this modification to vary from a very mild to a very severe change. We generally think this range of phenotypes will assume a normal curve, and there are mathematical expressions that will help those who are so inclined to understand the principles involved. These are well covered by Willis[6] and Nicholas,[7] and I refer you to them for further explanation.

In addition to the polygenic defects that tend to show a continuous variation in the phenotype (for example, hip dysplasia), which we assume to be due either to the number of detrimental genes present or to certain genes or combinations of genes that cause milder or more severe effects on the phenotype (for discussion purposes, we are not considering the environment), there are what we call *threshold* traits. A good example of a threshold trait is polydactyly (extra toes) in guinea pigs. A very lucid discussion of Wright's (1934) work is presented by Willis (1989). In essence, if a guinea pig has any five of the eight genes involved in the production of polydactyly, it will have four toes; if not, it will have three toes. While the potential for threshold traits to be present in dogs is high, currently, none are well enough defined to influence our course of action.

The general characteristics of a polygenic trait follow:

1. As with a recessive trait, both the sire and the dam must contribute one or more of the genes that cause the abnormal phenotype in the offspring.
2. Unlike recessive traits, the contribution from the sire and dam need not be equal.
3. Since we do not know the number or the specific effect of the genes involved in polygenic traits in dogs, no predictable Mendelian ratios are associated with these traits.
4. Both sexes are affected with polygenic traits (excluding sex-limited traits), but not necessarily in equal numbers.
5. The trait may skip generations and may appear to be erratic in occurrence.

Since no specific Mendelian ratios are associated with polygenic traits, we cannot present typical pedigrees for these traits. Instead, we will present a Punnett Square for a three-gene trait and discuss the ramifications. With a three-gene trait, there are sixty-four potential genotypes.

Starting with a sire and dam that are both heterozygous for three separate but interrelated genes, there are eight possible combinations of these genes among the gametes of each parent. Each parent is *Aa Bb Cc* and would have the following gametes: *ABC, AbC, ABc, aBC, aBc, abC, abc* and *Abc*. This results in sixty-four potential genotypes among the offspring, as you can see in the Punnett Square shown as Table 4.2.

(6) Willis, M. B. *Genetics of the Dog*. New York: Howell Book House, 1989.

(7) Nicholas, F. W. *Veterinary Genetics*. Oxford: Clarendon Press, 1987.

Table 4.2

A Punnett Square for a three-gene trait.

Sire / Dam	A B C	A b C	A B c	a B C	a B c	a b C	a b c	A b c
A B C	AA BB CC	AA Bb CC	AA BB Cc	Aa BB CC	Aa BB Cc	Aa Bb CC	Aa Bb Cc	AA Bb Cc
A b C	AA bB CC	AA bb CC	AA bB Cc	Aa bB CC	Aa bB Cc	Aa bb CC	Aa bb Cc	AA bb Cc
A B c	AA BB cC	AA Bb cC	AA BB cc	Aa BB cC	Aa BB cc	Aa Bb cC	Aa Bb cc	AA Bb cc
a B C	aA BB CC	aA Bb CC	aA BB Cc	aa BB CC	aa BB Cc	aa Bb CC	aa Bb Cc	aA Bb Cc
a B c	aA BB cC	aA Bb cC	aA BB cc	aa BB cC	aa BB cc	aa Bb cC	aa Bb cc	aA Bb cc
a b C	aA bB CC	aA bb CC	aA bB Cc	aa bB CC	aa bB Cc	aa bb CC	aa bb Cc	aA bb Cc
a b c	aA bB cC	aA bb cC	aA bB cc	aa bB cC	aa bB cc	aa bb cC	aa bb cc	aA bb cc
A b c	AA bB cC	AA bb cC	AA bB cc	Aa bB cC	Aa bB cc	Aa bb cC	Aa bb cc	AA bb cc

For the purposes of discussion, we are going to assign hip dysplasia phenotypes based on OFA scoring to the various genotypes illustrated in our example. These are not real genotypes or the resultant phenotypes, since we do not know the number of genes involved in producing hip dysplasia. However, we do need to develop some idea of how polygenic traits are likely to work if we want to grasp why an approach used to control simple Mendelian traits would not apply effectively to polygenic traits.

The OFA phenotypic grades for *hip dysplasia* (HD) follow:

1. Excellent
2. Good
3. Fair

(These first three grades all receive an OFA number.)

4. Borderline
5. Mild
6. Moderate
7. Severe

(These final four do not receive an OFA number and are generally not considered to be breedable.)

As an example, let's say that the following facts apply:

1. Any dog that is homozygous dominant for all three pairs of genes is excellent and cannot transmit hip dysplasia to its offspring. Of the sixty-four, there is one dog with this genotype.
2. Any dog that is homozygous dominant for any two pair of alleles will be graded from excellent to moderate, independent of the effect of the third pair. There are nine dogs that fit this category, and all nine could pass one HD gene to their offspring.
3. Any dog that is homozygous dominant for one pair and heterozygous for the other two pairs or that is heterozygous for all three pairs would be graded fair. There are twenty dogs that fit this category, and all twenty could pass two or three genes to their offspring.
4. Any dog that is homozygous dominant for one pair, heterozygous for one pair, and homozygous recessive for the third pair; or that is homozygous recessive for one pair and heterozygous for the other two pairs would be graded borderline or mild. There are twenty-four dogs that fit this category, and all twenty-four could pass two or three HD genes to their offspring.
5. Any dog that has two pairs of homozygous recessive genes and one pair of either heterozygous or homozygous dominant would be graded as moderate and could pass two or three HD genes to its offspring. There are nine dogs that fit this category.
6. Any dog that is homozygous recessive for all three pairs would be graded as severe, and this dog would have to pass all three HD genes to its offspring. There is one dog that fits this category.

Let's put this data into the form of a standard curve, as shown in Figure 4.27.

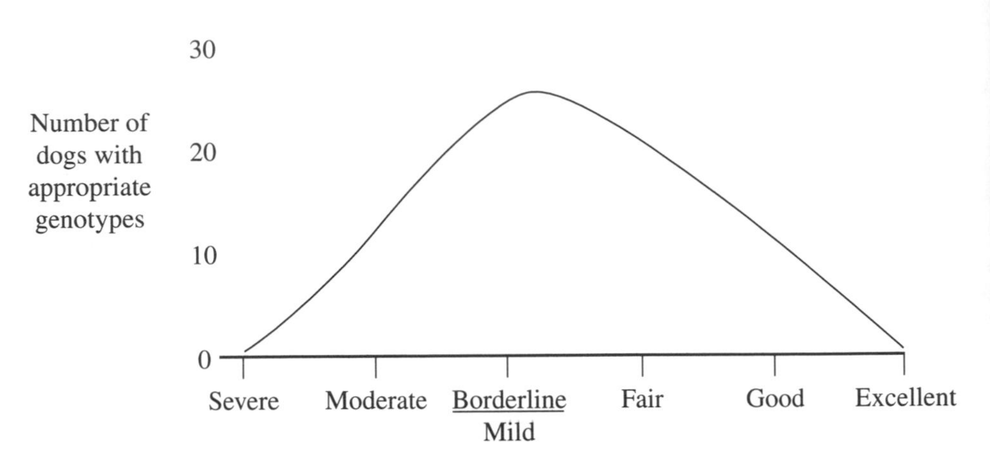

Fig. 4.27 *Approximation of the distribution of phenotypes with a three-gene polygenic trait.*

This example does roughly fit a standard curve, because we picked the starting genotypes and defined the phenotypes in such a way as to force them to fit. In the real world of dog breeding, HD does closely fit a standard curve, so something similar to this has to be happening. In addition, we have not factored in the changes in the phenotype that are caused by the environment.

Any model you choose to describe a polygenic trait is going to have some inherent liabilities, because we do not have sufficient real-world data on any polygenic trait in dogs to define a perfect system. Nevertheless, this model lets you see some of the general characteristics of a polygenic trait that are important to consider if you want to improve your dogs:

1. Sixty-three of the sixty-four genotypes would allow at least one HD gene to be passed to the offspring.
2. The better the phenotype, the smaller the risk of passing deleterious genes to the offspring.
3. The better the phenotype, the better the chance of good phenotypes among the offspring.
4. The poorer the phenotype, the greater the risk of poor phenotypes among the offspring.
5. Although other dogs could, in this model, pass three negative genes to their offspring, only one of the sixty-three dogs at risk has to pass all three negative genes to its puppies.

The model system I've described here is obviously complicated, and it involves only three genes. For a four-gene trait, there are sixteen possible gene combinations in the gametes and 256 possible genotypes among the offspring. Obviously, the more genes you add to the trait, the more complex the problem. Even so, the general rules hold:

- Do not breed affected dogs.
- The better the phenotype, the better the offspring.

Questions on Chapter 4

1. Illustrate a Punnett Square in which the dam is affected and the sire is heterozygous for a simple autosomal recessive trait.
2. List three general characteristics of an autosomal dominant trait.
3. Draw a typical pedigree using a family with four offspring for a sex-linked recessive trait in which the dam is a known heterozygote.
4. What is the typical Mendelian ratio for a dominant trait in which the sire is affected and known to be heterozygous and the female is phenotypically normal?
5. What is the expected Mendelian ratio for a polygenic trait that involves three genes?
6. Draw a typical pedigree using a family with four offspring for an autosomal dominant trait in which both parents are known to be heterozygous (carriers).
7. Why is the male the one that is usually affected with a sex-linked recessive trait?
8. What are the essential characteristics of a pedigree in order for a female to be affected with a sex-linked recessive trait?
9. If we are talking about polygenic traits, does the saying "like begets like" make sense? If so, why?
10. If we are talking about an autosomal recessive trait, when the parents are phenotypically normal, does the saying "like begets like" make sense? If so, why? If not, why?

Answers for Chapter 4

1.

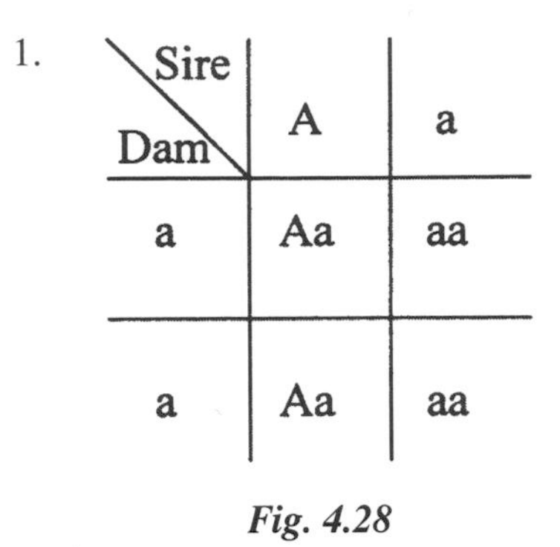

Dam \ Sire	A	a
a	Aa	aa
a	Aa	aa

Fig. 4.28

2. Any three of the seven general characteristics of autosomal dominant traits presented on page 38.

3.

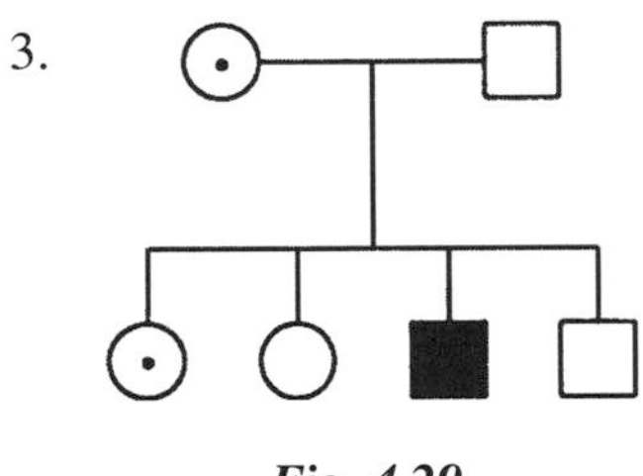

Fig. 4.29

4. 1:1 or 50:50 (half of the offspring will be normal and half will be affected)
5. Since we do not know the starting genotypes for the sire and dam with polygenic traits, there is no expected Mendelian ratio.
6. The dog with the normal phenotype (and thus genotype) in this pedigree could be either male or female; either is correct (see Figure 4.30).

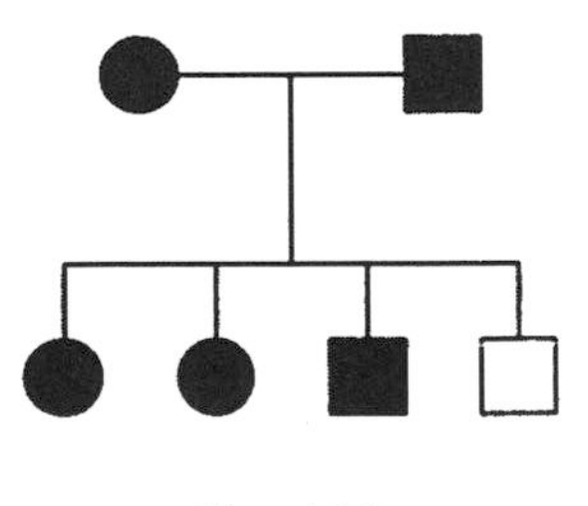

Fig. 4.30

7. Because the male has only one X-chromosome (the other is a Y), any recessive gene present on that chromosome will express itself.

8. The sire must be affected with the trait.
9. Yes, it does make sense. It is generally accepted that with polygenic defects, a severely affected animal either has more genes for the trait of concern, or the genes he/she has produce more severe phenotypic changes than occur in a mildly affected animal. No matter which is the case, the better the phenotype, the better the chance that an offspring will be normal. Obviously, the reverse will also be true.
10. No, it doesn't make sense. With an autosomal recessive trait, an animal that is heterozygous (a carrier) will have a perfectly normal phenotype, yet half the genes that cause the trait (*Aa*) can be present in that (phenotypically) normal dog. The end result is that if you breed a carrier to this dog, 75 percent of the offspring will be either carriers or affected. Even if you breed a genotypically normal dog to this animal, half the offspring will be carriers.

CHAPTER 5

Tables and Probabilities

In this chapter, you'll find all tables used in this book for test-mating probabilities, probability of the occurrence of affected offspring, distribution probabilities of a specific genotype or phenotype and related data. It is my intent that you refer back to this chapter rather than look throughout the book for a table you need to help you make a decision regarding a particular problem. For each table, I explain how it is to be used and what situations to use it in. In the following chapters, I will refer back to this set of tables as needed to show you how to use them.

Test-Mating Tables for Autosomal Recessive Traits (Simple Recessive Traits, Single-Gene Recessive Traits)

Table 5.1

Probability that an unknown animal is homozygous dominant *(AA)* for a given autosomal recessive trait when bred to an animal that is a carrier (Aa, heterozygote) for that trait.

Number of normal offspring	*Probability the unknown animal is homozygous dominant (AA, noncarrier)*	*Number of normal offspring*	*Probability the unknown animal is homozygous dominant (AA, noncarrier)*
1	25.0%	9	92.5%
2	43.7%	10	94.4%
3	57.8%	11	95.8%
4	68.4%	12	96.8%
5	76.3%	13	97.6%
6	82.2%	14	98.2%
7	86.6%	15	98.7%
8	90.0%	16	99.0%

For a test-mating to hopefully yield viable results, you must know the genotype (for the trait you are studying) of one of the dogs in the mating pair. The alternative is to know the frequency of the trait in the general population of the breed. I will discuss this alternative later in this chapter.

Table 5.1 should be used only with an autosomal recessive trait and when the mate with the established genotype is known to be heterozygous (a carrier, *Aa*). The requirement for a test-mating using this table is that the test-mate animal must be a carrier (heterozygote). Therefore, it is not necessary that the same dog or bitch be used if additional matings are required to get sufficient data to make a decision. Any animal of the appropriate sex can be used, as long as it is a known carrier. The puppies in each litter are added together, and you then check the table for that number of puppies to get the appropriate probability.

Remember that anytime a dog or bitch produces an affected offspring, it is a proven (defined) carrier, independent of how many normal puppies it has produced in previous litters. Since the probability that the test-mated animal is *AA* (homozygous dominant) is only 86.6 percent with seven puppies and 90 percent with eight puppies, the use of heterozygotes for test-mates in breeds that average four or fewer puppies per litter is rarely recommended for prospective studies on bitches. Prospective test-matings are those in which you intentionally breed a bitch (or dog) to a carrier (heterozygote) in order to determine its genotype. Carrier test-matings for bitches producing four or fewer puppies per litter is not recommended, because two litters will almost surely be required; thus, the test-matings may take up half or more of the breeding life of the bitch being tested, and you still might not get a probability you will be satisfied with. Since sires can be bred to multiple bitches, data accumulates much more rapidly, and this restriction may not apply.

Retrospective test-matings are a different matter; these are matings that have already taken place, and you later discover the genotype of the mate. Of course, you always take advantage of a situation like this to determine as much as you can about the genotype of your animal, even if your intent was not test-mating when the breeding took place. Depending on the trait in question, you may get the appropriate information months or even years after the dogs were mated. Even so, it may still be very useful for what it tells you about the offspring.

Lastly, as you will see in Table 5.3, heterozygote test-matings may be useful when combined with homozygous recessive test-matings, even in breeds with characteristically small litters.

Table 5.2

Probability that an unknown animal is homozygous dominant *(AA)* for a given autosomal recessive trait when bred to an animal *affected (aa)* with that trait.

Number of normal offspring	*Probability the unknown animal is homozygous dominant (AA, noncarrier)*	*Number of normal offspring*	*Probability the unknown animal is homozygous dominant (AA, noncarrier)*
1	50.0%	9	99.8%
2	75.0%	10	99.9%
3	87.5%	11	—
4	93.8%	12	—
5	96.8%	13	—
6	98.4%	14	—
7	99.2%	15	—
8	99.6%	16	—

Table 5.2 presents the probabilities that the dog or bitch being tested is homozygous dominant *(AA)* for the gene in question when bred to a homozygous recessive *(aa)* test mate. Remember that the genotype of the test-mate dog (or bitch) is what has to be known for a test-mating to occur. Therefore, if a second mating is required to accumulate sufficient data on the animal being tested, the second mating does not have to be made to the same dog or bitch. It can be made to any dog or bitch that has the correct genotype, and the results are cumulative. If you look at the data in Table 5.2, you will see that with three puppies, you have a certainty of 87.5 percent, and with four puppies, there is a 93.8 percent certainty that the bitch (or dog) being tested is homozygous dominant *(AA)* for the gene in question. It is for this reason that we recommend homozygous recessive test-matings for breeds that produce small litters (three or four puppies). However, even in this situation, breeds averaging one or two puppies per litter make this approach to determining the genotype of a given bitch nearly impractical. With males, even in one- or two-puppy litter breeds, this still remains a practical method of determining genotype and can be quite useful, especially with matadors.

Table 5.2a is so labeled because it also deals with test-mating to an affected animal. Using this table as presented requires that you start the test-mating with a dog that has a 50-percent chance of being a carrier (and thus a 50-percent chance of being normal *AA*). It is a more accurate method of calculating probabilities, and with small numbers of offspring, it presents a useful increase in determining whether a dog will be genetically normal for a given trait. With larger numbers of offspring, it makes little difference which table you use. This is the Bayesian method of calculating carrier status; the table presented here is adapted from a paper by E. A. Murphy.[1]

Table 5.2a

Probability that a dog with a 50-percent risk of being a carrier is in reality homozygous dominant *(AA)* for a given autosomal recessive trait when bred to animals that are *affected (aa)* with that trait using the Bayesian method of calculation.

Number of normal offspring	*Probability the unknown animal is homozygous dominant (AA, noncarrier)*	*Number of normal offspring*	*Probability the unknown animal is homozygous dominant (AA, noncarrier)*
0	50.0%	7	99.2%
1	66.6%	8	99.6%
2	80.0%	9	99.8%
3	88.9%	10	99.9%
4	94.2%	15	—
5	97.0%	20	—
6	98.5%		

Adapted from E. A. Murphy.

(1) Murphy, E. A. and G. S. Mutalik. *The Application of Bayesian Methods in Genetic Counseling,* 19:126–151. Hum. Hered., 1969.

Table 5.3

Probability (in percentages) that an unknown animal is homozygous dominant *(AA)* for a given autosomal recessive trait when bred to animals that are either heterozygotes *(Aa,* carriers) or homozygous recessive *(aa,* affected) for that trait.

		Number of Unaffected Puppies when Bred to Homozygous Recessives (aa, affected)								
		0	1	2	3	4	5	6	7	8
Number of Unaffected Puppies When Bred to Hetero-zygotes (Aa, carrier)	0	Na	50	75	87.5	93.8	96.8	98.4	99.2	99.6
	1	25	62.5	81.3	90.6	95.3	97.7	98.8	99.4	99.7
	2	43.7	71.7	85.9	92.8	96.5	98.2	99.1	99.6	99.8
	3	57.8	78.9	89.5	94.7	97.3	98.7	99.1	99.7	99.8
	4	68.4	84.2	92.1	96.0	98.0	99.0	99.3	99.8	99.9
	5	76.3	88.1	94.1	97.0	98.5	99.3	99.5	99.8	99.9
	6	82.2	91.1	95.6	97.8	98.8	99.2	99.6	99.9	
	7	86.6	93.3	96.7	98.3	98.9	99.4	99.7	99.9	
	8	90.0	94.9	97.5	98.7	99.4	99.6	99.9		
	9	92.5	96.3	98.1	99.0	99.5	99.7	99.9		
	10	94.4	97.2	98.5	99.3	99.6	99.8	99.9		
	11	95.8	97.8	98.9	99.4	99.8	99.9			
	12	96.8	98.4	99.2	99.6	99.8	99.9			
	13	97.6	98.8	99.4	99.7	99.9				
	14	98.2	99.1	99.5	99.8	99.9				
	15	98.7	99.3	99.6	99.8	99.9				
	16	99.0	99.5	99.7	99.8	99.9				

Adapted from Anne Sanders, personal communication, 1987.

Table 5.3 gives the probability that an animal is homozygous dominant for a given trait when bred to both homozygous recessive and heterozygous animals for that trait. This table is especially useful with retrospective test-matings where the genotype of the test-mate dog was not known at the time of the mating. The data for the two types of matings is combined. For example, if your bitch produced four puppies when bred to a carrier, and two puppies when bred to an affected dog, and all of the offspring are phenotypically normal, then there is a 92.1-percent chance that your bitch is genetically normal.

Remember that it is not essential that a breeding was intended to be a test-mating in order for a test-mating to occur. The data is just as valid, whether or not that was your intention. So if a situation arises in which your dog was bred to either a carrier or to a dog that later developed an autosomal recessive trait, why not use the data to improve your knowledge about the genotype of your own dogs?

Table 5.4 gives the risks of an animal being homozygous dominant for a given trait when bred to a number of mates when you have no specific knowledge of the genotype of any of the animals to which he/she was bred. In other words, this is a random-mating test-mating table. In order for a table like this to be useful, you must know something about the frequency of the trait—and thus the gene(s)—in the general population of dogs within a given breed. At the moment, there is a paucity of such information. It is clear, however, that with the advent of open registries, such data is becoming available. I will discuss this situation much more extensively in Chapters 7, "The Interpretation and Use of Pedigrees to Determine the Probable Mode of Inheritance of a Trait" and 8, "Test-Mating."

Table 5.4

Chance that a dog will be homozygous dominant *(AA)*
for a given autosomal recessive gene when bred to a partner population
with a given frequency of that gene and all offspring are normal.

Number of Matings	Frequency of Carriers in Population: 5%			10%			25%		
	Number of Dogs in the Litter: 1	5	10	1	5	10	1	5	10
	%	%	%	%	%	%	%	%	%
1	2	7	9	5	14	17	10	31	38
5	11	31	38	21	53	61	41	84	91
10	22	53	61	37	78	85	65	97	99
20	38	78	85	61	95	98	88	99	
30	52	90	94	75	96	99	99		
40	62	95	98	84	99		99		
50	70	98	99	90	99				
60	77	99		94	99				
70	82	99		96	99				
80	86	99		98	99				
100	91	99		99					
150	97	99							

Table 5.4 is very specialized and is most useful with dogs that have produced large numbers of offspring (matadors). Further, to use this table, you must know the frequency of carriers in the general population of the breed. Using this table, you can approximate the chance that a dog will be free (homozygous dominant) of the gene(s) for any given trait for which you have the appropriate information. As with all the above tables, whenever an animal produces an affected offspring, that animal is a proven (defined) carrier, independent of the number of normal puppies produced. This table is not used if you know the specific genotype for the trait in question of any of the dogs your animal is bred to. The other tables are much more efficient with known genotypes.

To use this table, let's say that your dog has produced fifty puppies in ten matings, and you know nothing about his genotype in regard to *craniomandibular osteopathy* (CMO), a recessive trait. But you do know that the frequency of dogs affected with CMO in your breed is 2 percent. Using the Hardy-Weinberg law, you can calculate a carrier frequency of 24.2 percent for this trait. Using Table 5.4, your dog has ten matings, averaging five puppies per litter (fifty puppies). Use the portion of the table with a frequency of 25 percent, and you find that your dog has about an 97-percent chance of being genetically normal for that trait.

This table allows us to estimate the genotype of matadors. At the present time, we know what is negative about matadors. That is, we know from gossip what diseases they produce, but we know nothing of what is good about them; we collect no information about what diseases they do *not* produce. It is essential that we start gathering data about the good points of matadors, and this is discussed extensively in chapter 10.

It is important to understand that if we have accurate information on the traits a dog produces, we also get accurate information on the traits he does *not* produce. This is why open registries are so important in the control of genetic disease. Knowledge about matadors (if it is accurate and complete) allows us to predict their genotype for all traits that occur in the breed, as long as we know the frequency of the trait within that breed. All clubs that have had the courage to generate a survey of the frequency of genetic defects in their breed have a running start on those clubs that still choose to bury their heads in the sand.

An additional table to be used with autosomal recessive traits involves the mating of the sire to his own daughters. This type of test-mating evaluates the sire for the presence of all undesirable recessive genes he may carry.

Table 5.5

Probability that a sire still carries undesirable recessive genes when bred to his own daughters.

Litter size without an affected offspring	*Probability* for a litter of given size*	*Litter size without an affected offspring*	*Probability* for a litter of given size*
1	88%	11	52%
2	78%	12	52%
3	71%	13	51%
4	66%	14	51%
5	62%	15	51%
6	59%	16	51%
7	57%	17	50%
8	55%	18	50%
9	54%	19	50%
10	53%	20	50%

*Multiply the probability for each litter produced together to get the overall risk for the sire.

To understand how to use this table, suppose that a sire is bred to four of his own daughters, producing four litters of five, six, seven and eight puppies, and all are phenotypically normal. The appropriate litter percentage probabilities are 62, 59, 57 and 55, respectively. These are multiplied together:

$$0.62 \times 0.59 \times 0.57 \times 0.55 = .114 \times 100 = 11.4\%$$

There is an 11.4 percent chance that the sire still carries an undesirable recessive gene. The opposite, of course, is also true. There is an 88.6 percent chance that the sire carries no undesirable recessive genes.

How useful is such information? In my opinion, very useful, but we do not have enough general information on the frequency of defects in purebred dogs. It is essential that we start collecting it. With a few breeds, we have some reasonable information on frequency. Using Newfoundlands as an example, the breed averages 5.8 puppies per litter, so Newfoundlands in a test-breeding situation could easily have produced the four litters discussed above. From a survey on this breed conducted by the Newfoundland Club of America in 1989, we have a rough estimate of the frequency of twenty-seven traits in this breed. Of these twenty-seven traits, seventeen have a carrier frequency higher than 11.4 percent. In Newfoundlands, then, this tested sire becomes a better risk than selecting an unknown male for seventeen separate traits. This is the type of data needed if breeders are to try to control genetic disease in purebred dogs. This point is be discussed extensively in Chapter 8, "Test-Mating."

Instead of this sire producing no affected puppies, let's assume that he produces a puppy with PRA in the six-puppy litter. Both he and his daughter, the mother of that litter, become proven carriers (they produced an affected puppy) of PRA. You, of course, are not happy with that, but you have now test-mated the other three daughters against a proven carrier. Using Table 5.1, these three daughters have a 76.3 percent (5 puppies), 86.6 percent (7 puppies), and 90 percent (8 puppies) chance of being homozygous dominant for PRA (noncarriers). When we do a test-mating, we should use all the information the mating provides.

The last table I will introduce in this section is the empiric, or *a priori,* risk that related animals carry as a result of being related to a dog or bitch affected with an autosomal recessive trait. This, of course, is a minimum risk, since other (perhaps unknown) related animals that are affected or are carriers could increase the chance of each of these dogs carrying the gene in question.

Table 5.6

Risk of being a carrier if related to an affected dog (autosomal recessive trait).

	Degree of relationship	*Minimum Carrier risk*
1 = Parent, progeny	1	100.0%
2 = Full brother/sister	1	66.6%
3 = Grandparents, aunts, uncles, half-brothers or sisters, grandchildren	2	50.0%
4 = Niece, nephew	2	33.3%
5 = Great-grandparent, first cousins, half-aunts and uncles, great grandchildren	3	25.0%
6 = Great-great-grandparents, first cousin once removed, second cousins	—	12.5%
7 = Great-great-great-grandparent, first cousin twice removed, third cousins	—	6.25%

Test-Mating Table for Autosomal Dominant Traits

Since autosomal dominant traits express themselves in the phenotype of animals that are heterozygous for dominant genes, tables are not necessary to establish the genotype, because the genotype is rarely hidden as it is with recessive traits.

There are what are called *incomplete dominants*—dominant traits with incomplete penetrance. These are dominant traits in which the dominant genotype is said to be present, but the appropriate phenotype is not shown or expressed. The most common example of an incomplete dominant in dogs is von Willebrand's disease. This is a bleeding disorder of dogs, which apparently occurs in many breeds. However, based on clinical pathologic tests, the affected dogs often do not show the defect in hemostasis phenotypically. This is a puzzling situation, and it is discussed more extensively in chapter 10.

Test-Mating Table for Sex-Linked Recessive Traits (X-Linked Traits)

Table 5.7

Probability that an unknown female is homozygous dominant *(AA)* for a given sex-linked recessive trait when bred to any nonaffected male.

Number of normal male offspring (only male offspring are counted for this test)	*Probability that the unknown female is homozygous dominant (AA, noncarrier)*
1	50.0%
2	75.0%
3	87.5%
4	93.8%
5	96.8%
6	98.4%
7	99.2%
8	99.6%

Since any mating of a female to a phenotypically normal male is a test-mating for sex-linked traits, nearly all females, in any and every breed, that have produced offspring have an established probability that they carry or do not carry a sex-linked gene. The problem is we do not collect this information and make it available to breeders in those breeds that are known to have sex-linked traits among their defects. With the exception of new mutations, there is no reason for sex-linked traits to persist in dogs, except that no one has paid much attention to them, and no one has pointed out how to control them. If you can recognize the defect and count to eight, you can control sex-linked traits. This statement is true even in small-litter breeds. If a breed averages three or four puppies per litter, any bitch producing two litters is likely to produce four males in them. If she produces four males and all are phenotypically normal, there is a 93.8-percent chance that she is not a carrier.

Tables for Use in Predicting the Production of Affected or Carrier Offspring with Autosomal Recessive Traits

Sum of Digits

Figure 5.1 shows the probability of producing an affected (homozygous recessive) puppy from parents with dogs of known genotype for a given trait among the parents' ancestors.

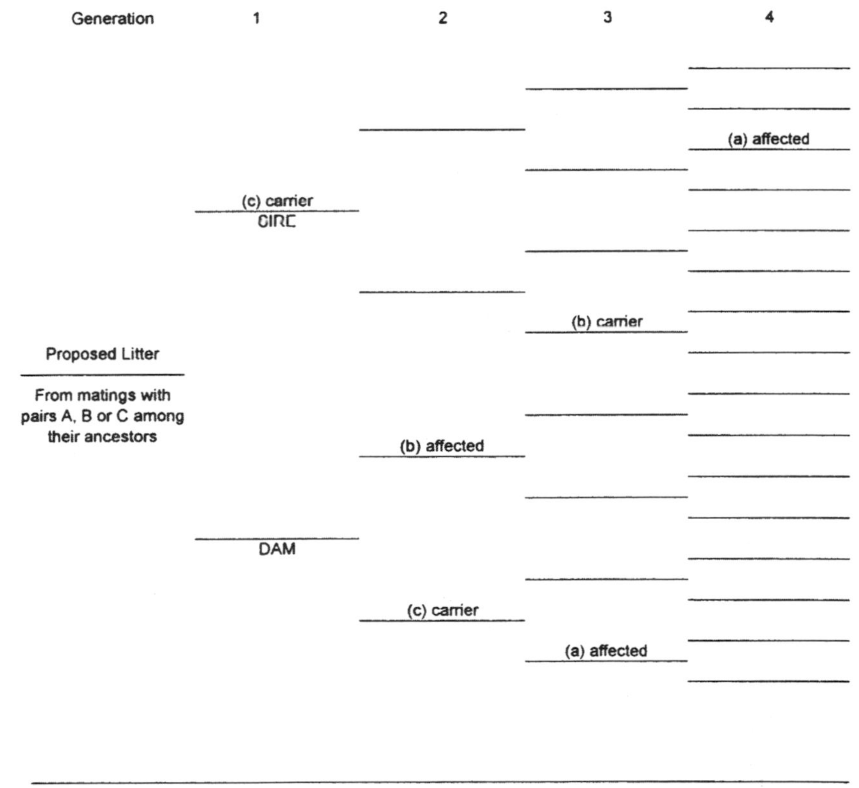

Fig. 5.1 Pedigree for sum of digits.

Table 5.8*

Probability of producing a homozygous recessive (affected) puppy using sum of digits.

Sum of digits	*Probability for an affected puppy*		
	AA(1)	*AC*(2)	*CC*(3)
2	100.0%	50.0%	25.0%
3	50.0%	25.0%	12.5%
4	25.0%	12.5%	6.25%
5	12.5%	6.25%	3.13%
6	6.25%	3.13%	1.56%
7	3.13%	1.56%	0.78%
8	1.56%	0.78%	0.39%

(1) Affected-affected combination *(a-a,* Fig. 5.1)
(2) Affected-carrier combination *(b-b,* Fig. 5.1)
(3) Carrier-carrier combination *(c-c,* Fig. 5.1)
*Adapted from Fisher, T. M. *Genetic Counseling,* 63:37–42. Med. Vet. Pract., 1982.

Figure 5.1 shows examples of three genetic combinations. In the combination of *a-a,* there is an affected animal in generation #3 and an affected animal in generation #4, sum of digits 3 + 4 = 7. Look under sum of digits, row #7, column #1 *(AA,* affected-affected), and you find that each puppy has a 3.13-percent risk of being affected in the proposed litter.

In the combination of *b-b,* there is an affected animal in generation #2 and a carrier animal in generation #3, sum of digits 2 + 3 = 5. Look under row #5, column #2 *(AC,* affected-carrier), and you find that each puppy has a 6.25-percent risk of being affected in the proposed litter.

In the combination of *c-c,* there is a carrier in generation #1 and a carrier in generation #2, sum of digits 1 + 2 = 3. Look under row #3, column #3 *(CC,* carrier-carrier), and you will find that each puppy has a 12.5-percent chance of being affected in the proposed mating.

Whether you decide to mate a particular dam and sire with any possible combination of phenotypes among the antecedents should be dependent on the severity of the trait and the frequency of the trait in the breed in question. If the risk in the proposed mating is higher than the average risk in the breed involved and the trait is a severe one, the mating is probably not a good idea.

Another way to arrive at the same answers as in the sum of digits follows.

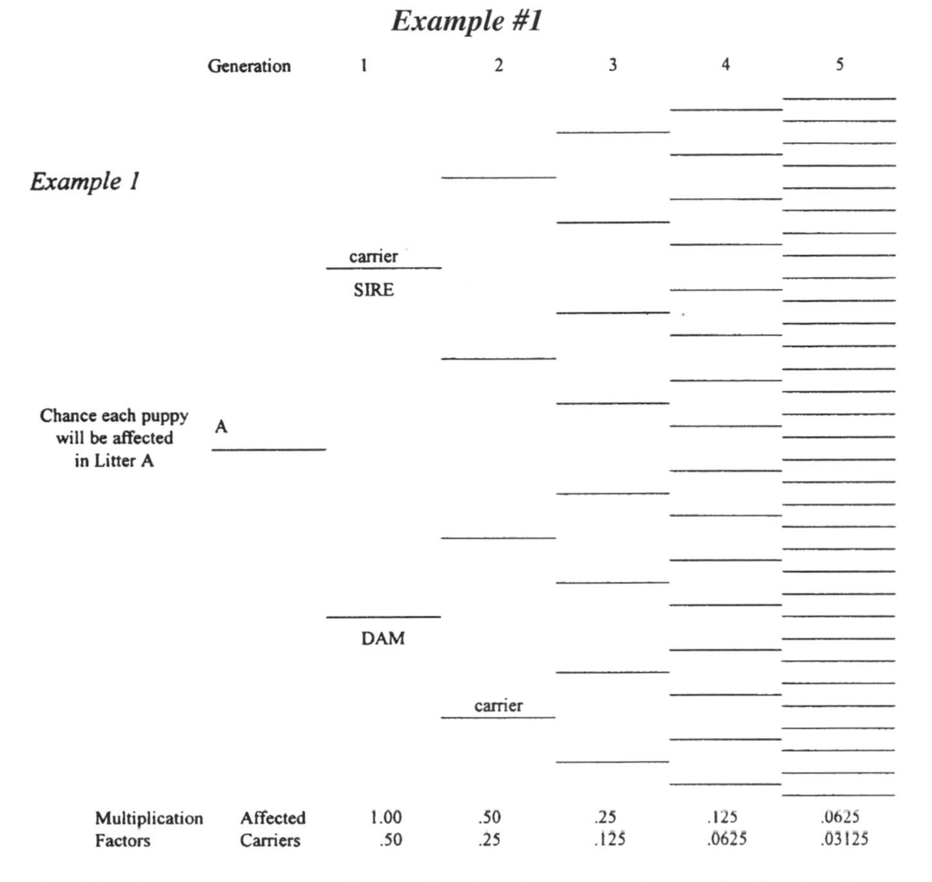

Fig. 5.2 *Five-generation pedigree showing the appropriate multiplication factors for animals of known genotype in any of the five generations to establish the risk each puppy in litter A has to develop a specific autosomal recessive trait.*

In Example #1, there are carriers in generations #1 and #2, using the carrier multiplication factors

$.50 \times .25 = .125 \times 100 = 12.5$ percent

the same as the carrier-carrier example in sum of digits.

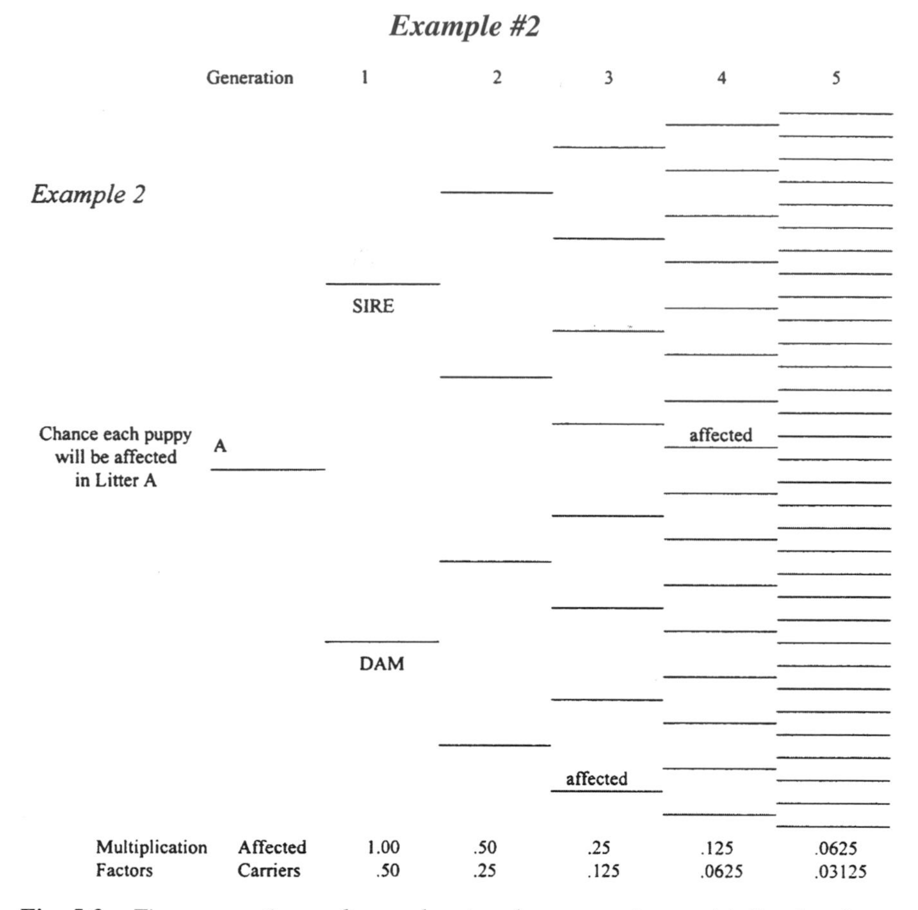

Fig. 5.3 *Five-generation pedigree showing the appropriate multiplication factors for animals of known genotype in any of the five generations to establish the risk each puppy in litter A has to develop a specific autosomal recessive trait.*

In Example #2, there are affected dogs in generations #3 and #4. Using the appropriate multiplication factors for affecteds,

$.25 \times .125 = .03125 \times 100 = 3.125$ percent

the same as the affected-affected example in sum of digits.

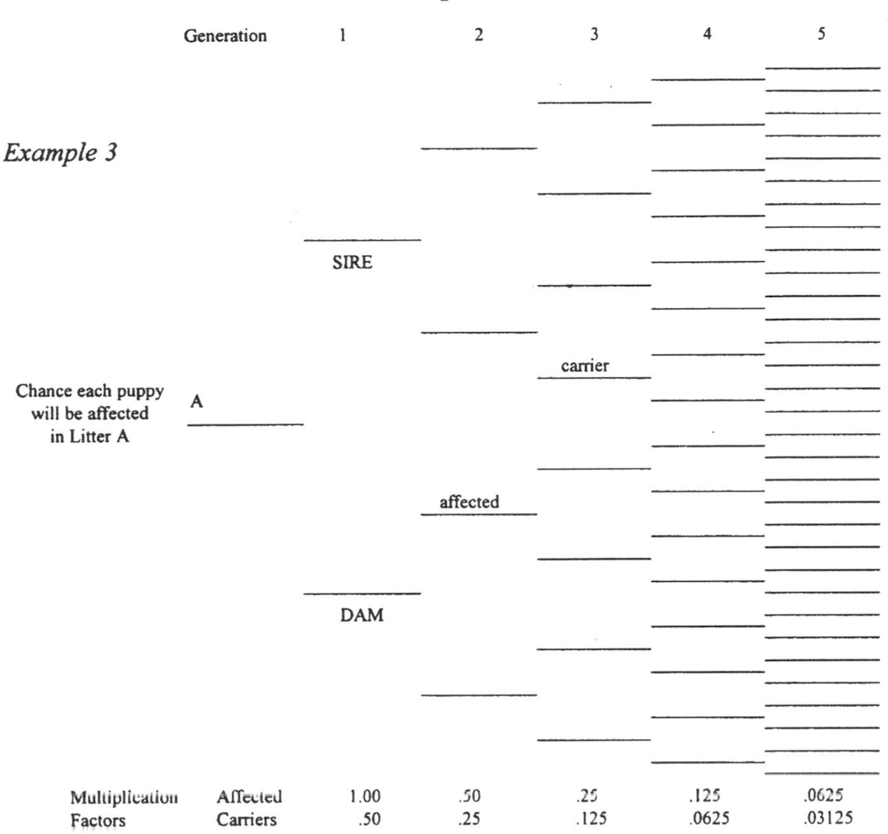

Fig. 5.4 *Five-generation pedigree showing the appropriate multiplication factors for animals of known genotype in any of the five generations to establish the risk each puppy in litter A has to develop a specific autosomal recessive trait.*

In Example #3, there is a carrier in generation #3 and an affected in generation #2. Using the appropriate multiplication factors for each,

$.125 \times .50 = .0625 \times 100 = 6.25$ percent

the same as the affected-carrier example in sum of digits.

It is important to remember with the above three examples, as well as with sum of digits, that you must have information on the dogs on both the sire's and dam's sides of the pedigree. If you have data on just the sire's side or just the dam's side, you will not be able to predict the outcome of any mating. Further, only the data closest to the proposed mating counts in the evaluations. All data on affecteds or carriers behind the closest-known carrier or closest-known affected is crossed off, since the risk is summarized in the closest relative. For example, in Figure 5.5, we have crossed off all known phenotypes and genotypes behind those most closely related to the proposed litter.

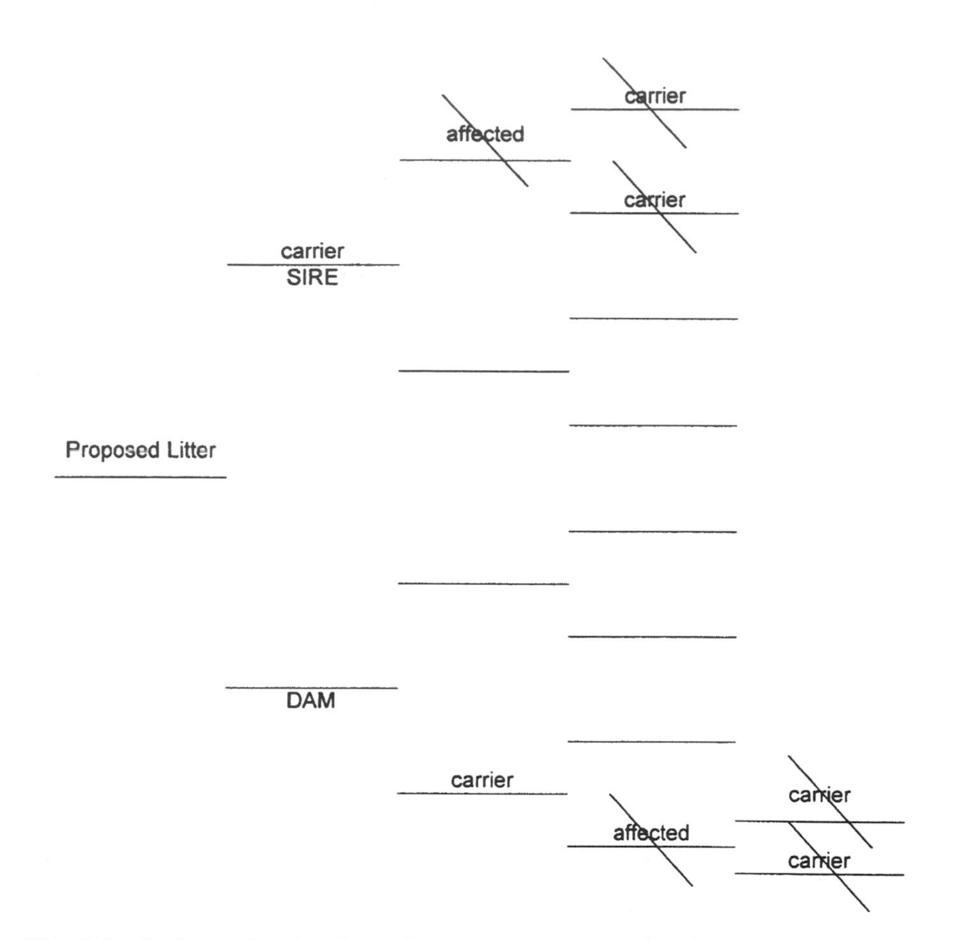

Fig. 5.5 *Pedigree showing that only dogs most closely related to the proposed litter are used when calculating the risk each dog in the litter has to develop a given trait.*

A third method of predicting the production of affecteds in a given litter is that used by G. M. Grant.[2] His tables allow you to predict both affecteds and carriers in the offspring of a proposed mating.

The tables are based on four-generation pedigrees of phenotypically dominant animals for which the occurrence of homozygous recessives or heterozygotes among their ancestors is known.

(2) Grant, G. M. *A Method to Predict the Probabilities of Homozygous Recessive and of Heterozygotes,* 67:393–396. J. Hered., 1976.

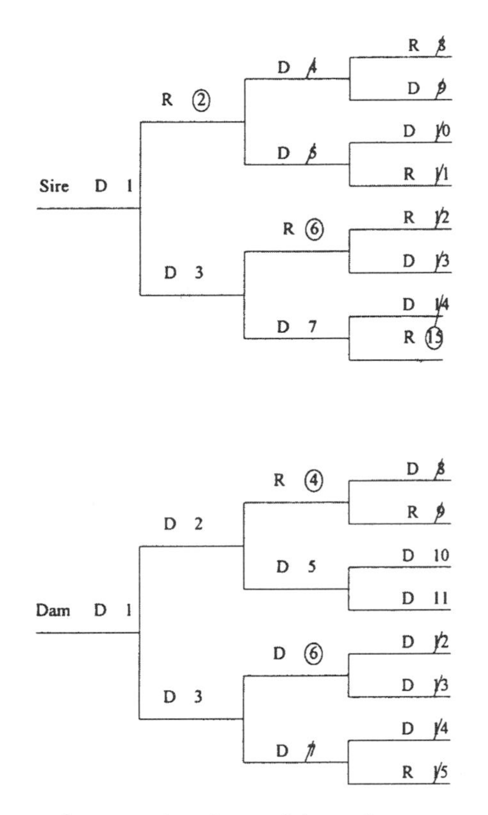

Fig. 5.6 *Pedigrees of prospective sire and dam whose progeny probabilities are to be evaluated.*

To understand how to use these tables, assume that the prospective mating of the sire and dam whose pedigrees are given in Figure 5.6 is to be evaluated. Each animal in the pedigrees is designated *D* or *R* to indicate either a dominant or recessive phenotype, and the animals are numbered in the sequence shown. Then, commencing from the lowest code number, circle the code numbers for all homozygous recessives in ascending numerical order. As you circle each code number, cross off all ancestors of that animal. Thus, in the pedigree of the sire in Figure 5.1, circle #2 and cross off 4, 5, 8, 9, 10 and 11. Then, circle #6 and cross off 12 and 13; finally, circle #15. The circled code numbers then are listed in ascending numerical order to give the code combination for that pedigree—for example, for the sire, 2-6-15.

You repeat the process for the pedigree of the dam, but to understand the procedure for known heterozygotes in a pedigree, assume that ancestor #3 in the dam's pedigree is known to have produced recessive phenotype progeny. In such a case, circle one only (either one) of its parents, and cross off the remaining parent and all ancestors of both parents. The code combination for the dam is then 4-6.

Table 5.9 lists all possible code combinations, along with a code letter for each. This letter is the key to the column for the sire, or row for the dam, in Table 5.10. In Table 5.10, at the intersection of the sire's column (under the appropriate code letter) and the dam's row (adjacent to the appropriate code letter), the upper figure is the probability that the progeny in the fifth generation will be homozygous recessive. The lower figure is the probability that a dominant phenotype progeny would be heterozygous. The lower figure subtracted from 100 is the probability that the progeny will be homozygous dominant. For the pedigrees of Figure 5.6, the code letter for the sire is B and for the dam C, so these probabilities are 16.7 percent and 60.0 percent.

Given the 232 possible code number combinations in Table 5.9, the method allows simple prediction for the possible 53,824 (232^2) matings.

Table 5.9*

Possible code number combinations that can be derived from a pedigree and the code letter for each.

1-	A	4-10-12	E	5-8-14	E	6-10-14	E	8-10-13	G	9-11-13-15	F
2-	B	4-10-12-14	E	5-8-15	E	6-10-15	E	8-10-13-14	F	9-11-14	G
2-6	B	4-10-12-15	E	5-9	F	6-11	E	8-10-13-15	F	9-11-15	G
2-6-14	B	4-10-13	E	5-9-12	E	6-11-14	E	8-10-14	G	9-12	H
2-6-15	B	4-10-13-14	E	5-9-12-14	E	6-11-15	E	8-10-15	G	9-12-14	G
2-7	B	4-10-13-15	E	5-9-12-15	E	6-14	F	8-11	I	9-12-15	G
2-7-12	B	4-10-14	E	5-9-13	E	6-15	F	8-11-12	G	9-13	H
2-7-13	B	4-10-15	E	5-9-13-14	E	7-	F	8-11-12-14	F	9-13-14	G
2-12	B	4-11	E	5-9-13-15	E	7-8	E	8-11-12-15	F	9-13-15	G
2-12-14	B	4-11-12	E	5-9-14	E	7-8-10	D	8-11-13	G	9-14	H
2-12-15	B	4-11-12-14	E	5-9-15	E	7-8-10-12	G	8-11-13-14	F	9-15	H
2-13	B	4-11-12-15	E	5-12	E	7-8-10-13	G	8-11-13-15	F	10-	J
2-13-14	B	4-11-13	E	5-12-14	D	7-8-11	D	8-11-14	G	10-12	H
2-13-15	B	4-11-13-14	E	5-12-15	D	7-8-11-12	G	8-11-15	G	10-12-14	G
2-14	B	4-11-13-15	E	5-13	E	7-8-11-13	G	8-12	H	10-12-15	G
2-15	B	4-11-14	E	5-13-14	D	7-8-12	E	8-12-14	G	10-13	H
3-	B	4-11-15	E	5-13-15	D	7-8-13	E	8-12-15	G	10-13-14	G
3-4	B	4-12	E	5-14	E	7-9	E	8-13	H	10-13-15	G
3-4-10	B	4-12-14	D	5-15	E	7-9-10	D	8-13-14	G	10-14	H
3-4-11	B	4-12-15	D	6-	F	7-9-10-12	G	8-13-15	G	10-15	H
3-5	B	4-13	E	6-8	E	7-9-10-13	G	8-14	H	11-	J
3-5-8	B	4-13-14	D	6-8-10	D	7-9-11	D	8-15	H	11-12	H
3-5-9	B	4-13-15	D	6-8-10-14	G	7-9-11-12	G	9-	J	11-12-14	G
3-8	B	4-14	E	6-8-10-15	G	7-9-11-13	G	9-10	I	11-12-15	G
3-8-10	B	4-15	E	6-8-11	D	7-9-12	E	9-10-12	G	11-13	H
3-8-11	B	5-	F	6-8-11-14	G	7-9-13	E	9-10-12-14	F	11-13-14	G
3-9	B	5-6	C	6-8-11-15	G	7-10	E	9-10-12-15	F	11-13-15	G
3-9-10	B	5-6-14	C	6-8-14	E	7-10-12	E	9-10-13	G	11-14	H
3-9-11	B	5-6-15	C	6-8-15	E	7-10-13	E	9-10-13-14	F	11-15	H
3-10	B	5-7	C	6-9	E	7-11	E	9-10-13-15	F	12-	J
3-11	B	5-7-12	C	6-9-10	D	7-11-12	E	9-10-14	G	12-14	I
4-	F	5-7-13	C	6-9-10-14	G	7-11-13	E	9-10-15	G	12-15	I
4-6	C	5-8	F	6-9-10-15	G	7-12	F	9-11	I	13-	J
4-6-14	C	5-8-12	E	6-9-11	D	7-13	F	9-11-12	G	13-14	I
4-6-15	C	5-8-12-14	E	6-9-11-14	G	8-	J	9-11-12-14	F	13-15	I
4-7	C	5-8-12-15	E	6-9-11-15	G	8-10	I	9-11-12-15	F	14-	J
4-7-12	C	5-8-13	E	6-9-14	E	8-10-12	G	9-11-13	G	15-	J
4-7-13	C	5-8-13-14	E	6-9-15	E	8-10-12-14	F	9-11-13-14	F	NIL	K
4-10	F	5-8-13-15	E	6-10	E	8-10-12-15	F				

*Taken from Grant, G. M. *A Method to Predict the Probabilities of Homozygous Recessive and of Heterozygotes,* 67:393–396. J. Hered., 1976.

Table 5.10*

Probabilities (expressed as percentages) that progeny of a particular mating will be either homozygous recessive (upper figure in each block) or heterozygous (lower figure in each block) if of dominant phenotype.

DAM Code letter from Table I	SIRE Code letter from Table I										
	A	B	C	D	E	F	G	H	I	J	K
A	†	50.0	33.3	30.0	28.6	25.0	22.7	20.0	16.7	12.5	0
		100.0	100.0	100.0	100.0	100.0	100.0	100.0	100.0	100.0	100.0
B	50.0	25.0	16.7	15.0	14.3	12.5	11.4	10.0	8.3	6.3	0
	100.0	66.7	60.0	58.8	58.3	57.1	56.4	55.6	54.5	53.3	50.0
C	33.3	16.7	11.1	10.0	9.5	8.3	7.6	6.7	5.6	4.2	0
	100.0	60.0	50.0	48.1	47.4	45.5	44.3	42.9	41.2	39.1	33.3
D	30.0	15.0	10.0	9.0	8.6	7.5	6.8	6.0	5.0	3.8	0
	100.0	58.8	48.1	46.2	45.3	43.2	42.0	40.4	38.6	36.4	30.0
E	28.6	14.3	9.5	8.6	8.2	7.1	6.5	5.7	4.8	3.6	0
	100.0	58.3	47.4	45.3	44.4	42.3	41.0	39.4	37.5	35.2	28.6
F	25.0	12.5	8.3	7.5	7.1	6.3	5.7	5.0	4.2	3.1	0
	100.0	57.1	45.5	43.2	42.3	40.0	38.6	36.8	34.8	32.3	25.0
G	22.7	11.4	7.6	6.8	6.5	5.7	5.2	4.6	3.8	2.8	0
	100.0	56.4	44.3	42.0	41.0	38.6	37.0	35.2	33.1	30.4	22.7
H	20.0	10.0	6.7	6.0	5.7	5.0	4.6	4.0	3.3	2.5	0
	100.0	55.6	42.9	40.4	39.4	36.8	35.2	33.3	31.0	28.2	20.0
I	16.7	8.3	5.6	5.0	4.8	4.2	3.8	3.3	2.8	2.1	0
	100.0	54.5	41.2	38.6	37.5	34.8	33.1	31.0	28.6	25.5	16.7
J	12.5	6.3	4.2	3.8	3.6	3.1	2.8	2.5	2.1	1.6	0
	100.0	53.3	39.1	36.4	35.2	32.3	30.4	28.2	25.5	22.2	12.5
K	0	0	0	0	0	0	0	0	0	0	‡
	100.0	50.0	33.3	30.0	28.6	25.0	22.7	20.0	16.7	12.5	

*Taken from Grant, G. M. A Method to Predict the Probabilities of Homozygous Recessive and of Heterozygotes, 67:393–396. J. Hered., 1976.

†All homozygous recessive

‡All homozygous dominant

All three of the above methods of predicting the occurrence of an affected or carrier offspring in a given litter are based on the same genetic principles expressed in slightly different ways. So use the one that you understand the best and is easiest to use. It is important to remember and to understand that the use of any of the three is based on knowledge of the phenotype and genotype of specific animals in a pedigree. So, if we want to understand what is likely to happen in a given mating, we must be willing to make the essential information available. We must be willing to talk about dogs that have defects or that produce them if we want to control genetic disease. We must be willing to register such dogs in open registries so that verifiable information becomes available for use by breeders in the production of healthy, winning dogs.

Product and Sum Rules

The last bits of information we need in order to calculate risks and to establish genotypes (or, more accurately, *potential* genotypes), are the *product rule,* the *sum rule, conditional probabilities,* and the *dilution rule.*

The product rule states that when two or more independent events occur, the probability that both will occur simultaneously and in a particular manner can be calculated. When genes assort randomly or independently, the probability of two or more outcomes simultaneously occurring is equal to the product of the individual probabilities. This rule, of course, is the basis for all three methods of predicting the occurrence of an affected puppy in matings in which we know the genotype of specific individuals in the pedigree.

As an example of the use of the product rule, let's take a heterozygous male *(Aa)* and a heterozygous female *(Aa)* and examine all possible combinations of genes that could occur when they are mated. In each sperm and in each ovum, there is a 50:50 chance that an *A* or an *a* could occur, so the possible risks for each occurrence follow:

$$M_A \bullet F_A = (.5) \times (.5) = .25 = 25 \text{ percent}$$
$$M_A \bullet F_a = (.5) \times (.5) = .25 = 25 \text{ percent}$$
$$M_a \bullet F_A = (.5) \times (.5) = .25 = 25 \text{ percent}$$
$$M_a \bullet F_a = (.5) \times (.5) = .25 = 25 \text{ percent}$$

The possibility of getting a dominant or a recessive gene from either parent is independent of getting a dominant or a recessive gene from the opposite parent. Therefore, all four possible outcomes have an equal probability (25 percent), which is the product of the respective risks.

If we are interested in a generalized outcome and the probabilities associated with it, we use the *sum rule.* The outcomes must be independent and mutually exclusive in order to use this rule. For example, if we ask the question, "What is the chance of getting a dominant gene and a recessive gene in an individual?" and we don't care which gene is from the father or which gene is from the mother, then we sum the individual probabilities. In the above example, the probability of M_A F_a is .25, and the probability of M_a F_A is .25. Thus, the overall probability according to the sum rule is equal to

$$.25 + .25 = .50 = 50 \text{ percent}$$

Let's look at this in a pedigree and see how it works in practice.

In Figure 5.7, bitch #2 is a known carrier of an autosomal recessive trait. The sire, dog #1, is genetically normal for the trait. As offspring of bitch #2, each of the puppies in litter a has a 50:50 chance of having bitch #2's mutant gene passed to them (the dilution rule).

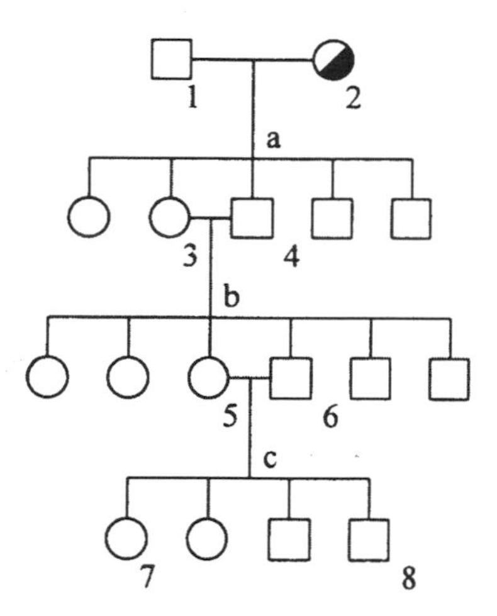

Fig. 5.7 *Pedigree illustrating the product rule, the sum rule, and the dilution rule.*

Using the product rule, the chance that both bitch #3 and dog #4 received the gene is

$.5 \times .5 = .25$ or 25 percent

Remember that the individual carrier risk for bitch #3 and dog #4 is still 50 percent.

Let's ask the question, "What is the risk for bitch #5 and dog #6, and all other puppies in litter b?" Since bitch #3 and dog #4 each have a 50-percent chance of having the mutant gene, their puppies each have a 25-percent chance of receiving that gene from each of their parents. Using the sum rule, the risk for bitch #5 and dog #6 and all other puppies in the litter is

$.25 + .25 = .50 = 50$ percent

The same analysis applies to all the puppies in litter c. Since both parents have an equal chance of being a carrier, there is no dilutionary effect, such as is seen in the mating between dog #1 and bitch #2 in Figure 5.7.

Conditional Probability

Now let's take a look at *conditional probability.* A conditional probability is one in which the probability we want to determine is based on a specific occurrence that is related to or dependent on a contingent occurrence.

Let's take a simple example we may all be interested in. What is the chance that a phenotypically normal littermate of a dog that is affected with an autosomal recessive trait is, in fact, a carrier of that trait? Since the outcome and specific condition are not independent, we cannot use the product rule. Let's call the conditional probability P_C. To solve for P_C, we must consider the probability of the specific condition that includes the outcome, as well as the outcome of the probability of interest.

P_a = *probability of any offspring of 2 carriers being a carrier* = .50

P_b = *probability of any offspring of 2 carriers being phenotypically normal* = .75

$$P_c = \frac{P_a}{P_b} = \frac{.5}{.75} = .666 = 66.6\%$$

The probability that a phenotypically normal littermate of an affected dog is a carrier is 66.6 percent.

The Dilution Rule

The dilution rule states that if a carrier (Aa) or affected (aa) dog or bitch is mated to a dog or bitch that is known to be genetically normal for that gene, the offspring will have half the risk of the carrier or affected parent for that gene.

For discussion purposes, let's go back to Figure 5.7. In this figure, bitch #2 is a known carrier of a recessive trait (there is a 100-percent chance that she is a carrier). She is bred to male #1, who is known to be homozygous dominant (a noncarrier) for the gene in question. Since she has a 50:50 chance of transmitting either the normal or the recessive gene to each of the offspring in litter a, the risk of each offspring is 50 percent (half her risk, which is 100 percent). The normal genotype of the sire assures us that the risk for each puppy cannot be more than half the dam's risk (he "dilutes" her risk).

These simple probability rules will be very helpful throughout our discussion of risks and the transmission of genes and traits. We must remember that in any discussion of probabilities, we are dealing with averages; the variations that occur due to small sample sizes should not cause us to abandon our long-term goals.

Tables Giving the Probabilities for the Distribution of Phenotypes and/or Genotypes for 1:1 and 3:1 Mendelian Ratios for Litter Sizes 4 Through 10

One of the more difficult aspects of genetics that a breeder has to grasp is the random distribution of traits and genotypes within a litter. If we say with a recessive trait that matings between carriers will result in three normal and one affected puppy in a litter of four, many people believe that we will always get three normal and one affected, or that in a litter of eight, we will always get six normal and two affected. The 3:1 ratio for matings between heterozygotes is an *average* ratio, and so the chance for other distributions to occur is always there. If we have a large number of matings and offspring to evaluate, there will always be a close approximation to the 3:1 expected ratio, but for any specific litter, the distribution may be quite different.

In 1932, B.L. Warwick developed a set of probability tables for various Mendelian ratios. These tables are as valid today as they were when they were developed. I am going to present Warwick's data for 3:1 and 1:1 Mendelian ratios for litter sizes of four to ten, because these are the ones that breeders are most likely to encounter. If, for some reason, you become interested in other ratios, they are available in Warwick's original work.[3]

If you refer back to Chapter 4, you will see that 1:1 Mendelian ratios are most likely to be encountered in the following situations:

1. A homozygous autosomal recessive bred to a heterozygote *(aa × Aa)*
2. A heterozygous female for a sex-linked recessive trait bred to a normal male *XX × XY* counting only male offspring
3. A heterozygote for an autosomal dominant trait bred to a normal mate *(Bb × bb)*
4. The normal distribution of sexes one male, one female (although there is generally a slight excess of males)

Referring again to Chapter 4, you will see that a 3:1 Mendelian ratio is generally encountered in the following situations:

1. For autosomal recessive traits, a heterozygote *(Aa × Aa)* bred to a heterozygote results in three phenotypically normal and one affected offspring.
2. For autosomal dominant traits, a heterozygote bred to a heterozygote *(Bb × Bb)* results in three affected (two heterozygotes, one homozygote) and one normal offspring.
3. For sex-linked recessive traits, a heterozygous female bred to a normal male (XX × XY), counting both male and female offspring, results in three normal and one affected (the affected offspring is always a male).
4. For a sex-linked dominant trait, a heterozygous female bred to an affected male (XX × XY) results in three affected and one normal offspring (the normal offspring is always a male).

(3) Warwick, B.L., 1932. Probability Tables for Mendelian Ratios with Small Numbers. Texas Agric. Exper. Stu. Bull. 463. 18 pp.

Table 5.11

Frequencies of various phenotypic combinations expected to occur in litters of 4.*

Combinations		*Dominant:Recessive*	*Dominant:Recessive*
D	*R*	*1:1*	*3:1*
4	0	6.25%	31.6%
3	1	25.0%	42.2%
2	2	37.5%	21.1%
1	3	25.0%	4.7%
0	4	6.25%	0.4%
		100.0%	100.0%

*As calculated by Warwick.

Table 5.12

Frequencies of various phenotypic combinations expected to occur in litters of 5.*

Combinations		*Dominant:Recessive*	*Dominant:Recessive*
D	*R*	*1:1*	*3:1*
5	0	3.1%	23.7%
4	1	15.6%	39.5%
3	2	31.3%	26.4%
2	3	31.3%	8.8%
1	4	15.6%	1.5%
0	5	3.1%	0.1%
		100.0%	100.0

*As calculated by Warwick.

Table 5.13

Frequencies of various phenotypic combinations expected to occur in litters of 6.*

Combinations		*Dominant:Recessive*	*Dominant:Recessive*
D	*R*	*1:1*	*3:1*
6	0	1.6%	17.8%
5	1	9.4%	35.6%
4	2	23.4%	29.7%
3	3	31.2%	13.2%
2	4	23.4%	3.3%
1	5	9.4%	0.4%
0	6	1.6%	0.02%
		100.0	100.0

*As calculated by Warwick.

Table 5.14

Frequencies of various phenotypic combinations expected to occur in litters of 7.*

Combinations		*Dominant:Recessive*	*Dominant:Recessive*
D	*R*	*1:1*	*3:1*
7	0	0.8%	Not given
6	1	5.5%	Not given
5	2	16.4%	31.2%
4	3	27.3%	17.3%
3	4	27.3%	5.8%
2	5	16.4%	1.2%
1	6	5.5%	0.1%
0	7	0.8%	0.01%
		100.0%	—

*As calculated by Warwick.

Table 5.15

Frequencies of various phenotypic combinations expected to occur in litters of 8.*

Combinations		*Dominant:Recessive*	*Dominant:Recessive*
D	*R*	*1:1*	*3:1*
8	0	0.4%	10.0%
7	1	3.1%	26.7%
6	2	10.9%	31.2%
5	3	21.9%	20.8%
4	4	27.3%	8.7%
3	5	21.9%	2.3%
2	6	10.9%	0.4%
1	7	3.1%	0.04%
0	8	0.4%	—
		100.0%	100.0%

*As calculated by Warwick.

Table 5.16

Frequencies of various phenotypic combinations expected to occur in litters of 9.*

Combinations		*Dominant:Recessive*	*Dominant:Recessive*
D	*R*	*1:1*	*3:1*
9	0	0.2%	7.5%
8	1	1.8%	22.5%
7	2	7.0%	30.0%
6	3	16.4%	23.4%
5	4	24.6%	11.7%
4	5	24.6%	3.9%
3	6	16.4%	0.9%
2	7	7.0%	0.1%
1	8	1.8%	0.01%
0	9	0.2%	—
		100.0%	100.0%

*As calculated by Warwick.

Table 5.17

Frequencies of various phenotypic combinations expected to occur in litters of 10.*

Combinations		*Dominant:Recessive*	*Dominant:Recessive*
D	*R*	*1:1*	*3:1*
10	0	0.1%	5.6%
9	1	1.0%	18.8%
8	2	4.4%	28.2%
7	3	11.7%	25.0%
6	4	20.5%	14.6%
5	5	24.6%	5.8%
4	6	20.5%	1.6%
3	7	11.7%	0.3%
2	8	4.4%	0.04%
1	9	1.0%	—
0	10	0.1%	—
		100.0%	100.0%

*As calculated by Warwick.

The use of these tables is fairly straightforward. Suppose that someone tells you they crossed two dogs that they were told carried a gene for Scottie Cramp (an autosomal recessive trait), because they had both produced before, and all five puppies they got were normal. Then they said, "I don't believe this trait is inherited, because if it is inherited, with five puppies, shouldn't we have gotten at least one affected?" Look at Table 5.12 under the 3:1 ratio (carrier *Aa* × carrier *Aa* = 3 normal, 1 affected), and you find that 23.7 percent of the time, you expect to get five normal and no affected puppies. This is the chance distribution of phenotypes that we expect in any statistical situation. But you often hear people make statements like the one above because they have not been apprised of these kinds of distributions. Hopefully, these tables that Warwick developed will help them more fully grasp standard distributions.

Questions on Chapter 5

1. Your bitch was bred to a Labrador Retriever male and produced 9 puppies, all normal. You later heard this male had produced 3 cases of PRA (autosomal recessive). This litter is now 5 years old and all are still normal.

   a. What is the chance this bitch is homozygous dominant?

   b. What is the chance these puppies are carriers?

   c. What about this sire's other puppies?

2. A sire was bred to 5 of his own daughters, producing 5, 7, 9, 6 and 7 puppies in these matings. All of his offspring were normal.

   What is his chance of being homozygous dominant (normal) for all major defects?

3. A Bedlington Terrier sire produced 20 litters with 20 different bitches and had a total of 110 puppies. The frequency of 5 reported diseases in this breed is 10%; of 4 separate diseases, the frequency is 25%; of 2 diseases, the frequency is 5%. Among these 20 bitches, 2 had produced renal cortical hypoplasia (autosomal recessive) in other litters, 1 bitch had 6 puppies with this sire, and the other bitch had 5 puppies with him. All these puppies were normal. He produced one case of cataracts (autosomal recessive).

   a. What is this sire's chance of being genetically normal for the 5 diseases having a frequency of 10%?

   b. For the 4 diseases with a frequency of 25%?

   c. For the 2 diseases with a frequency of 5%?

   d. What is his chance of being homozygous dominant for renal cortical hypoplasia?

   e. What is the risk of the other 18 bitches carrying renal cortical hypoplasia?

   f. What about his puppies in regard to cataracts?

   g. What about the bitches he was bred to in regard to cataracts?

   h. What do you think about this sire? Is he any good?

4. A Westie sire was bred to 7 bitches, producing a total of 26 puppies. The owner later discovered that 2 of the bitches had produced CMO (craniomandibular osteopathy, autosomal recessive) puppies in other litters: one in a litter of 3, the other in a litter of 4. In addition, the owner of the sire heard that 1 of the 7 bitches had CMO. He produced 4 puppies with her. This was later confirmed by asking the owner directly if the bitch had CMO. None of his puppies developed CMO.

   What is the chance that he is homozygous dominant (genetically normal) for CMO?

5. A Bull Terrier was a great-grandson of a bitch that produced acrodermatitis, an autosomal recessive trait in this breed. The owners decided to test-mate him to an affected bitch. He had 6 puppies with her, all normal.

   What's his chance of being homozygous dominant for this trait?

6. The great-granddam on the sire's side of your Golden Retriever bitch produced a puppy that developed PRA. Your bitch is a great dog conformation-wise, and you have no knowledge of any other serious traits in her background. You checked out a sire that's a good match for her, but his great-great-grandsire on the dam's side had PRA.

   a. What is the chance of producing a PRA-affected puppy in this litter?

   b. What is the chance of producing a carrier puppy in this litter?

7. The grandmother of your German Shepherd bitch produced a case of hemophilia B, a sex-linked recessive trait. The *a priori* probability that your bitch is a carrier is 25%. However, your bitch has already had 2 litters by outcross males that were known to be normal for this trait. There were 7 male puppies in the 2 litters, all normal for this trait.

   What is the chance your bitch is really normal—not a carrier for this trait?

8. You are talking with a friend of yours, a Bernese Mountain Dog breeder. He tells you he crossed a dog and a bitch that he was told were carriers for cerebellar hypoplasia (autosomal recessive) and got a litter of 9, all normal. He says he thinks genetics is all baloney, because none of the puppies were affected.

   a. What do you think?

   b. How often does this happen?

Answers for Chapter 5

1. a. Use Table 5.1, since the sire is a carrier (he is not affected himself, and he produced affected puppies). With 9 puppies, there is a 92.5% chance that the bitch is homozygous dominant (genotypically normal) for this trait.

   b. Since the sire is a carrier, all 9 puppies in this litter have a 50% risk of being carriers.

   c. Since the sire is a carrier, all his puppies have at least a 50% risk of being carriers. In one or more of his litters, the bitch was also a carrier (they produced affected puppies). In those litters, his phenotypically normal offspring have a 66.6% chance of being carriers.

2. a. Use Table 5.5, multiplying the 5 probabilities together:

   $.62 \times .57 \times .54 \times .59 \times .57 = .0641 \times 100 = 6.41\%$

   There is still a 6.41% risk that he is a carrier and a 93.59% chance that he is homozygous dominant (genotypically normal) for all major traits.

3. a. Use Table 5.4, the frequency 10%, and 5 puppies per litter, and you will find that he is 95% sure to be genetically normal for these 5 diseases.

   b. Use Table 5.4, the frequency 25%, and 5 puppies per litter, and you will find that he is 99% sure to be genetically normal for these 4 diseases.

   c. Use Table 5.4, the frequency 5%, and 5 puppies per litter, and you will find that he is 78% sure to be homozygous dominant for these 2 diseases.

   d. Use Table 5.1 with 11 puppies, and he is 95.8% sure to be free of this gene.

   e. Since our description of this family of dogs gave no indication of the status of the other 18 bitches, and since the sire is likely to be genetically normal for this trait, he provides no useful data in regard to the other 18 bitches and renal cortical hypoplasia. Therefore, we have no useful data on the other 18 bitches and this trait, so we can make no comment on this disease.

   f. Since he produced cataracts (an autosomal recessive trait), each of his puppies has *at least* a 50% chance of being a carrier.

   g. Nineteen of the 20 (1 produced cataracts) bitches bred to him have been test-mated (partially) for cataracts. He averages 5.5 puppies per litter, and all were normal for cataracts. So these 19 bitches have an average chance of being about 79% genetically normal for cataracts. If you knew the number of puppies each bitch produced with him, you could get an exact risk for each of them.

h. Overall, this is a very good sire. He has an excellent chance to be free of 9 diseases, plus renal cortical hypoplasia. He has a fair chance to be free of 2 or more diseases. It's true that he produced a case of cataracts, but if he is bred from now on to bitches that are homozygous dominant for this trait, he won't do that again. We know his puppies have a 50% chance of carrying cataracts, and that possibility has to be considered if you want to breed them. You also know they are not carrying 10 other diseases, at least from his side. This is the type of information we need if we are going to prevent genetic disease in dogs.

4. a. Use Table 5.3 to answer this question, since he was bred to both carrier and affected bitches. The sire has a 98.9% chance of being genetically normal for CMO.

5. a. Use Table 5.2 with 6 puppies, and he has a 98.4% chance of being normal.

6. a. You can use one table (Table 5.8) and 4 figures (5.1 through 5.4) to answer this question. Using sum of digits (Figure 5.1, great-grandparent #3, great-great-grandparent #4–#7) and Table 5.8, AC column, you get 1.56%. Using any one of the 3 figures multiplying .125 (carrier, great-grandparent) and .125 (affected, great-great-grandparent), you get 1.56%. The risk of producing a puppy that develops PRA is 1.56%.

b. To determine the risk of producing a carrier in this litter, you need to use Figure 5.5 and Tables 5.8 and 5.9. Using Figure 5.5, the great-granddam of your bitch on the sire's side is bitch #5, so you pick either one of her parents and cross the other off—say dog #10. Look #10 up in Table 5.9, and the code letter is J. Again, using Figure 5.5, there are 2 great-great-grandsires on the dam's side—dogs #12 and #14. Pick either one, but not both, and look it up in Table 5.9; the code letter is J. Now look up J,J in Table 5.10, and you have a 1.6% (rounding off 1.56%) chance of an affected puppy and a 22.2% chance of producing a carrier in the proposed litter.

7. Since, with a sex-linked trait, any male is a test-mate for a potential carrier female, use Table 5.7. With 7 normal male offspring, she has a 99.2% chance of being a noncarrier for hemophilia B.

8 . a. Genetics is really not baloney, and this is a common reaction of people who do not understand the statistical aspects of random distribution. But the first priority is to determine whether the dog and bitch were really carriers. How "good" is his information? Remember that if either one—the dog or the bitch—was not a carrier, we would expect all puppies to be normal. For our purposes here, let's say both dogs were carriers. You can give him a specific answer if you use your tables.

b. Using Table 5.16, plus the 3:1 ratio (crossing 2 carriers), you find that a 9:0 distribution occurs 7.5% of the time.

CHAPTER 6

The Interpretation and Use of Pedigrees to Determine the Genetic Status of Given Dogs

Pedigrees are interesting documents. There are two general types of pedigrees. The first is the *linear pedigree* we generally see with purebred animals and which is usually presented with three or four generations. I call this a *buyer's pedigree* because it is among the papers you are given when you buy a purebred dog. Figure 6.1 shows the general structure of a pedigree as it is usually presented to purchasers of purebred animals.

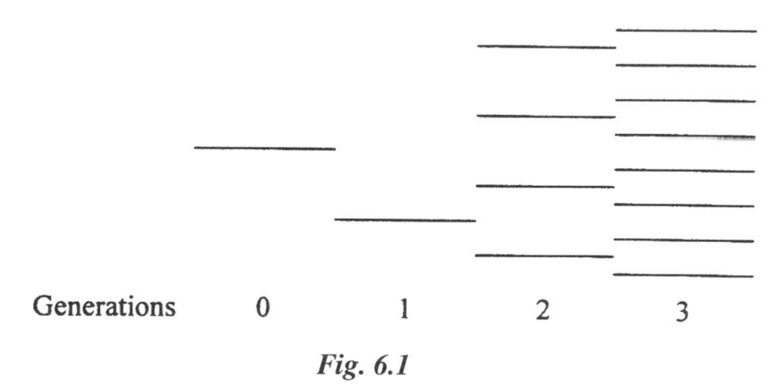

Fig. 6.1

In this case, generation zero is the dog you purchase; generation one, its parents; generation two, all four of its grandparents; and generation three, all eight of its great-grandparents. If the dog is already registered, the pedigree shows the registered name of the dog you purchase and the registered names of its direct antecedents. It may or may not show other components, such as the titles won by any of the dogs listed or whether they have an OFA or CERF number. But this is generally all the information you expect to find on a typical pedigree. It serves its purpose; that is, it tells you the direct lineage of your dog and provides you with the names of its direct ancestors. It is also of some limited use in the control of genetic disease.

The second type of pedigree, we might call a *geneticist's pedigree* (for want of a better name). I spent all of Chapter 3 giving you the symbols used in this type of pedigree and showing you how to assemble one. This pedigree shows not only the direct parental lineage of the dog in question but other related dogs within the family. The general structure of this type of pedigree as it is presented in the analysis of an autosomal recessive trait is illustrated in Figure 6.2.

A PRIORI
PARENTAL
CARRIER
RISK

Generations

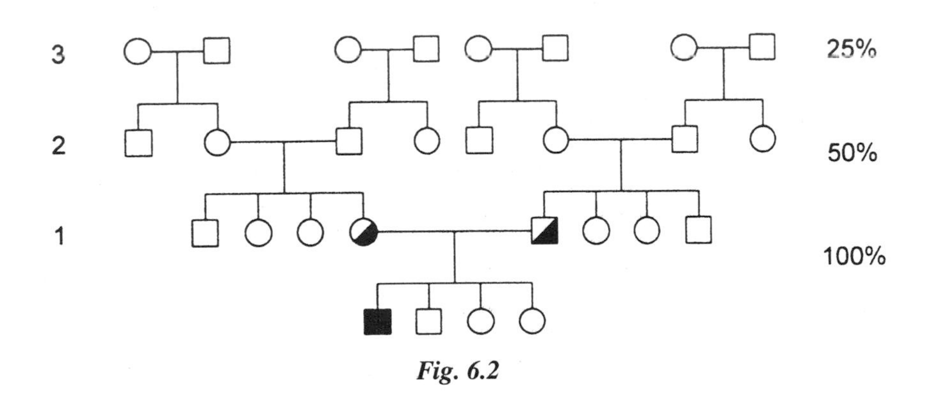

Fig. 6.2

Our goal in this chapter is to turn both the buyer's and the geneticist's pedigrees into *breeders' pedigrees.* Particularly those breeders whose goal it is to produce healthy, winning dogs. Four things are needed:

1. Knowledge about your dogs, especially correct parentage
2. Knowledge about the traits that occur in your dogs and what your dogs produce, which requires followup on the offspring of your dogs
3. Honesty and a willingness to record the data in a manner that makes it retrievable and useful to you and other breeders
4. Knowledge about how to interpret the pedigrees and how to use them to give you the least possible risk of producing puppies that develop genetic disease

As you proceed through this chapter, you will find that the essence of this whole system is based on the principle that *the more we know, the better the job we can do.* You will also come to the realization that there is a great deal about genetic disease in dogs that we don't know.

Let's start with buyer's pedigrees and see what we can glean from the information that is typically provided. You must keep in mind that breeders generally do the best they can to avoid selling dogs that are affected with genetic diseases, especially if they are going to other breeders or potential breeders. So you may be looking at your dog's pedigree because you heard that its brother or sister developed a given disease rather than your own dog being affected.

It is important to remember as we try to control genetic disease *that the only time we care if a dog carries a defect is when he/she has produced offspring or is likely to produce offspring.* Carriers themselves are phenotypically normal, healthy dogs the vast majority of the time and give the owner no more risk or added costs for care than a homozygous dominant animal. Therefore, we don't bother to search for carriers just to search for carriers or to point a finger at someone. We search for carriers to decrease or prevent genetic disease.

Let's examine a typical buyer's pedigree for an autosomal recessive trait (see Figure 6.3). For discussion purposes, we will name each dog in the pedigree, number them using Grant's system, and label the generations according to Fisher's sum of digits and the multiplication system (refer to chapter 5).

Generations	1	2	3	4
				8 Albert
			4 John	
				9 Judy
		2 Tom		
				10 Mike
			5 Jane	
				11 Janet
	1 Jack SIRE			
				12 Leroy
			6 Ken	
				13 Sara
		3 Mary		
				14 Sam
			7 Alice	
				15 Tammy
Alphonso				
				8 Terry
			4 Joe	
				9 Terri
		2 Bob		
				10 Dick
			5 Jean	
				11 Kate
	1 Jill DAM			
				12 Slim
			6 George	
				13 Dorothy
		3 Sandy		
				14 Albert
			7 Bobbi	
				15 Candy

Fig. 6.3 *A typical buyer's pedigree.*

Buyer's Pedigrees

Autosomal Recessive Traits

With an average generation time (the time it takes for a dog to be born, grow up and reproduce) in dogs of two-and-a-half to three years, the pedigree in Figure 6.3 represents 12-and-a-half to fifteen years of breeding. That is about twice the length of time the average breeder remains actively involved, according to the AKC, and perhaps half the length of time that a veteran or long-term breeder might be involved. Breeding dogs is a time-consuming avocation, which means that we should try to wring all of the information we can out of a pedigree. This time span is also one of the major reasons we should have open registries for genetic diseases: so that data is not lost when an individual drops out of the game or is forgotten by veteran breeders as the years pass.

Example #1

Let's say that Figure 6.3 is a Pointer pedigree and that Alphonso's full sister Angel developed English Pointer Dwarfism (an autosomal recessive trait). Since this is an autosomal recessive trait, what can we say for sure about this pedigree?

Since no other data is available, Alphonso's minimum risk for being heterozygous (a carrier) for the trait is 66.6 percent. Since, with an autosomal recessive trait, the gene must occur on both sides of the pedigree, both Jack and Jill, his parents (and also the parents of Angel) are proven carriers (they produced an affected dog). Since the parents (generation #1) are proven carriers, each of Alphonso's four grandparents (generation #2) has a minimum risk of 50 percent; each of the eight great-grand-parents (generation #3) has a risk of 25 percent; and each of the sixteen great-great-grandparents (generation #4) has a 12.5 percent risk. These are *a priori* (it has to be true) risks, and we are barring or ignoring mutation as a possible cause.

Why do we just ignore mutation? Aren't mutations possible? Yes, mutations are possible, but they are clearly not very common, and since this is a recessive trait, a mutation would have had to occur in both Jack and Jill (or their immediate anteced-ents), or we should have seen the disease earlier in one or both of the families. Since breeders seldom knowingly breed affected animals, and since, in this type of pedi-gree, only breeding animals are depicted, it should not be a surprise that we find no affected animals shown; so we cannot, from this type of pedigree alone, rule out a mutation.

This takes us back to an earlier statement: *There is a whole lot about genetic disease in dogs that we don't know.* One of the things we don't know is the mutation rate for any genetic disease in dogs. So we cannot make even a reasonable guess as to the likelihood that the affected puppy is the result of a mutation in both Jack and Jill. If we took a standard mutation rate of 1/100,000 gametes and tried to roughly apply it to this situation, there would be much less than one chance in 10 million that a mutation would occur in both Jack and Jill, resulting in the production of the affected bitch Angel. So we tend to ignore mutation as a cause of affected dogs with a recessive trait.

If it is not mutation, where did the trait come from? Since only one dog appears on both the sire's and dam's sides of the pedigree, our best guess is Albert. If Albert did introduce the gene, then John and Tom on the sire's side and Bobbi and Sandy on the dam's side have to be carriers. Since Albert appears on both sides of the pedigree, his risk of being the culprit is 25 percent (12.5 + 12.5), whereas the risk for any of the other great-great-grandparents is 12.5 percent. Remember, this does not mean that Albert is indeed the carrier, but he is our best guess. From Example #1, using a buyer's pedigree, we can determine the genotype of the parents and the minimum risk of the carrier state for all of the other dogs depicted.

Why do we want to know the risk that a dog or bitch has to be a carrier? This leads us to another of the things we do not know about the genetics of dogs. We have a rough estimate of the frequency of the carrier state in only four of the 300 or 400 breeds of dogs. These four are Cairn Terriers, Bichons Frises, Scottish Terriers, and Newfoundlands. But if we did know the carrier risk for a given disease in most breeds, we could tell if the use of various dogs in this pedigree would be likely to increase or decrease the chance of producing an affected puppy with that trait compared to outcrossing into the general population of dogs in the breed. Let's say this trait is luxated patellas in Cairns. The estimated general frequency of carriers of luxated patellas in Cairns is 29.2 percent. Therefore, with the exception of Albert, who we think introduced the trait, and John and Bobbi, the son and daughter of Albert, any of the great and great-great-grandparents of Alphonso have less risk of producing the disease than any dog in the general breeding population of the breed as a whole. This, by inference alone, includes Bob and Mary, the grandparents of Alphonso that are not in the direct lineage of Albert. It is for this reason that good information on the frequency of traits in the various breeds of dogs is of the utmost importance.

Example #2

Let's say that Figure 6.3 is a Miniature Schnauzer pedigree and that Mary (dog #3) on the sire's side and George on the dam's side have both produced renal cortical hypoplasia (an autosomal recessive trait) in past litters (which makes George and Mary proven carriers). What's the chance Alphonso will be affected or a carrier? Using sum of digits or the multiplication method, the risk that he will be affected is 3.13 percent. Using Grant's method, the risk that he is a carrier is 32.3 percent. We need to remember here that although we can gain information from this type of pedigree, that the pedigree itself does not provide us with the data that starts us off. The pedigree does not show the affected puppies. We have to find that out from other sources.

This brings us to the third area where we lack knowledge about the genetic diseases of dogs. We need to know the age by which if a dog does not have the disease he/she will not develop it. If we know, for example, that seven months is the cutoff point (either they have it or will not develop it) for renal cortical hypoplasia in Miniature Schnauzers, and Alphonso is eight months old, then the question of whether he will develop the disease is easily answered. He is eight months old, and he is not affected, so he will not develop the disease. Further, the question may have been answered if we had used the battery of tests available for renal dysfunction on him at an early age. This becomes extremely important in the control of genetic disease when we consider traits like PRA, cataracts and epilepsy, where in most breeds, a cutoff point has not been established. From Example #2, using a buyer's pedigree, we can predict the minimum risk of the occurrence of a trait and the minimum risk of carrier status if we know the genotype of dogs on both sides of the pedigree. We say *minimum risk* because there may be other unknown carriers among the ancestors.

Example #3

Let's say that Figure 6.3 is an American Cocker Spaniel pedigree that you received from the AKC when you bought and registered Alphonso. The pedigree shows that Jack, Jill, Bob, Mary, Jane, Ken, George and Bobbi all had CERF numbers (Canine Eye Registration Foundation certificates of normalcy) at ages ranging from two to four years. What's the chance Alphonso will be affected with or carry for cortical cataracts, an autosomal recessive trait that generally occurs by two-and-a-half years of age in this breed? If this is all the information you have, you cannot answer this question, because you have no knowledge about the carrier status of any dog in the pedigree or whether any dog in the pedigree is affected with the trait (excluding the named dogs above). A CERF number tells you that the phenotype is normal but tells you nothing about the genotype.

This pedigree epitomizes the problem of stamping or validating a dog as "normal" when the method of validation says nothing about the genotype of the dog(s) involved. The AKC's recently adopted practice of placing OFA and CERF numbers on AKC-certified pedigrees seems to imply that these animals are "approved" for breeding, when both the OFA and CERF clearly state that these are phenotypic evaluations of the clinical states of the dogs at the time of examination. It is not a good practice, since it gives breeders a false sense of security, which an organization like the AKC should understand. In terms of disease control or prevention, the information a breeder needs relates to the *genotype*—not the phenotype—of the dogs in any pedigree. From Example #3, we can see that knowing that the phenotype of a dog is normal does not help us to predict or prevent genetic disease when breeding from that individual.

In the first three examples, the problems are fairly straightforward, but how about more complicated situations in which multiple carriers or affected dogs are in the pedigree? In these cases, you use a combination of the dilution, sum and product rules. As a starting point, remember that an affected dog has a 100 percent chance of transmitting the abnormal gene to all of his offspring, and a carrier or potential carrier has half of his or her own risk of transmitting the gene to each of his offspring.

In examples four and five (Figures 6.4/6.4a and 6.5/6.5a), the risk of each dog in the litter being affected is shown above the line, and the risk for carrier status is below the line (defined or proven carriers and affected dogs are written out). In each case, only phenotypically normal dogs are bred, and we are also assuming that each dog that is not specifically identified as a carrier or affected is genetically normal—at least until we assign a potential risk for each dam and sire. We are not asking the conditional probability for each dam and sire (since we do not know the status of their littermates).

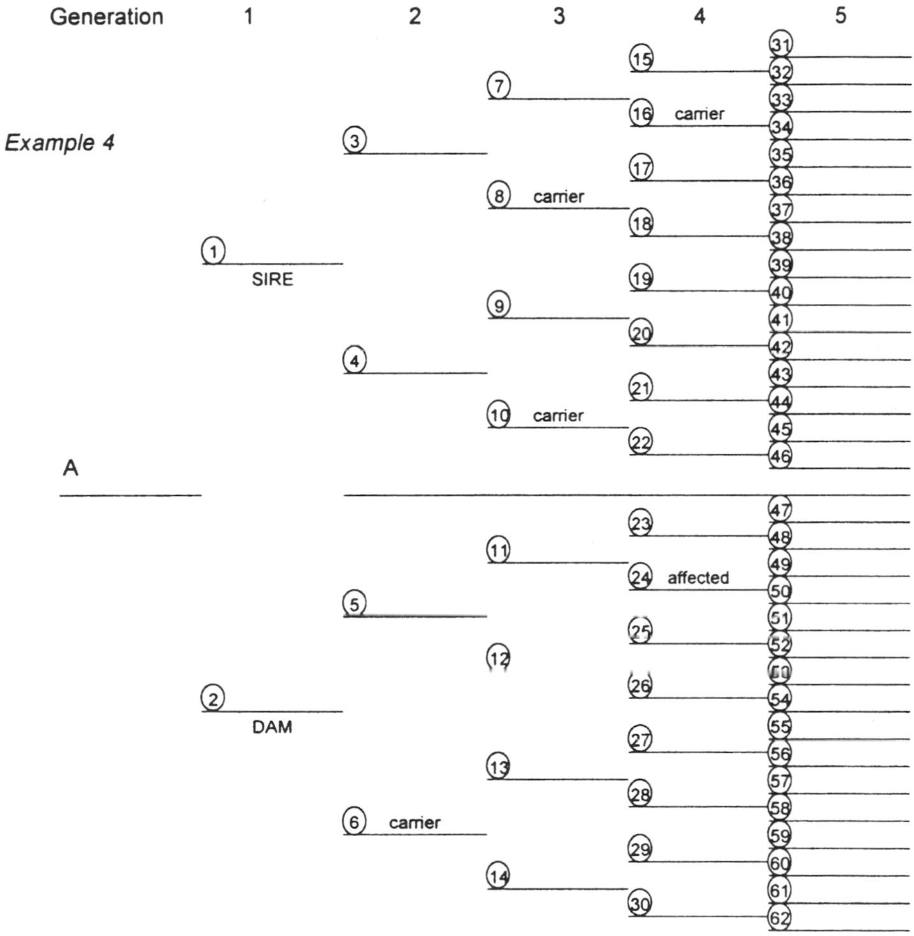

Generation 1 2 3 4 5

Example 4

15
7
16 carrier
3
17
8 carrier
18
1
SIRE
19
9
20
4
21
10 carrier
22
A
23
11
24 affected
5
25
12
26
2
DAM
27
13
28
6 carrier
29
14
30

31 32 33 34 35 36 37 38 39 40 41 42 43 44 45 46 47 48 49 50 51 52 53 54 55 56 57 58 59 60 61 62

Fig. 6.4 *Buyer's pedigree showing multiple carrier and affected dogs in the lineage with an autosomal recessive trait.*

Questions:

What is the risk each dam and sire has of being affected, a carrier or a potential carrier in this pedigree?

What is the risk each puppy in litter A has of being a carrier or affected?

What is the risk of having at least one affected puppy in litter A when there are four puppies in the litter?

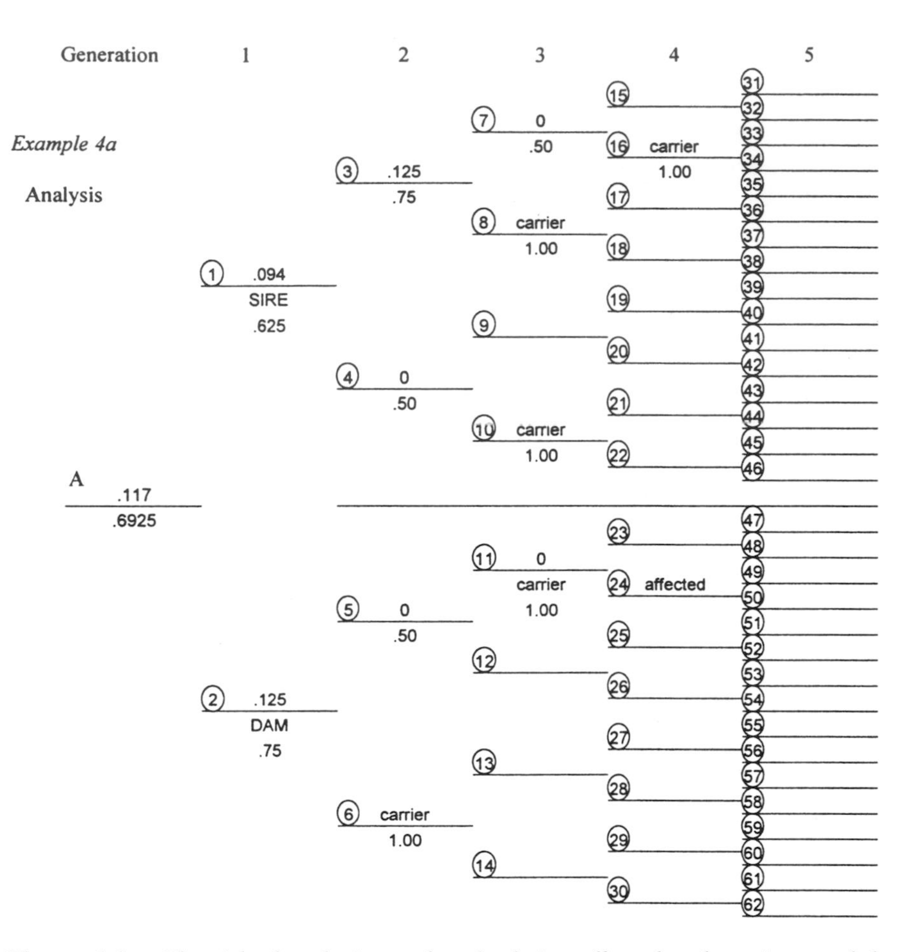

Figure 6.4a *The risk of each sire or dam for being affected and carriers, and the risk of each puppy in litter A of being affected or a carrier.*

Answers:

The risk for each dam and sire for being affected is above the line, and the risk of being a carrier or potential carrier is below the line.

Each puppy in litter A has an 11.7 percent (.117 × 100) chance that it will be affected.

Each puppy in litter A has a 69.25 percent (.6925 × 100) chance that it will be a carrier (heterozygote).

The risk that there will be at least one affected puppy in a litter of 4 is 46.8 percent.

Let's analyze pedigree 6.4 and see what happens (Figure 6.4a), starting on the sire's side with the carrier (#16) in generation #4. In this case, she must be a proven carrier (have produced an affected dog), since neither of her parents is affected. Her offspring, dog #7, has a 50:50 chance of being a carrier and, in this case, since the sire is apparently normal, no chance of being affected. Dog #7 is crossed with bitch #8, a proven carrier (neither of her parents is affected). Dog #7 has a 25 percent chance of throwing the abnormal gene (dilution rule), and bitch #8 has a 50 percent chance of throwing the gene. Using the product rule (.25 × .50), there is a 12.5 percent risk of male #3 being affected and a 75 percent (.25 + .50 sum rule) risk of his being a carrier. We know that he is not affected, because he is phenotypically normal. He was mated to a bitch (#4) that has a 50:50 chance of being a carrier (her mother is a proven carrier). Their offspring (dog #1) has a 9.4 percent chance of being affected as a result of that mating (product rule: .375 × .25 × 100). His carrier risk is 62.5 percent (sum rule: [.375 + .25] × 100). We know that he is not affected, because he is phenotypically normal.

On the dam's side of pedigree 6.4, bitch #24 is affected, so her son, dog #11, is a defined carrier (he must be a carrier, since his mother is affected). He is mated to bitch #12, who has no known carrier risk to produce a son (#5) that has a 50:50 chance of being a carrier (dilution rule). The son (#5) is mated to a proven carrier (bitch #6) to produce the dam (#2) of litter A. Her risk of being affected is 12.5 percent (.25 × .5 × 100: product rule), and her risk of being a carrier is 75 percent ([.25 + .50] × 100: sum rule). We know that she is not affected, because she is phenotypically normal.

Dog #1 becomes the sire, and bitch #2 becomes the dam of litter A, with their attendant risks. The risk that each puppy in litter A will be affected is 11.7 percent (.312 × .375 × 100: product rule), and the risk that each will be a carrier is 58.75 percent ([.312 + .375] × 100: sum rule). With four puppies in the litter, the risk that at least one puppy will be affected is 46.8 percent ([.117 + .117 + .117 + .117] × 100: sum rule or .117 × 4 × 100: sum rule).

Exactly the same type of analysis is required for Figure 6.5. See if you come up with the same answers I show in Figure 6.5a. Remember that in pedigree 6.5, there are some known affected and carrier dogs behind a known affected dog. You only need to use the dogs closest to litter A, and those behind them are crossed off.

Remember that we will cross off all dogs in the direct lineage behind any animal for which we can be absolutely sure of the genotype (proven and defined carriers and affected dogs).

Questions:

What is the risk of each dam and sire for being affected, a carrier or a potential carrier?

What is the risk for each puppy in litter A for being affected or a carrier?

What is the risk of having at least one affected puppy in litter A if there are five puppies in the litter?

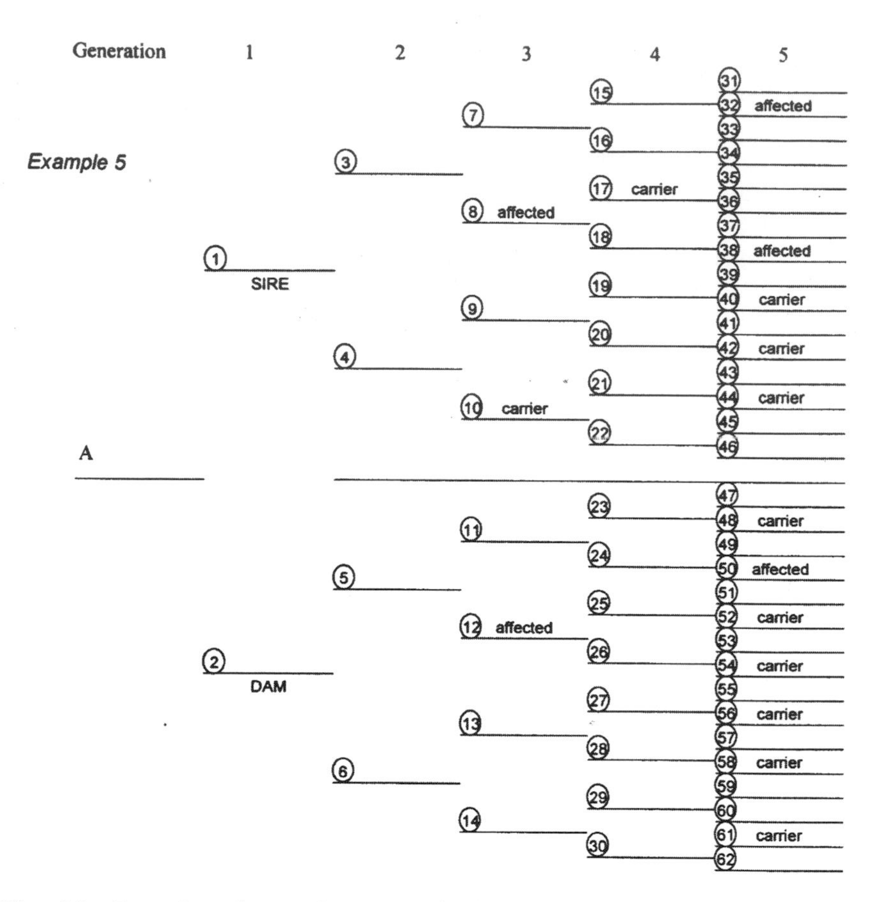

Fig. 6.5 *Buyer's pedigree showing multiple carrier and affected dogs in the lineage with an autosomal recessive trait.*

Answers:

The risk each dam and sire has of being affected is above the line, and the risk each has of being a carrier or potential carrier is below the line.

Each puppy in litter A has an 11.8 (1.118 × 100) percent chance that it will be affected and a 68.7 (.687 × 100) percent chance that it will be a carrier (heterozygote).

There is a 59.0 (.118 × 100 × 5) percent chance that there will be at least one affected puppy in litter A if there are five puppies in the litter.

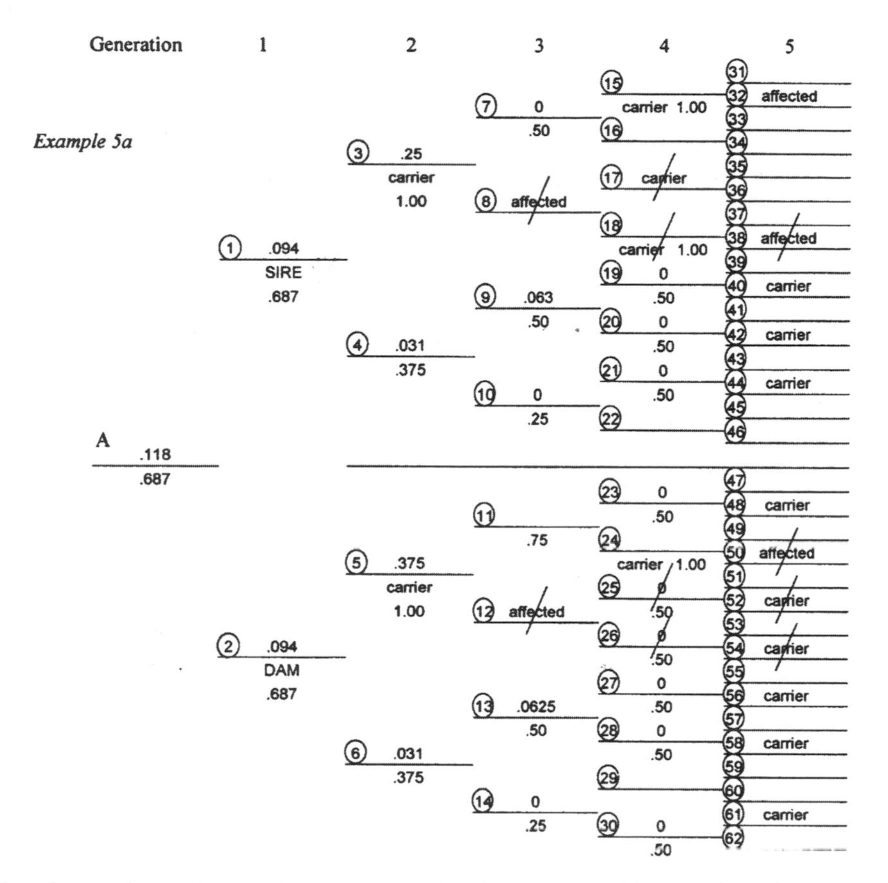

Fig. 6.5a *The risk each dam and sire in this lineage has of being affected, a carrier, or a potential carrier; and the risk of each puppy in the litter for being affected or a carrier.*

Sex-Linked Traits (Recessive)

Example #6

Let's go back to Figure 6.3 and say that this is a Kerry Blue Terrier pedigree and that you own Alphonso. You are told that Charlie, a full brother of Mary, who is the grandmother of Alphonso, had hemophilia B. This is a sex-linked recessive trait in this breed. No other dog in the pedigree as shown has hemophilia B, but we don't know about Alphonso yet. What's the chance that Alphonso has the disease or is a carrier?

There is no chance that Alphonso is affected. The analysis goes like this. Since a full brother of Mary is affected, her mother, Alice, must be a carrier (she does not have the disease, so she cannot be homozygous). So Mary has a 50 percent chance of inheriting that gene from her mother. However, Mary's relationship to Alphonso is through her son Jack. Since this gene is on the X-chromosome, if Jack had the gene, he would also have hemophilia B and would be a hemizygote (there is no hidden carrier state for males with sex-linked traits). So Alphonso cannot be affected, and he cannot be a carrier (or he would be affected), since his mother, Jill, is not a carrier. As far as this particular pedigree goes, the disease stops with Mary.

Example #7

What if we said that Jerry, the full brother of Bob (Alphonso's grandfather), had hemophilia B? What's the risk to Alphonso?

The answer is again none. There is no chance that Alphonso will get the disease. The analysis goes like this. Bob's mother, Jean, has to be a carrier, since she does not have the disease herself but produced Jerry, who does have it. But she did not pass it to Bob, or he would be hemizygous and affected. Bob is phenotypically and thus genotypically normal, so the disease stops with Jean as far as this particular pedigree is concerned.

Example #8

Suppose that Jim, a full brother of Sandy (Alphonso's other grandmother), had hemophilia B. What's the risk to Alphonso?

Alphonso has a 12.5-percent chance of being affected with hemophilia B. The analysis goes like this. Bobbi, Sandy's mother, does not have the disease, so she cannot be homozygous and is therefore a proven carrier, since she produced Jim, who is affected. So the *a priori* risk for Sandy becomes 50 percent, and for her daughter, Jill, it is 25 percent; thus, for Alphonso, the risk is 12.5 percent. If either Sandy or Jill had other normal male offspring, the risk for them and thus for Alphonso might be reduced if we used Bayesian calculations as discussed in Chapter 5.

Example #9

Let's say that Bob, the grandsire of Alphonso on the dam's side, had hemophilia B, and no other dogs in pedigree 6.3 were affected. What is the risk that Alphonso will develop the disease?

Alphonso's risk is 50 percent. What is the chance that Joe, Terry, Terri and Dick have the gene? What is the chance that Kate has the gene for hemophilia B? Kate's chance is 100 percent; she has to carry it.

Let's look at the reasoning behind the stated risks. The disease is sex-linked, so it is on the X-chromosome. Bob has the disease, so he is hemizygous for the trait. Bob throws the X-chromosome (and therefore the gene) to all of his daughters and none of his sons, because he gives his sons the Y-chromosome. Consequently, Jill must get the gene from Bob, and she is, therefore, a defined carrier. Since we know that she has the gene and does not have the disease, she cannot be homozygous, and Alphonso's risk becomes 50 percent. How about Joe, Terry, Terri and Dick? The three males cannot have the gene for hemophilia B, or they would be affected, since it is a sex-linked trait. It is possible that Terri has the gene (although unlikely), but we cannot tell from this type of pedigree, since we have no other information on her. There is no reason to think she has it, because we can account for the disease through other animals. Since Bob has the disease (his father is normal; even if he were not normal, he would not pass the gene to his son), it had to be passed by his mother, Jean. Her risk is 100 percent. Since Jean has the gene and her father, Dick, is normal, the gene had to come from her mother, Kate. Kate's risk is, therefore, 100 percent.

Remember, with sex-linked traits in the male, the disease can only come from the mother, and it does not have to be on both sides of the pedigree. As a result, unless a male is affected, you always look at the female side of the pedigree.

Figure 6.6 shows a buyer's pedigree for a sex-linked trait. This could be viewed as a Miniature Schnauzer pedigree with the trait hemophilia A. As you can see, there are eight carriers and one affected animal in this pedigree. However, as you will see by the analysis of the pedigree in Figure 6.6a, only one of these nine dogs has any influence on litter A.

Questions:

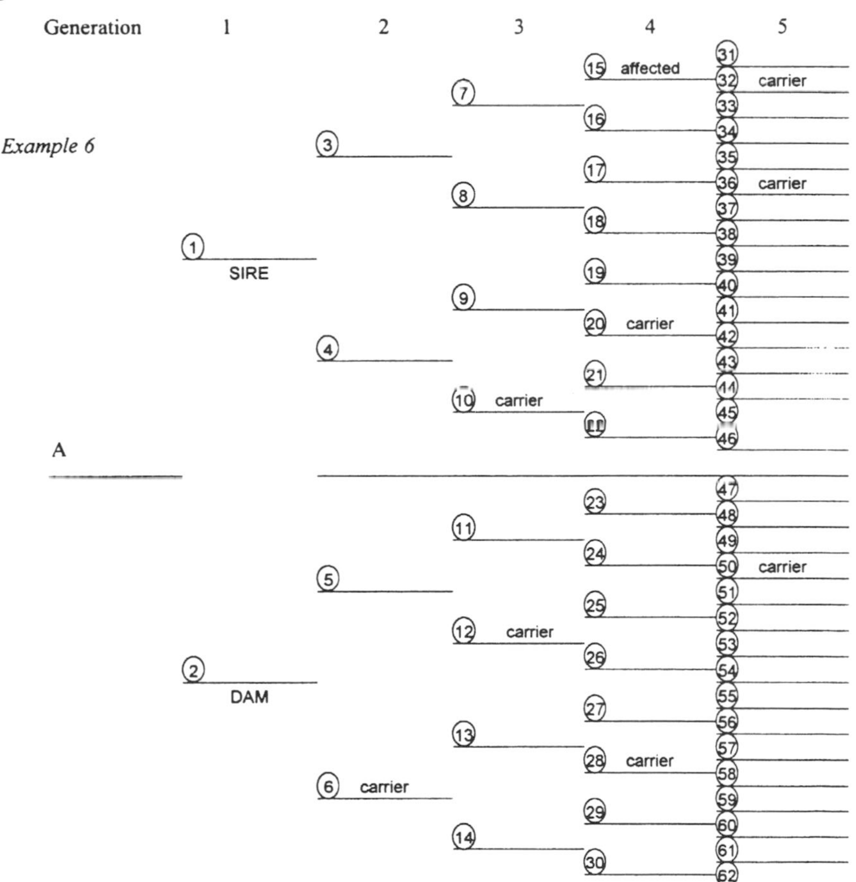

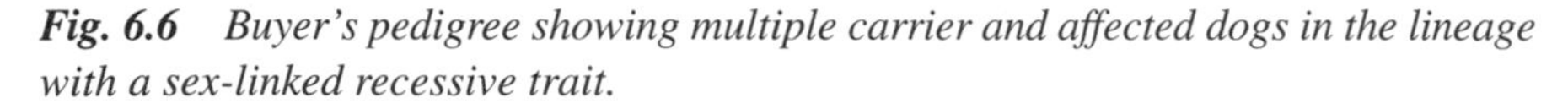

Fig. 6.6 *Buyer's pedigree showing multiple carrier and affected dogs in the lineage with a sex-linked recessive trait.*

What is the risk that each male in litter A will be affected?

What is the chance that a female in litter A will be a carrier?

What is the chance that a female in litter A is affected?

If there are three males in litter A, what is the chance that one will be affected?

Answers:

Each male has a 25 percent chance of being affected.

Each female has a 25 percent chance of being a carrier.

Although there was a risk that dogs 1, 5, 9, 11, 13 and 17 could be affected (it is shown) in this pedigree, they are presented as being phenotypically normal, so they must also be genetically normal for this trait.

There is no chance that a female in litter A will be affected.

There is a 75 percent chance that at least one male will be affected if there are three males in the litter.

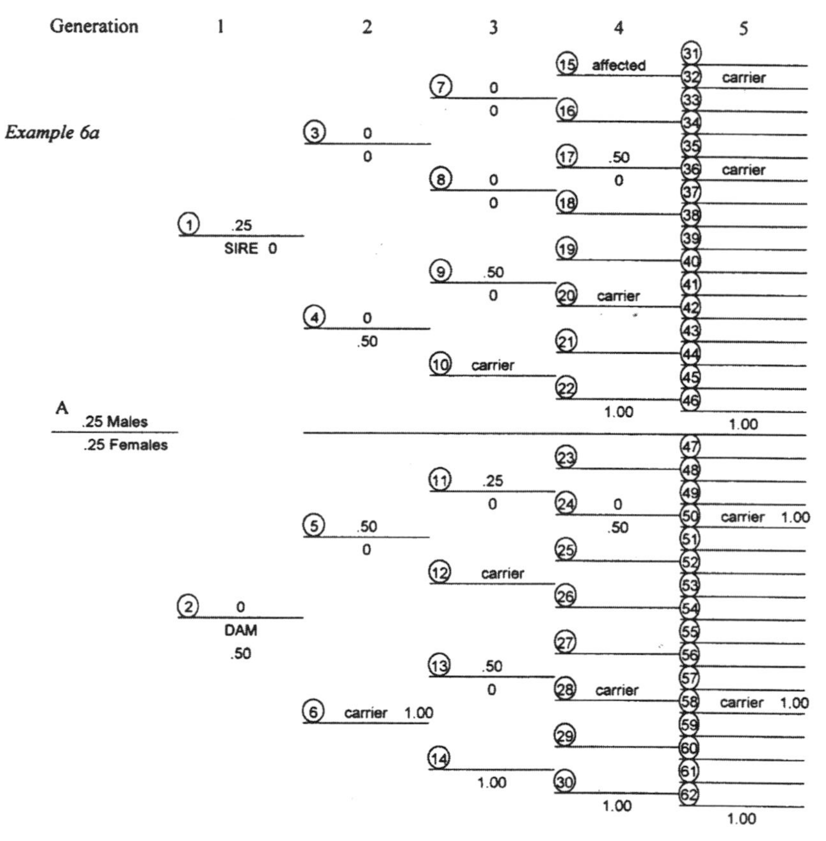

***Fig. 6.6a** Buyer's pedigree showing the risk of various dogs in the lineage as the result of known carrier and affected dogs when a sex-linked recessive trait is involved.*

Dog #15 in generation #4 is affected as a result of his mother (bitch #32). Since this is a sex-linked trait on the X-chromosome, and he throws the Y-chromosome to his sons, dog #7 is phenotypically and genetically normal. Even though bitch #36 in generation #5 is a carrier, her son (#17) does not show the trait, so he is genetically and phenotypically normal. The same applies to bitch #20 and her son (#9) and bitch #10 and her son (#4); since the males don't show the trait, they must be phenotypically and genetically normal. Since males must show the trait (they are hemizygous) if they have the gene, any phenotypically normal male is also genetically normal. On the dam's side of the pedigree, female #50 is a carrier, so her daughter has a 50:50 chance of being a carrier, but her son (#11) blocks further transmission of the gene in this pedigree. The same applies to bitches #12 and #28, and even though they are known carriers, their sons #5 and #13 block the trait. Bitch #6, a proven carrier, does influence litter A through her daughter (#2), the dam of litter A. She (#2) has a 50:50 chance of being a carrier. Since dam #6 is a carrier, her mother (#14), grandmother (#30) and great-grandmother (#62) must be carriers, since in each case, the appropriate male is phenotypically normal. Since dam #2 had a 50 percent chance of being a carrier, each of her sons has a 25 percent chance of being affected, and each daughter has a 25 percent chance of being a carrier. In this pedigree, there is no chance a daughter can be affected and no chance a son could be a hidden carrier.

Analyze pedigree 6.7, and see if you get the same answers I show in Figure 6.7a.

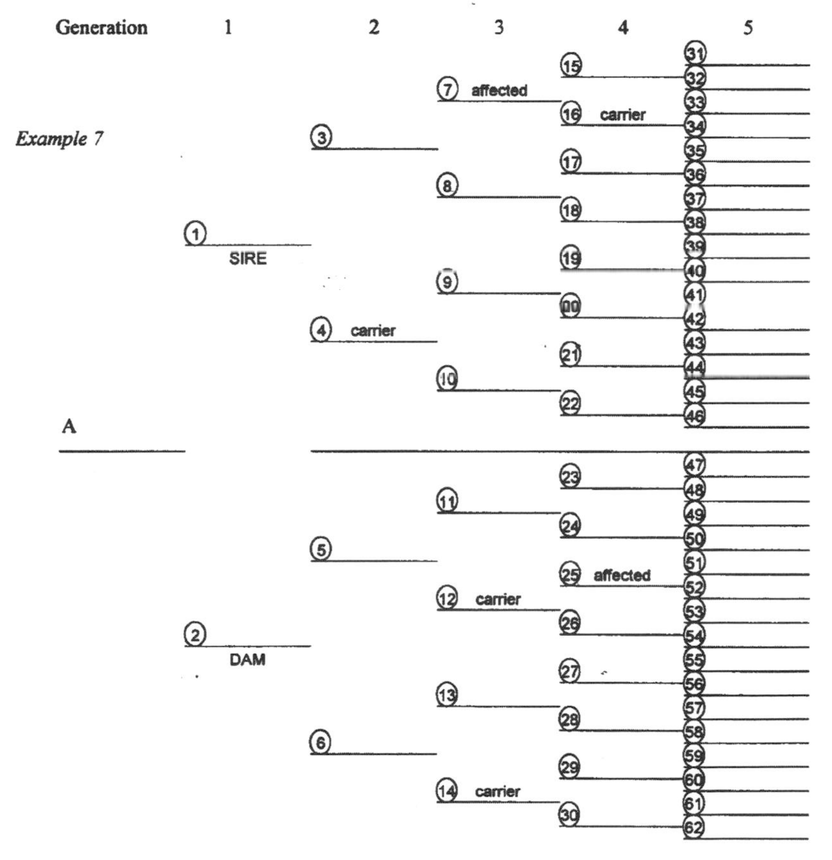

Fig. 6.7 Buyer's pedigree showing multiple carrier and affected dogs in the lineage with a sex-linked recessive trait.

Questions:

What is the chance that a male in litter A is affected?

What is the chance that a female in litter A is a carrier?

What is the chance that a female in litter A is affected?

What is the chance that bitch #34 is a carrier?

What is the chance that bitches #46 and #62 are carriers?

What is the chance that bitch #26 is a carrier?

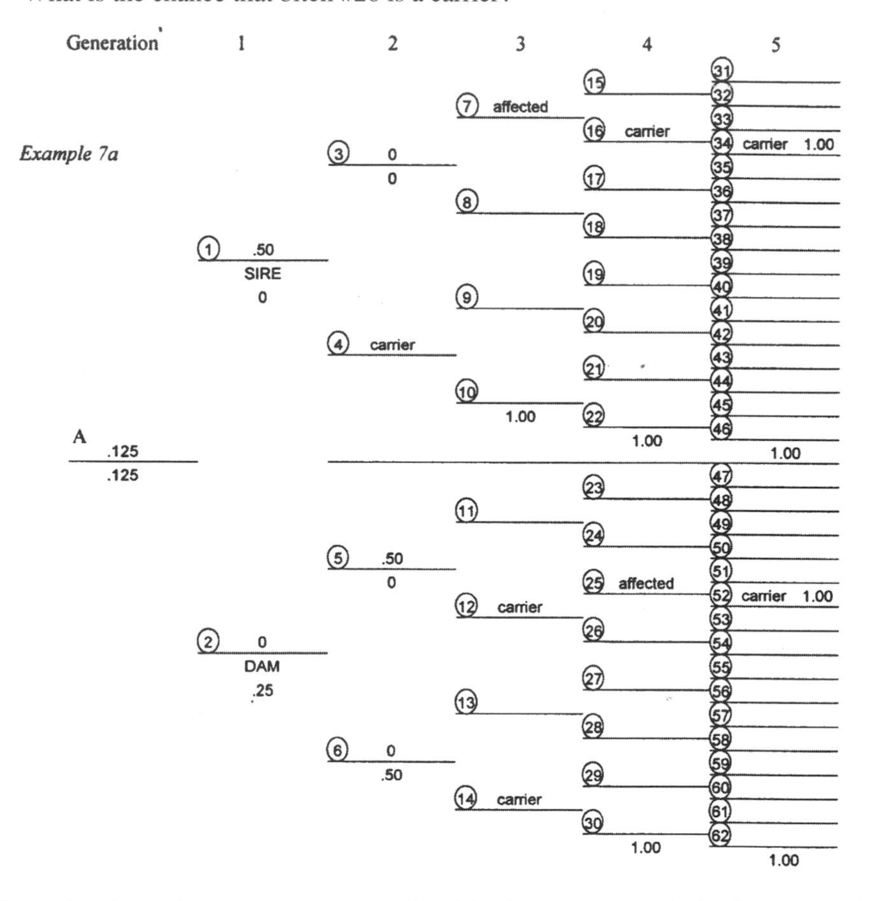

Fig 6.7a Buyer's pedigree showing the risk of various dogs in the lineage as the result of known carrier and affected dogs when a sex-linked recessive trait is involved.

Answers:

There is a 12.5 percent chance that a male in litter A will be affected.

There is a 12.5 percent chance that a female in litter A will be a carrier.

There is no chance that a female in litter A will be affected.

There is a 100-percent chance that bitch #34 is a carrier.

There is a 100-percent chance that bitches #46 and #62 are carriers.

Since we can account for the carrier status of bitch #12 through her sire dog (#25), there is no need for bitch #26 to be a carrier, and I would assume that she is genetically normal.

Although there was a risk that dogs #1 and #5 could be affected (it is shown) in this pedigree, they are presented as being phenotypically normal, so they must also be genetically normal for this trait.

Again, as with autosomal recessive traits, the risks we calculate are minimum risks, because other unidentified carriers may be in the pedigree. Accurate calculation of risks is always dependent on full knowledge about the dogs involved in a pedigree, which of course, is the reason open registries are so important in disease control.

Autosomal Dominant Traits

This discussion is aimed at deleterious (harmful) traits that you are generally selecting against. If the trait is beneficial (such as in hair coats and colors in some breeds of dogs), you may find dominants on both sides of a pedigree, because you are selecting dogs for breeding based on that trait being present. Keeping this in mind, we can proceed. The trait does not and can not skip generations. So if the individual the pedigree (see Figure 6.8) describes is affected with a dominant trait, at least one parent must show the trait.

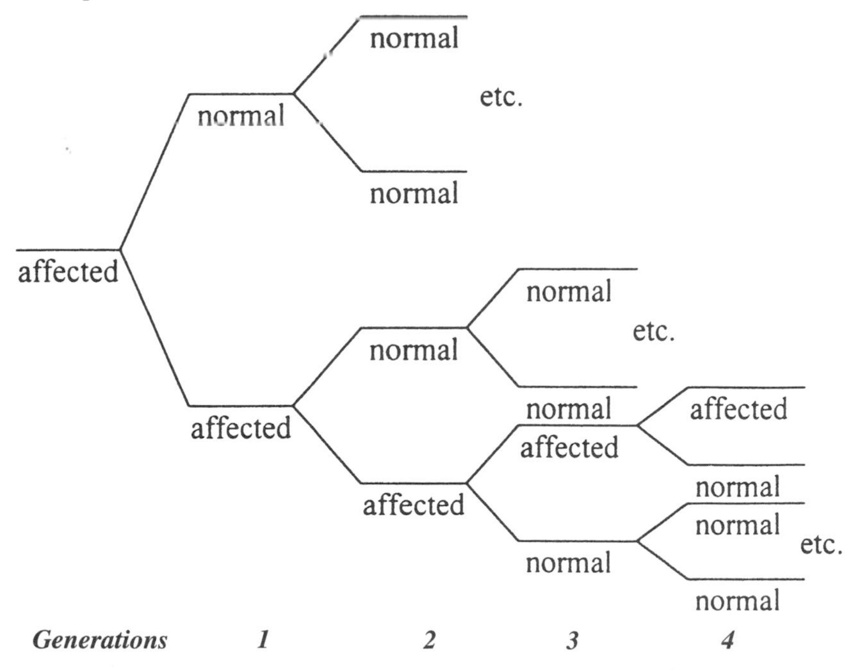

Fig. 6.8 *Pedigree illustrating an autosomal dominant trait.*

All normal dogs are both phenotypically and genetically normal for the trait depicted.

The individuals showing the trait are generally (but not always) heterozygotes (they have only one copy of the gene). The trait then follows the side of the pedigree of the affected parent (male or female). At this point, in nearly all cases, you can forget the opposite side of the pedigree, because all the individuals listed there should be phenotypically normal and genetically normal, including all littermates (because if a littermate shows the disease, one parent must be affected). On the affected side, one of the grandparents must show the trait, and the opposite side is generally again free of the disease. This pattern extends back *ad infinitum* or until you come upon the initial mutation causing the disease. This type of pedigree does not distinguish the statistical aspects of a dominant trait. With a dominant trait, we expect, on the average, to have 50 percent of the offspring affected with the disease and 50 percent to be phenotypically and genetically free of the disease. Further, it does not show that we expect both males and females to be affected approximately an equal number of times. All normal dogs are both phenotyptically and genetically normal.

Incomplete Autosomal Dominant Traits

With an incomplete dominant trait such as is proposed for von Willebrand's disease, all bets are off. You cannot distinguish this type of trait using this type of pedigree. Luckily, there are very few incomplete dominant traits reported in dogs.

Sex-Linked Traits (Dominant)

This mode of inheritance cannot be distinguished from an autosomal dominant trait using this type of pedigree, because both males and females are affected as they are with an autosomal dominant trait. What you cannot illustrate with this type of pedigree is that all daughters of an affected male are affected, and all sons of an affected male are normal when bred to a phenotypically normal female. Since this is a dominant trait, a female cannot carry this gene without being affected, so a phenotypically normal female is also genetically normal.

Polygenic Traits

Polygenic traits are like autosomal recessive traits in that both sides of a pedigree must be involved. I know of no polygenic trait in dogs in which only the dam or only the sire can transmit all of the genes required to produce an affected offspring. Polygenic traits differ from autosomal recessive traits in that both parents do not have to be equally involved in producing the defect. One parent may carry one or perhaps two genes for the trait, while the other may have three, four or more, depending on how many genes are implicated.

Polygenic traits also differ from recessive traits in that we cannot give accurate statistical predictions on the number of affected offspring or whether there is likely to be affected offspring from a given mating, as we can with recessive traits. Like a recessive trait, since both sides must be involved, we can attempt to determine the source of the gene by finding the same individual on both sides of the pedigree, but we do that with even less certainty than we do with a recessive trait.

Many breeders like to label a trait "polygenic" because they believe they can place the blame on the opposite side, leaving their own dog sparkling clean. Unfortunately, they are misinformed.

Geneticists' Pedigrees

Pedigree 6.9 is the type of pedigree used by geneticists when analyzing a pedigree for mode of inheritance of a trait, as well as determining the risk various individuals have to develop the disease or to carry one gene for the trait, thus putting their offspring at risk for the disease.

If you are a breeder, I strongly recommend that you develop such a pedigree for your own kennel. Figure 6.9 is left blank (no trait illustrated) as your own original should be left blank. For discussion purposes, we will use this pedigree throughout the rest of the chapter, labeling it 6.9a, 6.9b, and so on so that you can see how useful it is in analyzing various traits in various litters. If you create such a pedigree for your breeding, you can do the same thing.

As we use this pedigree, we will add arrows and/or numbers to make the discussion easier. They will change with each illustration. I have not labeled the generations in this pedigree (although it is roughly laid out by generation), because in most cases, it is very difficult to do so in canine pedigrees. It is difficult to do because of the short generation time and because both males and females are used multiple times with multiple mates, often crossing generations. Therefore, to apply the information we developed in Chapter 5, you will have to count generations, going either forward or backward, depending on the questions being asked. In this chapter, we will concentrate on how to use this type of pedigree, and in Chapter 7, we will set up guidelines for both prospective and retrospective test-matings.

In Example #1, we are using three figures: Figure 6.9 to show you "your" pedigree, Figure 6.9a to show you the first affected dog (the propositus), and Figure 6.9aa to add the defined carriers. In all other examples, we will use one figure to illustrate all aspects of a trait.

Autosomal Recessive Traits

Example #1

Let's say that Figure 6.9a is an Airedale Terrier pedigree illustrating the trait *cerebellar ataxia* (CA), which is autosomal recessive in this breed.

Dog #100 (arrow) in litter x, born in 1991, developed the disease. What can we deduce about the genotype of the other dogs in the pedigree? Since dog #100 developed the disease, both his parents are now proven carriers, and they are so marked on the pedigree. Dog #13 is the only dog common to both sides of the pedigree. He is

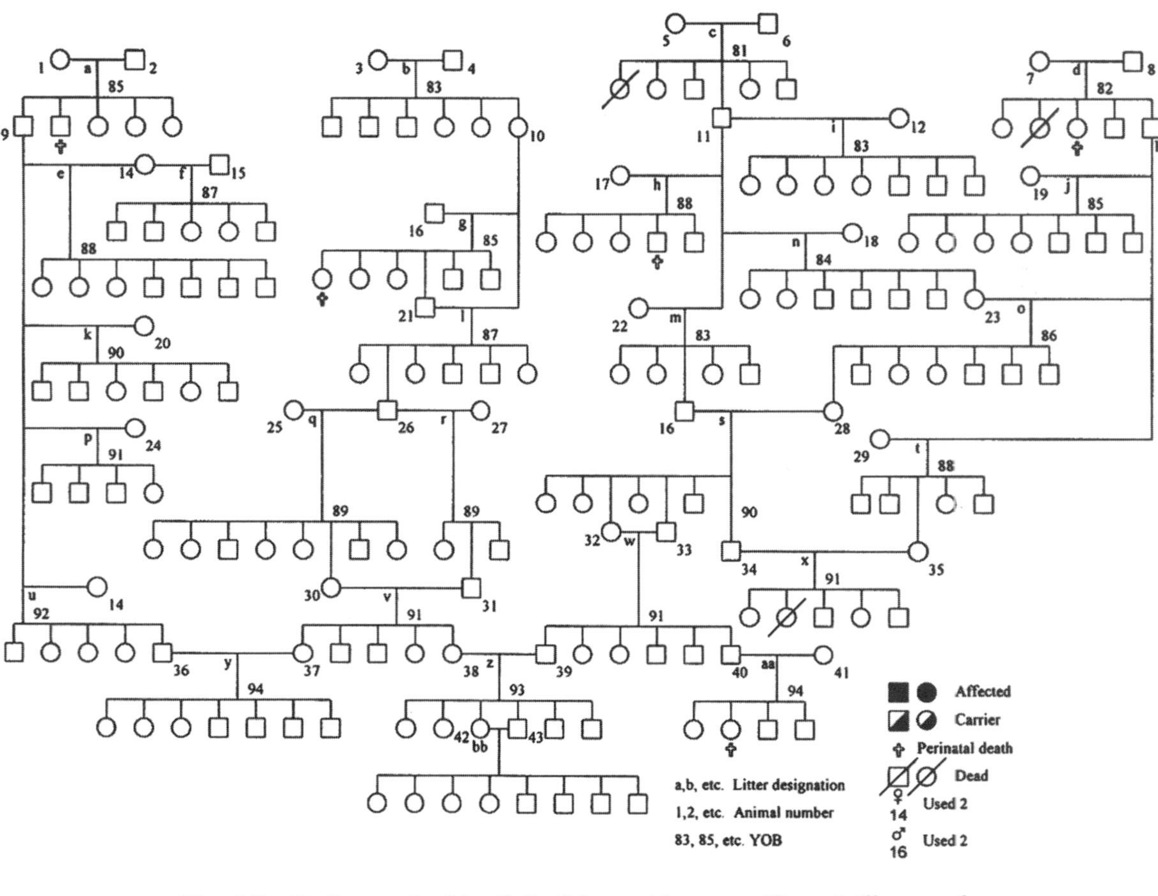

Fig. 6.9 *Pedigree of a "family" of dogs with no specific trait illustrated.*

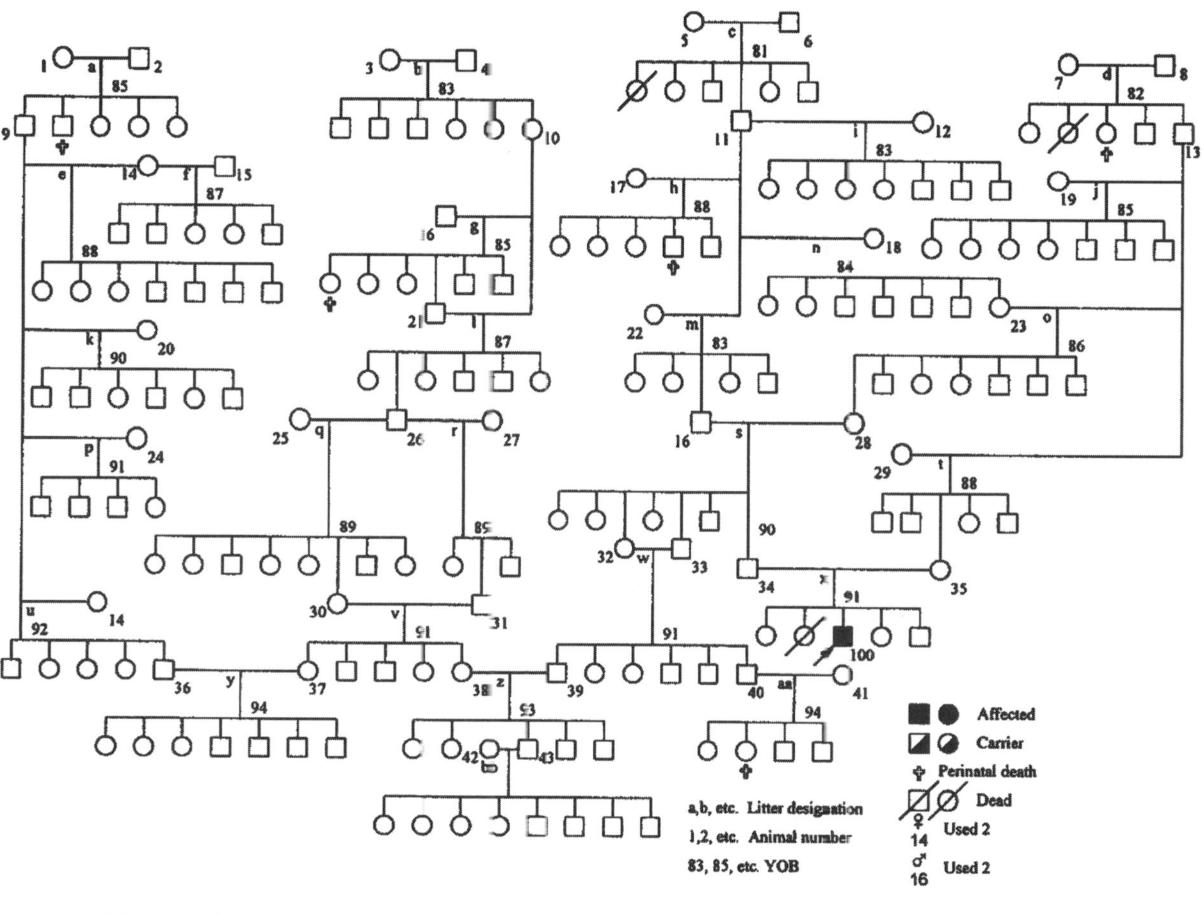

Figure 6.9a *Pedigree of a "family" of dogs illustrating cerebellar ataxia, a recessive trait.*

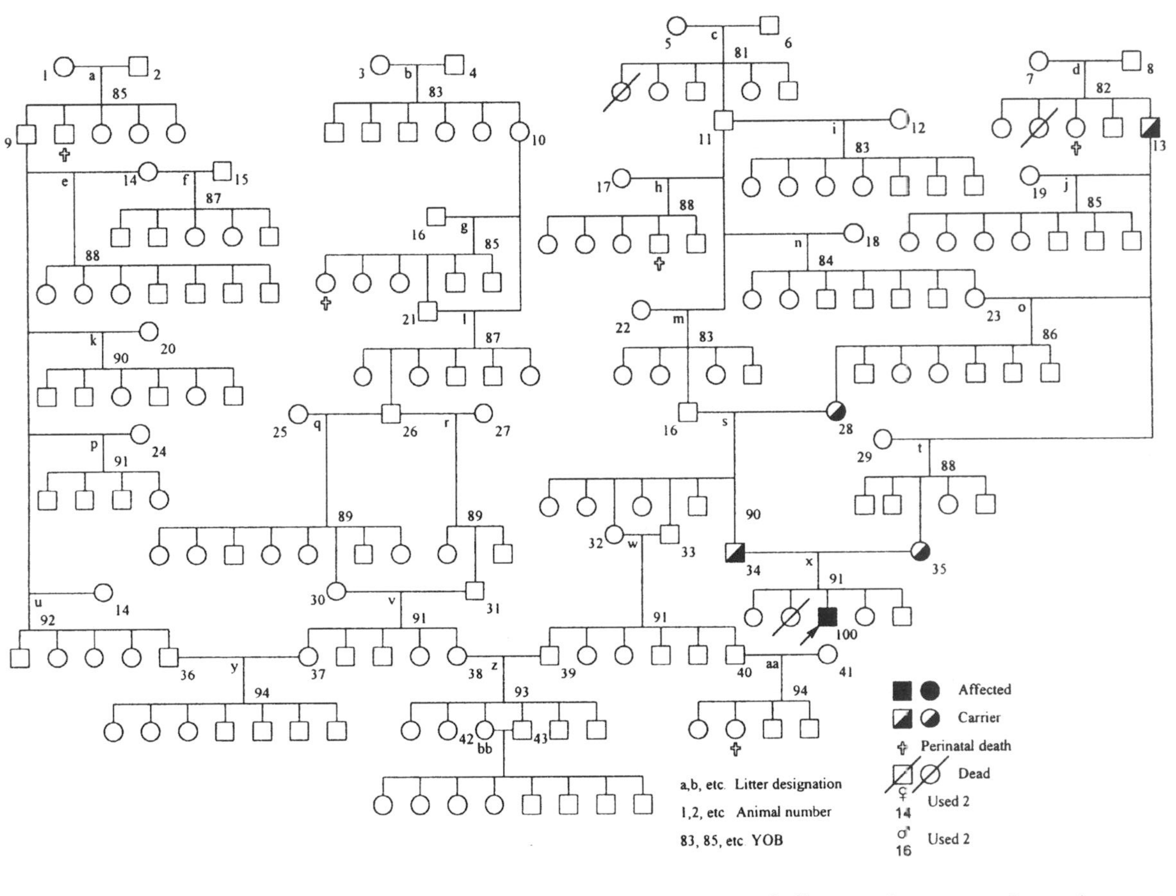

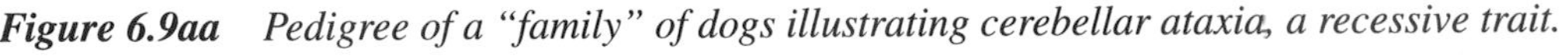
Figure 6.9aa *Pedigree of a "family" of dogs illustrating cerebellar ataxia, a recessive trait.*

the great grandsire on the sire's side and the grandsire on the dam's side of dog #100. While we can never be 100 percent certain that this is the case (since we have no data on this trait regarding dog #16 or bitch #23 and bitch #29, which are the only other possible sources of the gene), we are going to approach the analysis from the standpoint that dog #13 is the culprit. If he were not the source, then dog #16 or bitch #23 and bitch #29 would have to be carriers, and we have no data that suggests that this is the case. In a situation in which you have no specific knowledge about a gene in certain dogs in the pedigree you are working with, you should do your best to rule it in or out, if you can, by asking for information from anyone who might have historical knowledge about the phenotype or genotype of dogs related to them.

Dog #13 is therefore a defined carrier and is so marked in the pedigree (see Figure 6.9aa). Since dog #13 is a carrier, bitch #28 has to be the source of the gene we know is present in dog #34. She is marked as a carrier, and she accounts for the gene on the sire's side of litter x. Bitch #35 must be a carrier, accounting for the gene on the dam's side, which would come directly from dog #13, and she is so marked (see Figure 6.9aa). We now have three bitches (#19, #23 and #29) and one dog (#16) that have been retrospectively test-mated for cerebellar ataxia, since we know the genotype (heterozygotes) of the animals they were mated to.

Using Table 5.1 (see pg. 55), their respective chances of being genotypically normal for the CA trait are 86.6 percent, 86.6 percent, 76.3 percent and 86.6 percent. All the puppies in litters j, o, s and t have a 50:50 chance of carrying the gene for CA, and the phenotypically normal puppies in litter x have a 66.6-percent chance of carrying the gene for the trait.

Let's say that you own bitch #42 (litter z) and are strongly considering mating her to dog #43, her full brother. Whether you proceed is dependent on the risk of producing a CA-affected puppy in that litter. What is the risk?

You would determine the risk in the following manner. Since bitch #28 is a defined carrier, bitch #32 and dog #33 each have a 50:50 chance of carrying the CA gene. Each has a 25-percent chance of passing the gene to the puppies in litter w. Using the sum rule 25 + 25 gives each puppy in the litter a 50-percent risk of carrying the CA gene. Dog #39, a member of litter w, is outcrossed, diluting the CA gene so that each puppy in litter z has a 25-percent chance of carrying the CA gene. Therefore, bitch #42 and dog #43—members of litter z—each have a 25-percent chance of carrying for the CA gene (litter aa based on dog #40 has the same risk as litter z). Using the product rule ($.25 \times .25 = 0.625 \times 100 = 6.25$ percent), there is a 6.25-percent chance that each puppy will have CA in the proposed litter bb.

From the data we have here, no dogs other than the ones specifically mentioned have a risk of carrying the gene for CA. This is a major advantage of an open registry. You know where the gene is, and you can calculate the risk each dog in a pedigree has to carry for that gene.

Example #2

Let's say that Figure 6.9b is a Beagle pedigree and that dog #31 (arrow) developed progressive retinal atrophy at 4-and-a-half years of age and bitch #102 (arrow)

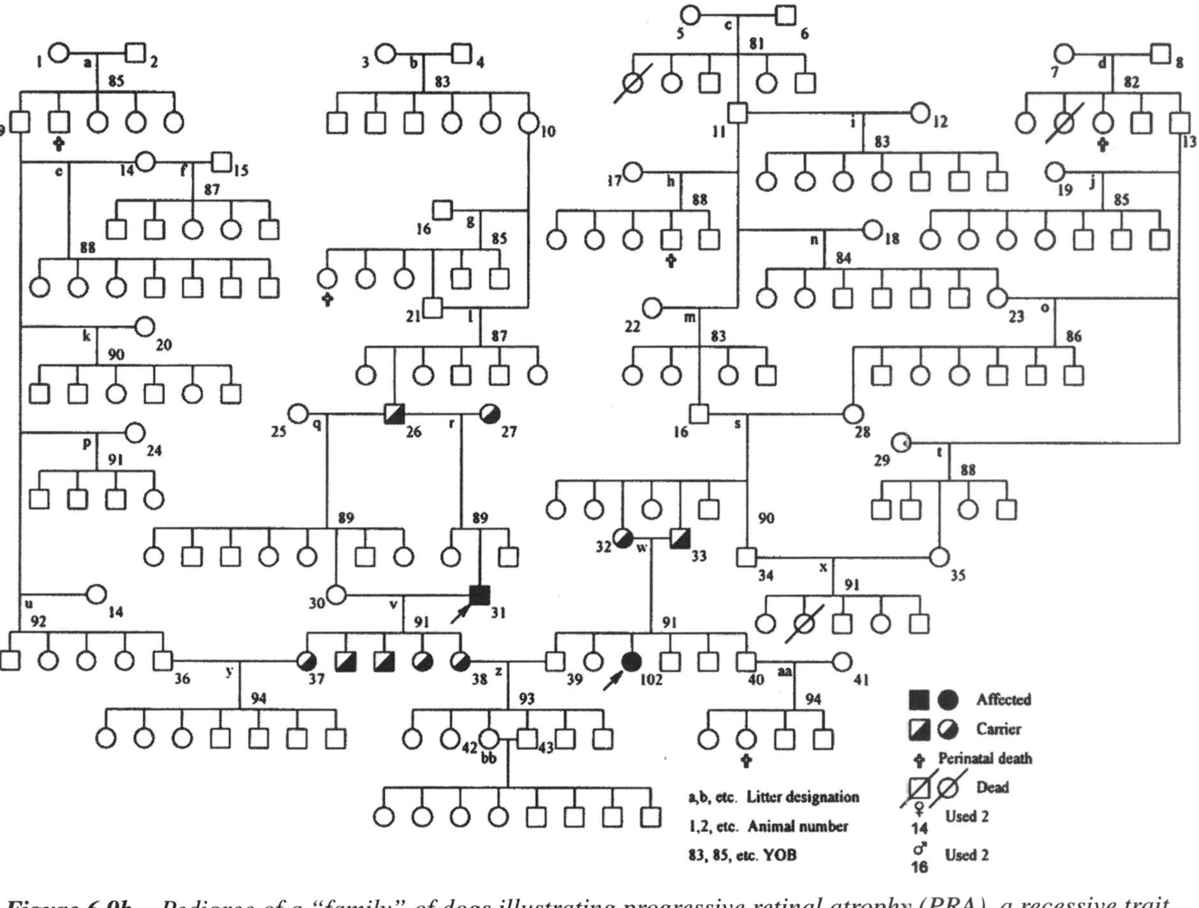

Figure 6.9b *Pedigree of a "family" of dogs illustrating progressive retinal atrophy (PRA), a recessive trait.*

developed PRA at three years of age. PRA has been found to be inherited as an autosomal recessive trait in all breeds studied to date. With this information, what can we tell about the dogs in pedigree 6.9b?

Dogs #26, #27, #32 and #33 are proven carriers, since they produced affected puppies. Dogs #21 and #10 (the granddams of an affected dog) and #16 and #28 (the grandsires of an affected dog) each have a 50:50 chance of carrying the PRA gene.

Dogs #16 and #10, #22 and #11, as well as #23 and #13, as the great-granddams and sires of an affected dog, each have an *a priori* risk of 25 percent for carrying the PRA gene. Dogs #16 and #10 are each in the pedigree line twice.

Bitch #10, through a mating with dog #16, produces dog #21. And, again in a mating with her son, dog #21, she produces the sire (#26) of the affected dog (#31). Dog #16 is in both pedigree lines as a great-grandsire of dog #31 and as a grandsire of bitch #102. In fact, dog #16 all by his lonesome could account for both the sire and dam's sides for bitch #102 and for the sire's side of dog #31. We have no other information on the relatives of bitch #27 since she is an outcross, but there is no doubt that she is a carrier.

The most likely conclusion here is that dog #16 is a carrier, although there is no absolute proof that that is the case. Bitch #25 has been test-mated to dog #26, a proven carrier, producing eight phenotypically normal puppies. She has a 90 percent chance of being free of the PRA gene (see Table 5.1). Bitch #30 has been test-mated to an affected dog (#31), producing five puppies. There is a 96.8 percent or 97.0 percent chance that she is a noncarrier for the PRA gene (see Tables 5.2 and 5.2a). However, all her puppies are defined carriers, since their sire is affected. Dog #36 has been test-mated to bitch #37, a defined carrier, producing seven puppies. He has an 86.6 percent chance of being a noncarrier for PRA.

However, these puppies were born in 1991 and, at this point, we cannot be sure that none of them will be affected. All unknown puppies in litters q and y have a 50:50 chance of carrying the PRA gene, since one parent is a known carrier in each case. Using the conditional-probability equation (see chapter 5), each of the unknown puppies in litters r and w have a 66.6 percent chance of being carriers. Since the sire in litter v is affected, every puppy in that litter is a defined carrier. There is a 16.7 percent chance that each puppy in litter z will develop PRA ($.5 \times .333 \times 100$; the product rule, chapter 5) and an 83.3 percent chance that they will be carriers ($[.5 + .333] \times 100$; the sum rule, chapter 5). Keep in mind that these puppies were born in 1993. They could, in fact, have PRA and have not yet shown clinical signs of the disease.

The proposed mating between bitch #42 and dog #43 is very high risk, even if neither of these dogs has PRA. The risk of producing PRA in each of the puppies in the proposed litter bb is 17.6 percent (product rule, chapter 5).

So far in our analysis of pedigrees 6.9a and b, we have learned which dogs are defined carriers or likely to be carriers, which dogs have been test-mated, the risk that specific dogs or sets of dogs present to develop one of the diseases involved, as well as the risk given matings have of producing disease. Remember that this is all based on knowledge of affected dogs and knowledge that the traits are autosomal recessive.

If we have good information on all traits occurring in this set of dogs (and we could have, because this is "your" pedigree), then we have a lot more information that has not yet been spelled out. Go back to pedigree 6.9 and look at all of the dogs that do not have CA and, more important, could not have the disease, because for the most part (barring new mutations), you can trace genes through a pedigree. The same is true in pedigree 6.9b—some dogs could not have the gene for PRA and *lo and behold,* now you can tell which ones.

If both diseases had been described in one family instead of two breeds, you would also see that some dogs carry for one trait but are free (or likely to be free) of the other. You will find this to be very useful when we discuss strategies of disease control in Chapter 8, "Test-Mating."

Polygenic Traits

With polygenic traits, we cannot present typical pedigrees, because these diseases are often sporadic in occurrence, and as I said in Chapter 4, we do not know the number of genes involved in the production of any polygenic trait in dogs. That, however, does not mean that pedigrees are of no use in your attempts to control polygenic traits.

The typical buyer's pedigree is clearly of limited value because of the following:

1. Breeders tend to avoid the use of affected dogs.
2. We cannot calculate the specific risks associated with any given dog.
3. Most important, we cannot "see" the littermates of dogs in the pedigree.

It is for these three reasons that putting the "normal" phenotypic status of a dog on this type of pedigree is of little value to the breeder.

Now let's look at a geneticist's pedigree illustrating the polygenic trait hip dysplasia (see Figure 6.9c). In three interrelated "families," dog #9 produced the trait with two bitches (#14 twice and #24), but not with bitch #20. Given the fact that puppies in litter k fit the phenotype you want, I would certainly use them before I picked a puppy for breeding from any of the other three litters sired by dog #9.

Despite the fact that 50 percent of the puppies produced by bitch #14 were dysplastic when she was bred to dog #9, all were normal when she was bred to dog #15. While I can't provide an exact risk for dog #15, I believe that it bodes well for him, although I would have liked to see a few more normal puppies in litter f.

Dog #16 (litter m) is phenotypically normal himself (he would get an OFA or PennHip number), but three of his four littermates have HD. He is not a good pick, and in this case, 50 percent of his puppies were affected, and his son produced the disease when he was bred to his own dam.

Despite the fact that dog #11 produced HD when bred to bitches #12, #17 and #22, he did not produce the disease when bred to bitch #20. I cannot give you a

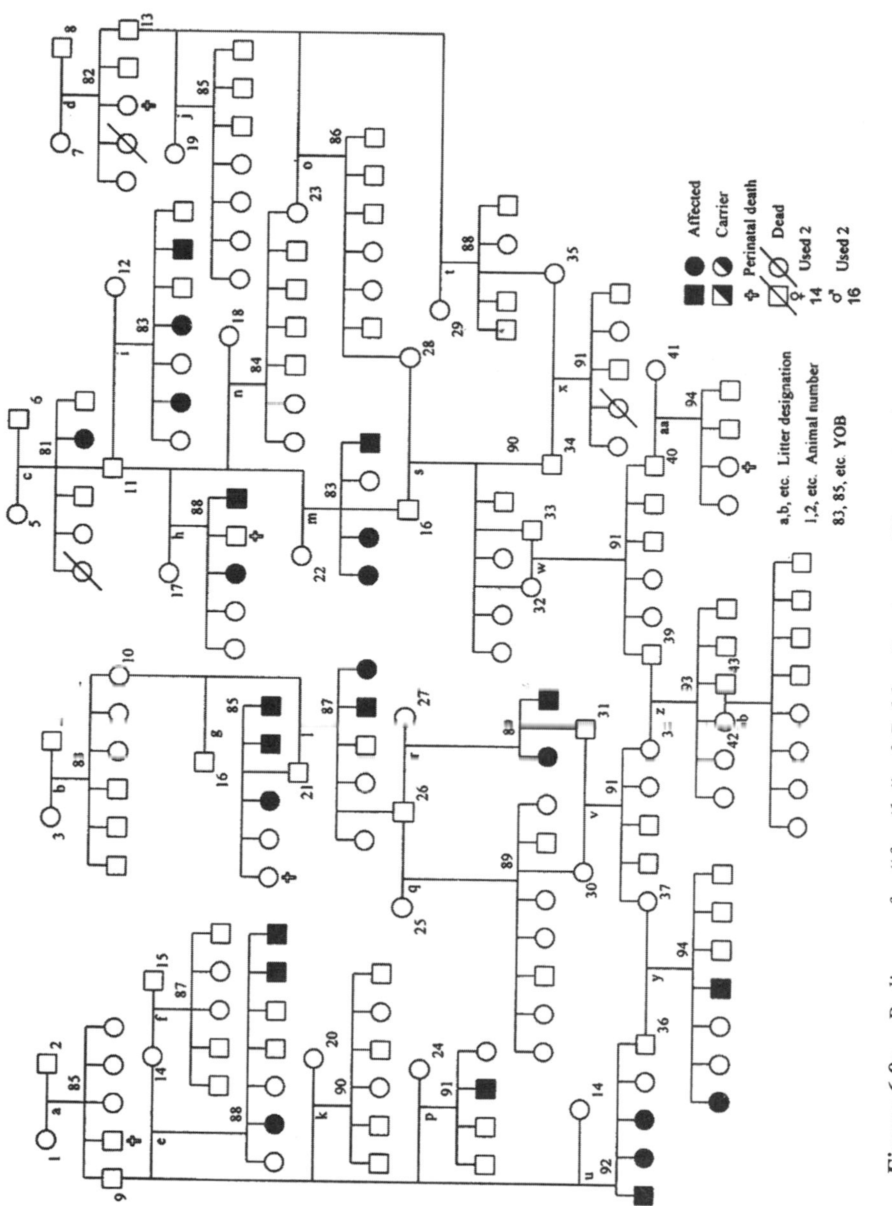

Figure 6.9c *Pedigree of a "family" of Golden Retrievers illustrating hip dysplasia, a polygenic trait.*

specific risk for bitch #18, but I can say that I would like to see a litter from dog #15 and bitch #18, given that they are a good phenotypic match.

Pedigrees are clearly of use in trying to select breeding stock to reduce the frequency of polygenic traits, even though we cannot attach specific risks to dogs as we can with single-gene traits. I believe this type of selection will lead to a reduction of the frequency of polygenic traits in a kennel, and as we shall see in the following chapters, this is not the only tool we have. Remember, the point of importance here is that we get to "see" families of dogs—not just the progenitors.

Questions for Chapter 6

1. Pedigree 6.10 is a typical buyer's pedigree. Alphonso, whose pedigree it is, developed CMO (craniomandibular osteopathy) at five months of age. CMO is an autosomal recessive trait.

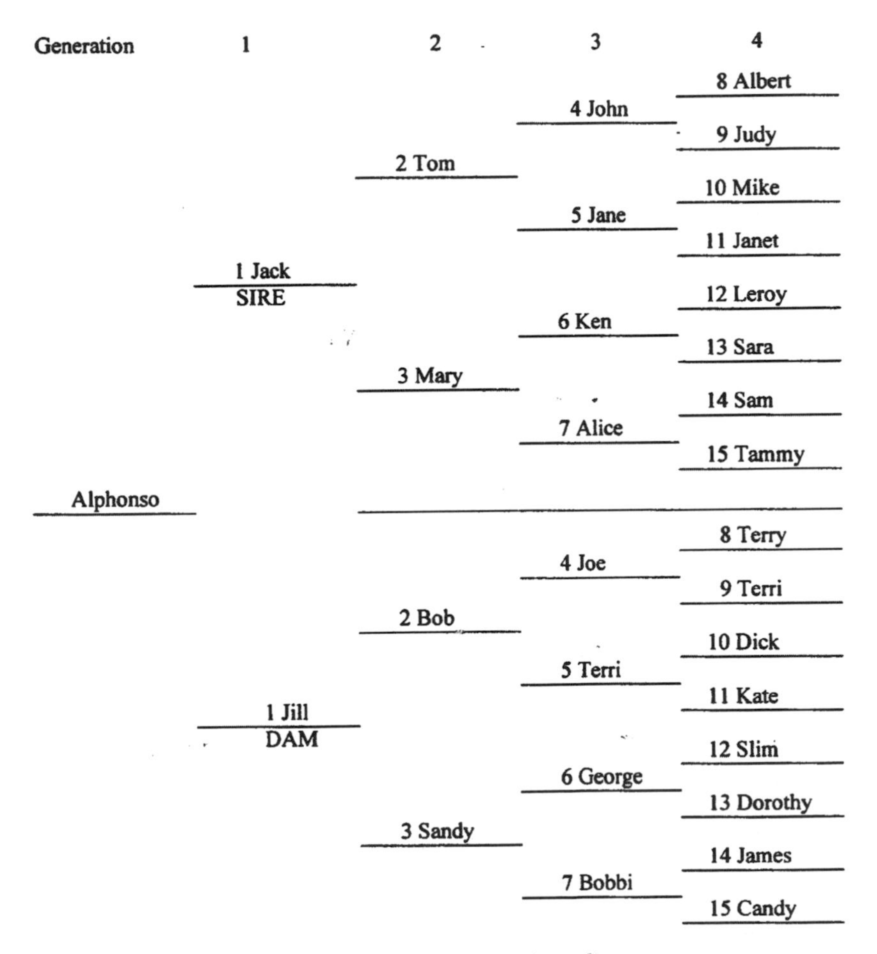

Fig. 6.10 *A typical buyer's pedigree.*

a. Name the dog or bitch (or both) that is likely to be the original source of the gene causing the problem in this pedigree.

b. Name the proven carriers in this pedigree.

c. What is the chance that Bobbi (#7 on the dam's side) and John (#4 on the sire's side) are carriers?

2. Figure 6.11 shows a buyer's pedigree with six known carriers of anasarca, an autosomal recessive trait.

   a. Show the carrier risk and the chance each dog has of being affected in the pedigree for which it is appropriate. The carrier risk is below the line, and the affected risk is above the line.

   b. Can you determine the carrier risk behind each marked carrier as well as the risk in front of each carrier? If so, what are the risks for each appropriate dog?

   c. If there are three puppies in litter a, what is the risk that at least one will be affected?

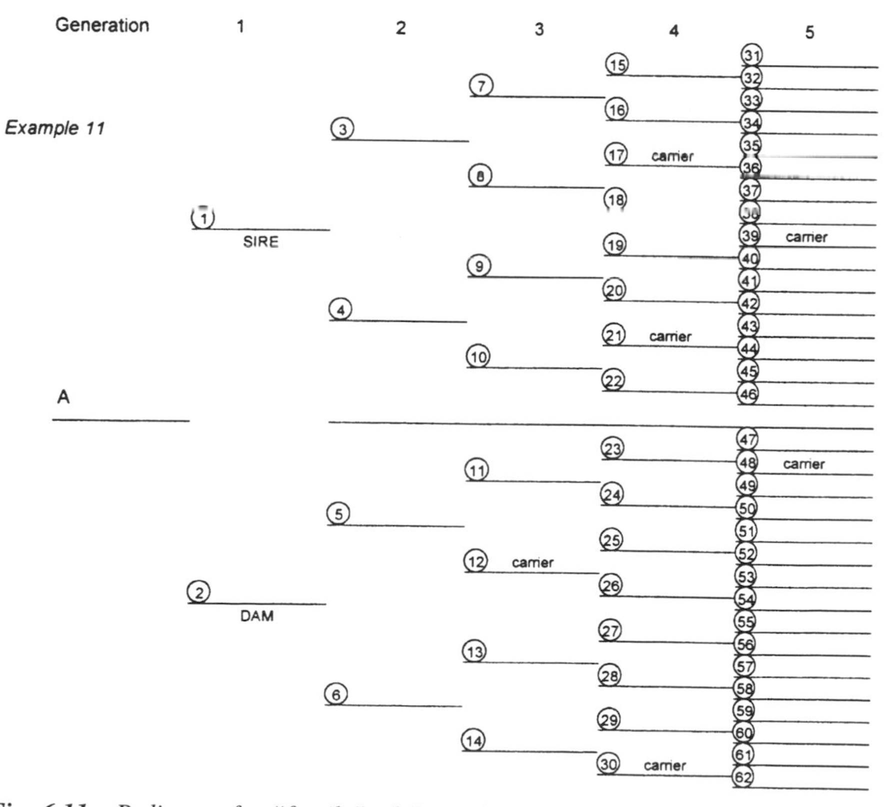

Fig. 6.11 *Pedigree of a "family" of dogs showing multiple carrier and affected dogs with anasarca, an autosomal recessive trait.*

3. Figure 6.12 could be considered an Irish Terrier pedigree showing a sex-linked trait termed X-linked myopathy.

   a. Evaluate pedigree 6.12 and show the risk each appropriate dog has to be affected (above the line) or a carrier (below the line), both anterior and posterior to the identified dogs.

   b. What is the chance that bitch #62 is a carrier?

   c. What is the chance that dog #3 is a hidden carrier?

4. Figure 6.13 presents a geneticist's pedigree of a "family" of Labrador Retrievers with PRA (progressive retinal atrophy), which is an autosomal recessive trait. There are six affected dogs shown in this pedigree.

   a. Mark both proven carriers (they produced the disease) and defined carriers (they are offspring of an affected dog or bitch) in the usual fashion.

   b. What is the chance that dog #9 is genotypically normal for this trait?

   c. What is the chance that bitches #19, #23 and #29 are homozygous dominant (genetically normal) for this trait?

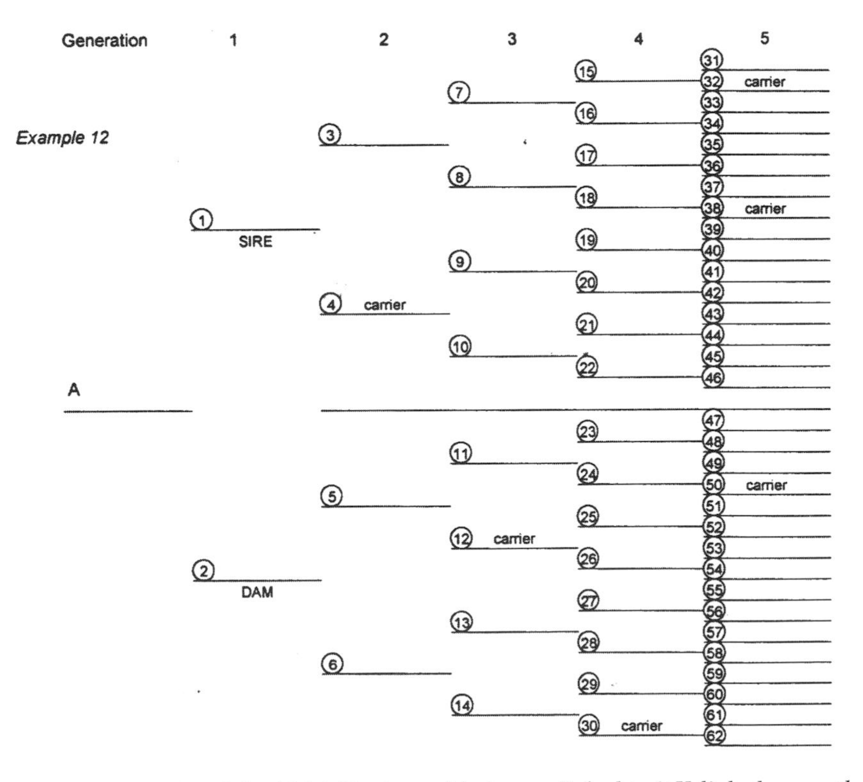

Figure 6.12 *A "family" of Irish Terriers with the sex-linked trait X-linked myopathy.*

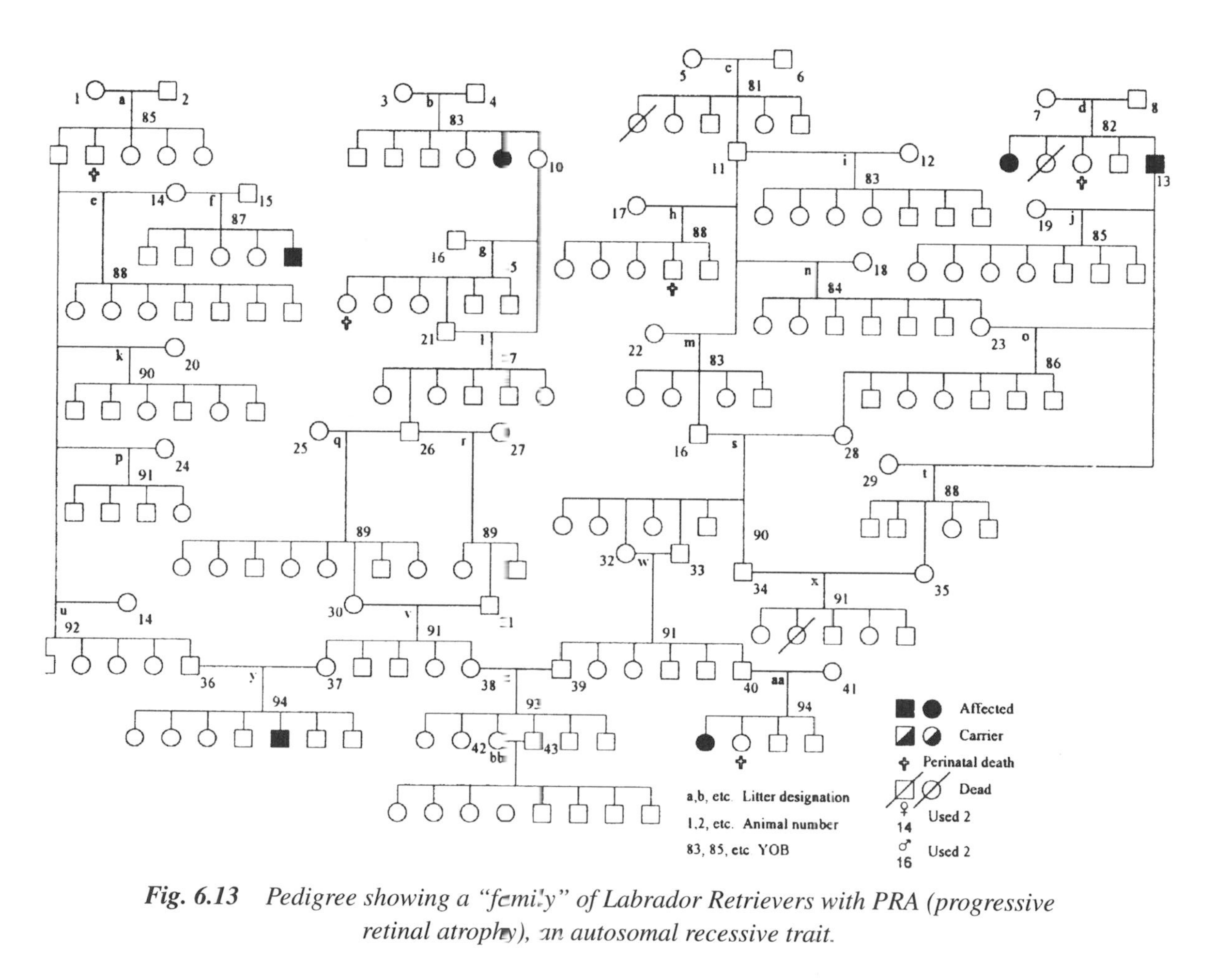

Fig. 6.13 *Pedigree showing a "family" of Labrador Retrievers with PRA (progressive retinal atrophy), an autosomal recessive trait.*

d. What is the risk that bitch #10 is a carrier?

e. What is the risk that dog #26 is a carrier?

f. What is the risk that bitch #20 is a carrier?

g. What is the risk that dog #11 is a carrier?

Answers for Chapter 6

1a. There is no clear-cut source for this gene in this pedigree. There is no animal in this pedigree on both the sire and dam's side. Terri is in the pedigree twice, but only on the dam's side. Since a potential source for this type of trait must be on both sides of the pedigree, the "blame" cannot be placed on her (at least not exclusively on her). This illustrates the problem of a buyer's pedigree, which is that we can determine nothing about the littermates of Alphonso's progenitors, and somewhere in this "family," there must be other affected dogs.

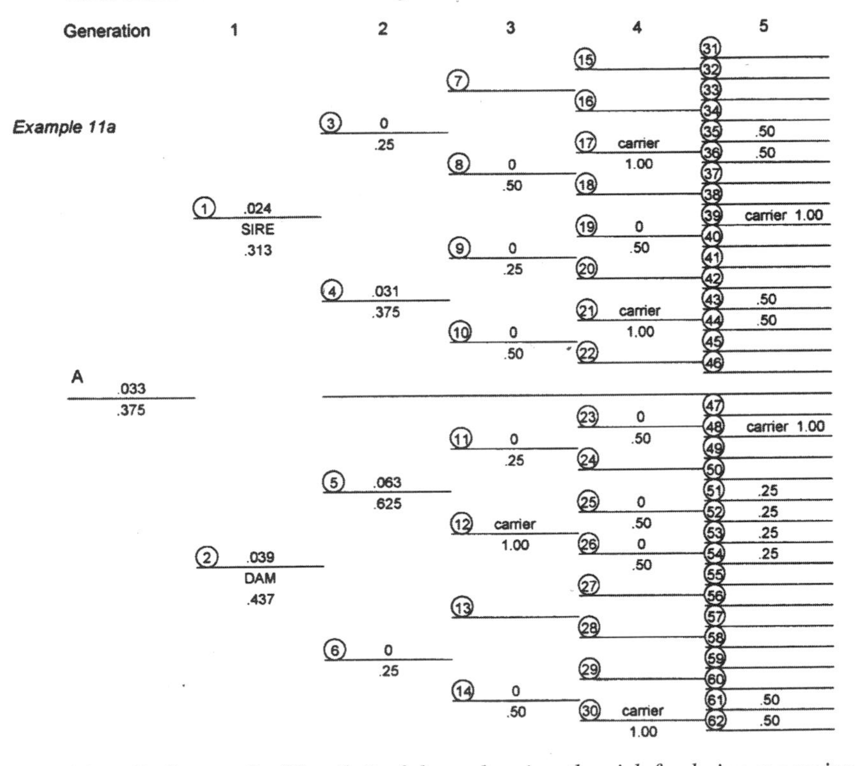

Fig. 6.11a Pedigree of a "family" of dogs showing the risk for being a carrier or affected for the autosomal recessive trait anasarca.

b. Jack and Jill.

c. The risk is the same for both Bobbi and John, since they are both great-grandparents of Alphonso: 25 percent.

2a. Figure 6.11a shows the risks for the affected and/or carrier state for each appropriate dog in the pedigree in Figure 6.11.

b. Figure 6.11a also shows the risk for each appropriate dog behind the marked carriers.

c. 0.099 or 9.9 percent.

Although there was a risk that dogs #1, #3, #5, #11 and #15 could be affected (it is shown) in this pedigree, they are presented as being phenotypically normal, so they must also be genetically normal for this trait, and therefore, they cannot have a gene to pass to their daughters.

3a. Figure 6.12a shows the risk each appropriate animal in the pedigree has to be affected (above the line) or a carrier (below the line).

b. 100 percent: Bitch #62 is a defined carrier with a sex-linked trait.

c. There is zero chance that dog #3 is a hidden carrier, since males are hemizygous for sex-linked traits and show the disease if the gene is present. There is a 12.5 percent chance he is affected.

4a. Proven and defined carriers are marked on Figure 6.13a. Bitch #14 is in the pedigree twice. With litter f, she is shown to be a proven carrier, and of course, this status still applied when she was used as the dam of litter u five years later. All offspring of dog #13 are defined carriers, since he is affected.

b. 96.8 percent (Table 5.1, chapter 5).

c. Bitches #19 and #23, 99.2 percent; bitch #29, 96.8 percent (Table 5.2, chapter 5).

d. 66.6 percent (conditional probability)

e. It depends on how you want to calculate the risk of dog #26:

i.) Going backward from the affected dog in litter y, dog #26 is his double great-grandparent, giving him a risk of 50 percent (25 + 25).

ii.) Coming down from his dam, bitch #10, bred to her own son, dog #21, the risk is 49.9 percent (33.3 + 16.6).

iii.) Probably the best way to assess the risk of dog #26 is to assume the gene that reached bitch #37 originated from bitch #10, her

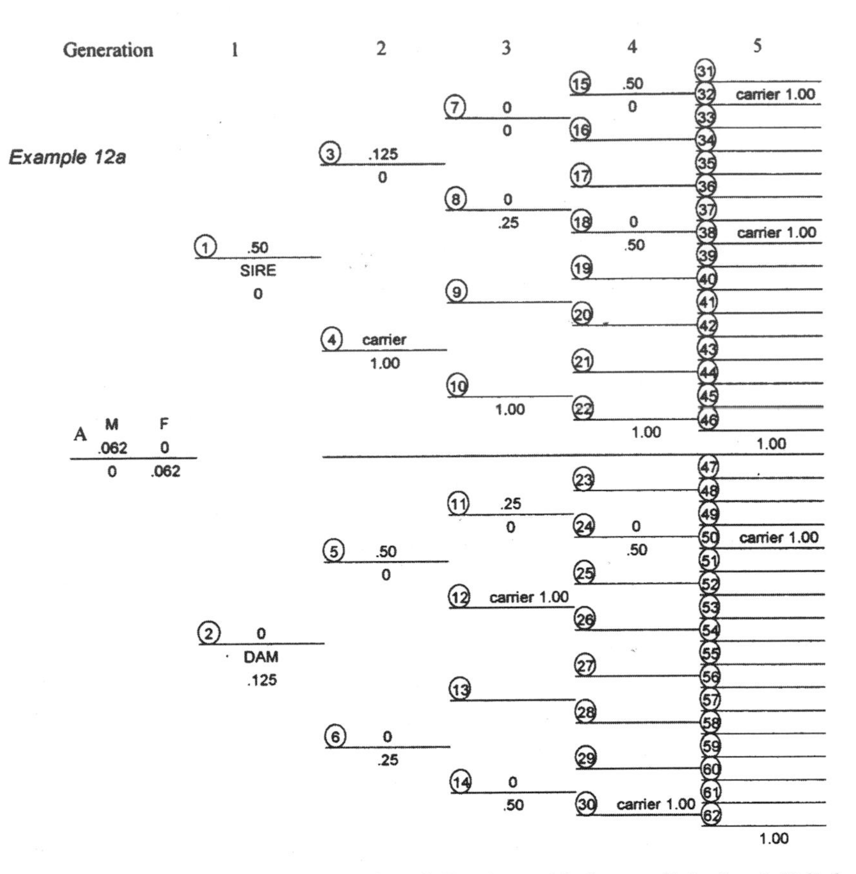

Fig. 6.12a *Pedigree of a "family" of Irish Terriers with the sex-linked trait X-linked myopathy showing the risk that an animal will be affected (above the line) or a carrier (below the line).*

great-grandmother (unless you have specific information showing that bitch #25 or #27, which are both outcrosses, could be a carrier). The only way the gene could get to bitch #37 is through dog #26, making him a defined carrier. Therefore, the risk that dog #26 is a carrier is 100 percent.

f. Since dog #9 has a 96.8-percent chance of being homozygous dominant for the PRA gene, we can make no determination about the genetic status of bitch #20 for this trait. My assumption would be that she is normal.

g. The location of dog #11 in this pedigree and the information we have on his offspring does not allow us to draw specific conclusions about his genetic status in regard to this trait. My assumption would be that he is genetically normal, because there is no information to the contrary.

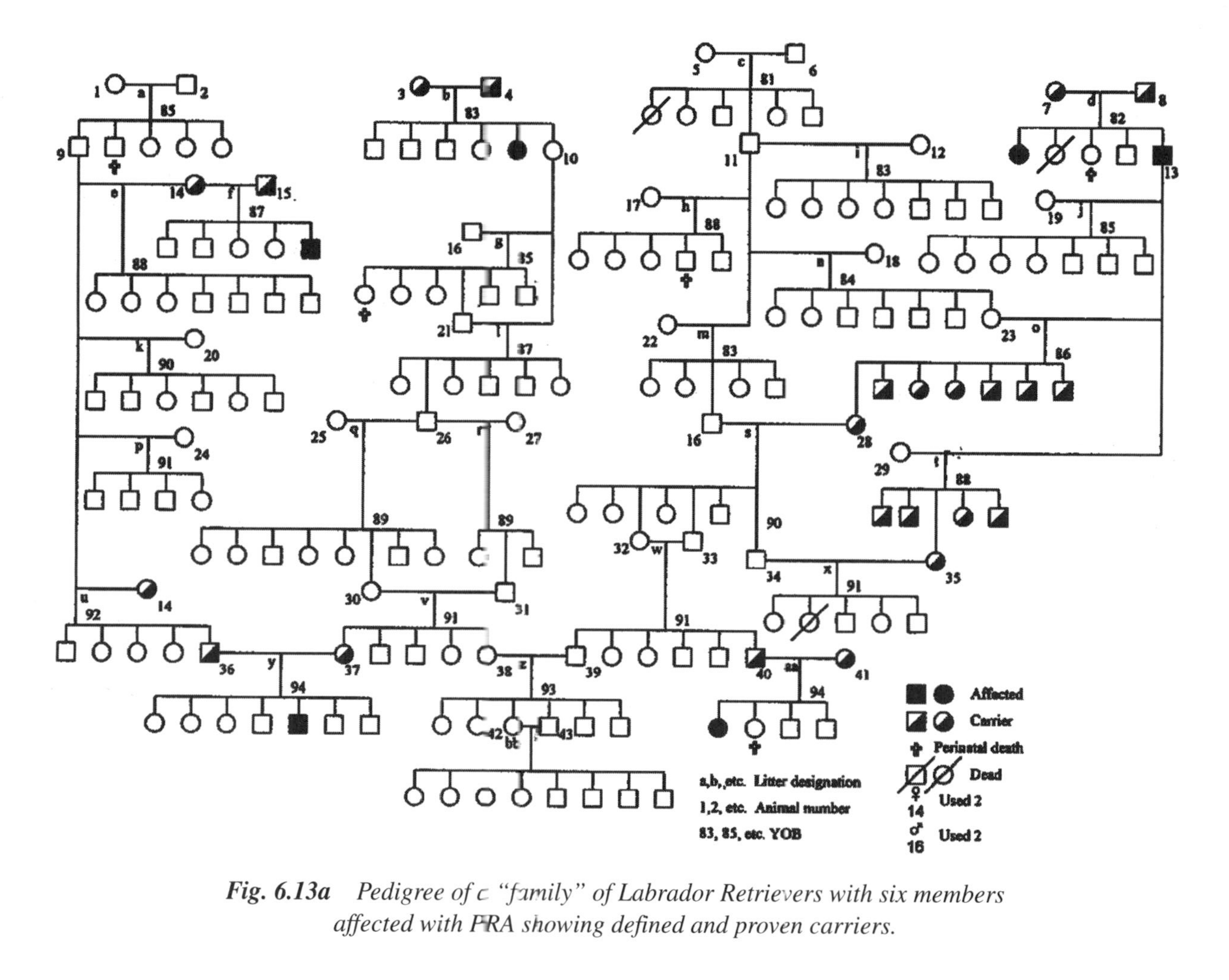

Fig. 6.13a *Pedigree of a "family" of Labrador Retrievers with six members affected with PRA showing defined and proven carriers.*

CHAPTER 7

The Interpretation and Use of Pedigrees to Determine the Probable Mode of Inheritance of a Trait

In Chapter 6, we learned to use pedigrees to determine the possibility a dog has to develop or to be a carrier of a given trait. But pedigrees are also useful to estimate whether a trait is inherited and its likely mode of inheritance.

The approach I will use in this chapter is straightforward and, to an extent, simplistic. Some may say it is too simplistic, but I do not believe I can turn you into a genetic counselor with this book alone. Therefore, my approach here is to present inheritance as if there are no situations that cause inheritance patterns to modify and present themselves as deviations of the patterns I describe. For example, if certain sex-limited traits occur in males, you might think a disorder is sex-linked. If the disorder affects only females, you will see a pattern that I do not describe here. So adequate and accurate background data is necessary to help you avoid this problem. Further, the accurate determination of the mode of inheritance for any trait requires that you have accurate and consistent diagnosis of the trait under consideration. If you have different diagnoses for the same disease, it is obvious that no pattern is likely to develop that will allow you to estimate the mode of inheritance for a trait.

It is my belief that if you follow the patterns presented here, you will be correct a high percentage of the time, and the strategies you use to control the traits you want to breed away from will, in fact, reduce the frequency of the disease in your kennel. Whenever possible, you should pool your data with that of other breeders, because generally speaking, the more cases you have to analyze, the more accurate you will be in reaching a decision.

Isolated Cases of a Given Disorder

If a single case of a disease occurs in your line, you cannot, based on that case alone, determine whether that disorder is inherited. If there is some reason to believe that it might be inherited, you can take some steps to protect yourself.

Some reasons that may suggest that a single case in your line may be inherited follow:

1. The disease has occurred in other "families" in your breed, but has never been definitively shown to be inherited.
2. It is thought to be or known to be inherited in other breeds.
3. It is thought to be or known to be inherited in other species.

If this disorder or problem is minor (it causes no serious problems for the dog), you may want to ignore it and proceed with your breeding program. If the problem occurs in an offshoot breeding (in a mating in which, for some reason, you are not keeping any of the offspring for breeding and are not planning to use the parents again), you may just want to forget that the disorder surfaced at all.

However, if the disease is a serious one and occurred in the main aspect of your line (you are going to propagate these dogs), you may want to take certain steps to protect yourself as completely as possible.

First, even if the occurrence is a single case, you can make some reasonable assumptions about the disorder in terms of potential inheritance:

1. If the disorder is a single case, the parents must be phenotypically normal for the trait, so you can rule out dominance (except, of course, for a new mutation).
2. If a female is affected, you can generally rule out sex-linkage.
3. This leaves two potential alternatives: autosomal recessive and polygenic modes of inheritance.

At this point, you apply the same ground rules you would apply if you knew the trait was inherited. Specifically, you calculate the risks that related dogs would have to carry the trait and select dogs for breeding that carry the least risk. Retrospective test-matings may have occurred, and if so, you can make more specific determinations for the risk that a given dog or bitch has to carry this potentially inherited trait. All you are doing here is selecting dogs that minimize the chance that this potentially inherited disease may spread in your line. Despite the fact that the typical advice you will generally get if you approach your veterinarian with a problem like this is "Don't remate these dogs and outcross to get rid of the trait," this may very well not be in the best interests of your line for various reasons.

Perhaps the best advice I can give is that if you are faced with a serious disease central to your line, remate the dogs and determine whether it is genetic. Otherwise, the disorder is very likely to plague you for a very long time. Remember, the tables showing the risk that a given dog is a carrier can also provide an estimate of whether this disease is inherited.

For example, if you remate the dogs making the assumption that both are proven carriers (whether it is recessive or polygenic), and you get eight puppies and all are normal, you can state for a recessive trait that there is a 90-percent probability that the trait is not inherited (chapter 5, Table 5.1). For a polygenic trait, you cannot give a specific risk, but you can say that it is reasonable to assume that the trait is unlikely to be inherited.

Multiple Cases of a Given Disorder

Figure 7.1 presents a pedigree of a family of dogs in which a given trait has appeared five times over a period of eight years. The question, of course, is "Is it inherited?" If so, what is the likely mode of inheritance? The information you have is that the condition is not common in your breed, at least to your knowledge. There is no report of this disorder being inherited in other breeds, at least to your knowledge.

What do you do now? Whether or not the trait is inherited, at this point, with five cases occurring on one side of your pedigree, you must be thinking that it certainly could be inherited. If so, how do you analyze the situation? You proceed as you did before. In no case was a parent affected with the disease, so it is extremely unlikely that it is dominant if it is inherited. Both males and females are affected in about equal numbers, and a female is affected when the sire is phenotypically normal, so it can't be sex-linked. That leaves autosomal recessive and polygenic traits.

If the trait is an autosomal recessive, you expect, on the average, 25 percent of the puppies in affected litters to be affected. There are nineteen puppies in the affected litters, and five—about 25 percent—are affected. Further, the general description of the characteristics of a recessive trait (that the trait tends to skip generations and there is an increased consanguinity; chapter 4) are present here. In addition, if you assume that bitch #12 and dogs #11 and #13 are proven carriers (which they must be, if the trait is inherited), you can account for the presence of the gene in all the other parents, because they are all descendants of these three dogs. You still can't rule out a polygenic trait at this point, but an assumption that it is recessive is a good place to start.

At this point, if you followed the general advice most veterinarians give and did not remate the parents of the first three affected dogs, you still would have produced the two affected dogs in litter x. If you follow the advice that you should not breed the littermates of affected dogs or other offspring of dogs that have produced the trait, you would wipe out the whole right side of the pedigree, starting from litter z. If you remember that dog #16 is the son of a dog that produced the disease, you now wipe out everything in the pedigree to the right of litter y, and three quarters of your pedigree is up in smoke.

What do you do now? You proceed exactly as we did in Chapter 6, making the assumption that the trait is inherited, and you select dogs for breeding that have the least risk of carrying the genes for this putative inherited trait. At this point, you may

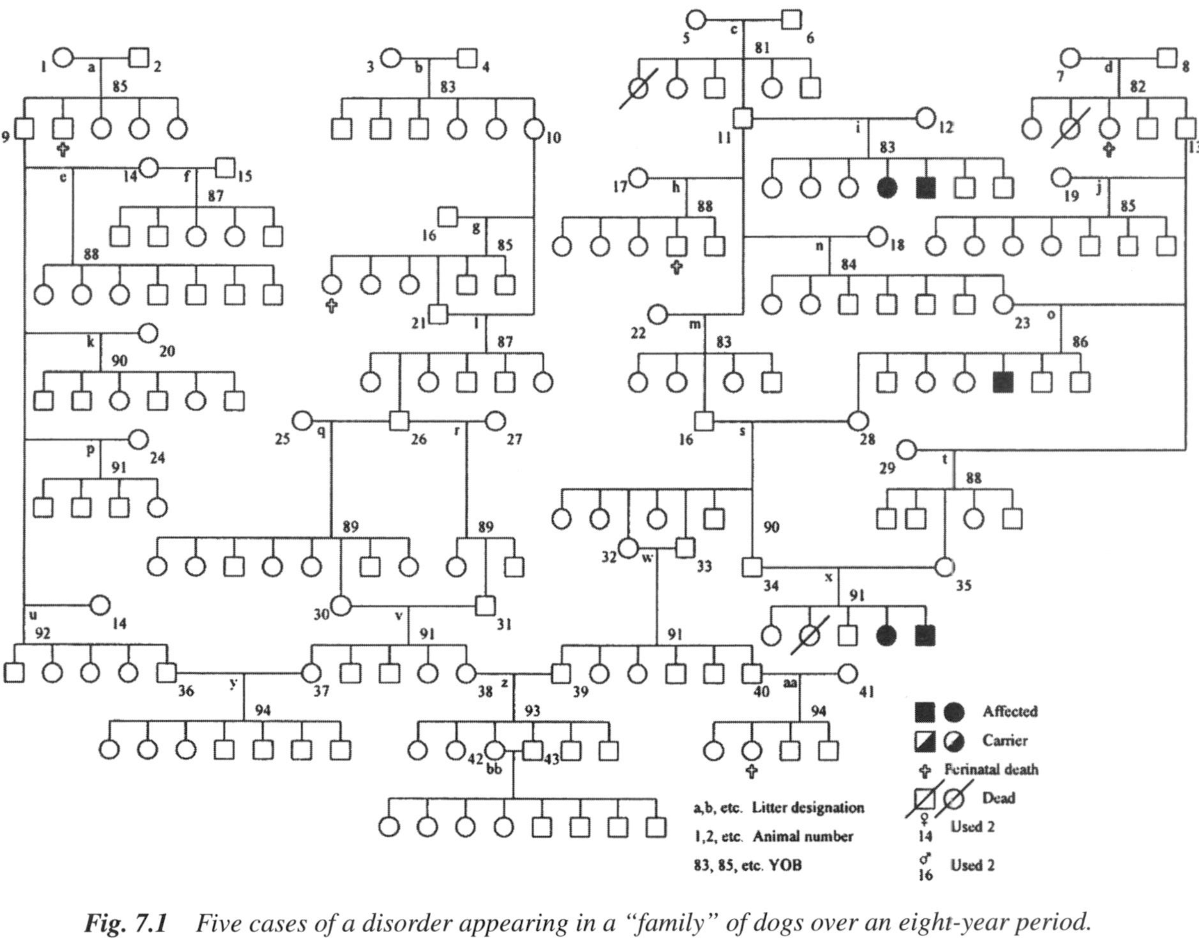

Fig. 7.1 *Five cases of a disorder appearing in a "family" of dogs over an eight-year period.*

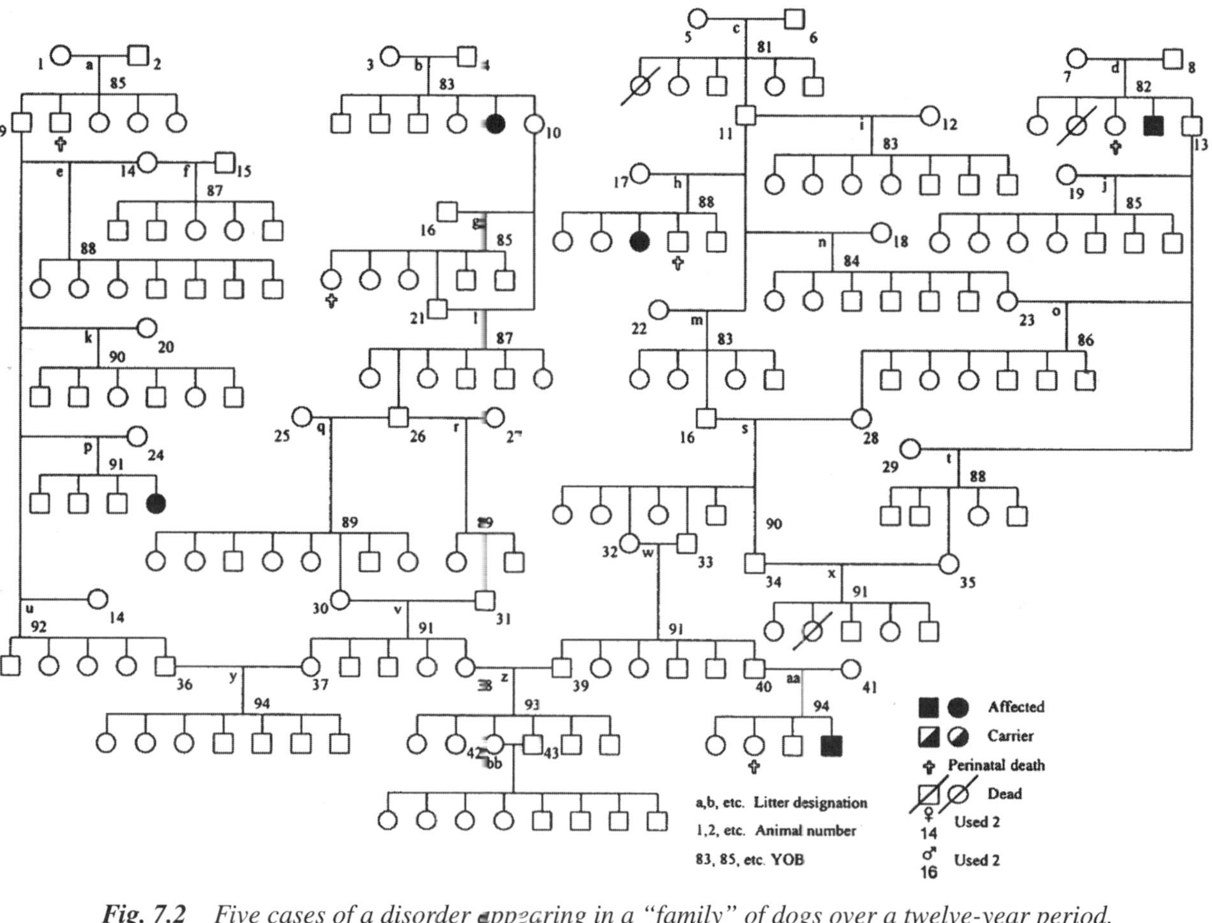

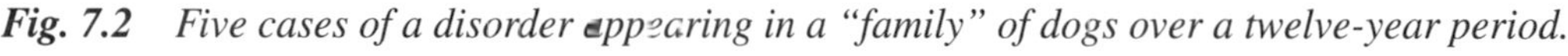

Fig. 7.2 *Five cases of a disorder appearing in a "family" of dogs over a twelve-year period.*

want to test-mate the dogs to prove for certain whether the condition is inherited. In any case, if you proceed correctly, you minimize the long-term risk of perpetuating this disorder.

In Figure 7.2, we present another situation in which multiple cases of a disorder appear in this pedigree.

As you can see, again, there are five affected dogs, but the distribution of the trait is entirely different. Remember, if you had not drawn your own pedigree, it would be difficult to "see" the difference in the distribution of this trait. Let us say, for argument's sake, that the trait depicted in Figure 7.2 is the same trait with the same ground rules we had for Figure 7.1 (not common in your breed and not known to be inherited in other breeds). Would you draw the same conclusion for the trait in Figure 7.2 that you did for the same trait in Figure 7.1? I wouldn't. The difference in the time period over which the disease occurred (eight years, Figure 7.1; twelve years, Figure 7.2) is not important here. But if you mark in the putative proven carriers in Figure 7.2, you find that you need nine dogs to account for all the cases in Figure 7.2 compared to three dogs in Figure 7.1. So you ask yourself, "If this is not a common disease in the breed, where did all of these carriers come from?" Although all nine dogs are in the same pedigree, they are not closely related, so no increased consanguinity is present. Although the trait is spread over several years ('82, '83, '88, '91 and '94), it is not really skipping generations. The disorders are appearing independent of one another, and the disease cannot be traced from one case to the next. I would draw the conclusion that the trait depicted in pedigree 7.2 is not inherited, despite the fact that there are five affected dogs among twenty-four total offspring in the affected litters (21 percent).

In Figure 7.3, we have nine cases of a disease occurring in the pedigree: seven males and two females. Is the trait likely to be inherited, and if so, what is the probable mode of inheritance?

You begin the analysis the same way you did in the previous examples. Of the eight parents of the affected dogs, only one is affected. If this condition is inherited as a dominant trait, we would expect at least one affected parent for each litter that has affected offspring. Further, we would expect half of the offspring to be affected. There are twenty-seven total offspring, and only nine are affected (33 percent). On the basis of these two parameters, we can rule out autosomal dominant as a likely mode of inheritance. With 33 percent of the offspring affected, it could certainly be a recessive trait, and in the litter in which one of the parents is affected, half of the offspring (three) are affected. With a recessive trait, we expect a 1:1 ratio of affected to normal if one of the parents is affected. Clearly, the condition, if it is inherited, could be recessive. It also could be polygenic, because it is not possible to distinguish between a polygenic and a recessive trait based on the information presented in this pedigree.

What is the chance that it is a sex-linked recessive trait? Pretty good based on the following. The only time a female is affected (litter w), the sire is also affected, which is a requirement for a sex-linked recessive trait. This, of course, means that dam #32 is also a carrier. We also know that dam #32 is a carrier, because a male

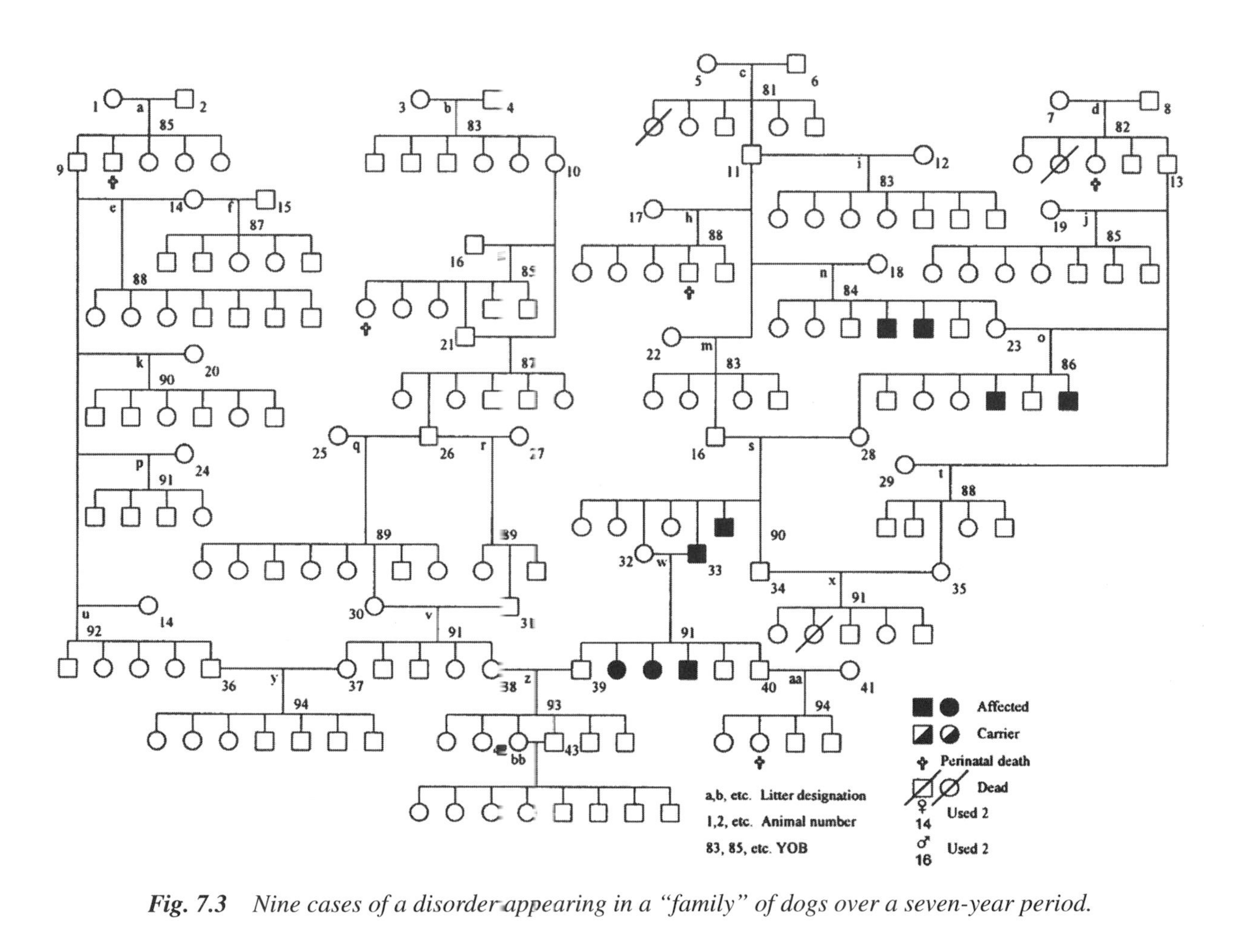

Fig. 7.3 *Nine cases of a disorder appearing in a "family" of dogs over a seven-year period.*

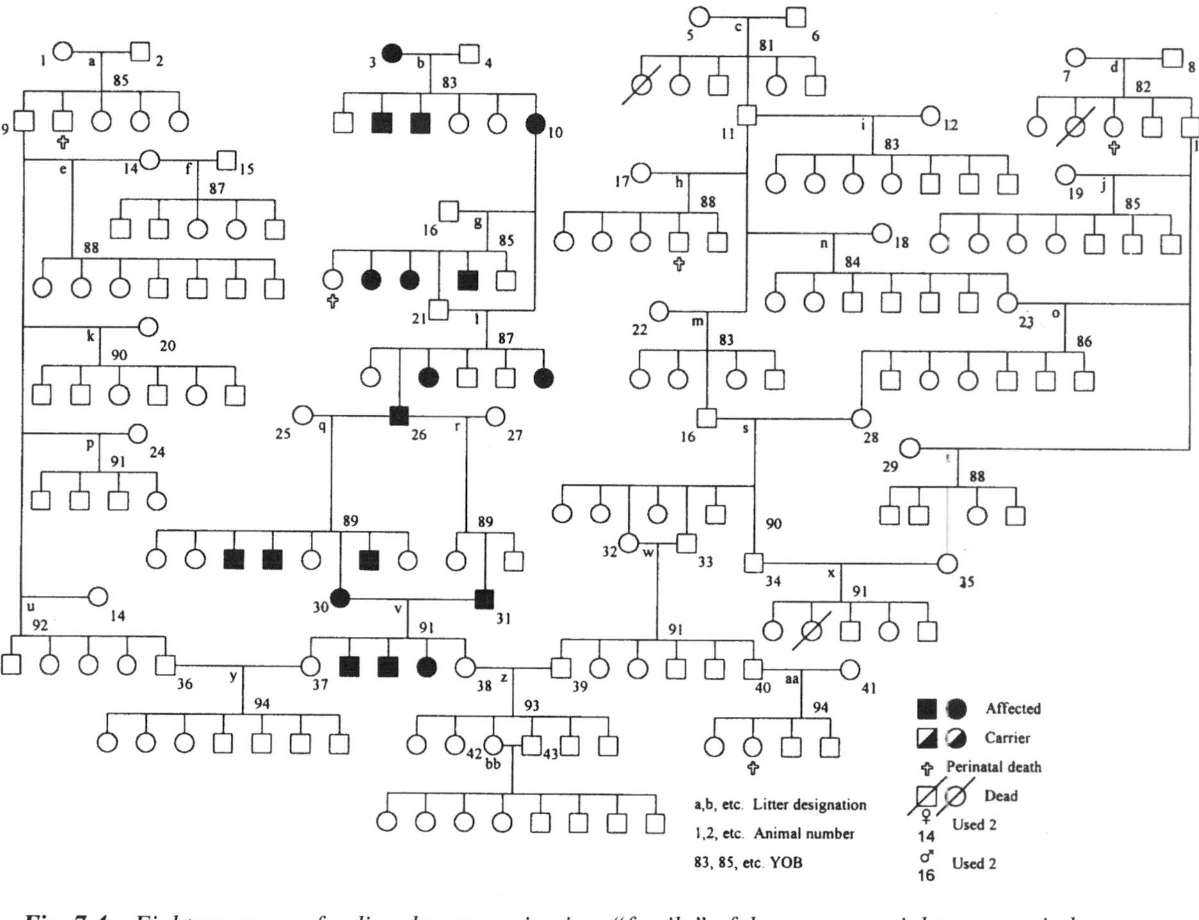

Fig. 7.4 *Eighteen cases of a disorder appearing in a "family" of dogs over an eight-year period.*

puppy in litter w is affected, and a male cannot get an X-chromosome from his father. Further, in litters n, o and s, there are a total of ten females, none affected. With a recessive trait, we expect an equal ratio of affected males to affected females, and although the ratio we see here is statistically possible, it is not probable. In addition, there are a total of fifteen males in the litters that contain affected dogs, and seven of them are affected (48 percent). With a sex-linked recessive trait, you expect half of the male offspring to be affected if the dam is phenotypically normal. None of the four dams used in these matings has the disease. A sex-linked recessive is the best choice for the mode of inheritance for this trait.

You could prove this point by test-mating an affected female (if they can bear offspring) to any normal male, and you expect all males and no females to be affected. Why worry about the difference between a sex-linked recessive and an autosomal recessive trait? Because if it is a sex-linked trait, the disease has run its course in this pedigree. It is over, and you do not have to do anything else to prevent the disease from recurring. The only dogs that could pass this trait on are males #16 (in the central part of the pedigree), #39 and #40. Since they are phenotypically normal, they must be genotypically normal if this is a sex-linked trait.

In Figure 7.4, we have the central portion of the pedigree afflicted with a trait that seems to be affecting about an equal number of males and females. What is the probable mode of inheritance? Again, we start out in exactly the same way as we did before: by looking at the phenotypic status of the parents.

In Figure 7.4, in each case in which there is an affected dog in the litter, at least one of the parents is affected. This alone should make you think of a dominant trait. There are seventeen affected puppies among a total of thirty-four in the litters containing affected puppies (50 percent). A 1:1 ratio is expected with a recessive trait if one of the parents is affected and the other is a carrier, and it is expected with a dominant trait if the affected parent is heterozygous.

The telling mating in this pedigree is between bitch #30 and dog #31, both affected. If the trait is recessive, we expect all the puppies to be affected, and if it is dominant, we expect three-fourths of the puppies to be affected. In litter v, three out of five puppies are affected, and the conclusion I would draw from this pedigree is that a dominant trait is illustrated.

How do we know it is not a sex-linked dominant? We know it is not a sex-linked dominant trait, because a requirement for that mode of inheritance is that all daughters of an affected male must be affected. In litter v, females #37 and #38 are phenotypically and, since this is a dominant trait, genetically normal. Why are we interested in the mode of inheritance here? Again, because the trait automatically stops without you needing to do anything else. The only animals being carried on in this line are females #37 and #38, and they are genetically normal; you can prove that to your own and anyone else's satisfaction by analyzing "your" pedigree.

Figure 7.5 presents a series of seven cases of a disorder that occurred over a ten-year period in this pedigree. What is the probable mode of inheritance? You start the same way as always. Are any of the parents affected? No, so it can't be dominant. What is the sex ratio? There are four males and three females affected, so it cannot be

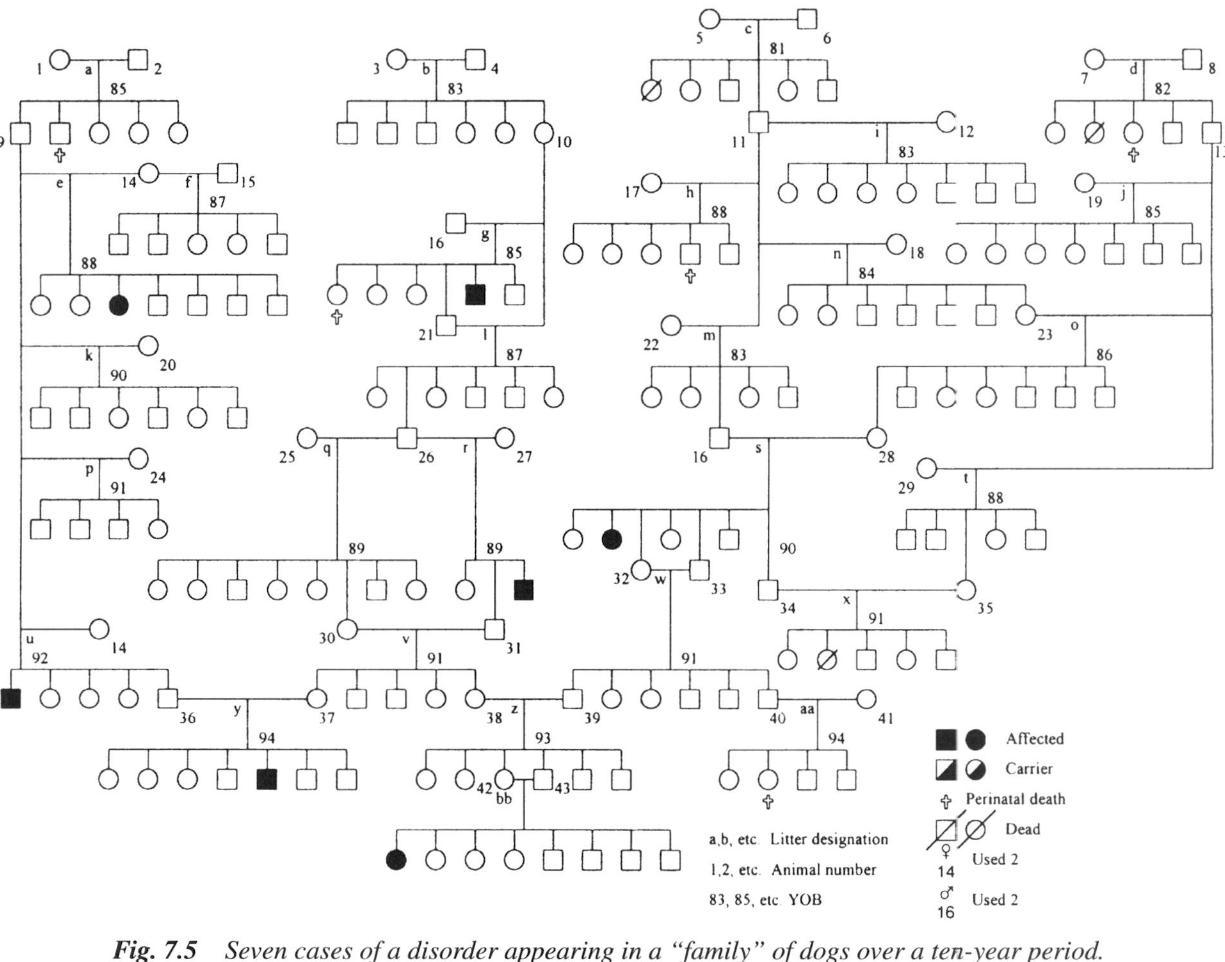

***Fig. 7.5** Seven cases of a disorder appearing in a "family" of dogs over a ten-year period.*

sex-linked. This leaves an autosomal recessive or a polygenic trait. What is the best choice? The trait skips generations, but both polygenic and recessive traits do that with equal facility. Both parents are normal in each case in which an affected animal is present in a litter. Again, this is a common finding with both recessive and polygenic traits.

At this point, you might ask, "Is this trait inherited?" To me, it looks like it is inherited, based on the following:

1. Dog #16 produced an affected puppy in two separate litters.
2. Dog #9 and bitch #14 produced an affected puppy in their first litter, and the disease recurred when they were remated.
3. A clear-cut pathway for the gene or genes causing the trait leads to the other three affected dogs.

Is the trait autosomal recessive? There are seven affected puppies among a total of forty-three puppies in the affected litters (16 percent). We expect 25 percent of the puppies to be affected with an autosomal recessive trait when both parents are phenotypically normal. But only four more affected puppies are needed to give us 25 percent in this pedigree. So, it could still be recessive or polygenic. Can we resolve this dilemma?

The answer is "no" with any real degree of certainty using the number of dogs involved. Willis delves into the statistics of this situation using the Chi-squared test on *a priori* expected results and a method of correcting the *a priori* data.[1] I strongly recommend that you read Willis if you are interested in this aspect. Looking at this situation, my best guess is that this trait is likely to be polygenic, and if you use the methods described by Willis, you will come to the same conclusion.

What difference does it make if it's polygenic or not? The basic difference is that there are several dogs in this pedigree that have been test-mated, and if the trait is recessive, you can give specific results for those test-matings. If the trait is polygenic, you cannot give specific results. For example, if this trait were recessive, bitch #14 and dog #9 must be carriers, so dog #15 and bitches #20 and #24 are test-mated, and they would have a 76.3-percent, 82.2-percent and 68.4-percent chance, respectively, of being genetically normal for this trait (see Table 5.1).

Aside from the immediate benefits you can derive (more accurate knowledge about dogs in the pedigree) from knowing the mode of inheritance of a trait in your line and breed, this knowledge is needed for DNA analysis to develop for use in more accurately ascertaining the genetic status of your dogs.

The last point I want to make in this chapter is that the decisions we are talking about here are those you need to make for your own kennel. Is there a chance that if you make a decision based on the situation I described here that you could be wrong? Of course there is. But you are generally not in a position to generate sufficient data

(1) Willis, M. B. *Genetics of the Dog*, pp. 352–354. New York: Howell Book House, 1989.

in your own kennel such that your decision would have the accuracy necessary for a publishable paper. If you wait for that, you may never make the decision that gives you the best chance to protect your dogs and the people who buy them.

I expect to be roundly criticized for this chapter, as every geneticist and veterinarian finds loopholes and objections to what I have said, but if you follow the typical advice currently given to today's breeders, the genetic status of your dogs will remain a mystery, and we will maintain the sorry state of affairs we face with genetic diseases of dogs at the present time.

Questions for Chapter 7

1. a. What is the most likely mode of inheritance for the trait shown in Figure 7.6?
   b. Why?
   c. What is the chance that bitch #5 is genetically normal?
   d. What dogs are proven carriers for this trait?

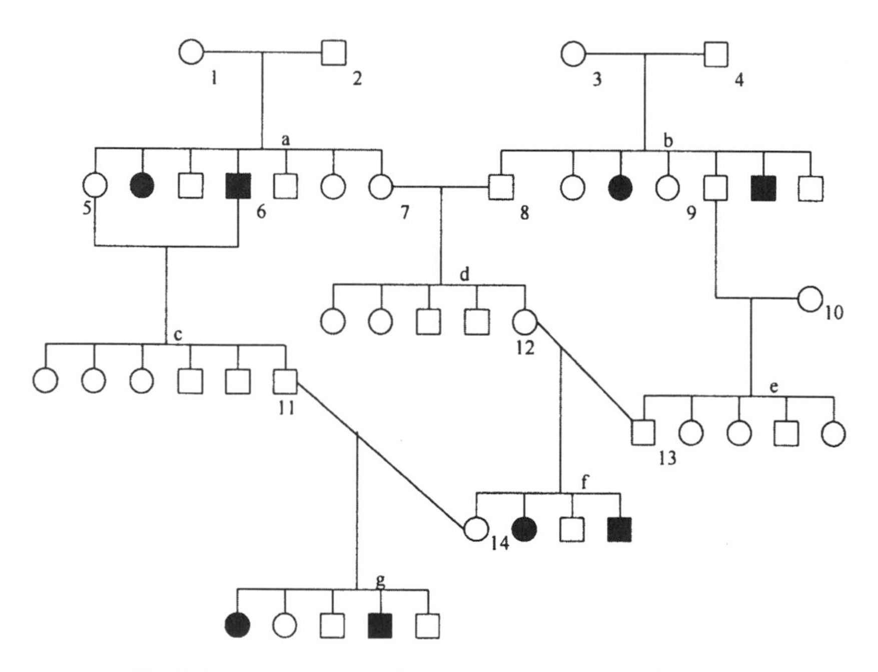

Fig 7.6 *A "family" of dogs containing seven affected puppies.*

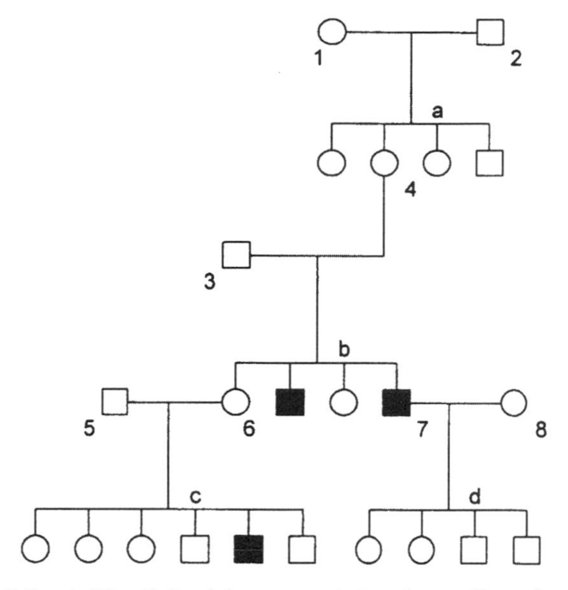

Fig. 7.7 *A "family" of dogs containing three affected puppies.*

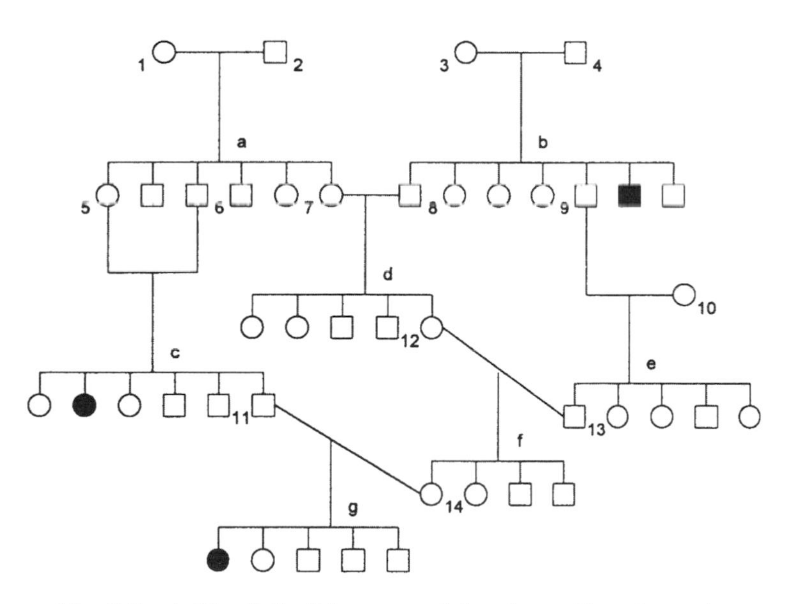

Fig. 7.8 *A "family" of dogs containing three affected puppies.*

2. a. What is the most likely mode of inheritance for the trait shown in Figure 7.7?

   b. Why?

   c. What is the genetic status of bitch #1?

d. What is the genetic status of dogs #2 and #5?

e. What dogs are proven carriers for this trait?

f. What is the chance that the two bitches in litter b are carriers?

g. What is the chance that all three bitches in litter c are carriers?

3. a. What is the most likely mode of inheritance for the trait shown in Figure 7.8?

   b. Why?

   c. What would you do with these dogs to more firmly establish the mode of inheritance?

   d. Which dogs in this pedigree are proven carriers?

4. a. What is the likely mode of inheritance of the trait shown in Figure 7.9?

   b. Why?

   c. What is the genetic status of bitch #1 in regard to this trait?

   d. What is the genetic status of dog #7 in regard to this trait?

   e. Could this trait be sex-linked dominant?

   f. Why?

   g. What is the genetic status of litter d?

   h. Could this trait have any other mode of inheritance?

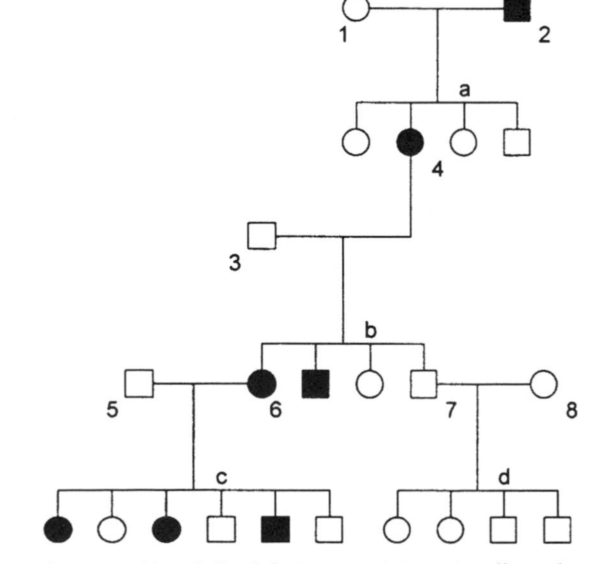

Fig. 7.9 *A "family" of dogs containing six affected puppies.*

5. We decided in the discussion of the pedigree in Figure 7.1, a pedigree of an autosomal recessive trait, that bitch #12 and dogs #11 and #13 were proven carriers and that they accounted for the presence of the gene that reached the two puppies in litter x.

   a. What other dogs are proven carriers in this pedigree?

   b. What dogs have been test-mated in pedigree 7.1?

   c. What is the chance that each of the test-mated dogs is genetically normal?

   d. Which dogs have at least a 50-percent chance of being carriers for this trait?

   e. What is the risk that each puppy in litters z, aa and bb has to be a carrier?

6. We have decided that Figure 7.3 presents a pedigree of a sex-linked recessive trait. That being the case,

   a. Which dogs are proven carriers?

   b. Which bitches have been test-mated?

Answers for Chapter 7

1. a. Autosomal recessive (for Figure 7.6).

   b.

      i.) All parents of affected dogs are phenotypically normal.

      ii.) The sex ratio is about even—four males and three females among the affected dogs.

      iii.) The trait skips generations.

      iv.) About 25 percent (seven affected, twenty-two total) of the puppies in affected litters have the disorder.

   c. 98.4 percent; Table 5.2.

   d. #1, #2, #3, #4, #11, #12, #13 and #14

2. a. A sex-linked recessive (for Figure 7.7).

   b.

      i.) About half the males (three affected, seven total) in affected litters are affected.

      ii.) There are no affected females among a total of eight females in the affected litters.

iii.) Both females in litter d are phenotypically normal, although their sire is affected.

iv.) All females producing affected puppies are phenotypically normal.

c. She is a defined carrier (she must be a carrier).

d. They are genetically normal for this trait.

e. Bitches #1, #4, #6 and #8.

f. Each bitch in litter b has a 50-percent chance of being a carrier (dilution rule).

g. There is a 12.5 percent risk that all three bitches in litter e are carriers (.5 × .5 × .5 = .125 = 12.5 percent; product rule).

3. a. You cannot determine the specific mode of inheritance of this trait with the data presented.

b.

i.) A dominant trait can be ruled out, because all six parents producing affected offspring are phenotypically normal.

ii.) You can rule out a sex-linked trait, because two females (litters c and g) are affected when their sire is phenotypically normal.

iii.) This leaves both autosomal recessive and polygenic as possible modes of inheritance. For a recessive trait, if you got the classical distribution of 25 percent affected, you would expect four-and-a-half affected puppies in the litters with affected puppies. We have three affected puppies, which is not far enough away from four-and-a-half to make a statistically valid prediction. In fact, with eighteen total puppies and a 3:1 ratio, you would expect a distribution of fifteen normal: three affected 17.04 percent of the time (taken from Warwick's table but not provided in chapter 5). Therefore, we do not have sufficient data to distinguish between an autosomal recessive and a polygenic trait.

c. To resolve whether this is a recessive or a polygenic trait, I would breed the affected male to one or both of the affected females (provided, of course, that they can produce offspring). If one phenotypically normal puppy is produced in one or both litters, I would rule out autosomal recessive.

d. Dogs #3, #4, #5, #6, #11 and #14 must carry at least one gene for the trait, whether it is autosomal recessive or polygenic.

4. a. Autosomal dominant

   b.

      i.) At least one parent of each litter that has an affected puppy is affected.

      ii.) About 50 percent of the offspring in affected litters are affected.

      iii.) Males and females are affected with about equal frequency in all three affected litters (three males, four females).

      iv.) The trait does not skip generations.

   c. She is genetically normal (she does not show the trait).

   d. He is genetically normal (he does not show the trait).

   e. No.

   f. If the trait were sex-linked dominant, all three females in litter a would have to have the disease, since an affected sire throws his affected X-linked gene to all of his daughters.

   g. They are all genetically normal (they do not show the trait).

   h. It is possible that the trait is autosomal recessive, since if one mate of a pair is affected and the other is a carrier, you expect a 1:1 ratio (one affected to one normal puppy) in the litter produced. However, for that to be true in this pedigree, all three outcross mates (bitch #1 and dogs #3 and #5) would have to be carriers. Even if there was a 33 percent carrier rate for this disorder in the general population of the breed, the chance that all three mates would be carriers is only 3.6 percent. The most likely choice for mode of inheritance for the trait depicted in Figure 7.9 is still an autosomal dominant.

5. a. Bitches #23 and #35, and dog #34.

   b. Bitches #19 and #29 against dog #13, a proven carrier.

      Bitches #l7, #18 and #22 against dog #11, a proven carrier.

      Since dog #34 is a proven carrier, either sire #16 or dam #28 or both must be carriers. If both are not carriers, then the one opposite the carrier has been test-mated, but we cannot tell which is which, so we gain no data here.

   c. Bitch #19 has an 86.6 percent chance of being homozygous dominant.

      Bitch #29 has a 76.3 percent chance of being genetically normal.

      Bitches #17 and #22 are the same as bitch #29.

      Bitch #18 is the same as bitch #19 (Table 5.1).

d.

   i.) Dogs #5, #6, #7 and #8, and the parents of bitch #12.

   ii.) All phenotypically normal puppies in litters i, o and x.

   iii.) All puppies in litters c, d, h, j, m, n, s and w.

e. 25 percent for each puppy in all three litters (dilution and sum rules).

6. a. Bitch #18 and her mother, and her direct female antecedents, back to the original mutation. Bitches #23, #28 and #32.

   b. Any bitch bred to any male in this pedigree and producing at least one male puppy has been test-mated. If any of her puppies are affected, she is a proven carrier. If all her male puppies are normal, you can determine the chance that she is genetically normal using Table 5.7. For example, bitch #14 produced nine normal male puppies in litters e, f and u, so she has better than a 99 percent chance to be genetically normal for this trait. Bitch #10 produced six normal male puppies in litters g and l, so she has a 98.4 percent chance of being homozygous dominant for this trait. Further, since we know that a sex-linked recessive trait is prevalent in this breed, any bitch that has been bred and has produced at least one male puppy, and whose puppies are all phenotypically normal for this trait, has been test-mated; we can determine her chance of being genetically normal by counting her normal male offspring. Except in the case of a new mutation, there is no reason for a sex-linked recessive trait to be a problem in purebred dogs.

CHAPTER 8

Test-Mating

Background

There is no subject in canine genetics that is more misunderstood by geneticists and breeders alike than test-mating (T-M). Detractors imply that T-M is done willy-nilly and that it costs far too much for any "practical" or "good" breeder to undertake. The claim is also made that doing a T-M is like searching for a needle in a haystack, and that you are spreading defective genes far and wide when you do one. Many suggest that the offspring of T-Ms should be "put down" or, if they are more squeamish, "put to sleep," because we should not have these "horrible carriers" of defects wandering around, for they will be the downfall of our wonderful breed. I was once told by a breeder that no "good" Irish Setters exist in America any longer because of all of the test-matings that had been done for PRA.

I have heard such statements from veterinarians, geneticists and breeders, which to me indicates that whoever is doing the talking has not really thought about the process and the correct use of T-M at all.

Before we discuss T-M per se, let's talk about these general statements and try to identify reality. As to T-M willy-nilly: A number of years ago, I was in Geillo, Norway talking to a well-known and respected geneticist (although he does not usually work with dogs), who said that T-M was not a practical approach to the control of genetic disease because: 1) too many matings are wasted searching for dogs that "may" have the gene; 2) it takes too long; 3) it costs too much.

In regard to point #1, I asked him, "Would you T-M a Cocker Spaniel for grey Collie syndrome [a disease only reported in the Collie]?" He said "No," and I asked him why. He answered, "Because the gene can't be there; it occurs only in Collies." I said, "Good thinking!"

Then I asked him if he would T-M a Rough Collie for grey Collie syndrome if he knew that the dog was of pure Bellhaven stock (the grey Collie gene is not present in the pure Bellhaven line). He said no, and I asked him why. He said, "Because the gene can't be there; it does not occur in that line." I said, "Good thinking!"

The discussion continued, and I said, "I know you don't believe in T-M, and I now know that you would not T-M a dog that could not have the gene in question. But, if you did decide to T-M a dog, under what circumstances would you do it?" He said, "I guess I would do it when I knew the gene could be present." Again, I said "Good thinking!"

This leads us to our first rule for test-matings:

Rule one. Do not test-mate a dog or bitch unless you know it has a higher risk of carrying the gene in question than is present in the general population of the breed.

On a practical basis, this means you generally only consider T-M animals that are first- or second-degree relatives of an affected dog.

In regard to our geneticist's second point, "It takes too long," it is clear that the point he makes here is an important consideration in regard to some genetic diseases. The fact is that some of them—for example, PRA—take such a long time to develop that it makes prospective test-mating a difficult approach to use to protect your line against that defect. However, the vast majority of genetic diseases are not late onset. For example, Cairn Terriers have thirty-two diseases reported, and PRA, epilepsy and Hashimoto's disease consistently occur after two years of age (they may also occur before two years of age). Scotties have thirty-six diseases, and four (the same three as in Cairns plus Addison's disease) occur after two years of age. Bernese Mountain Dogs have forty-three genetic diseases, and four (AIHA, PILA, RACL and epilepsy) consistently occur after two years of age. So, while late onset of a disease is certainly a consideration as to whether that disease is a candidate for prospective test-matings, it only applies to a limited number of diseases. This leads us to our second T-M rule:

Rule two. As a general rule, do not prospectively test-mate dogs for diseases that usually produce clinical signs after two years of age.

Why two years of age? This is an arbitrarily generated number that was chosen because many, if not most, breeders do not breed their bitches until after they have had their screening tests (OFA, CERF, GDC) completed and because most genetic diseases are detected before two years of age.

Does this rule mean that I would never T-M a dog for a disease that has a late onset? No, under certain circumstances, this could still be a useful approach. Remember, in a T-M, when the first case of the disorder occurs, you have the data you need to call a dog a carrier. Even in late-onset diseases like PRA, the first case could occur at one-and-a-half to two years of age. Further, specifically with PRA, a properly conducted electroretinogram may allow detection of an affected dog as early as eight or ten months of age. So, if a specific dog is central to your pedigree or if he has the potential to develop into a matador, it may well be worthwhile to determine whether he is a carrier. Therefore, in specific cases, you may want to alter your approach depending on the circumstances involved.

The fact remains that in the vast majority of cases, you are not maintaining dogs for long periods of time for a disease to develop. Despite all of the hullabaloo about having to hold dogs for several years to get the results of a T-M, it is more a phantom argument than a real one.

The last point my geneticist friend made was that T-Ms cost too much. The way I look at it, T-Ms shouldn't cost any more than any other mating you make. So, I asked him why he thought T-Ms cost too much. He answered, "Well, what do you do with all of the offspring? You can't sell them—they are carriers."

So I asked him, "When was the last time you heard of a dog being bred that was not a carrier of something?"

He said, "Well, all dogs probably carry for one or more defects, and besides, even if a dog was totally genetically normal, you couldn't tell from the offspring, because the opposite member of the mating would still transmit half of his or her defective genes to the puppies."

"If that is the case, that all dogs carry something, what would you do with all these puppies?"

He said, "I'd sell them."

So I pointed out that if you can sell all of these other carriers, why can't you sell carriers that are produced in a test-mating?

Of course, there is no reason why you cannot sell the offspring produced in a T-M. Remember, the carrier of a defect is perfectly healthy and will make as good a pet as any other dog. Further, the carrier should be neutered so it cannot be bred by well-meaning but less astute persons who may purchase it. As far as I am concerned, however, this is not a different process from what should be applied to any purebred dog that is sold as a pet. The important point to remember is that if a dog or bitch is neutered, it could carry for 100 different defects, and it would not matter, because it could not pass any of them on.

"Well," you say, "if I sell one of these puppies, how much should I charge for it?"

You should charge exactly what you charge when you sell any pet puppy.

"Well," you say, "if I sell these puppies, how am I going to observe them to see if they develop the disease I am testing for?"

That's easy to answer. You include the necessity of having the puppy examined for the trait in question as part of your sales contract. If the test is expensive, you agree to pay for the examination and the tests you require. Collect the money for the sale of the puppy, and pay for the examination when it is completed.

Remember, you have an ethical obligation to tell anyone who purchases any of these dogs exactly what's going on. If you have read and studied the previous chapters, you can give the purchaser an exact risk that the puppy will develop the disease you are testing for. If the puppy develops the disease, you should do what you should do with any puppy you sell that develops a genetic disease. Offer to take the puppy back and refund their money, replace the puppy with another healthy one or offer to pay for the correction of the defect to the extent of the original purchase price. All of these are standard operating procedures with most good breeders I know.

"What a mess!" you say. "How can I tell a purchaser that this dog may develop a disease?"

What you have just done is state one of the major problems we have with purebred dogs today. Not enough breeders tell purchasers of purebred dogs that the dog they buy has a risk of developing a genetic defect. The buyer purchases the dog and expects (as he or she should) to get a healthy dog, because they are not told anything except that all of the dogs the breeder sells are healthy and that they have never had anything bad in their line.

If you have done your homework on your own dogs and on the mate you chose, you should be able to make reasonable predictions on what your dog might develop (including this T-M) and on what he or she is unlikely to develop. So the fact is that you give them bad news and good news.

You will be surprised to learn how much people respect honesty. This leads us to our third rule of T-M:

Rule three. You are obligated to tell any purchaser of any puppy from a test-mating exactly what risk the puppy has to develop a genetic disease or to be a carrier of that defect.

One of the constant arguments against T-M that I hear is that T-M somehow causes the quality of the offspring produced to be inferior to the offspring in a non–T-M breeding. I find this argument to be irrational and, as it is applied sometimes by some people, downright dumb. There is no reason for the quality of T-M offspring to be less than that found in any other type of mating as far as I am concerned. This predicament is sidestepped if we follow our fourth rule for T-Ms:

Rule four. Never breed to an animal that is of lesser quality than what you want to represent you, your line and your breed just because you are making a T-M.

This rule is one you should follow when you make any mating if you want to produce quality offspring. Further, it applies to conformation, obedience, hunting and working qualities, depending on your individual goals as a breeder. Again, I find the argument that T-M reduces the quality to be irrational, because we generally find carriers because they have produced a defect. Therefore, the more a dog is bred, the clearer the picture will be regarding his or her genotype. Matadors, the best dogs in the breed, are the ones that are most likely to be identified as carriers. Obviously, these are the dogs that are best fitted to be used as a foil in a T-M. If we use quality animals in all T-M situations, how will that decrease the quality of an individual line and, by extension, the entire breed? The fact is, it won't decrease the quality, and this, too, becomes a shadow argument. The problem that often arises in T-M situations is that some people want to buy the puppies as breeding stock, because good dogs are involved in the T-M. If they are not good dogs, why bother to T-M them?

Let's talk for a moment about PRA and a dog we will call Barney. He is a super representative of the breed, winning his championship easily and going on to take numerous all-breed Bests in Show and Specialties. He is a matador. Unfortunately, he develops PRA at four-and-a-half years of age. You use him as the sire in a T-M of your bitch.

What do you do if someone observing this T-M litter says, "That's a superb puppy, and I want him/her for breeding? I'll give you $4,000 [or whatever is a lot of money to you]."

For sure, this will happen when you have puppies from a dog like Barney. I would not sell a puppy for breeding that has a 50 percent or higher risk of carrying a gene for a trait as severe as PRA without an ironclad agreement that the dog will not be offered or used as a public stud. I would require that the dog be registered in an open registry such as GDC with the attendant risk attached, and to be sure that this happens, I would do it myself. I would require that offspring of the dog be registered in an open registry with the appropriate risk attached so that potential purchasers of the offspring would have an outside accurate source of information about the dogs. I would require that the purchaser sign an agreement stating that he/she understands the risk of PRA involved and that clearly defines what that risk is. Lastly, I would have to be assured that the purchaser understands how to handle the breeding of a dog with a risk like this, and if I was not convinced they knew how, I would not sell them the dog while it was intact, no matter what they offered.

As a rule, all puppies produced in test-matings that are left intact, for whatever reasons, should be registered with an open registry documenting their attendant risk, no matter what trait is involved.

It is not my goal in this book to tell everyone, "Hey, you can breed carriers, it's okay," but I do recognize reality. I believe many people would sell Barney's son for $4,000. Remember, it is your dog. You own him, and if you choose to sell him, obviously you can. My point here is that if you choose to sell a dog like this in a situation in which he is likely to be used for breeding, why not do it as safely as you can?

What about the idea that T-M produces many extra carriers that would not have come into being if the dog were just bred in the routine manner? Remember rule one: We never T-M a dog or bitch unless the animal has a high risk of being a carrier. For argument's sake and to give us a starting place, let's say the dog we are testing has a 50 percent chance of being a carrier. To keep things even in these comparisons, let's put the dog in a situation in which it has a 99 percent chance of being shown to be genetically normal. We will do this by a T-M of the animal against an affected mate, and a known carrier mate, by diluting the trait and by randomly mating the dog. Random-mating (breeding a dog without knowledge of the genotype of any of its mates) is the alternative type of mating that most people are arguing for when they oppose T-M, even though they might not realize it.

Using Tables 5.1 (T-M against a carrier) and 5.2 (test-mating against an affected), you will find that sixteen puppies are required to reach the 99-percent level against a carrier, and eight puppies are required to reach the 99-percent level against an affected dog. On the average, half of the puppies will be carriers (eight puppies) when a carrier is used, and all eight puppies will be carriers if it is against an affected mate. So in both cases, eight carriers will be produced.

Now let's look at dilution. To dilute a gene, you must mate your dog to a genetically normal mate. If you do that, then in each generation, the risk that any offspring will be a carrier is cut in half and, of course, so is the risk that a carrier will be produced. Remember that to dilute a gene in this manner, you cannot rebreed the same generation; you must use a member of the new generation for each mating.

Let's look at Table 8.1.

Table 8.1

Production of carriers by dilution of a gene to the 99 percent chance that the offspring is genetically normal (eight puppies/litter).

Generation	*Years*	*Matings potential carrier × normal chance puppy will be genetically normal*	*Number of carrier puppies produced*
1	2.5	50.0%	4
2	2.5	75.0%	2
3	2.5	87.5%	1
4	2.5	93.8%	0.5
5	2.5	96.8%	0.25
6	2.5	98.4%	0.125
7	2.5	99.2%	0.062
TOTAL	17.5		7.937

You can see from Table 8.1 that, to be sure the final set of puppies is 99 percent sure to be free of the gene, you must produce eight carriers (actually, 7.937), just as if you test-mated your dogs. In addition, you must spend 17.5 years doing it.

Now let's try to prove that a dog is 99-percent sure to be free of a gene in a random-mating situation. We need to look at Table 5.4. Let's look at an average of ten puppies per litter, since any fewer puppies per litter makes the situation worse. If the gene is distributed in the general population of your breed with a frequency of 5 percent, you would need fifty litters or 500 puppies to be 99-percent sure your dog is normal. On the average, the dog you are breeding will be a carrier half the time (his risk is 50 percent), so you have 250 puppies, each of which has a 50:50 chance of being a carrier. By just breeding your dog in the general population of your breed, you will, on the average, produce 125 carriers before you can be sure he has a 99 percent chance to be genetically normal. If the frequency is 10 percent, you need thirty litters, or 300 puppies. Again, half the time, he will be a carrier; the other half he won't, so 150 puppies are at risk. On the average, 50 percent will be carriers, so 75 carriers are produced at this frequency before you can be sure he has a 99 percent chance to be genetically normal.

Now let's look at a frequency of 25 percent carriers in the general population. In this case, you need ten litters, or 100 puppies. Using the same ground rules as before, you will produce an average of 25 carriers at this frequency. Despite any arguments to the contrary, the way to produce the most carriers is by random-matings. All other methods of controlling the gene are more accurate and more certain. The fact that most purebred dogs are randomly mated regarding genetic disease is what accounts for the current sorry state of purebred dogs as far as the prevalence of genetic disease is concerned. While programs designed to control genetic disease are beginning to develop in some breeds, for the vast majority of breeds and breeders, attempts to control genetic disease appear to be, at best, a whimsy.

Prospective Test-Mating

What I have done in this chapter so far is to try to lay to rest those arguments that spring to the fore the moment T-M is mentioned. Now let's look at using T-M as a control procedure. Before we start, we probably need to establish some terminology. The dog you are test-mating, the one for which you want to determine the genotype, is the *test mate*. The animal you will T-M against, the dog with the known genotype, is the *foil*.

Point 1

Never T-M a dog or bitch that lacks characteristics that identify them as highly desirable representatives of the breed. In other words, don't waste your time on a dog or bitch that does not have the potential to become a matador, a highly productive member of the breed. If you are going to breed a dog or a bitch to see what pops out, don't bother with a T-M, because this animal is unlikely to have any influence on your line or the breed as a whole.

A dog or bitch becomes a candidate for a T-M when you believe it has the characteristics on which you want to base your line—in other words, dogs whose genetic influence is likely to be long-term. Don't worry about minor traits such as inguinal hernias, retained testicles, hypothyroidism, a crook in the tail or a missing tooth. Surely, these are undesirable features in a dog, but you can live with them, and so can the people who buy your dogs.

For a dog to be a candidate for a T-M, the disease of concern should be a severe, debilitating disorder, and he/she should have a high risk of carrying the gene in question (first- or second-degree relative of an affected dog). Such diseases as PRA, cataracts, glaucoma, sebacious adenitis, Vogt-Koyanagi-Harada syndrome, dwarfism and renal dystrophy are the types of diseases of concern here—in other words, diseases that generally occur after the puppy is sold, are expensive to diagnose and difficult and expensive, if not impossible, to treat. It is very undesirable to incorporate such traits into the genetic background of your line. Prevention by T-M and eliminating proven carriers from your breeding program is a very reasonable alternative in such situations.

Point 2

You generally intend to T-M your dog against one specific trait—the one you know about and the one that concerns you. This, of course, is and should remain your primary goal. However, since all dogs are likely to be carriers for more than one trait, in reality, you are going to T-M your dog against whatever diseases your foil is known to carry. If the foil is a matador with multiple matings behind him, you may be able to determine the genotype of your dog for several diseases, not just the one of most concern to you. In addition, the foil acts as a T-M against any diseases your dog is known to carry. All that is needed is to examine the puppies produced for all diseases that either dog is known to carry for, and we expand our knowledge of the genetic makeup of both lines of the breeding partners.

Any time you gain knowledge about the genetic makeup of dogs that are used for breeding, you are better able to plan your program for disease prevention. Of course, accurate record-keeping regarding these traits is an essential part of a breeding program.

Point 3

Your test-matings should be designed to determine whether or not a dog or bitch carries a specific deleterious gene before you incorporate its offspring into your line. If you plan the matings well, they should become part of your breeding program. The dog or bitch you choose as a foil should allow your program to progress. That is, the offspring should be at least as good and hopefully better than your own foundation stock. If you choose the foil well, the puppies should be highly desirable, showable stock—as good as with any other mating you might make. The problem many breeders have in accepting T-M is that they know a specific defective gene may be present in the offspring. Since T-M should only be used with high-risk dogs, what happens to the offspring if you do not T-M? Does the gene go away? Half the time it may, and the other half, it won't. What do you do with the offspring of these "regular" matings? Do you sell them? If so, what do you tell the buyers? It seems to me that those who frown on T-M are really saying that it is better to be ignorant about the genetic makeup of your stock than it is to be knowledgeable about it. The fact is that, at the present time, 30 percent or more of all purebred dogs produced have or develop a genetic defect. In my opinion, that is a sorry state of affairs, and it is the result of mating dogs without knowing their genetic makeup or that of potential mates. The reason you T-M is to alleviate that problem. You cannot change the current situation by closing your eyes.

The old idea that the basic purpose of a dog show is to determine the qualifications of a dog as breeding stock is obsolete and should be abandoned. Dog show wins should be one parameter you use to determine a dog's breeding worth. There are other parameters just as important as winning (some suggest that they are more important), and these include temperament and the genetic background of the dog in regard to genetic disease. I would not suggest that you should breed a dog that could not win a show or compete well in any working trial, but a show should be fun and enjoyable in and of itself, and there should be no implication or requirement that the winner should be bred. Offspring of a T-M should provide all of what any purebred dog should provide. In my opinion, they should participate in conformation shows, Obedience trials and other organized performance activities. They should be used for hunting or for whatever other aspect of purebred dogs is appropriate to the breed and a breeder's or owner's own goals. The fact that you know about the genetic makeup of these animals allows you to prevent disease either by not breeding them or, if you elect to breed, by giving you the knowledge that you have to breed them with care.

Knowledge about the genetic makeup of your stock can never cause a worse situation than the blind breeding so routinely practiced at the present time.

Retrospective Test-Mating

A retrospective test-mating (R-T-M) is a mating for which, when it takes place, there is no knowledge about the genotype of either dog in regard to a specific trait. So the knowledge about the genotype becomes available after you have bred the dog or bitch. An example is a dog to whom you bred your bitch when he was two years old and then develops PRA when he is four years old. The fact that he developed the disease at four does not mean that he did not have the genes for the trait when he was two. He had the genes; you just did not know it. So your bitch had an R-T-M. The unpleasant fact of life is that this situation occurs routinely in purebred breeding. The problem occurs when you fail to use this situation to gain the knowledge needed about the genotype of your dogs to prevent disease. If your bitch had seven puppies and none developed PRA, she is 99.2 percent sure to be free of the gene for PRA, and you do not know it. In addition, all seven of these puppies are defined carriers, and any buyers of breeding stock are not made aware of it.

In order to use R-T-M on a routine basis, some mechanism must be in place that allows you to determine the genotype of dogs on a routine basis. That mechanism is an open registry (I cover registries much more extensively in Chapter 9, "Registries and Prioritizing Genetic Diseases").

First, we probably should define an open registry. An *open registry* is a registry in which all animals are identified in respect to phenotype and, when possible, in respect to genotype. All information on all dogs is available to other breeders. This is different from *closed registries,* which are the prototype registries found in the United States. Examples of closed registries are the *Orthopedic Foundation for Animals* (OFA) and the *Canine Eye Registration Foundation* (CERF). In closed registries, the only information available to breeders is on those animals that are phenotypically normal. Again, the word *phenotype* means the observable properties of an animal (structural and functional) produced by the interaction of that animal's genotype and the environment. For example, with hip dysplasia, you might have a normal (excellent, good, fair) or dysplastic (borderline, mild, severe) phenotype based on a radiograph. It is what you observe or measure in an animal in regard to the trait in question. With *sebaceous adenitis* (SA), you might have a normal SA, subclinical

SA, or clinical SA phenotype based on a skin biopsy and, where appropriate, clinical signs.

Okay, we now have a nice distinction between an open and a closed registry, but from a breeder's standpoint, what difference does it make?

With single-gene traits, especially those with late onset, such as sebaceous adenitis, PRA and epilepsy, it makes all the difference in the world. An open registry allows you to retrospectively test-mate your dogs. That is, it allows you to genotype your dogs based on matings that may have taken place many months or even years ago. The single requirement for this is the knowledge of the genotype of one of the animals involved in the mating. This, of course, you can obtain from an open, but not a closed, registry.

An example of how retrospective test-mating works follows. Since all dogs, on the average, carry defective genes (perhaps as many as four or five), every mating is, in fact, a test-mating. Our current problem, since we do not identify affected dogs, is that we do not know what the test-mating is for. Remember, it is a test-mating, whether or not that was your intention. It is also a test-mating even if it occurred before the dog developed the disease or before you knew the dog produced the disease.

As an example of how retrospective test-mating takes place, let's take Charlie, a Standard Poodle. His breeding history is recorded in the pedigree in Figure 8.1.

Charlie was born in 1982. He was radiographed for hip dysplasia, had a CERF examination and produced his first litter in 1984. He was subsequently bred twenty-five more times, producing a total of 174 puppies—an average of 6.69 puppies per litter, which is about right for a Standard Poodle. In 1987, a bitch puppy of Charlie's developed a skin disorder and was diagnosed as having *sebaceous adenitis* (SA). The first report of SA in Poodles was in 1987, so the disease was not known as an entity prior to this time. A second puppy, a male in the same litter, developed clinical SA in 1988, and the breeder withdrew Charlie from public stud. Charlie himself never developed clinical SA. In 1989, two more of Charlie's puppies, born in 1985, showed up with SA. Even though Charlie was clinically normal, he was biopsied for SA in 1990, and it turned out that he was subclinically affected.

So where are we now? Well, since Charlie is affected, all 174 of his puppies are defined carriers. Does this make Charlie a "bad" dog? Not in our opinion. In fact, he is a champion and has produced twenty-nine champions—16.6 percent of all of his offspring. And that's not a bad track record by any means! Is Charlie's owner a disreputable breeder? Not in our opinion. The disease was not known when Charlie was first used at stud, and twenty-five of his twenty-six matings were complete before his first affected puppy was detected. He made one more mating and was withdrawn from stud when a second affected puppy was found. There was no way the breeder could have known Charlie was affected and, in fact, he did not find out Charlie was affected until 1990, well after he was withdrawn from stud. Charlie still has not shown clinical signs of SA; he is a true subclinical case.

So where are we as a result of Charlie? Well, if we use the knowledge that Charlie is affected, we can do something about the disease. Twenty-three bitches have been

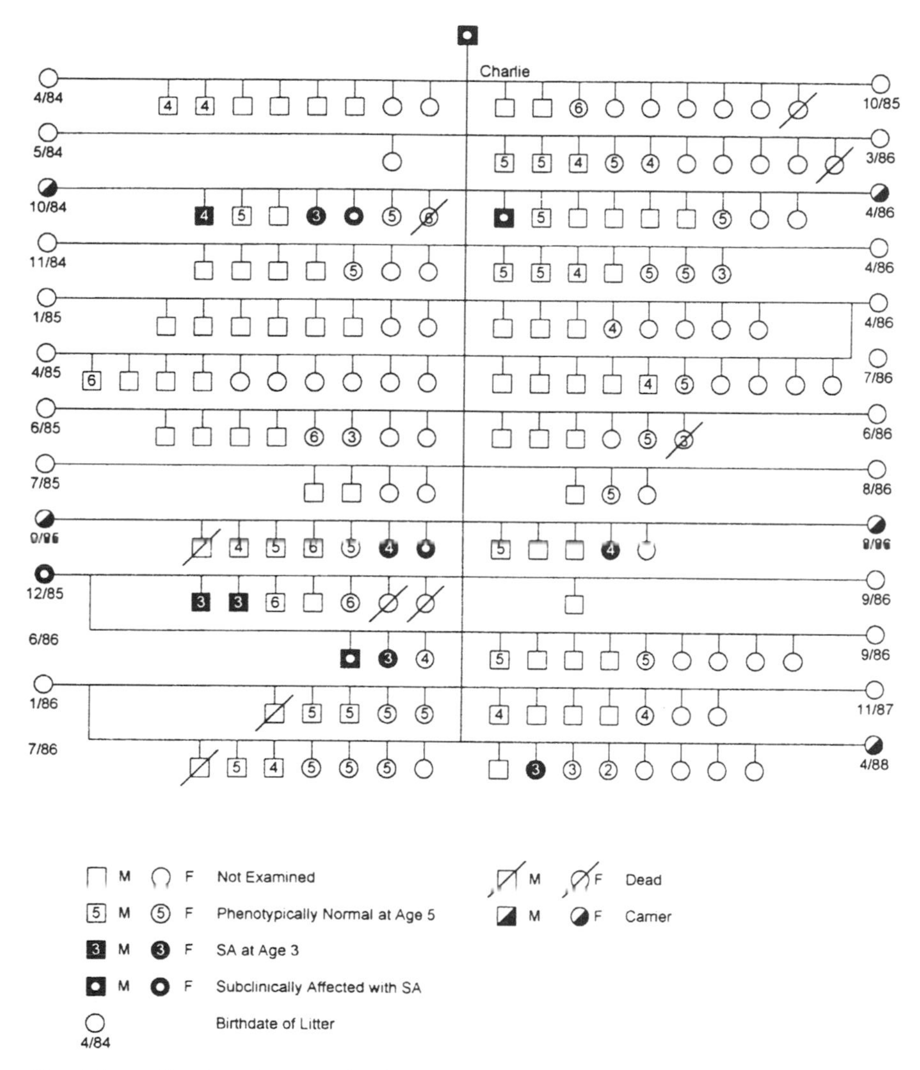

Fig. 8.1 *Offspring of a Standard Poodle sire subclinically affected with sebaceous adenitis (SA).*

test-mated for SA, and at this point, six of these bitches have proven to be carriers. How about the rest? It is probably true that the puppies from many of these matings are spread out or lost. But, if four puppies can be *randomly* located from any of these matings and all four are normal, the bitch is 93.7 percent sure to be free of the SA gene. All that is required to establish any dog's clear status is to check the offspring that have been born. Happily, many of the puppies will be at the right age, and useful data can be collected. In addition, all 174 of Charlie's puppies are defined carriers, correct? Many of them have already been bred. Thus, any animal bred to one of Charlie's puppies has been test-mated to (at a minimum) a carrier. Therefore, if you *randomly* evaluate seven of their puppies and all are normal, the mate is 86.6 percent sure to be free of the SA gene. Remember that none of this information about the genetic makeup of these dogs would be available if we did not know that Charlie was subclinically affected.

So the first thing we need to do is to thank Charlie's owner for having the courage to tell us. It's true that Charlie got us into trouble, but it's also true that he provided us with the means to get out of trouble if we are wise enough to use it. If we examine the offspring of these random test-matings we will surely find both bitches and dogs that have an excellent chance to be free of this gene.

Obviously, it is not desirable to have dogs that transmit diseases like SA, PRA or epilepsy, but with an open registry, you can use the information correctly to select dogs with a greatly reduced risk of having the gene(s) in question. At present, the only alternative to an open registry is to stumble along blindly as we have been, praying that the puppies in our next litter are normal.

CHAPTER 9

Registries and Prioritizing Genetic Diseases

Registries

Purebred dog breeders have been challenged by the problem of genetic disease for a considerable number of years. The vast majority, if not all, would do just about anything within reason to be able to guarantee that puppies of their breeding would develop no major genetic problems. In order to make such a guarantee, breeders realized that they needed information about the genetic propensities of their dogs. As a result, in the 1960s, the first of the canine disease registries came into being—the *Orthopedic Foundation for Animals* (OFA) to control hip dysplasia, a major disease of many breeds of dogs. In the 1960s, many breeders refused to openly discuss genetic disease in their dogs, so the OFA started as a closed registry. In the late 1970s and 1980s, breeders began to realize that more information needed to be made readily available if they were really serious about preventing genetic disease. As a result, the concept of open registries was developed to provide information on both the phenotype and the genotype of dogs used in specific breeding programs.

A closed registry releases information only on those dogs that are phenotypically normal. (Remember that the *phenotype* is what can be seen or measured in a dog. The coat and eye color, the type of ears, the tail set, the appearance of hips on a radiograph and the white blood cell count are all phenotypes.) The OFA and the *Canine Eye Registration Foundation* (CERF) are examples of closed registries. The OFA registers normal hips, elbows, patellae, shoulders and hocks as separate entities. Unfortunately, if a dog has normal hips and diseased elbows, the OFA will certify the hips as normal but will not disclose that the elbows are abnormal; nor will the OFA indicate whether the elbows have been examined. If the hips are normal (at two years of age or older), OFA will grade the hips and give the dog an OFA number that indicates that the hips are normal, but it will not discuss any structural abnormalities present in the same dog. The CERF closed registry is a little different, since it works only with eyes. CERF will not issue a number to any dog that has any eye abnormality—be it PRA, cataracts, corneal dystrophy or any other ocular abnormality—that seriously interferes with the dog's normal functions. Dogs with minor abnormalities that are not known to progress and do not interfere with function may be certified. CERF does not divulge information on any dog with serious defects. Data in both these registries is made available to all qualified researchers with the stipulation that the anonymity of affected dogs be maintained. The AKC has elected to add OFA and CERF numbers to the registration documents and certified pedigrees of dogs carrying those numbers.

In an open registry, all data on an animal is made available to breeders, whether the dog is phenotypically normal or is affected with one or more diseases. If a dog has normal hips and abnormal elbows, both pieces of data are made available and both are reported, even if the request is only for hips. Open registries are the new kids on the block. They are brand-spanking new as this book goes to press and are just getting their feet on the ground. The first two open registries started at almost the same time: PRA Data Inc. and the West Highland White Terrier WATCH program.

PRA Data Inc. was started by Georgia Gooch (Woodinville, Washington), a Labrador Retriever breeder in late 1989 and 1990. In 1991, she published her first PRA report on affected dogs, and a second was published in 1992. At the present time, data is available on 262 affected Labradors. Data on each dog listed in the reports includes clinical findings, AKC registration number, the name of the owner and/or breeder, and a six-generation pedigree. A release has been signed for each dog registered openly acknowledging the presence of the disease in that dog. In all cases, the owners of the dam and sire are notified that an offspring of their dog is in the registry and that their dogs are at least proven (obligate) carriers of the disease.

The Westie WATCH (West Highland Anomaly Task Council) program began in 1989 and is somewhat broader-based. WATCH registers craniomandibular osteopathy, Legg-Perthes disease and hip dysplasia. Diagnosis of these disorders is through the OFA, which cooperates with this program. WATCH registers both phenotypically normal and affected dogs. In addition, it collects research data on copper toxicosis (an inherited liver disease of Westies, Bedlington Terriers and several other breeds) to further knowledge on the mode of inheritance and clinical parameters of the disease in this breed. They also notify the owners of the sire and dam that their dogs have at least one offspring in the registry and that these dogs are at a minimum proven (obligate) carriers of the gene(s) causing the disease.

For a dog to be entered in the WATCH registry, a firm diagnosis of the phenotypic status of the dog, normal or affected, is required, as well as a release signed by the owner and/or the dog's breeder acknowledging that this information can be released to the public. WATCH does not publish lists of dogs affected with these disorders or dogs related to them. Instead, for a nominal fee ($5 at present), it will provide breeders with any of the following reports:

1. A clearance report on any dog that has been test-mated, giving the chance that the dog (male or female) is free of the gene in question

2. A list of affected dogs available for test-mating

3. A pedigree showing affected dogs, obligate carriers and the risk that related dogs carry the gene(s) of concern
4. Reports on any dog affected with any of the registered diseases and their first-degree relatives

WATCH also provides a test-mating verification service. Further, it has an alerting service individuals can use to request any information that alters the genetic status of their dog or bitch in regard to any of the traits in the registry, even if that happens after the request was made. There is no charge to register a dog, whether it is affected, phenotypically normal or genotypically normal.

The broadest-based open registry at the present time is the Institute for *Genetic Disease Control* (GDC), housed in Davis, California. The GDC began operations in 1990. It has both an open disease registry and a research registry, which collects data on the clinical and genetic aspects of a disease until sufficient information is available to be of use to a breeder in selecting animals for breeding. When sufficient data becomes available, all dogs in the research registry are placed in an open registry and all information is made available to breeders. There is no charge to register affected dogs for any of the diseases, and charges for phenotypically normal dogs vary with the trait being registered. Reduced rates are charged when multiple dogs in a litter are registered, in order to obtain as much information as possible on the offspring of a given dam and sire.

At the present time, the *Poodle Club of America* (PCA) registers PRA (progressive retinal atrophy) and SA (sebaceous adenitis) with GDC. The *Cairn Terrier Club of America* (CTCA) registers CMO, Legg-Perthes, hip dysplasia and luxated patellae (slipped kneecaps) and has a research registry for portosystemic shunts (a disease in which blood bypasses the liver causing severe clinical signs) with GDC. The *Bernese Mountain Dog Club of America* (BMDCA) registers histiocytosis and mastosarcoma (both inherited tumors) with GDC and has a research registry with it for all other tumors that occur in that breed. The *Great Pyrenees Club of America* (GPCA) has a research registry for Pyrenees dwarfism with GDC. A large group of California Labrador Retriever breeders registers hips and elbows with GDC and has formed a research registry for epilepsy with this organization. Numerous individuals from various breeds have wanted their dogs in an open registry and have selected GDC for this purpose.

Like WATCH, GDC does not publish information on affected dogs. Instead, for a small fee ($10 at present), it provides the following data:

1. All data it has on the dog for which you request information and his/her offspring
2. Any information it has on his/her full brothers and sisters and half-brothers and sisters (all offspring of the parents of the dog)
3. Any information it has on the parents, their full brothers and sisters and half-brothers and sisters (all offspring of the grandparents of the dog)
4. Any information it has on the grandparents

In this way, an inquiry results in full data on the family of the dog you are interested in, including all titles that the dog, his parents and his grandparents have earned that are on file.

The latest entry into the field of open registries is the OFA soft-tissue registry, which began in 1997. The intent is to begin a registry for heart defects and hypothyroidism in early 1996. With this registry, breeders will have the option of placing their dogs in either a closed or open registry. If they place them in the closed aspect of the registry, only normal dogs will be identified and published, and if they place them in the open aspect of the registry, data on both normal and affected dogs will be published. At present, reports on dogs as families are not anticipated.

The interesting point in regard to registries is that the AKC refuses to acknowledge GDC-registered normal dogs, even though the criteria for phenotypic normalcy and for diagnosis of hip and elbow disease is identical to that of OFA, although GDC registers the normal dogs at a younger age. The GDC uses the same diagnosticians (members of the American College of Veterinary Ophthalmology) as CERF and has the identical diagnostic criteria for normal and affected dogs as CERF. GDC requires annual evaluations, as does CERF, yet AKC still will not recognize GDC-registered phenotypically normal dogs. Of course, if AKC recognized the GDC registry, it could no longer state that information on affected dogs is not available.

In addition to the above registries that are really outside of parent clubs, the Alaskan Malamute Club of America, the Miniature Schnauzer Club of America, the Portuguese Water Dog Club of America and the Inland Empire Collie Club clearly had to have working open registries, or they could not have made the inroads they have in controlling genetic disease in their breeds. The Portuguese Water Dog Club publishes the names of dogs affected with PRA in its national magazine, the *Courier*. Further, the *Courier* does not allow any Portuguese Water Dog to be advertised unless that ad provides current information on the CERF number, the OFA number, and the storage-disease status of the dog or bitch being advertised. This policy is rare among national club magazines and newsletters.

Registries, of necessity, must be the backbone of control of genetic disease in dogs. Control of genetic disease is a complicated problem, revolving around the provision of and use of information about the genetic makeup of dogs. If a registry is to be effective in the control of disease, the starting point must be the dog affected with a given trait. From that point, with autosomal and sex-linked recessive traits, the risk that related phenotypically normal dogs carry (are heterozygous for) the gene for that trait can be calculated. Polygenic traits are more complicated, but even so, there are established procedures (progeny testing) that allow the evaluation of the genetic makeup of a dog or bitch so that it can be determined whether an animal is likely to produce more healthy offspring than another dog might produce. Dominant traits are easy, because in most instances, only the affected dogs have the genes for the trait, and phenotypically normal dogs are also genetically normal. For this reason, there are relatively few dominant traits that cause long-term problems in dogs.

You do not have to be around dog breeders (purebred or otherwise) very long before you realize that the vast majority of these breeders do not have the background to allow them to draw the most accurate conclusions about the genetic makeup of a phenotypically normal dog based on a disease occurring in one of its first-degree relatives. For the most part, dog breeders are talented people, and they can and do effectively produce winners in conformation, obedience, working and hunting situations. But they are not geneticists. With these facts in mind, any disease registry that purports to be effective in the control of disease must provide the information that breeders need in a form they can use.

What information should a registry provide to breeders? First, just providing the knowledge that a dog in a given pedigree has a genetic disease is a major step above the knowledge that a dog is phenotypically normal, since a normal phenotype tells you nothing about the genetic makeup of the dog in regard to disease. This alone is a major help. But if the goal of any registry is to provide breeders with the information necessary for them to prevent genetic disease in the offspring they produce, then just naming affected dogs will not cut the mustard. We must remember that we are trying to help breeders, not geneticists.

Most breeders do not fully understand the genetic implications of having a dog with a genetic disease in a pedigree. Further, the average length of time a person remains as an active breeder is about six years, so even if we taught the current crop of breeders all about genetic disease, we would have to do it all over again in six years. In other words, we are operating with a perpetual kindergarten. I have talked with numerous people who have quit breeding purebred dogs and asked them why they quit. By a large margin, the most common answer was "I produced dogs that had diseases I could not live with, so I stopped breeding dogs." Frequently, the answer was something like this: "People I sold dogs to came back to me and told me the problems they had, that their dogs were sick, or blind or had died, and how much money they had spent. I couldn't handle it. I didn't know what to do, so I gave up." No one wants to produce dogs that have or develop genetic diseases, especially after that dog has bonded with the owners and their children. Clearly, that is not the goal of purebred dog breeders. But they need help to change that situation.

If a registry truly wants to help breeders produce normal, healthy dogs, it should provide as much information as possible on the genetic makeup of breeding stock, which includes data on the entire family. Further, that information should be as current and up-to-date as possible. Rather than accepting published lists of phenotypically normal and affected dogs, which a breeder might still be using after the list is two or three or more years old, breeders should be encouraged to request current information on any dog they are considering for breeding purposes. That information should include data on the whole family, indicating that a given animal is affected with a deleterious trait or the risk it carries, or is free of the gene(s) for any trait in the registry that is known to occur in that breed. Is that possible? Sure it is. Right now. Today. We have the computers and technology already in our hands. We just need to get off our collective duff and do it. We need to forget the ways we handled disease yesterday and quit avoiding the fact that diseases occur. We need to forget the registries we had yesterday, because it is obvious that they did not accomplish what we thought they would. It's time to get out of the 1960s and move into the new millennium.

Prioritizing Genetic Defects

Since all dogs (or nearly all) carry several genes for genetic defects, if you want to control the defect in an effective manner, it is necessary to prioritize those genes. It is necessary to prioritize the genes because most dogs don't carry just one or two abnormal genes; they have four or five or more. For example, we know that Cairn Terriers have about 5.0 and Newfoundlands 4.5 defective genes per dog on the average. We don't have as good information on most dog breeds, because effective surveys have not yet been conducted. Many breeders, breed clubs and apparently the AKC believe that the less you talk about a problem, the more likely it is to go away. This is clearly not the case, because breeders have been trying to hide problems for years and none have gone away. It takes effective and continued selection to reduce the prevalence of a genetic defect.

Take Collie eye, for example. A group of breeders, with the help of Dr. William Yakely, reduced the prevalence of this disorder by 38 percent over a three-year period in the Northwest, while in the rest of the United States, it remains a widespread problem. This same group of breeders reduced the prevalence of gray Collie syndrome to negligible levels a couple of years earlier. There are other examples, like the Portuguese Water Dog Club of America, that made major inroads on hip dysplasia and all but eliminated the breed's storage-disease problem in just a few short years. The Alaskan Malamute Club of America greatly reduced the prevalence of Malamute dwarfism, although there was some disagreement on what to do with carriers.

So it is clear that genetic diseases can be controlled, but they cannot be controlled by being hidden. In fact, hiding the defects, rationalizing them, minimizing them and, in some cases, flat-out lying about them is causing the puppy-lemon laws like the one recently passed in Florida to come into being. No sane breeder and no one interested in purebred dogs, for any reason, wants to see this happen—but folks, whether we like it or not, it is happening.

Can we do anything about it? Of course, but not by sitting on our hands, keeping our mouths shut, closing our eyes and letting our dogs go blind, become crippled, have fits and suffer from other conditions that make them unfit to be show dogs, hunting partners, obedience competitors and, most important, good pets and companions. Breeders love their dogs (at least, most of them do), and the people they sell them to bond with the dogs, and they become part of the family. This is what we want to happen with dogs: We love them, they love us and provide great pleasure and satisfaction in our lives. Is it any wonder that people are upset when their dogs go blind, become crippled or develop a disease that may cost several times the original purchase price of the dog? Not to my mind. I believe they have a right to be upset, and the buyers do, too.

It is clearly time for breeders, breed clubs, the AKC and the veterinary profession to come to grips with the problem to preserve the integrity, health and well-being of our canine friends.

If 30 percent to 40 percent of our dogs have a defect themselves and, in addition, carry four or five genes for other deleterious traits, isn't the situation almost impossible to resolve? The answer to that is clearly "Yes, unless something is done to put order into the picture." We must prioritize the traits, working on those that harm our dogs first and putting on the bottom of the list those things that do little harm or that we can readily correct. We have to quit thinking like we did in 1920 and look at the real situation as it is in the present. I hate to tell you this, but all dogs are not perfect, and since that is true, we have to decide what we can live with and what we cannot. Why is it that we can cut the tails and ears off a dog and show it, but we can't repair an inguinal hernia and show it? They are both (for the most part) for cosmetic purposes. Who makes rules that require an inguinal hernia to become equivalent to PRA or cataracts or Malamute dwarfism in terms of selection? The AKC needs to reconsider some of its rules and adopt a more sensible and realistic approach to the realities of nature and dog breeding. However, given that the dog-breeding situation is as it is today, how do you solve the problem?

You Prioritize!

Step one. Since every time you breed dogs, you get whole dogs, not just eyes or hips or elbows or hearts, you should always look at the whole dog first. The whole dog is composed of somewhere between 10,000 and 110,000 genes; we are not sure of exactly how many, but it should be obvious that it is easier to control one or two or even five genes than it is to control 100,000. Therefore, you must choose a dog (or dogs) for breeding that will allow you to accomplish your goal(s), be it conformation, hunting, obedience or the production of quality pets. If your goal is to win in conformation competition, it will do you no good to produce an animal with superb hips if it fails to win. You will not be satisfied with the dog, even though it is healthy. So you must pick the *whole dog first.* Of course, it will be best if you can select three, four or even five dogs that fit this category to allow secondary selection parameters to be introduced. However, with a few exceptions, this is not essential—it just makes life easier.

Step two. There are some traits that override the primary selection parameters (conformation, hunting and working abilities). In my opinion, one of these and perhaps the only one is temperament. It should be obvious to those of us involved with purebred dogs that the public (including legislators) is upset about the potential for physical harm that exists with dogs. We need to come to grips with the fact that many people, perhaps most people, cannot handle some of the dogs produced by breeders. They are not familiar with aggressive dogs and do not have the knowledge or skills to handle them. This, of course, causes many problems, hence the breed-specific and all-breed legislation that has swept the United States. Although the problem may be more severe with some breeds than with others, in reality, it applies to all dogs. I have seen massive efforts by the AKC, parent and regional specialty clubs and all-breed clubs to modify proposed legislation in order to bring it into a more realistic evaluation of and correction for the problem. These efforts meet my hearty approval.

However, I have seen little effort by any of these organizations to get at the heart of the problem—that is, the dogs themselves.

The number of dog bites tends to be proportional to the size of a breed's population, although perhaps not completely so. There is also a clear variation in the intensity and severity of the attacks. However, it should be obvious that such breeds as Golden and Labrador Retrievers, Collies and Poodles bite more people than do Bull Terriers. This is not because they are more aggressive, but because there are more of them—lots more. This, of course, applies to all breeds, not just the four mentioned here. **We need to make it clear in a straightforward and unambiguous way that it is always unacceptable to breed dogs with poor temperament.** We can argue ad nauseam about what poor temperament is, but we cannot accept it in our breeding stock, no matter how good a dog's other characteristics may be.

Although I am not a behaviorist (nor do I intend to become one), I offer this opinion realizing that it does not cover all aspects and that there are *some* extenuating circumstances in *some* cases. **Dogs that bite people and other dogs, dogs that continually growl and exhibit aggressive behavior toward people and other dogs, dogs that more than once upset or interfere with conformation shows or field obedience and other trials (and the first time should be documented) should not be bred independent of all other factors.**

The AKC should instruct judges that such behavior is unacceptable in dogs and that these dogs *must* be excused from the ring or trial for any and every instance of such temperament. It is most important that they be excused on the first offense, because we cannot document the second offense without the first being in place. Those dogs exhibiting poor show-ring or trial behavior twice should be permanently excused from any competitive event. Those judges that cannot or will not excuse dogs for poor behavior should themselves be relieved of judging approval—permanently.

Over a period of time, if we continually select against poor temperament, and if all of our clubs and judges exert the peer pressure necessary to make this a standard selection parameter against poor behavior, we will again regain the trust of our dog-buying public.

Step three. We have now selected our breeding stock—that is, a dog (hopefully, dogs) that fulfills our good-citizen requirement as well as our requirement for a winning phenotype, be it in conformation, hunting, obedience, working or serving as a good pet and companion.

Good breeders with some experience with dogs in their line or kennel should know which diseases are present in their stock. There may be some excuse for new breeders or ones who have produced relatively few litters not being aware of what their stock carries, but there is no excuse for the breeder who sold them that stock not telling them which disorders are involved with the line. Good breeding practices require ethical behavior. If you know which traits can be found in your stock, you know what to select against, which means that something that is good and correct for one line may be inappropriate for another. So it should be understood that all breeders will not be facing exactly the same problems at the same time.

Since there is an average of four or five defective genes per dog, and since it is difficult to select against more than one (or perhaps, if you are lucky, two) trait(s) at a time, you need to prioritize the disorders. In Table 9.1, I present my opinion of a prioritization scheme—a hierarchy of disagreeability of genetic traits. As you study the table, you will see that a given trait may fall into more than one category. The more categories it fits, the less desirable it is, so the more severely it should be selected against. This table is not intended to be a list of the only diseases that should be selected against; they are examples, and there are hundreds of other diseases that belong in one or more of the categories. Further, no breed of dogs is exempt from this table. Just because I have not mentioned a disease that occurs in your breed does not mean that no such disease occurs in your breed. Further, just because you do not have a severe trait in your line or kennel does not mean that you should not select against the less-severe traits.

After you select your breeding stock, know what traits occur in your stock and prioritize the traits, you know what to look out for in the mate. It is true that it is difficult to determine which traits will be present in your selected mate, because breeders tend to avoid telling others about those traits, to minimize them or to outright lie about them, but you now have a starting point and can ask appropriate questions, which will help you block the occurrence of a trait or eliminate the gene from your line or kennel. Most of the dilemma about identifying dogs that carry genes for specific traits could be eliminated by open registries. An open registry identifies dogs that are affected with or carry specific defects, as well as those dogs that are phenotypically and genotypically normal for such traits.

Table 9.1

Hierarchy of disagreeability of a genetic trait.

Severe Traits

1. **Painful disorders**

   Examples: glaucoma, craniomandibular osteopathy, hip dysplasia, entropion, portocaval shunts, dermatomyositis, cancer

2. **Disorders that disfigure, maim or otherwise render an animal nonfunctional**

   Examples: English Pointer dwarfism, cataracts, retinal dysplasia and detachment, Malamute chondrodystrophy, PRA, deafness

3. **Lethal disorders**

   Examples: malignant histiocytosis, inherited kidney disease, anasarca, globoid cell leukodystrophy, Portuguese Water Dog storage disease

4. **Disorders requiring treatment for the life of the animal**

   Examples: grey Collie syndrome, diabetes, epilepsy, copper toxicosis

5. **Disorders requiring surgical correction for the animal to survive or live relatively painlessly**

   Examples: esophageal achalasia, ventricular septal defects, elbow dysplasia, distichiasis

6. **Disorders that are difficult to control**

   Examples: multigene traits; late onset traits, such as sebaceous adenitis, subaortic stenosis, osteochondritis dissecans

Mild Traits

7. **Disorders that are readily treatable and respond well to therapy**

   Example: hypothyroidism

8. **Disorders requiring one-time surgery that is highly successful and principally cosmetic**

   Examples: inguinal hernia, umbilical hernia, mild tooth misalignment (these are equivalent to tail docks and ear crops), unilateral cryptorchidism

9. **Disorders that prevent an animal's use for the purpose for which it was bred**

   Examples: Samoyed albinism, correct color, mild bite, dentition, gait abnormalities

CHAPTER 10

Breed Clubs and Control of Genetic Disease

Wherever we turn, there are dog clubs . . . and more dog clubs . . . and still more dog clubs! The American Kennel Club is the epitome of an all-breed club and the master registry for more than a million dogs a year. Operating under the rules set down by AKC are the national and regional specialty breed clubs, the all-breed clubs, as well as the obedience, hunting and other clubs devoted to a variety of breed-specific performance activities. It seems like everyone is yelling at them about genetic disease. Some are yelling "STOP! Don't talk about disease—nobody will buy our dogs!" Others shout, "Do something to prevent disease, or nobody will buy our dogs!" Which way should we jump? Which way should we turn? Where do we go from here? What should we do? Everyone seems to be asking questions, but answers seem to be few and far between.

The reason answers are few and far between is because nobody is sure what the problem is, how widespread it is and how severe it is. Unfortunately, the AKC can't respond adequately to the problem, because it does not have the data, and in fact, it has no effective way to get at it. To be fair, the AKC is trying. It has asked the parent clubs what their problems are and has received answers. Unfortunately, the answers were not well-thought-out, because most parent breed clubs do not have the data to supply reasonable answers.

The first thing most breed clubs need to do is assess the problem. They need to determine what is happening in their own breeds. For the most part, they have not done that, and it is an essential step if they want to change the current situation.

A few clubs have tried to assess the situation—specifically, the Cairn Terrier Club of America, the Newfoundland Club of America, the Bichon Frise Club of America and the Scottish Terrier Club of America. There may well be others that have similar data of which I am not aware. These clubs have conducted surveys involving both normal dogs and dogs affected with various diseases. Among the diseases included in the surveys were a number that were known to be genetic based on data developed in that breed or in other breeds.

From this data, we could calculate the frequency of the various genetic diseases that were reported. From the frequency data, we could calculate a carrier rate for the various genetic diseases in each breed based on the Hardy-Weinberg law, and from this, we could derive the average genetic burden for each dog in the breed.

The data for each breed is presented in tables 10.1 through 10.4. In each case, the data is presented in a similar manner: first, the name of the disease, then the mode of inheritance, if known (or whether it is undetermined), the frequency of the disease in the survey population and what I call a "guesstimate" of carrier frequency based on the Hardy-Weinberg law. If we add up the frequencies of the various genetic diseases, we end up with the percentage of affected dogs in the general survey population. If we add up the frequencies of carriers and divide by 100, we arrive at the average number of genetic diseases carried by each dog in the survey population. The four breeds mentioned above are remarkably similar as to the frequency of genetic disease in their respective populations and the number of diseases each dog carries.

Table 10.1

Genetic diseases of Cairn Terriers.

Disease	Mode of inheritance*	Frequency	Guesstimate of carrier frequency (percent carriers)
Hard-tissue diseases			
1 Legg-Perthes	Poly	0.8/100	16.2%
2 CMO	R	0.9/100	17.0%
3 Hip dysplasia	Poly	0.25/100	9.5%
4 Panosteitis	Und	0.2/100	8.4%
5 Patellar Luxation	Und (R)	3.2/100	29.2%
6 OCD	Poly	0.4/100	11.7%
7 Cleft palate	Poly	0.7/100	15.2%
8 Tailless	Und	0.1/100	6.1%
9 Crooked tail	Und	0.2/100	8.4%
10 Undershot bite	Und	1.7/100	22.6%
11 Overshot bite	Und	1.3/100	20.2%
12 Missing teeth	Und	3.0/100	28.6%

Disease	Mode of inheritance*	Frequency	Guesstimate of carrier frequency (percent carriers)
Neurologic diseases			
13 Globoid cell leuk	R	0.1/100	6.1
14 Epilepsy	Und	0.4/100	11.7%
15 Over- aggressiveness	Und	1.3/100	20.5%
16 Shyness	Und	1.0/100	18.0%
Ocular diseases			
17 PRA	R	0.1/100	6.1%
18 Entropion	Und	0.2/100	8.4%
19 Cataracts	Und	0.4/100	11.7%
20 Glaucoma	Und	0.2/100	8.4%
Blood/Heart diseases			
21 von Willebrand's	Und (D?)	.002/100	.002%
22 Heart defect	Poly	0.9/100	17.0%
Soft-tissue diseases			
23 Rheumatoid arthritis	Und (?)	0.4/100	11.7%
24 Inguinal hernia	R	2.3/100	26.4%
25 Umbilical hernia	R	4.1/100	32.2%
26 Skin allergies (atopy)	Und	2.6/100	27.0%
27 Autoimmune disease	Und	0.03/100	1.0%
28 Anasarca (Bulldogs)	R	0.1/100	6.1%
29 Cryptorchid	Und (R?)	2.3/100	26.4%
30 Monorchid	Und (R?)	9.5/100	42.6%
31 Retractable testes	Und (R?)	1.4/100	20.8%
32 Portocaval shunt	Poly	0.2/100	8.4
		40.28	**503.6**

*R = Recessive, Poly = Polygenic, D = Dominant, Und = Undetermined

Table 10.2

Genetic diseases of Newfoundlands.

	Disease	Mode of inheritance*	Frequency	Guesstimate of carrier frequency (percent carriers)
Hard-tissue diseases				
1	Hip dysplasia	Poly	21/100	49.6%
2	Undershot bite	Poly	3.4/100	30.0%
3	OCD	Poly	2/100	24.0%
4	Elbow dysplasia	Poly	1.8/100	23.2%
5	Patellar luxation	Und	0.7/100	15.2%
6	Overshot bite	Poly	0.5/100	13.1%
7	Wobbler syndrome	Und	0.2/100	8.6%
8	Kinked tail	Und	—	—
Cardiac diseases				
9	SAS (Auto. D. ?)	Poly	0.8/100	16.2%
10	PDA	Poly	—	—
11	VSD	Poly	—	—
Ocular diseases				
12	Entropion	Poly? D?	5.3/100	35.4%
13	Ectropion	Und	1.9/100	23.6%
14	Eversion Nictating Membrane	R?	1.1/100	18.6%
15	Dermoid cyst of the cornea	Und	0.1/100	6.0%
16	Diamond or pagoda eye (kinked eyelid)	Poly	—	—
17	Medial Canthal Pocket syndrome	Und	—	—
Soft-tissue diseases				
18	Allergic dermatitis	Und	12.6/100	45.7%
19	Hypothyroidism	Und	7/100	38.4%
20	Umbilical hernia	R	1.8/100	23.2%
21	Retained testicle	R	1.4/100	20.8%
22	Bloat	Und	0.8/100	16.2%
23	Allergies	Und	0.6/100	14.2%

24 Megaesophagus=	Und	—	—
Neurologic and behavioral diseases			
25 Trembling	Und	3.5/100	30.4%
26 "Rage" syndrome over-aggressiveness	Und	—	—
		66.5	**452.4**

*R = Recessive, Poly = Polygenic, D = Dominant, Und = Undetermined
=Indicates that the trait occurs in this breed, but the frequency has not been determined.

Table 10.3

Genetic diseases of Bichons Frises.

Disease	Mode of inheritance*	Frequency	Guesstimate of carrier frequency (percent carriers)
Hard-tissue diseases			
1 Missing teeth	Und	0.9/100	17.0%
2 Hip dysplasia	Poly	1/100	18%
3 Legg-Perthes	Poly	0.3/100	10.2%
4 Elbow dysplasia	Poly	0.09/100	6.0%
5 Patellar luxation	R, Poly?	1/100	18%
6 Overshot bite	Und	1/100	18%
7 Undershot bite	Und	3.9/100	31.6%
8 Cleft palate	Poly	0.6/100	14.2%
Neurologic diseases			
9 Epilepsy	Und	0.6/100	14.2%
10 Aggressive	Und	0.9/100	17.0%
11 Shyness	Und	2.1/100	24.6%
12 Deafness	Und	0.1/100	6.1%
13 Hydrocephalus	Und	0.5/100	13.0%
Ocular diseases			
14 Ectropion	Und	0.09/100	6.0%
15 Entropion	Und	0.4/100	11.7%

	Disease	Mode of inheritance*	Frequency	Guesstimate of carrier frequency (percent carriers)
16	Corneal dystrophy	R	1/100	18.0%
17	Juvenile cataracts	R?	0.3/100	10.2%
18	Glaucoma	Und	0.1/100	6.1%
19	Cataracts	Und	2.2/100	25.2%
20	PRA	R	0.4/100	11.7%
21	Blocked tear ducts	Und	0.8/100	16.2%
Blood/Heart diseases				
22	von Willebrand's	IncD	0.04/100	0.04%
23	PDA	Poly	0.4/100	11.7%
24	VSD	Poly	0.1/100	6.1%
Soft-tissue diseases				
25	Umbilical hernia	R?	3.9/100	31.6%
26	Inguinal hernia	R?	0.3/100	10.2%
27	Ciliary dyskenesia	Und	0.7/100	15.2%
28	Autoimmune disorders	Und	0.4/100	11.7%
29	Cleft lip	Und	0.3/100	10.2%
30	Cryptorchidism	R?	1.7/100	22.6%
31	Monorchidism	R?	3.7/100	31.0%
			29.8	**463.3**

*R = Recessive, Poly = Polygenic, D = Dominant, Und = Undetermined, IncD = Incomplete Dominance

Table 10.4

Genetic diseases of Scottish Terriers.

	Disease	Mode of inheritance*	Frequency	Guesstimate of carrier frequency (percent carriers)
Hard-tissue diseases				
1	Achondroplasia	R?, D?	.06/100	4.7%
2	Cleft palate	Poly	.06/100	4.7%
3	CMO	R	.06/100	4.7%
4	Hip dysplasia	Poly	.06/100	4.7%
5	Legg-Perthes	Poly	.06/100	4.7%
6	Patellar Luxation	R?, Poly?	1.2/100	19.5%
7	Missing teeth	Und	1/100	18.0%
8	Overshot bite	Und	0.2/100	8.4%
9	Tail kink	Und	0.2/100	8.4%
10	Undershot Bite	Und	2.1/100	24.7%
Eye diseases				
11	Cataracts	R?, Poly?	1.1/100	18.8%
12	Glaucoma	Und	.06/100	4.7%
13	PPM, persistent pupillary membranes	Und	.4/100	11.7%
14	PRA, progressive retinal atrophy	R	.06/100	4.7%
Vascular and immune mediated diseases				
15	Immune mediated SLE, CAH, HA, thrombosis	Und	0.4/100	11.7%
16	Heart disorders PDA, SAS, VSD	Poly	0.2/100	8.4%
17	von Willebrand's disease	R	0.2/100	8.4%
Neurologic and behavioral diseases				
18	Aggressiveness	Und	1.7/100	22.6%
19	Cerebellar ataxia	R	0.5/100	13.0%

Disease	Mode of inheritance*	Frequency	Guesstimate of carrier frequency (percent carriers)
20 Epilepsy	Und	3/100	28.6%
21 Scottie cramp	R	3.2/100	29.3%
22 Unstable temperament	Und	0.1/100	6.1%
Skin and endocrine diseases			
23 Addison's disease	Und	0.2/100	8.4%
24 Atopic dermatitis	Und	5.5/100	35.8%
25 Demodectic mange	Und	1.9/100	23.6%
26 Diabetes	Und	0.3/100	10.2%
27 Hashimoto's disease hyperthyroidism	R	6.4/100	37.7%
28 Inguinal hernia	Und, R?	0.6/100	14.2%
29 Seborrhea (greasy coat)	Und	0.2/100	8.4%
30 Umbilical hernia	Und, R?	0.7/100	15.2%
Soft-tissue diseases			
31 Cystinuria	X-R	0.4/100	11.7%
32 Cryptorchidism	Und, R?	.06/100	4.7%
33 Deafness	R?	1.2/100	19.5%
34 Monorchidism	Und, R?	.06/100	4.7%
35 Myasthenia gravis	R	.06/100	4.7%
36 Portocaval shunts	Poly ?	.06/100	4.7
		33.56	**474.0**

*R = Recessive, Poly = Polygenic, D = Dominant, Und = Undetermined, X-R = Sex-linked recessive

Breed clubs at all levels must take an active role in educating their members about the problems in their breeds and use their influence and peer pressure wherever possible to point their members in a direction that will remedy the situation.

No breed is free of genetic diseases, but many breed clubs and their members lack adequate knowledge about the diseases that plague them.

Point 1—Frequency of Defects

Of the dogs reported in the various surveys, 40.3 percent of the Cairns, 66.5 percent of the Newfoundlands, 29.8 percent of the Bichons and 33.5 percent of the Scotties have a genetic defect of some kind. Approximately 40 percent of all dogs produced in these four breeds have a defect, and in my opinion, that is a serious problem. Further, I do not believe this situation is unique to these four breeds. Most dog breeds probably produce similar numbers of dogs with abnormalities. Some may have a few less, some a few more, but all most likely have a problem. This distribution of genetic diseases is, of course, the reason this book is needed.

A quick survey of the list of defects reported to occur in each of these four breeds reveals that many of the defects reported are not severely detrimental to the health of the dog. Some of these, many call faults rather than diseases—such as overshot and undershot bites (unless they are very severe), crooked tails, umbilical and inguinal hernias (unless they are severe) and one or two missing teeth. I tend to agree with such a classification, but nevertheless, all are genetic. It is also easy to determine from the lists presented that some of the diseases are very severe, inexorably leading to death, blindness or a debilitating and poor quality of life. It is these differences that led us to the prioritization of defects discussed in Chapter 9.

The important point for a breed club and its members is that genetic traits are common in purebred dogs (as they are in crossbred dogs) and that they are widely distributed in the various breeds. I believe it is an obligation of breed clubs, through their members, to make strong efforts to reduce the frequency of genetic defects in their breeds. It is important to glean from this data that no one's skirts are totally clean, and while it may be possible to point a finger at a given line for producing one specific trait, they rate a clean bill of health for various other traits. There are no dogs or lines that are free of *all* defects. The question is not whether genetic defects are present; it is which ones the breeder is dealing with. If you know which dogs carry for which defects, you can prevent disease.

Point 2—Modes of Inheritance

A quick scan of the data presented in Tables 10.1 through 10.4 shows that for over half of the traits reported in each breed, the mode of inheritance has not been determined. While we tend to accept the idea that the mode of inheritance for a given trait is the same in two different breeds, the factual data that supports that idea is certainly sparse. This lack of knowledge about the mode of inheritance of a trait is a major handicap in genetic counseling, as well as in delineating markers and genes by DNA analysis. There should be a major push to determine the mode of inheritance for those traits where such information is not available. Breed clubs can and should join forces to alleviate this handicap. Once the mode of inheritance for a given trait is determined in one breed, a single crossbreeding to another breed will, in most cases, be all that is required to determine if it is the same gene in both breeds. There may be some exceptions to this generality, but in the vast majority of cases, both the clinical and genetic data will apply to both breeds.

Some people take exception to determining the mode of inheritance for a trait on the grounds that they are producing dogs with defects. However, unless something is done in this regard, we will be forever producing dogs with defects, because adequate counseling cannot be provided without this data. In most cases, with breeder and breed-club cooperation in gathering the necessary preliminary data, only one or two prospective matings will be necessary to prove the mode of inheritance for a trait.

Determining the mode of inheritance for diseases in their breeds must be a priority item for breed clubs. In many cases, DNA analysis may allow us to short circuit some of the requirements needed to produce the scientific data necessary to prove the mode of inheritance.

Point 3—Frequency of Carriers

Determining the frequency of carriers in the general population of dogs within a breed provides the data necessary for breeders to understand how a dog that produced one or two totally normal litters suddenly produces one or more defective puppies in a third litter. Such data is very hard to obtain, and I know of no rock-solid data that allows us to estimate the frequency of the various genes within the general population of a breed. As far as I know, there is no such data available anywhere.

What I have done in Tables 10.1 through 10.4 is break all of the rules of genetics, all of the rules for data collection, all of the rules of mathematics and probably all of the laws found anywhere on this planet to derive a "guesstimate" of carrier frequency for each trait reported in their respective surveys by the Cairn, Newfoundland, Bichon, and Scottie clubs. I used the Hardy-Weinberg Law to do this dastardly deed.

Every geneticist in the world will probably say, "Horrors, horrors, horrors! What have you done? You can't do that! The data must be wrong!"

If I were hanging from a cliff by my hands over the Grand Canyon, there would be a mad rush by every true hard-working geneticist everywhere to rush out and stomp on my fingers so that I would fall 5,000 feet to my well-deserved, excruciatingly painful death.

"You can't use the Hardy-Weinberg law on polygenic traits, you dummy! It's for single-gene traits." I know that. "Are you crazy? You can't use the Hardy-Weinberg law if the mode of inheritance for a trait is unknown. The answers must be wrong, wrong, WRONG!" I know that, too, but I did it anyway. I am a bad boy!!!

The fact is that you must have some understanding of how traits occur in a set of dogs, and this can only come through an understanding of how carriers are distributed in the general population of a breed. It is for this reason that I have broken the rules in order to present in a coherent fashion the data that will allow breeders to come to grips with the problem of genetic disease.

Are these surveys perfect? NO! Is the data absolutely correct? NO! But to my knowledge, it is the best data available at the present time on the distribution of carriers in a breed. We should accept better data with more accurate estimates anytime it is presented without qualm. We should reject all of the bickering about this data, unless it is accompanied by better, more useful, information.

So folks, complain about these surveys and calculations all you want. It's okay with me. But such information is essential if you want to approach the control of genetic disease in a logical manner. The old adage *outcross, and you will get rid of a trait* doesn't work, and it is obvious that it doesn't, because at least 40 percent of all dogs we produce have a defect of one kind or another. We must take into consideration the distribution of traits and carriers as they occur in dogs.

This distribution is not at all like it is in people. The carrier rate for most traits in dogs is strikingly higher than it is for nearly any trait in people. Outcrossings and matadors account for the major part of this difference in distribution of carriers, and as a result, outcrossing in dogs is as risky as close inbreeding is among people. The only solution is to know the traits that occur in your animals and the specific risk for the carrier status of your own dogs, along with the risk that dogs in the general population of your breed have for those same traits. This is the essential basis for open registries. It is imperative that we know the genetic status of both dogs in a given mating if we want to prevent disease.

From the information presented in Tables 10.1 through 10.4, we surely should be able to see that if we follow that oft-given advice *don't breed carriers,* we will never breed another dog in any breed in the entire world. All dogs carry for some defect; the question becomes, "What defect is involved, and what defects does the potential mate carry for?" If we can solve that problem through open registries, we can control genetic defects and greatly reduce the production of those defects that are seriously harmful to our canine friends.

I fervently wish that I knew the exact, perfectly correct distribution of carriers for each trait that occurs in each breed of dogs right now. **But that's not the way the world is today.** I would be delighted if I could tell you the exact mode of inheritance for each trait in each dog breed at this very moment. **But that is not the way the world is today.** I would be the happiest man around if I could look at a dog and tell you exactly what defective genes that specific dog has. **But that's not the way the world is today.** I would be ecstatic if I could tell you that DNA analysis was going to solve all of our problems tomorrow or even the next day. **But that's not the way the world is today.** In fact, I believe that most, if not all, of us reading this book will have died before accurate DNA analysis is readily available to identify the genetic status of an animal regarding a specific trait for the majority of traits that occur in dogs.

I submit to you, the reader, that the information presented in Tables 10.1 through 10.4 is the best data available today to assist a breed in controlling genetic disease. I do this without trepidation, because as far as I know, it is the only data on the distribution of traits in a given breed available today.

Point 4—Where Do We Stand Now?

I have talked to hundreds of breeders and owners of purebred dogs over the years, and these are the most common comments I hear: "My, isn't it a shame genetic disease is growing rampant in purebred dogs?" "Genetic disease is getting worse and worse." "In some breeds, it seems that all the dogs have a disease." "Genetic disease is becoming more of a problem every day." The fact is, I don't really know how fast genetic disease is growing as a problem or if it is increasing at all. There are no baseline studies available that allow me to tell how bad it was ten or twenty years ago, and there are few studies available that tell me what the status is right now.

Is genetic disease growing as a problem or not?

The reports available from the four breeds discussed in this chapter may allow us to determine what is happening in purebred dogs—whether the problem is getting better or worse. But at the present time, we have little or no information that allows us to give pat answers to the question.

CHAPTER 11

For the Breeder

If you have stayed with me this long, you are probably thinking by now, "Okay, buddy, you have given us the lowdown on how to calculate the risks that a given dog has to be genetically normal for a trait, to carry for a trait, to produce the trait or to develop the trait. Now what do we do?" And my answer to you is, "That's easy, you do just about the same thing you always do, but you gather and use a little more information."

Item 1—Know Your Own Dogs

For the person just starting out in breeding, this is a tough problem. The reason it's tough is that if the person you bought your bitch from had told you everything you needed to know (as he or she should have), you probably wouldn't have bought the bitch. Instead, you may very likely have bought your bitch from someone who did one or more of the following things:

a. Prevaricated and said their dogs have no problems at all.

b. Told you that there are problems in their dogs, but they are all minor.

c. Avoided talking about problems by pointing out the bitch's good qualities instead.

d. Said the only major problem in their dogs was hypothyroidism and explained that this is treatable, which it is.

e. Said here's the bitch, she's a winner, take her or leave her.

f. If you are very lucky, you may have bought your bitch from someone with the integrity to tell you the truth and the savvy to explain the facts of life to you.

In all except the last case, you obviously cannot go back to the seller now and expect to get any more information than you were already given just because you explain why you need it. If you are in this situation and you do have a quality bitch based on whatever parameters you have decided to set for yourself (conformation, obedience, working, hunting and so on), the only thing you can do about her is to close your eyes, pray and breed her. Within two, three or four litters, you will have information about her genetic status if you are wise enough to do what all good breeders should do: **Follow your puppies and find out what happens to them.** This is one of the hardest things for a breeder to do, because if you call someone and there is a problem, what do you say? If you started the situation out correctly when you sold the puppy, you are in good shape and the owner will appreciate your call. You need to tell the truth to all those who have bought your puppies: that you are trying to determine what traits occur in your breeding so that you can prevent disease in the next litter(s) and that you will be calling them when the puppies are one to two years old. Tell them you do follow up on the puppies you produce, and then do it at the appropriate time. Give them your phone number and ask them to call you if their dogs develop a genetic disease. **But you need the information, and to guarantee that you get it, it is your obligation to follow up, not the new owner's obligation to report to you.** You will be surprised at how much your clients appreciate your concern.

When inquiring about a puppy for a friend of mine who asked me to help her pick a puppy, I talked to a Golden Retriever breeder and asked about diseases that occurred in her line. She told me that she didn't think she had any serious problems, because none of her buyers had called her to tell her so. I asked her if she followed up on her puppies by calling the buyers. She told me, "No, I have had at least 500 puppies over the last ten years, and that would be too much work." So I said, "Ten years, fifty-two weeks in a year, 520 weeks, you would only have to make little more than one call a week." She said she didn't have time to do that, but folks, I do not believe that an average of one call a week should be too much of a job. Needless to say, my friend did not buy a puppy there. Remember, with only a little bit of extra effort, you can get the information you need.

Once you have determined what traits are carried in your dog's family, you can begin to apply the data.

Experienced breeders should know what traits occur in their lines. In my opinion, if they don't know the traits that occur in their lines, I would hesitate to think that the word "breeder" applies to them. Instead, I would suggest that you think of them as "people who mate dogs."

At this point, I am assuming that you are a breeder—not someone who "mates dogs"—and that your goal is to produce healthy dogs that win in whatever category you have set as your main objective.

Since you know what traits occur in your dogs, you must know which dogs are affected with those traits. If you know which dogs are affected, you can determine the risk each dog you own has to carry for each trait in your line. Do not be surprised if each dog you have carries for three, four or more defects. This is the situation you must deal with, and it will not go away just because you don't like it. *You,* as a breeder, have to deal with this reality.

So, using the techniques we developed in chapters 5 through 8, assign a risk for each trait that could be carried by each dog that you are considering as a potential breeding animal, both males and females. If you elect to sell some of these animals as pet stock, be sure they are neutered. If you elect to sell them as potential breeding stock, it is, in my opinion, your obligation to tell each purchaser the exact risks you have calculated for the dogs they buy.

Item 2—Prioritize the Traits

In chapter 9, we discussed prioritizing traits. I outlined some reasons for prioritization and presented a few examples. At this point, you need to clearly establish your priorities, which traits you can't live with and those, although not desirable, you can co-exist with. Write them down so that you do not find yourself adjusting your priorities to fit what you find. As a breeder, at least one that admires your own dogs, you must take into account that horrible disease "kennel blindness" and try to assure yourself that this disorder, the bane of so many breeders, is not playing a major role here. In my opinion, temperament is one of the problems that is often overlooked based on "kennel blindness." Then set an objective to eliminate the most severe trait and to minimize the risk of producing those traits that are of lesser concern. Once you set your objective, stick with it and use the myriad techniques we have discussed to reduce the risks your puppies have to develop a defect.

Item 3—Pick the Whole Dog First

Why pick the whole dog first? Why not just pick a healthy dog that doesn't carry for any defects? The reason to pick the whole dog first is simple. Most people (it would be nice if it were all people) have a goal when they breed a bitch. That goal may be to win at conformation, to produce a capable hunter or working dog or to produce a quality pet. In any of these cases, the breeder is producing a dog that is composed of 100,000 or so (no one knows the exact number) genes that make up all of the characteristics embodied by that animal. In other words, the whole dog is evaluated to decide whether or not the animal fulfills the breeder's expectations. So you pick the whole dog first, because it is easier to control a few genes than it is to control the 100,000 genes that make up the whole dog. Unfortunately (or perhaps fortunately), every time you breed a bitch, you get whole puppies. You cannot just breed eyes or hearts or hips, although I am sure there are times you wish you could do just that because you like the rest of the puppy.

If you start out with a conformation dog that fails to win a class in thirty outings, you will spend a long time trying to mold those 100,000 genes into the desired shape, and in the end, you will probably fail. If you start out with a hunting dog that can't find a bird if it's tied to his nose, it will take many generations to bring his or her offspring to the point where they can win a field trial. If your goal is to produce a good pet, and the dog you start with takes the arm off someone who bends over to talk to your child or takes a chunk out of the buttock of your boyfriend because he kisses you, there is clearly a lot of work to be done in your breeding program. In order to avoid these problems (because they are very complex, and dealing with them will be very time-consuming), you pick a dog for breeding because it has the characteristics that generally fulfill your goals. The old adage about not being able to make a silk purse from a sow's ear is very appropriate in the matter of selecting breeding stock.

You should also never pick an ugly dog for breeding just because it is genetically normal for PRA. You should never pick a hunting dog for breeding that can't find the duck blind (much less the duck), just because it does not produce hip dysplasia. You should never pick a dog for breeding that does not have the characteristics that fulfill your goal just because it has gene(s) that would be useful in a test-mating.

If you do any of these things, your breeding program will go backward instead of forward. So your goal here is to pick dogs for breeding that represent the best available qualities. Since you already know the genetic makeup of your own dogs in regard to disease, your problem is to pick a complementary mate and to determine its genetic status in regard to the traits you know occur in your own dogs. Therefore, you should pick three or four potential mates, determine their individual risk factors and use the best match to fulfill both your goals as a breeder and your attempt to prevent disease.

Item 4—Determine the Risks for the Potential Mate

Currently, determining the risks for the various diseases of the potential mates is the most difficult part of selecting a mate; this is the information most breeders hide, because they believe their studs will not be used and their puppies will not be sought if they tell the truth about what their stock produces. Unfortunately, as the situation now stands, the fact is that if a disturbingly large number of breeders were to tell the truth about their dogs, most people would not seek them out. Breeders looking for mates for their animals prefer to use dogs whose owners tell them what they want to hear. This preference is based on the mistaken belief that many, if not most, dogs are genetically normal for all traits. So in searching for this mythical genetically normal dog, breeders overlook the information they need to breed their own dogs safely. Breeders who tell the truth about their dogs are routinely vilified by many of their peers—the same peers who praise owners who mold the truth to better serve their ends. At the risk of repeating myself, I want to say again that, for the most part, the phenotype does not reveal the genotype for nearly every major defect in dogs. I say again that closed registries provide little defense against genetic disease.

So what is a breeder to do? Unfortunately, with a few exceptions, the best information available comes from gossip. Gossip is not always correct, that's for sure, but it is more likely (or at least as likely) to be correct than the information from an owner who states that "My dogs don't produce defects." Support of open registries by breed is the only rational solution to the problem.

So my best suggestions at present are to use whatever information is currently available in open registries like the Institute for *Genetic Disease Control* (GDC). Then work your way into the inner circles of your breed so that gossip becomes available to you, and use that information to protect your dogs and line from genetic defects.

The last point I want to make in this section regards *imports*—those dogs and bitches brought in from foreign countries. It does not matter if they come from Great Britain or any other part of Europe, the Near East or the Orient: For the most part, there is no gossip about these dogs because you are not in the inner circles of that breed in that country. Therefore, these dogs always look great. There is no gossip about them available. Let me point out that in about three or four generations, the defects they carried in with them will create plenty of gossip. Remember when you import or export a dog that its defective genes as well as its normal genes go with it.

Item 5—Know How to Use Your Information

I say again that you do about the same thing you always do, but you gather and use a little more information.

For this discussion, I am going to use Scottish Terriers and the *Scottish Terrier Club of America* (STCA) as an example, although the same information is available on Bichons Frises, Cairn Terriers, and Newfoundlands, because their parent clubs have also gathered the basic necessary information on the frequency of various traits in their breeds.

I am going to describe two dogs you are considering as potential studs for your bitch, which I will also describe. Whether you are into Scotties or some other breed, remember that the phenotype of both of these studs is complementary to your bitch (they are a good match, and the stud has the potential to correct any flaws in type that you perceive in your bitches). Remember as we go into this analysis that Scotties average about four puppies per litter, and the data would be stronger in those breeds averaging more than four puppies per litter.

Both dogs described here would be considered *matadors*—that is, they have already contributed more than their fair share to the gene pool of this breed as a whole.

Scottie Matador #1

Born April 1990

He has had thirty litters, producing 123 puppies.

He is a champion, has won three Bests in Show and was Best of Breed at the annual national Specialty.

He has produced thirty-one champions, and 25 percent of all his get are champions.

He has both a GDC and CERF number to his credit, so he is phenotypically normal for both hard-tissue and ocular disease. He is also normal on physical examination for luxated patellae.

Scottie Matador #2

> Born September 1991
>
> He has sired twenty-two litters, producing a total of ninety-three puppies.
>
> He finished his championship easily, with wins that include two five-point majors. He won two Bests in Show, he has his CD, and he won the national specialty in 1994.
>
> He has produced eighteen champions; 19.3 percent of all his get are champions.
>
> He has both a GDC and CERF number to his credit, so he is phenotypically normal for both hard-tissue and ocular diseases. He is also normal on physical examination for luxated patellae.

These are the two males that complement the needs and characteristics you see in your own bitch. Are they compatible? Would you breed to either or both these males? I would. I created them in such a way that there would be very little reason not to breed to them. So the answer to the question "Are they compatible?" obviously is yes.

This is your bitch. Again, she fits all of the general phenotypic characteristics you would like to see in a bitch in your breed.

She is two years old, a nice, typey little lady and you think she could go somewhere. She has a lovely temperament. So far, she is a champion, has won three Bests in Show and two regional Specialties. She has been radiographed and has normal hips and patellae. Patellae are also normal on physical examination. She was cleared by CERF and was normal at two years of age.

Like the matadors I created, this bitch is superb and would be bred by anyone I know. Would you breed her? Again, the answer obviously should be yes.

From the information I have provided at this point, I believe any reasonable person would consider these dogs to be compatible. But wait a minute—there is a problem here! The owners of these dogs just happen to be honest, forthright and ethical breeders, and they tell you the following:

The male dogs were clinically and phenotypically normal for all hard-tissue diseases known to occur in Scotties and did not have an ocular disease that would cause severe detrimental effects on vision as determined by CERF. Further, they believe they had an obligation to tell breeders who want to use these dogs as studs the exact status (to the best of their knowledge) of the genetic makeup of these dogs in regard to the diseases known to occur in Scottish Terriers. In addition, they do their best to follow up on the puppies their dogs produce so they can determine the genetic traits their dogs carry. They tell you that to the best of their knowledge (and they checked), their dogs are not related to any dog that has von Willebrand's disease or to a dog that has produced von Willebrand's, and on this basis, they decided not to have a DNA analysis done based on the cost of this procedure (at the present time, $135).

In my opinion, this is a reasonable decision, since a dog or bitch cannot have the gene for this disease if it is not related to a dog that has von Willebrand's disease or one that has produced it.

The owners of the studs told you their dogs have produced the traits shown in Table 11.1.

Table 11.1

Traits produced by the studs.

Matador #1		Matador #2	
Produced	*Carrier Status*	*Produced*	*Carrier Status*
1 Legg-Perthes	Proven	1 Undershot bite	Proven
2 Tail kinks	Proven	2 Luxated patellae	Proven
3 Cataracts	Proven	3 Cerebellar ataxia	Proven
4 Scottie cramp	Proven	4 Addison's disease	Proven

Since the dogs produced these traits, they are proven carriers of the disease. Since your bitch is a virgin, you realize that there is little direct information about her genetic status. You know that the bitch had a mild umbilical hernia that self-corrected at about six months of age. You began collecting any available information concerning related dogs. The bitch is found to have an uncle on her father's side with Scottie cramp, so her *a priori* risk of being a carrier of that trait is 33.3 percent (see Table 5.6). She has a first cousin once removed with Hashimoto's disease (autoimmune thyroiditis), so her *a priori* carrier risk for this trait is 12.5 percent (see Table 5.6). She has a littermate that is deaf, so her *a priori* carrier risk is 66.6 percent (see Table 5.6). We summarize her data in Table 11.2.

Table 11.2

Information on your bitch.

Disease	*Carrier Risk*
1 Umbilical hernia	Affected
2 Scottie cramp	33.3%
3 Hashimoto's disease	12.5%
4 Deafness	66.6%

What do you think of these three dogs now? Would you breed to the dogs? Would you breed from your bitch? Indeed, do you think they are breedable at all?

When I presented this identical data at four separate seminars with a total audience of over 400 or 500 attendees, the response of nearly all was universal: Nearly all said they would not use any of these dogs in a breeding program.

Here you have the exact situation you want. You have three top-notch dogs. You know the exact status of all three high-quality animals regarding all genetic diseases that have been reported in the breed. These dogs carry no more than the average number of genetic diseases that are known to occur in the breed, and you would not breed from this bitch or breed to the males?

Do you know now why people won't tell you about the disease status of their dogs? If you won't breed these dogs, what dogs will you breed? Do you believe that of all the Scottish terriers in the world, these are the only three that carry four genetic diseases? Remember, we have some information on this breed. Scotties carry, on the average, 4.7 defects per dog. Currently, the way you handle this situation is to blacklist dogs like these three and breed to dogs whose owners lie to you. Currently, we do things in exactly the reverse order of how we should do them. We ostracize people who tell us the truth and give our trust (and our stud fees) to the people who are not honest with us.

All right, let's see what happens if we breed these dogs. Remember, we know about the genetic makeup of both potential sires and the potential dam, and if you know that, you can prevent disease.

The fact is that it does not matter so much what the dog carries or what the bitch carries. It's the combination of the dog and the bitch that counts.

Shouldn't that be true????

In Tables 11.3 and 11.4, we will breed matadors #1 and #2 to your bitch and try to determine the risk that the resultant puppies will develop a genetic defect.

Table 11.3

Expected results if matador #1 is bred to your bitch.

He carries	*She carries*	*Risk that each puppy will be affected*
1 Undershot bite	1 Umbilical hernia	0
2 Luxated patellae	2 Hashimoto's disease	0%
3 Cerebellar ataxia	3 Deafness	0%
4 Addison's disease	4 Scottie cramp	0%

Table 11.4

Expected results if matador #2 is bred to your bitch.

He carries	*She carries*	*Risk that each puppy will be affected*
1 Legg-Perthes	1 Umbilical hernia	0%
2 Tail kinks	2 Hashimoto's disease	0%
3 Cataracts	3 Deafness	0%
4 Scottie cramp	4 Scottie cramp	8.2%

Lo and behold, matador #1 bred to your bitch produces no defects, but when matador #2 is bred to your bitch, there is an 8.2 percent chance that each puppy will develop Scottie cramp.

Not too bad, I say—and this is not dependent on luck, it's dependent on knowledge.

No! No! No! Is Padgett crazy? He knows it can't work this way. He wants us to think knowledge is better than ignorance. String him up! Shoot him! Hang him!

Well, be that as it may, instead of doing all of that nasty stuff to me, let's look at what would happen using the same parameters and breeding these two matadors and your bitch in the general Scottie population.

The following matings are based on the Scottie survey reported in 1995. While surveys are never perfect, this estimate is a whole lot better than guessing when you decide to undertake a mating.

The results of matings between an animal whose genotype is known (regarding genetic disease) and a randomly selected animal whose genotype is not known are shown in Tables 11.5 through 11.7. There is a 63 percent chance with matador #1 and a 99 percent chance with matador #2 that at least one of their puppies will be affected with one of the four diseases listed in the tables. Essentially, every litter will produce at least one puppy affected with one of the four diseases carried by your bitch. Are results like these to be expected when you breed to dogs with unknown genotypes even if you know all of the bad points your own dogs carry? Yes, it is what we should expect. Right now, today, 33 percent of all Scottish Terriers produced have a defect of one kind or another. How could we possibly reach 33 percent if something like this is *not* happening? Is this unique to Scotties? Of course not. All breeds have a similar risk; some will be higher and some lower, but none are free of risk.

Table 11.5

Expected results if matador #1 is bred to a randomly selected Scottie bitch (no specific knowledge of the bitch's genetic status).

Disease	*His risk*	*General risk*	*Risk for at least one affected puppy in the litter*
1 Legg-Perthes	100%	4.7%	4.8%
2 Tail kinks	100%	8.4%	8.8%
3 Cataracts	100%	18.3%	19.7%
4 Scottie cramp	100%	29.3%	29.8%
			63.1%

There is a 63.1 percent chance this breeding will produce at least one puppy with one of these diseases.

Table 11.6

Expected results if matador #2 is bred to a randomly selected Scottie bitch (no specific knowledge of the bitch's genetic status).

Disease	*His risk*	*General risk*	*Risk for at least one affected puppy in the litter*
1 Undershot bite	100%	24.7%	25.8%
2 Luxated patellae	100%	19.5%	20.4%
3 Cerebellar ataxia	100%	13.0%	13.7%
4 Addison's disease	100%	37.7%	39.5%
			99.4%

There is a 99.4 percent chance that this breeding will produce at least one puppy with one of these diseases.

Table 11.7

Expected results if your bitch is bred to a randomly selected Scottie male (no specific knowledge of the genetic status of the male).

Disease	*Her risk*	*General risk*	*Risk for at least one affected puppy in the litter*
1 Umbilical hernia	Affected	15.2%	63.8%
2 Scottie cramp	33.3%	29.3%	10.3%
3 Hashimoto's disease	12.5%	37.7%	4.9%
4 Deafness	66.6%	19.5%	27.3%
			106.3%

There is essentially a 100 percent chance that you will get at least one puppy with one of these diseases.

Many people will criticize me and this book because I have taken some liberties in these matings. We *cannot* make specific predictions as I have done here if polygenic traits are involved. I know that, but there is no other way to try to show you what is happening to your dogs and, more important, there is no other way to prevent genetic disease.

I say to you that although these numbers are not perfect, breeding with knowledge is a better way to proceed than the approach most breeders are currently taking with the vast majority of dog breeds today.

Sure, Doc! That's pretty neat—literally no affected dogs in these matings you dreamed up—but what if I can't find a dog that does not carry for all of the defects that I know occur in my dogs?

What do I do then?

The most likely situation you will run into is the one you just described. You can't find the perfect mate—the "wonder dog" that will prevent any disease from occurring in a given mating. Addressing this problem is why we spent a large part of chapter 9 on prioritization. Look at your hierarchy of disagreeability and avoid those dogs that are known to carry a high risk of carrying the same genes as your dog for severe disease. In the mating between matador #2 and your bitch, there is still an 8 percent risk that each puppy produced in that mating will contract Scottie cramp. On my scale of severity, Scottie cramp is less harmful than Legg-Perthes disease, cataracts and deafness—three diseases that are unlikely to occur in this litter, because you blocked them. I am not breeding for Scottie cramp any more than you are, but I would rather take the risk for Scottie cramp than I would for Legg-Perthes, cataracts or deafness. It is just good common sense that if you have to take the risk of producing a disease, you take the risk with the mildest disease you can. Three of the twelve disorders I listed for these three dogs are what I call *nonentities* as far as disease is concerned—umbilical hernia, tail kinks and undershot bites. What you must decide is that if you must take the risk of a disease occurring, would you rather it was a tail kink or Addison's disease. Once you have selected your potential stock to produce dogs that fulfill your particular goals, select from among them breeding stock that will be likely to produce the fewest and the mildest disorders.

Well, doctor, you have shown us how to prevent disease, but how about all those carriers you are producing and sort of strewing around our precious gene pool?

I think you are screwing up our gene pool with carriers!!! What do I do with all of these carriers?

You do the same thing with these puppies that you do with the puppies you are producing right now. *You sell them!!* Isn't that a reasonable thing to do? The difference here is that you can tell the purchaser the risk this puppy has to develop a defect, what that defect is, what to look for as far as clinical signs are concerned and the possible treatment. Isn't that better than selling or buying a puppy blindly? Remember that 40 percent or so of the dogs we produce right now have a defect of some kind. Most people who set out to purchase a dog don't know what they are buying. Many people don't know what they are selling, and almost nobody is doing what needs to be done to prevent disease, because everybody is hiding the genetic propensities of their dogs from everybody it is possible to hide them from. Every time we buy, sell or breed a dog, carriers are involved, so the question becomes not whether a given dog or bitch is a carrier—it is *what do they carry?*

Let's look at what happens with these two matadors and your bitch. Remember that with polygenic traits, more than one gene is involved, but for a defect to occur, each parent must contribute at least one gene to the production of that defect. So remembering that with traits like Legg-Perthes or undershot bites, a given parent may contribute more than one gene, for discussion purposes, we are going to address the situation as though it was one gene. Further, I strongly suggest that you handle the problem as if one gene were involved, because it is better than guessing, and because the data we really need is not presently available.

Since both males are proven carriers of four traits each, they will both transmit the genes for each trait half of the time. The other half of the time, they will transmit the normal gene. So each trait has a 50:50 chance of being carried on and a 50:50 chance of dropping out in each puppy produced. So each puppy, on the average, will inherit the gene for half of the diseases its sire had. On the average, then, each puppy will inherit the genes for two diseases from its sire—not all four diseases.

Now let's look at your bitch. Since she is affected with umbilical hernia, all of her puppies will carry one gene for that defect, and they will be defined carriers for that trait. Remember: That is half of the risk your bitch had. Since she was not a proven carrier of the other three traits associated with her, each puppy she produces will have half the risk that she has to carry the trait in question. For example, her risk for deafness is 66.6 percent, so the risk for each of her puppies is 33.3 percent (she has a

50:50 chance of transmitting the trait to her puppies). Therefore, the fact is that, on the average, half of all of the diseases (except umbilical hernia) will drop out. We will not know for sure which disorders are lost and which are retained, but on the average, each puppy will carry the same number of diseases as the parents, with half the risk for each disease. (Table 11.8 summarizes the risk each puppy carries for the various disorders each parent has.)

We have to keep in mind as we go through this process that we know there are at least thirty-six genetic diseases known to occur in Scottish Terriers. I believe that if the owners of these dogs are willing to acknowledge the diseases that they know occur, they are unlikely to be dishonest about any other disease that they know is present. I believe you will be as safe as it is possible to be (and a whole lot safer than if you got no information) from any of the twenty-five other diseases that occur in the Scottish Terrier.

Table 11.8

Carrier risk of the offspring when bred to dogs of known genotype.

Matador #1	*Disease*	*His/Her risk of being a carrier*	*Puppy risk of being a carrier*
1	Legg-Perthes	100%	50%
2	Tail kinks	100%	50%
3	Cataracts	100%	50%
4	Scottie cramp	100% with bitch #1	66.7%
Matador #2			
1	Undershot bite	100%	50%
2	Luxated patellae	100%	50%
3	Cerebellar ataxia	100%	50%
4	Addison's disease	100%	50%
Your bitch			
1	Umbilical hernia	Affected	100%
2	Scottie cramp	33.5% With matador #1 66.7% With matador #2	16.8%
3	Hashimoto's disease	12.5%	6.25%
4	Deafness	66.6%	33.3%

Each puppy has a minimal or no risk for the twenty-five other Scottie traits.

What do you do with puppies from these matings?

Simple: You sell them!

But if you sell them as pets, make sure they are spayed or neutered or on a nonbreeding registration. If you sell them as breeding stock, you are morally obligated to tell the purchasers the exact status of the dogs in regard to their genetic propensities.

The last topic I want to cover in this chapter is the indirect benefits that automatically occur when you have knowledge concerning the phenotypic and carrier status of the dogs you breed. With a breed like Scotties, which average three-and-a-half to four puppies per litter, at first glance, this will not appear to be a great help. But remember that when you know the genotype of a given animal in any mating, the opposite animal is test-mated for any disease for which the specific genotype is known. This works for traits that are known to have a recessive mode of inheritance. Therefore, the bitch is test-mated for cerebellar ataxia and cataracts, and the males are test-mated for umbilical hernia and deafness. With four puppies per litter, the degree of assuredness of the homozygous state is not high (68.4 percent; see Table 5.1), but remember that the data is cumulative, and other matings by the males or the bitch may give a very high degree of assuredness.

Breeds that normally produce seven or more puppies per litter are superb sources of additional information on the genetic propensities of your breeding stock. Clearly, this information should be recorded, used and passed on to purchasers of your puppies as it accumulates.

APPENDIX 1

Genetic Disease Predisposition by Breed

In this appendix, I list 308 dog breeds. The listings of breeds were obtained from the (AKC) and (UKC) registries, articles on rare breeds published in *Dog World* (July 1996) and, in a few cases, breeds published as having specific disorders, even though they were not listed by any of the above three sources. I believe living specimens of all the breeds listed here are present in the United States at this time.

The diseases reported, as well as the breeds reported to have had affected individuals, were obtained from the forty-five books listed in the Reference section of this book, information obtained from the (OFA), the Veterinary Medical Data Program at Purdue University, cases presented at Michigan State University and those reported in approximately 1,100 research papers, beginning in 1934.

The criteria for including a disease as genetic includes any or all of the following:

- The disease has been reported as being genetic in the breed involved.
- The disease has been reported to be genetic in other breeds.
- The disease has been reported as being genetic in other species.
- The disease follows family lines, and it occurs in multiple generations of a given line.

These criteria may be considered to be very loose or minimal as requirements for categorizing a disease as genetic and may have resulted in a few errors among the diseases included. However, the goal of this book is to prevent genetic diseases in breeding kennels as well as within breeds. If there are errors here, they are on the side of preventing the spread of a disease by recognizing the disorder as being genetic or very likely to be genetic.

The criteria for including a breed as having a genetic disease are fairly straightforward. Occurrence must be reported in at least one member of the breed by an adequately qualified veterinary diagnostician, be it a clinical specialist, an endocrinologist, a pathologist or another well-trained individual. Some will say, "My gosh, you have a horrible chance of making an error here." That may well be true, but there is no doubt that the best time to stop a genetic disease is when there is just one or, at most, a few cases. It behooves us to remember that if we believe even a small part of the Hardy-Weinberg law, with recessive traits, if 1 percent of the population is affected with a genetic disease, 18 percent of the population consists of carriers, and we have a major problem on our hands.

There are 532 genetic diseases listed in this book, which are spread out among fifteen diagnostic categories. However, if you add up the number of diseases listed for each category, you'll arrive at the number 437. This difference occurs for several reasons.

First, we have diseases with one name, such as Collie Eye Anomaly, which is reported as having a recessive mode of inheritance in twelve breeds and a dominant mode of inheritance in only one breed. Obviously, if there are two modes of inheritance, the diseases cannot be identical, even though the clinical signs or characteristics are so similar that we cannot distinguish between them. This difference is more readily apparent when we examine a disorder such as Glycogenosis (Glycogen Storage Disease), in which we have diagnosed dogs as Type II (two breeds), Type III (two breeds) and Type VII (six breeds) based on enzyme and, in some cases, DNA differences. These are clearly separate diseases, although they are difficult to separate based on clinical signs alone.

Second, in veterinary medicine, we have major problems in differentiating one disease from another, very similar, disease because the disease material is almost never available at one site so that accurate comparisons can be made. An example is the dwarfisms reported under Skeletal Disease. There are eighteen separately listed Dwarfism categories that contain twenty-five breeds and a large lump at the end called "Not Further Defined," which includes fourteen breeds. In one group, Pituitary Dwarfism, eight breeds are listed as the same, based principally on the fact that lack of a growth hormone seems to be involved in the etiology. Whether the disease is identical in these eight breeds is not clear, and it is likely that only DNA analysis will allow us to resolve this point. I list Giant Schnauzer and Scottish Deerhound Congenital Hypothyroid Dwarfism separately—not because we know for certain they are different, but because we are not sure they are the same. Many will complain, saying that Congenital Hypothyroid Dwarfism should not even be categorized under Skeletal Diseases at all, since it clearly has an endocrine etiology. All I can say is that I placed the diseases in the categories I thought would be the easiest place to find if you were trying to search out a diagnosis.

Third, the number of diseases per breed varies strikingly, as you will see when you go through this appendix. There are sixty-six breeds in which no disease has been reported to occur. Every one of these sixty-six breeds falls into the rare-breed category. I would like to clearly state at this point that genetic disease does occur in these breeds, but so few specimens of the breeds are available that they are unlikely to get to a university or other veterinary practice likely to report the disease in the literature. So if a disease like Hip Dysplasia occurs in a breed like the Treeing Tennessee Brindle and the radiograph is not sent to the OFA or the disorder is not reported in the literature, it would be missed in a review such as the one I have included here.

Another problem that relates to rare breeds is that it is difficult to collect enough cases of a given disorder to generate an acceptable clinical paper. Even though enough cases actually occur, the distribution of the dogs nationwide may make it impossible to pull the cases together for a report. These breeds with "no disease" are listed in this book in the hope that an awareness of them will lead to more complete reports in the literature.

Just as there are breeds with no reported occurrence of diseases within the population, there are other breeds in which a very large number of diseases is reported.

The largest number of dogs in the United States consists of those of mixed breeding (mutts, curs, crossbreeds and so on), and as would be expected, since they contain mixtures of most, if not all, breeds, they have far and away the most diseases. These dogs are reported to have 220 diseases. In a way, it surprised me that they had so few disorders, because—since they are a mixture of all breeds—one might expect them to have all diseases of all breeds. It may be that they do have many more disorders, since they are often left out when we report diseases by specific breed.

The breed with the most diseases reported is the Poodle (all three sizes), with 145, and as you will see, there are many breeds with over 100. As you go through the list of diseases by breed, you will find that there is a strong correlation between the number of dogs in the breed and the number of diseases reported in the breed. This is not a perfect one-to-one correlation, of course, and the reasons for the correlation are just about the opposite as those for "No Disease" in the rare breeds. To my way of thinking, this is what I would expect to find. I need to add one more point in this regard. Remember that the more animals available for a mutation to occur, the more likely a mutation will occur. The diseases tend to accumulate over the years, because almost no fancy of a specific breed has tried to do anything realistic to eliminate genetic diseases or to reduce the frequency in their breed. In those few breeds where such an initiative has been undertaken, I strongly applaud the efforts of those involved.

Systems and abbreviations for disease categorization.

System	Abbreviation
1 Alimentary	AL
2 Behavior	BE
3 Cancer	CA
4 Endocrine	EN
5 Hearing, Balance	HB
6 Heart and Vascular	HV
7 Hematopoietic, Lymphatic	HL

System	Abbreviation
8 Immune	IM
9 Integumentary	IN
10 Liver, Pancreas	LP
11 Muscle	MU
12 Neurologic	NE
13 Ocular	OC
14 Reproductive	RP
15 Respiratory	RS
16 Skeletal	SK
17 Urinary	UR

Breed (Synonyms)

1. Affenpinscher

   AL:10; **EN**:5B; **HL**:1; **HV**:13; **IM**:1; **IN**:6F,52; **MU**:19; **OC**:5H,12,14,27,41B; **RP**:2; **RS**:8; **SK**:9B,20,25,31,39,51

2. Afghan Hound

   AL:13,19B; **BE**:1; **EN**:5B; **HB**:1C; **HL**:26,41C; **HV**:16,19; **IM**:6; **IN**:22,49,51B,63; **LP**:5; **MU**:1; **NE**:1,45; **OC**:5B,11E,15, 23C,26,31,38,41B,45; **RP**:6; **RS**:4,5; **SK**:7,15,20,23,30,31,41A, 41B,41D,49,65B; **UR**:5,16

3. Ainu (*Ainu Dog, Ainu Ken*)

4. Airedale Terrier

   AL:13; **BE**:1; **EN**:3,5B,8; **HL**:21,24,41C; **HV**:1,4,16,18,20, 21; **IM**:1,2,6,8,11,12,14; **IN**:6C,6F,32,37,46,51B,53B,63; **LP**:2B,5,6B; **NE**:7K,8,9,12,19B,45; **OC**:5H,11C,15,17,20,36,37B, 41B,45; **RP**:2,12; **RS**:4; **SK**:13N,20,23,41A,43,46,58,59,64,65B; **UR**:9C,13B,16

5. Akbash

   EN:5B; **NE**:19B; **SK**:20,21,46

6. Akita (*Akita Inu*)

   AL:13; **EN**:5B; **HB**:1C,2A; **HL**:16,35; **IM**:1,9,12; **IN**:47,53B; **LP**:6B; **NE**:12,27B; **OC**:5A,20,23D,33B,41B,45,52; **SK**:2,7,20,31, 41A,41D,41E; **UR**:13B

7. Alapaha Blue Blood Bulldog

8. Alaskan Malamute

   AL:13,19B; **BE**:1; **CA**:2B; **EN**:5B; **HL**:12,17,20,21; **HV**:13, 16,18,19,21; **IM**:1,2,6,7,8,14; **IN**:6C,11,32,63,66A; **LP**:3B,7; **MU**:20; **NE**:3,19B,45; **OC**:5H,11E,12,15,19,20,23D,24,27,35,38, 40,41B; **RP**:2; **SK**:13A,19B,20,23,31,36,41A,41D,46,51; **UR**:3,13B

9. Alpine Dachsbracke

10. American Bulldog

    EN:5B; **SK**:20; **UR**:1B

11. American Eskimo (*American Eskimo Dog*)

    AL:19B; **BE**:1; **EN**:5B, **HL**:1,30,36; **HV**:13; **IM**:6,8,14; **IN**:6F,22,46,53B; **NE**:19B,31; **OC**:5H,15,20,23C,26,33B,41B; **RP**:2,4; **RS**:2,4,8; **SK**:19B,20,23,31

12. American Foxhound

    AL:9; **EN**:5B; **HB**:1B,1C; **HL**:18,31; **OC**:25; **RP**:2; **RS**:2; **SK**:20,42

13. American Hairless Terrier (*Rat Terrier*)

    IN:5A; **OC**:29C; **SK**:31

14. American Pit Bull Terrier

    EN:5B; **IM**:1; **IN**:33D,66A; **SK**:9B,20,31

15. American Staffordshire Terrier

    CA:2B; **EN**:5B; **HB**:1C; **HV**:13,18; **IN**:33B,63; **OC**:15,20,37B, 41B; **RP**:2; **SK**:9B,10,20,41A,65B

16. American Water Spaniel

    IN:6D,32,37,63; **NE**:19B; **OC**:5H,41B,44B; **RP**:2,4; **SK**:9B, 13S,20,23,31

17. Anatolian Shepherd Dog (*Anatolian Karabash*)

    EN:5B; **OC**:15,20; **SK**:20,30; **UR**:13B

18. Anglo-Francais de Moyen Venerie

19. Anglo-Francais Petite Venerie

20. Appenzeller (*Appenzell Mountain Dog, Appenzeller Sennenhund*)

    SK:41A

21. Argentine Dogo (*Argentinian Mastiff*)

    EN:5B; **HB**:1C; **IM**:1; **OC**:23C,26; **SK**:20

22. Ariegeois

23. Australian Cattle Dog (*Australian Queensland Heeler*)

    BE:1; **EN**:5B; **HB**:1B; **HL**:31; **IN**:20; **LP**:6B,7; **NE**:10,18; **OC**:5H,23C,29C,36,38,41B; **SK**:20,31,41A,41C,41F

24. Australian Kelpie (*Barb*)

    EN:5B; **IM**:2; **IN**:24,49; **NE**:7A; **OC**:36,41B; **SK**:20

25. Australian Shepherd

    BE:1; **CA**:2B; **EN**:5B; **HB**:1B; **HL**:31; **HV**:13,15,16; **IM**:1,2, 6,7,15; **IN**:37,49,51B,63; **LP**:3B,6B; **NE**:8,19B; **OC**:5H,7,8A,9, 15,23C,29C,32,33B,35,36,38,41B,43,44B,45,52; **RP**:2; **SK**:3,9B, 13B,13S,20,31,41A,46

26. Australian Terrier

    AL:19B; **BE**:1; **CA**:2B; **EN**:1,5B; **HV**:13; **IM**:1,2,7; **IN**:39, 51B; **LP**:3B,6B; **NE**:26; **OC**:5H,41B,44B; **RP**:2; **SK**:9B,20,25,28,31

27. Azawakh

    EN:5B

28. Barbet

29. Basenji (*Congo Dog*)

    AL:4,7,17,18,22; **EN**:5B; **HL**:31,36; **IN**:37,63; **NE**:19B,27C; **OC**:5H,8B,11E,13,15,20,38,41B,52; **RP**:2; **SK**:7,13S,20,40; **UR**:5,11

30. Basset Artesian Normand (*Bassett Artesian Normand*)

    IM:1; **SK**:61

31. Basset Bleu de Gascogne

32. Basset Fauve de Bretagne

33. Basset Hound

    AL:10,13,15; **BE**:1; **CA**:2B; **EN**:1,5B,8; **HL**:2,41C; **HV**:6,15, 16,18,19,20,21; **IM**:1,3,6,8; **IN**:6B,6D,8,12,15,37,38,51B,52, 63; **LP**:7; **NE**:19B,25,39,40; **OC**:5H,11E,14,17,20,21B,23B,23D, 27,29C,38,41B,42; **RP**:2; **RS**:5; **SK**:4,9B,19B,20,21,23,28,30,31, 41B,46,49,50,62,65B; **UR**:1B

34. Bavarian Mountain Hound (*Bayrischer Gebirgsschweisshund*)

35. Beagle

    AL:10,19B,21; **BE**:1; **CA**:2B; **EN**:5B; **HB**:1A,2A; **HL**:7,10,12, 20,24,36; **HV**:6,16,19,21; **IM**:1,2,6,9,10,12,14,15; **IN**:6A,8,12, 15,24,25,26,37,47,49,51B,63,66B; **LP**:3B,5,7; **NE**:4,7B,19B,23A, 25,27C,30,39,41,45,60; **OC**:5A,5H,6C,8A,11E,14,15,16,17,20, 21B,23E,26,27,29C,33B,34,35,37B,38,41B,42,44B,45,49; **RP**:2,4, 5,10; **RS**:2,8; **SK**:6,7,9B,13C,16,20,23,27,31,37,44,46,58,65B; **UR**:2,9A,12,13B,16

36. Bearded Collie

    EN:5B,8; **HV**:7,13,18,41C; **IM**:1,11,15; **IN**:8,12,47,52,53B, 63; **MU**:5; **NE**:19B; **OC**:5H,11E,20,27,41B,45; **RP**:2; **SK**:9B,20,31, 35B,41A,45B,46,64

37. Beauçeron

    EN:5B; **IM**:1; **SK**:20

38. Bedlington Terrier

    CA:2B, **EN**:5B; **IM**:1,15; **LP**:2A; **NE**:19B; **OC**:5H,15,20,23D, 26,27,33B,41B,44A,45,53; **SK**:20,23,43; **UR**:2,3,13B

39. Belgian Griffon

    OC:41B

40. Belgian Laekenois

    EN:5B, **SK**:20,41A

41. Belgian Malinois

    AL:13; **EN**:5B; **NE**:19B,58A; **OC**:5H,36,41B; **SK**:20,41A

42. Belgian Sheepdog (*Belgian Shepherd Dog, Belgian Groenendael*)

    EN:5B; **HV**:18; **IM**:15; **IN**:15,64; **LP**:4,6B; **MU**:19; **NE**:19B, 27C; **OC**:5H,36,41B,46; **RP**:1; **SK**:20,41A

43. Belgian Tervuren

    EN:5B; **HL**:28; **HV**:1; **IM**:1; **IN**:64; **LP**:6B; **NE**:19B; **OC**:5H, 35,36,41B; **RP**:1; **SK**:20,41A,64

44. Bergamasco (*Bergamese Shepherd*)

45. Berger de Picard

46. Berger de Pyrenees

    EN:5B; **NE**:27C

47. Bernese Mountain Do (*Bernese Sennenhund*)

    AL:13,15,19B; **BE**:1,3; **CA**:1A,2A; **EN**:5B,8; **HL:**10; **HV**:11, 13,18,20; **IM**:1,2,8,10,14,15; **IN**:6B,47,51B,53B,56,63; **LP**:1,7; **NE**:7K,19B,28,31,35A; **OC**:5H,16,17,20,35,41B,52; **RP**:2; **SK**:7, 9B,12,20,21,23,24,31,41A,41D,46; **UR**:10A

48. Bichon Frise

    BE:1; **EN**:5B,8; **HB**:1C; **HL**:21,41C; **HV**:13,21; **IM**:1,2,11, 15; **IN**:15,37,47,49,63,64; **LP**:6B; **NE**:19B,31,60; **OC**:5H,11E,17, 20,23C,26,27,41B,42; **RP**:2; **RS**:6; **SK**:9B,12,20,23,25,28,30,31, 35B,40,41A,45B,64; **UR**:22C

49. Billy

    OC:14

50. Black and Tan Coonhound (*American Black and Tan Coonhound*)

    AL:13; **CA**:2B; **EN**:5B; **HL**:21; **IM**:1,6,14; **IN**:37,49,63; **NE**:19B,31,38; **OC**:5H,6C,14,17,20,23C,29C,33B,41B; **RP**:2; **RS**:4; **SK**:20,31

51. Black Forest Hound

52. Black Mouth Cur

53. Black Russian Terrier

54. Bloodhound

    AL:13,15; **EN**:5B; **NE**:19B,57E; **OC**:17,20,21B,27,30,38,42; **RP**:2; **SK**:7,20,41B,59

55. Bluetick Coonhound

    AL:13; **EN**:5B; **HL**:31; **HV**:11,16; **IM**:1; **LP**:7; **NE**:19B,25, 38; **OC**:5H,20; **RP**:2; **RS**:4; **SK**:20,34

56. Bolognese

    BE:1

57. Border Collie

    AL:16; **EN**:5B; **HB**:1B; **HL**:3,18; **HV**:10,13,18; **IN**:8; **LP**:4, 6B,7; **MU**:1,11; **NE**:7C,10,18,19B,37,46,54B; **OC**:5H,8A,11E,23C, 27,29A,36,38,41B,44B,45; **RP**:2; **RS**:6; **SK**:10,20,36,41A,41D, 41E,50,64; **UR**:2

58. Border Terrier

    EN:2,5B; **HL**:38; **HV**:4,14,16, 21; **IN**:8; **LP**:2B; **NE**:4,48; **OC**:5H,14,41B,44B; **RP**:2; **SK**:6,10,19B,20,25,31,64

59. Borzoi (*Russian Wolfhound*)

    AL:13; **BE**:1; **EN**:5A,20; **HL**:10,25,28,30; **OC**:4,5H,33B,35, 38,41B,44A; **RS**:5; **SK**:7,20,21,35B,41E,65A

60. Boston Terrier

    AL:1,10,19B,23; **CA**:2B; **EN**:4,5B; **HB**:1C; **HL**:1,31; **HV**:7, 13,15,18,20; **IM**:1,6; **IN**:6B,6D,6E,22,33B,37,49,63; **NE**:7K,8, 9,18,19B,31; **OC**:1,5A,5G,11E,12,13,15,16,18,21A,22,23C,26,27, 29C,41B,42,48,50; **RP**:1,2,5,13; **RS**:7,9; **SK**:9B,10,13S,19B,20, 25,30,31,53,58,64,65B; **UR**:7,17

61. Bouvier des Flandres (*Bouvier*)

    AL:10,13,14,19B; **EN**:5B; **HB**:1C; **HV**:18; **IM**:1; **IN**:6C,6F, 63; **LP**:6B; **MU**:2; **NE**:19B; **OC**:5H,20,23B,33B,37B,38; **RS**:4; **SK**:9B,20,41A;45B,64; **UR**:2

62. Boxer

    AL:5,10,13,19B,23; **BE**:1; **CA**:2B; **EN**:4,5B; **HB**:1C; **HL**:11, 12,28,34,40,41C; **HV**:1,4,6,7,12,13,15,16,18,19,20,21; **IM**:1,6, 15; **IN**:2,6C,6F,21,24,32,37,48,49,63; **MU**:13; **NE**:5,19B,36,37, 48,54B; **OC**:5H,6C,11E,12,15,16,17,18,20,23D,27,37B,38,41B,42, 50; **RP**:2,13; **RS**:9; **SK**:7,9B,10,13S,20,21,23,31,36,41D,41E, 45B,49,50,54,58,59,60,64,65B; **UR**:1B,13B,22C

63. Boykin Spaniel

    EN:5D, **HV**:16; **SK**:20,31,41A

64. Bracco Italiano

    HL:41C

65. Braque D'Auvergne

    SK:20

66. Braque de Bourbannais (*Braque du Bourbonnais*)

    SK:20

67. Braque Français de Grand Taille

68. Braque Français de Petite Taille

69. Braque Saint-Germain

70. Briard

    AL:13,14; **EN**:5B; **IN**:49; **OC**:5H,6A,41B,47; **SK**:20,41A; **UR**:2,12,13B

71. Briquet Griffon Vendéen

72. Brittany (*Brittany Spaniel*)

    EN:5B; **HL**:20,24; **HV**:13; **IM**:4,7; **IN**:37,63; **LP**:6B; **NE**:7D, 19B,53,57A; **OC**:5H,17,23D,26,29E,41B; **RP**:2; **SK**:7,20,31,35B, 41A,41D,45B,64; **UR**:7

73. Brussels Griffon (*Belgian Griffon*)

    EN:5B; **HL**:27; **IN**:22; **OC**:5H,11E,12,15,16,41B; **SK**:9B, 20,31,32,45B

74. Bull Terrier

    BE:1; **CA**:2B; **EN**:5B; **HB**:1A; **HV**:11,18; **IM**:1,6,16; **IN**:4, 16,33B,37,63; **LP**:2B; **NE**:7K,8,32; **OC**:3,17,20,21A,27,29C,41B, 42; **RS**:3,4; **SK**:7,9B,10,20,41A,41C,41D,41E,41F; **UR**:9B,10B

    Bulldog (see **English Bulldog**)

75. Bullmastiff

    AL:13; **EN**:5B; **HL**:1; **HV**:4,16; **IN**:64; **NE**:7E,8,19B; **OC**:15, 17,20,21B,23C,38,41B,44B; **SK**:6,9B,10,20,28,41B,45B,60,65B

76. Cairn Terrier

    BE:1; **EN**:5B; **HB**:1C; **HL**:1,20,21,36,41C; **HV**:8; **IM**:1,6,11; **IN**:33B,37,39,63; **LP**:2B,3B,6A,7; **MU**:17; **NE**:7K,19B,25,31,43, 57G; **OC**:5H,16,20,23G,27,29C,39,41B,44B; **RP**:1,2; **SK**:1,9B,10, 12,20,25,31,35B,41A,45B,46,64; **UR**:1B,2,8

77. Canaan Dog

    EN:5B; **NE**:19B; **OC**:41B; **RP**:2; **SK**:20,41A

78. Canadian Eskimo Dog

    EN:5B

79. Cane Corso

    EN:5B; **SK**:13N,20

80. Carolina Dog

81. Catahoula Leopard Dog (*Louisiana Catahula Leopard Dog, Leopard Cur*)

    EN:5B; **HB**:1C; **LP**:3B; **OC**:5H; **SK**:10,20,41D,46

82. Caucasian Mountain Dog (*Caucasion Ovcharka*)

    SK:41A

83. Cavalier King Charles Spaniel

    AL:2,10,19B; **EN**:4,5B; **HL**:6,41C; **HV**:1,11,13,16,20; **IM**:1, 8,14; **IN**:6B,22,24,25,33A,63; **LP**:3B,5,6B; **MU**:13,14,16; **NE**:19B,20,31;

OC:5C,5H,11D,14,15,20,27,33B,37B,38,41B,44B, 45; **RP**:2; **SK**:9B,20,28,31,32,45B,49,64; **UR**:10C

84. Cesky Fousek

    SK:20

85. Cesky Terrier (*Bohemian Terrier*)

    EN:5B

86. Chart Polski

87. Chesapeake Bay Retriever

    AL:13; **BE**:3; **EN**:5B; **HL**:41C; **IN**:6C,8,37,63; **MU**:11; **NE**:7K,14,16,19B; **OC**:5D,6C,15,20,21B,41B,44B,45; **RS**:4; **SK**:7,20,31,41A,41D,41F,45B,64

88. Chien d'Artois

89. Chien Français Blanc et Noir

90. Chien Français Blanc et Orange

91. Chien Français Tricolore

92. Chihuahua

    EN:5B,8; **HL**:8,20,30; **HV**:7,11,13,16,18; **IM**:6; **IN**:6B,6D, 6E,8,37,63; **NE**:10,27D,31,46,56; **OC**:11E,18,20,23D,27,29C,41B, 42,50; **RP**:2; **RS**:6,8; **SK**:9B,17,23,25,28,30,31,32,35B,37,38, 40,41D,45D,49,50,64; **UR**:1B

93. Chinese Crested

    EN:5B; **IN**:5B; **LP**:6B; **SK**:13S,35B,45B,64

94. Chinese Foo Dog

95. Chinese Shar-Pei

    AL:4,11,12,14,15,19B; **EN**:5B; **HL**:15; **HV**:18; **IM**:1,6,12; **IN**:18,28,37,38,51B,54,63,65; **OC**:15,20,26,30,36,41B,42; **RS**:6,7; **SK**:9,20,31,41A,41D,64; **UR**:16

96. Chinook

    EN:5B; **SK**:20

97. Chow Chow

    AL:10,13,15; **EN**:1,5B,8; **HB**:1C; **HV**:16; **IM**:1,12; **IN**:6B, 6C,11,32,44,47,53B,61,64; **LP**:3B,5; **MU**:16; **NE**:4,7K,8,19B,31, 35B; **OC**:3,5A,5H,17,20,23C,23D,27,38,41B,52; **RS**:1,6; **SK**:6,20, 30,31,41A,41E,65B; **UR**:13B,22C

98. Clumber Spaniel

    EN:5B; **MU**:13; **NE**:19B; **OC**:15,17,20,27,30; **SK**:20,23,35B, 45B,64

99. Cocker Spaniel (*American Cocker Spaniel*)

    AL:5,9,10,19B,21; **BE**:1,3; **EN**:5B; **HB**:1C,2B; **HL**:1,13,21, 23,31,32,34; **HV**:6,7,11,13,15,16,17,18; **IM**:1,2,6,8,9,12,15; **IN**:8,9,12,15,21,28,33B,37,38,41B,44,47,48,53B,63,65; **LP**:1, 4,6B,7; **MU**:17; **NE**:7K,10,11,19B,27C,31,36,44,45; **OC**:5A,5F, 6C,11B,12,14,15,16,17,18,20,23B,23D,26,27,29C,30,33B,34,35, 38,41A,42,44B,45,50,51; **RP**:2,4,8,10; **SK**:1,6,7,9B,11,13D,17, 20,23,25,27,30,31,41B,41D,45B,52,59,62,64,65B; **UR**:13A,22C

100. Collie

    AL:3,13,16,20; **BE**:1; **EN**:5B; **HB**:1B,2B; **HL**:4,10,20,25; **HV**:13, 18,21; **IM**:6,7,9,15; **IN**:9,20,26,33B,36,37,46,47,48,49,50,53B,58,63, 64; **LP**:5,6B; **MU**:13;**NE**:7F,14,16,19B,46,53,54B,56,57G;**OC**:3,5H, 6C,8A,11D,11E,14,15,19,20,25,27,32,33B,35,38,41A,44B,50; **SK**:7,13S,20,21,30,31,33,34,41E,45B,48,54,64,97; **UR**:2,13B

101. Coton de Tulear

    EN:5B

102. Crossbreeds (*Mixed Breed, Mutt, Cur, Street Dog, Pound Dog, Pariah Dog, Pack Dog, House Dog*)

    AL:10,12,13,14,16,19,20,23; **BE**:1; **CA**:2B; **EN**:4,5B,6,8; **HB**:1A,1C,2B; **HL**:1,8,12,20,21,24,28,30,31,36,41C; **HV**:1,2,4, 6,7,11,13,15,16,18,19,20,21; **IM**:1,2,6,7,8,9,10,11,12,14,15; **IN**:2,3,6B,6C,6D,6E,6F,8,9,10,11,12,15,17,20,22,24,29,32,33B, 37,38,44,46,47,48,49,51B,52,53B,58,63,64,66; **LP**:1,2B,3B,4,5, 6B,7; **MU**:1,5,11,15; **NE**:4,7K,8,9,10,12,14,16,18,19B,23A,23B, 26,27D,31,33,36,38,39,42A,45,46,56,57E,57G,58A,60; **OC**:3,5H, 6C,8A,11E,12,14,15,16,17,19,20,21,22,23C,23D,25,26,27,29C, 30,31,33B,35,36,37B,38,40,41B,42,44B,45,50,51; **RP**:1,2,5,7,8, 11,13; **RS**:2,4,7,9; **SK**:1,5,7,9B,10,12,13S,17,19B,20,21,23,27, 28,30,31,32,34,35B,36,38,40,41A,41B,41D,41E,45B,46,49,50,58, 59,61,64,65B; **UR**:1B,2,5,7,11,12,13B,14,20,21,22C

103. Curly-Coated Retriever

    EN:4,5B; **HL**:41C; **IN**:6C,8; **OC**:5H,15,17,20,27,38,41B; **SK**:20

104. Dachshund

    AL:2,13,18,19B,25; **BE**:1; **CA**:2B; **EN**:4,5B; **HB**:1B,1C; **HL**:41C; **HV**:15,17,18; **IM**:1,5,6,8,12,15; **IN**:1,6B,6C,6D,6E,6F,

8,12,23,24,32,37,39,44,46,47,48,49,51B,53B,63,64; **LP**:1,3B, 6B,7; **MU**:8,16; **NE**:10,12,19B,45,54A,57G,60; **OC**:5H,8A,11E,12, 14,15,16,18,20,23D,25,26,27,29C,33B,35,36,38,40,41B,50,52; **RP**:2,3; **SK**:9B,13E,19B,20,23,25,30,31,41B,41D,44,45B,59,64, 65B; **UR**:1B,13B,22C

105. Dalmatian

AL:16,19B; **BE**:1; **EN**:5B; **HB**:1A; **HV**:6,17,18; **IM**:1,6,12; **IN**:19,24,37,46,53B,63; **LP**:3B; **MU**:7,17,20; **NE**:10,13,25,35C, 45,56,58B; **OC**:14,15,17,20,23D,25,33B,36,41B; **RS**:4,6; **SK**:20, 21,41C,41D,45B,58,64,65B; **UR**:2,20,22D

106. Dandie Dinmont Terrier

EN:4,5B,8; **LP**:6B; **OC**:5H,12,20,23D,27,29C,38; **SK**:10,15, 20,23,30,31,32

107. Danish Broholmer

108. Deutsche Bracke

109. Doberman Pinscher

AL:13; **BE**:1; **CA**:1B; **EN**:5B; **HB**:1C,2A; **HL**:5,41A; **HV**:1,5, 6,7,11,15,20; **IM**:1,2,6,9,12,14; **IN**:2,3,6B,6C,6F,9,10,22,33B, 41,45B,47,48,51B,53B,58,64,66B; **LP**:1,3B,5,6B,7; **MU**:4,5, 11,12; **NE**:4,17,18,45,53,54B; **OC**:5H,14,19,20,21B,31,33B,37A, 38,41B,43,44B,45; **RP**:10,14; **RS**:6; **SK**:1,5,7,8,10,19B,20,21, 27,28,31,34,35A,41A,41D,41E,45B,46,47,49,58,64,65A; **UR**:10E, 12,21

110. Dogue de Bordeaux

EN:5B; **IN**:29; **OC**:17,20; **SK**:20

111. Drentse Patrijshond (*Drentse Partijshond*)

AL:7; **HL**:17

112. Drever

113. Dunker

HB:1C

114. Dutch Kooiker Dog

NE:1

115. Dutch Shepherd

LP:6B; **SK**:41A

116. East Siberian Laika

117. English Bulldog (*Bulldog*)

    AL:10,13,14,15,21,23; **CA**:2B; **EN**:5B; **HB**:1A; **HL**:1,12,20,28; **HV**:11,15,16,18,19,21; **IM**:1,6; **IN**:2,6C,16,32,38,52,63; **NE**:18,31,56; **OC**:5H,14,15,16,17,20,22,27,38,42,44B,50; **RP**:1,2,3; **RS**:4,7,8,9; **SK**:1,9B,10,11,19B,20,30,31,40,41A,41D,53,55,58,60; **UR**:1B,2,13B,17,18,21,22C,22D

118. English Cocker Spaniel

    EN:5B; **HB**:1B,2B; **HL**:11,20,21; **HV**:4,6,16; **IM**:1; **IN**:37; **LP**:1,6B; **NE**:10; **OC**:5A,5H,6C,15,17,20,23B,23D,26,27,29C,30,33B,35,38,41A,42,44B; **RP**:2,10; **RS**:4; **SK**:6,20,31,45B,57,64; **UR**:10D

119. English Coonhound

    AL:19B; **NE**:38; **OC**:38

120. English Foxhound

    EN:5B; **HB**:1B; **HL**:31,38; **HV**:4; **IN**:51B; **LP**:1; **NE**:30; **SK**:20,45B,64

121. English Pointer (*Pointer*)

    AL:13; **BE**:1,2; **EN**:5B,8; **HB**:1C; **HV**:18; **IM**:1,6,15; **IN**:3,8,12,22,39,63; **LP**:1; **MU**:11; **NE**:19B,37,54A,57B; **OC**:5H,6C,11E,17,20,21B,33B,36,41B; **RS**:6; **SK**:7,9B,13F,14,20,21,41B,41D,41E,46,64

122. English Setter

    AL:16,20; **EN**:5B; **HB**:1A,2B; **HL**:9,20,30; **HV**:18; **IM**:1,6; **IN**:10,24,37,63; **LP**:5,6B; **NE**:10,23B,36; **OC**:5H,6C,14,17,20,21B,26,27,30,38,41B,42; **RS**:6; **SK**:10,20,31,41A,41D,45B,64

123. English Shepherd

    EN:5B; **SK**:20

124. English Springer Spaniel (*Springer Spaniel*)

    AL:9,13; **BE**:1,3; **CA**:1B; **EN**:5B; **HB**:1C; **HL**:14,20,32,41C; **HV**:7,13,14,18,21; **IM**:6; **IN**:6C,24,33B,35,38,41,44,51B,53B,63; **LP**:1,3B; **MU**:11; **NE**:7K,12,19B,22,23A,27C,35D,45; **OC**:5H,6A,11E,15,16,17,18,20,23D,27,30,33B,35,36,38,40,41A,44A,45; **RS**:4,6; **SK**:7,20,23,41A,41D; **UR**:2

125. English Toy Spaniel

    EN:5B, **HV**:13; **IN**:63; **LP**:3B; **OC**:5H,11E,44B; **SK**:9B,20,31,40,64

126. Entlebucher (*Entelbucher*)

    SK:20,41A

127. Epagneul Bleu de Picardie

128. Epagneul Picard

129. Epagneul Pont-Audemer

130. Estonian Hound

131. Estrella Mountain Dog (*Estrela Mountain Dog*)

132. Eurasier

133. Fell Terrier (*Patterdale Terrier*)

134. Field Spaniel

    EN:5B; **IM**:1; **IN**:6C,41; **NE**:19B; **OC**:5H,14,15,17,20,41B, 44B,45; **SK**:20

135. Fila Brasileiro

    EN:5B; **IM**:7; **OC**:20; **RP**:13; **SK**:20,41A

136. Finnish Hound

137. Finnish Lapphund

    HL:28; **OC**:23D; **SK**:20; **UR**:1B

138. Finnish Spitz

    AL:19B; **EN**:5B,8; **HL**:37; **HV**:8,16; **IM**:1,7,14; **IN**:3,47; **LP**:3B; **NE**:19B,60; **OC**:5B,8A,15,20,22,23D,27,41B; **RP**:2; **RS**:2, 8; **SK**:9B,13N,20,31; **UR**:16

139. Flat-Coated Retriever

    AL:19B; **EN**:5B; **HV**:21; **NE**:19B,30; **OC**:5H,6C,11E,16,17, 20,23C,38,41B; **SK**:20,21,31,41A,59

140. Fox Terrier

    AL:12,19A; **BE**:1; **CA**:1B,2B; **EN**:2,5B; **HB**:1C,2B; **HV**:7,15, 16,18,19,21; **IM**:1,15; **IN**:17,37,53B,63; **LP**:2B; **MU**:17; **NE**:7K, 8,12,19B,29,41,57G; **OC**:5H,11E,12,15,20,23D,29B,29C,38,41B, 50; **RP**:2,5; **SK**:7,9B,20,25,31,32,39,42,45B,49,50,64,65B; **UR**:2

141. French Bulldog

    AL:5,10; **EN**:5B, **HB**:1C, **HL**:1,20,21; **HV**:16; **IM**:1; **IN**:6C, 6F,15,38; **NE**:7K,19B; **OC**:5H,15,20,29C; **RP**:2,7; **SK**:6,9B,13G, 19B,20,23,31,41B,55,58,61

142. French Spaniel (*Epagneul Français*)

    SK:20

143. German Longhaired Pointer

    SK:20

144. German Pinscher

    EN:5B

145. German Shepherd Dog

    AL:4,6,12,13,16,19B,20,24,25; **BE**:1; **EN**:5B,7,8; **HB**:1C, 2B; **HL**:20,21,31,41C; **HV**:6,9,11,13,15,16,18,19,20,21; **IM**:1, 2,6,7,8,9,12,15; **IN**:3,9,17,22,24,30,31,35,44,47,48,51B,53B, 58,59,62,63,64,66B; **LP**:1,3B,5,6B,7; **MU**:1,8,10,12,18; **NE**:6, 7K,12,14,18,19B,24,27A,27B,57C; **OC**:5B,6C,8A,11E,14,15,17, 20,21B,23C,26,27,29C,30,33B,35,36,37B,38,41B,44B,45,52; **RP**:1,2,9,10; **SK**:5,7,9B,10,13N,19B,20,21,23,26,27,28,34,35B, 36,41A,41B,41D,41E,45B,46,49,50,58,59,63,64,65B; **UR**:1B,6,7, 13B,16,19,22C

146. German Shorthaired Pointer

    AL:13; **EN**:5B,8; **HL**:14,15,20,21,28,39,41C; **HV**:18; **IM**:1,6,7,10; **IN**:2,3,6C,39,63,66B; **NE**:23B,54B; **OC**:5H,6C,11E, 20,21A,21B,25,26,41B,48; **RP**:2,10; **SK**:12,19A,20,21,31,35B, 41D,45A,46,58,64

147. German Spaniel (*Deutscher Wachtelhund*)

    OC:15

148. German Wirehaired Pointer

    EN:5B; **HL**:41C; **IN**:6C,32; **OC**:5H,20,44B; **SK**:7,10,20,41A, 41D

149. Giant Schnauzer

    AL:8; **EN**:5B, **HL**:41C; **HV**:16,18,20; **IM**:1; **IN**:63,64; **NE**:19B,45; **OC**:5H,23B,41B,44B; **RP**:2; **SK**:9B,13H,13N,20,41A, 45B,64

150. Glen of Imaal Terrier

    EN:5B; **IN**:6F; **OC**:20; **SK**:20

151. Golden Retriever

    AL:13,16,18; **BE**:3; **CA**:1B,2B; **EN**:5B,8; **HL**:1,7,41C; **HV**:6,11, 16,18; **IM**:1,6,9,12; **IN**:3,17,22,24,29,33B,37,39,51B,53B,56,

63,64; **LP**:1,4,6B,7; **MU**:15,20; **NE**:7K,8,10,12,19B,34,47,53, 56,58A; **OC**:1,5A,5D,6A,11E,12,14,15,16,17,19,20,23D,26,27, 35,38,41A,44B,48,52; **RP**:2,7,8,9; **RS**:2,4,6; **SK**:5,7,9B,10,13S, 20,21,27,31,33,34,35B,41A,41C,41D,41F,45B,46,64,65B; **UR**:2,13B

152. Gordon Setter

    AL:13; **EN**:5B; **IM**:6; **IN**:8,12,39; **NE**:7G,19B; **OC**:5H,20,27, 31,41A,44B; **SK**:20,21,41A

153. Grand Anglo-Français

154. Grand Bassett Griffon Vendéen

    EN:5B; **SK**:36

155. Grand Bleu de Gascogne

156. Grand Gascon-Saintongeois

    HV:6

157. Grand Griffon Vendéen

    UR:2

158. Great Dane

    AL:12,13,15,19B; **BE**:1; **EN**:5B,8; **HB**:1B; **HL**:28,41C; **HV**:6, 11,13,15,18,20; **IM**:6; **IN**:2,3,6B,6C,9,37,48,63,66B; **LP**:5; **MU**:3,16; **NE**:7K,19B,57E; **OC**:5H,15,17,19,20,21B,23D,24,25,31, 33B,38,41B,43,44B; **RP**:1,2; **SK**:7,10,12,20,21,24,36,41A,41B, 41D,41E,45B,46,49,64,65A,65B; **UR**:1B,13B

159. Great Pyrenees (*Pyrenean Mountain Dog*)

    AL:15; **BE**:1; **EN**:5B, **HB**:1A; **HL**:14,18; **HV**:18; **IN**:39,63; **NE**:5,29,54B; **OC**:5H,17,20,31,35,38,41B; **RP**:2; **SK**:9B,13I,20, 31,41B,41D,45B,46,59,63,64,65B; **UR**:13B

160. Greater Swiss Mountain Dog

    AL:13,15; **BE**:1; **HL**:41C; **OC**:15; **SK**:20,41A,41D,46,64

161. Greenland Dog

162. Greyhound

    AL:12,13,19B,25; **EN**:5B; **HB**:1A; **HL**:41C; **HV**:7,15,20; **IN**:6B,6D,14,24,34; **MU**:1,6,11; **OC**:5H,11E,15,29C,35,36,37B, 38,41B,44B; **RP**:2; **SK**:7,20,21,41D,41E,54,56,58

163. Griffon Fauve de Bretagne (*Griffon Fauve de Bretagne*)

    SK:31

164. Griffon Nivernais

165. Hamiltonstovare

166. Hanoverian Hound

 RP:11

167. Harrier

 EN:5B; **IN**:37; **NE**:7K,30; **SK**:20,64; **UR**:2

168. Havanese

 EN:5B; **IM**:14; **LP**:7; **OC**:5H,15,27,38,40,41B; **SK**:31

169. Hovawart

 HV:18; **IN**:53B; **LP**:6B; **RP**:2; **SK**:20

170. Ibizan Hound

 AL:10; **EN**:5B; **HB**:1C; **HV**:4; **LP**:2B; **NE**:19B; **OC**:5H,31, 44B; **RP**:2; **SK**:20,35B,45B,60,64

171. Iceland Dog

172. Inca Hairless Dog

 IN:5B

173. Irish Red and White Setter

 SK:20

174. Irish Setter

 AL:12,13,15,16,19B,20,26; **BE**:1; **EN**:5B,8; **HL**:5,20,27, 41C; **HV**:11,15,20; **IM**:1,2,6,9; **IN**:3,6B,6C,22,33B,51B,53B,63; **LP**:5,6B,7; **MU**:9; **NE**:7K,8,19B,41,43,45,50; **OC**:5H,6A,11E,12, 15,17,19,20,21B,26,29C,33B,35,37B,38,41A,52; **RS**:4; **SK**:6,7, 9B,10,19B,20,21,29,36,41B,41C,41D,41F,45B,46,49,59,61,62,64, 65B; **UR**:1B,2

175. Irish Terrier

 EN:5B; **IN**:129; **LP**:6B; **MU**:10,15,16,19; **OC**:33B,41A; **RP**:2; **UR**:1B

176. Irish Water Spaniel

 EN:5B; **IM**:1; **IN**:6C,8,15; **OC**:5H,20,38,41B; **SK**:20,41A,64

177. Irish Wolfhound

 AL:13; **EN**:5B,6; **HL**:41C; **HV**:4; **LP**:6B,7; **OC**:5H,20,21B, 37B,41B,45; **SK**:7,20,21,41B,41D,41E,49,65B; **UR**:2,13B

178. Italian Greyhound

 AL:19B; **BE**:1; **EN**:5B; **HB**:1C; **HV**:15; **IM**:1; **IN**:6B,6C,6D, 6E; **NE**:19B; **OC**:5H,11E,23C,35,41B; **RP**:2; **SK**:9B,31,45B,64

179. Jack Russell Terrier

 EN:5B, **HB**:1C; **HL**:13; **IN**:8,33B,47,63; **MU**:13,17; **NE**:7K, 9,12,19B,29,46,54B; **OC**:11E,15,16,23D,27,29B; **SK**:20,25,31, 35B,64; **UR**:2

180. Jagdterrier

 IN:24

181. Japanese Chin

 EN:5B; **HV**:11; **OC**:5H,12,15,41B; **RP**:2; **SK**:13S,19B,20,28, 30,31

182. Japanese Pointer

 NE:23B

183. Japanese Retriever

 NE:10

184. Japanese Spaniel

 NE:23B; **SK**:28,30,31

185. Kai Dog

 EN:5B

186. Karelian Bear Dog (*Carelian Bear Dog*)

 HB:1C; **SK**:13N,20

187. Keeshond

 CA:1B; **EN**:1,4,5B; **HL**:41C; **HV**:11,13,16,18,19,21; **IM**:1; **IN**:11,24,32,63; **LP**:3A; **NE**:19A,19B; **OC**:5H,6C,16,23F,35,41B; **SK**:20,31,41A,41D,45B,64; **UR**:3,13B

188. Kerry Blue Terrier

 BE:1; **EN**:5B; **HL**:14,21; **IM**:1,2; **IN**:21,29,57; **LP**:1; **MU**:5; **NE**:7H,14; **OC**:3,5H,15,17,20,27,30,41B,50; **RP**:2,4,10; **SK**:10, 20,31,41B

189. Komondor

 AL:13; **EN**:5B; **IM**:1; **IN**:63; **MU**:5; **RS**:2; **SK**:20,35B,41A,64

190. Krasky Ovcar

191. Kromfohrländer

192. Kuvasz

AL:13; **EN**:5B; **HB**:1C; **HL**:41C; **OC**:5H,20; **RP**:2; **SK**:20,21,41A,41B,45B,46,64

193. Kyi-Leo

EN:5B; **IM**:1; **SK**:31

194. Labrador Retriever

AL:12,13,16,19B,20; **BE**:1; **CA**:2B; **EN**:5B,6,8; **HB**:1C; **HL**:20,21,28,41C; **HV**:2,6,13,18,20; **IM**:1,2,6,9; **IN**:3,15,17,22,29,33B,39,47,51B,53B,56,63,65,66B; **LP**:1,3B,5,6B,7; **MU**:7,10,11,16; **NE**:6,7I,8,12,16,18,19B,21,45,56,58B; **OC**:5D,6B,15,16,17,19,20,23D,27,29C,31,33B,37B,38,41A,44A,44B,45,47; **RP**:2,9; **RS**:2,4; **SK**:5,7,9B,10,13J,13M,20,21,27,31,32,35B,36,39,41A,41B,41C,41D,41E,41F,46,50,54,59,63,65B; **UR**:1B,2,5,13B

195. Lakeland Terrier

BE:1; **EN**:5B; **HL**:41C; **OC**:5H,15,23C,23D,29C,33B,38,41B; **RP**:2; **SK**:6,18,20,23,25,41B,45B,64; **UR**:2

196. Large Münsterländer

LP:4; **OC**:5D; **SK**:35B; **UR**:1B

197. Large Spanish Hound

198. Leonberger

EN:4,5B,8; **RP**:2; **RS**:4; **SK**:20,41A,41D

199. Lhasa Apso

AL:23; **EN**:4,5B; **HL**:25,41C; **HV**:20; **IM**:1,2; **IN**:15,22,32,37,53B,58,63; **NE**:19B,27D,31,41; **OC**:5H,11E,12,14,15,16,20,22,27,28,30,36,41B,42,50,51; **SK**:20,23,27,31,35B,37,45B,64; **UR**:2,13A,22A

200. Löwchen

EN:5B; **OC**:5H,41B; **SK**:25,31

201. Lundehund

AL:4,7,18,22

202. Lurcher

NE:35E

203. Maltese

    AL:23; **EN**:5B,8; **HB**:1A; **HV**:11,13,20; **IN**:22,53B,63; **LP**:6B; **NE**:19B,27D,31,49,60; **OC**:15,23D,26,41B,44B,50; **RP**:2; **RS**:8; **SK**:9B,20,31,35B,37,40,41D,45B,64

204. Manchester Terrier

    EN:5B; **HL**:41A; **IN**:6D,24,37,63; **LP**:3B; **NE**:8,19B,31; **OC**:5H,23C,29C,41B; **SK**:9B,20,25,31,35B

205. Maremma Sheepdog

    SK:20,31; **UR**:13B

206. Mastiff

    AL:13,15; **EN**:5B; **HV**:16,18,21; **IM**:1,6; **IN**:2; **NE**:19B; **OC**:11E,17,20,30,33B,38,41B,44B; **SK**:9B,10,20,41B,41C,41D,41E

207. Miniature Bull Terrier

    EN:5B; **NE**:19B; **OC**:20,29C; **RS**:9; **UR**:10B

208. Miniature Pinscher

    BE:1; **EN**:5B; **HB**:1C; **IM**:1; **IN**:6B,6D,22,37,53B; **LP**:3B; **NE**:42B; **OC**:5H,11E,20,23F,27,36,41B; **SK**:9B,13N,20,23,25,30,32

209. Miniature Schnauzer

    AL:2,12,16,19A; **BE**:1; **EN**:5B,6; **HL**: 9,12,17,20,24,41C; **HV**:7,16,17,18,19; **IM**:1,6,12; **IN**:6C,6F,7,8,13,37,48,58,63, 65; **LP**:3B,6B,7; **MU**:19, **NE**:11,19B; **OC**:5A,5H,8A,10,11E,15,20, 23D,26,27,29C,32,33A,35,37B,38,41A,43,44B; **RP**:2,10; **RS**:8; **SK**:9B,20,25,28,31,35B,45B,46,58,64; **UR**:3,5,13B,24A

210. Mudi

211. Neopolitan Mastiff

    EN:5B, **HV**:13; **IM**:14; **OC**:5H,14,17,20,21B,30,38,41B,42; **SK**:1,20,41A,50

212. New Guinea Singing Dog

    EN:5B

213. Newfoundland

    AL:12,13,15,19B; **BE**:1,3; **EN**:5B; **HV**:6,13,16,18,20,21, 41C; **IM**:1; **IN**:6B,47,48,63,64; **NE**:16; **OC**:5H,14,17,20,21B, 30,31,38; **RP**:2; **SK**:12,19B,20,21,30,31,41A,41B,41D,45B,49,64, 65B; **UR**:1A,2,10F

214. Norbottenspets (*Norbottenspets*)

215. Norfolk Terrier

    AL:19B; **EN**:5B; **HV**:4; **IM**:1; **IN**:37; **LP**:2B,6B; **OC**:5H,23C, 29C,35; **SK**:7,20,31,45B,64

216. Norwegian Buhund

    EN:5B; **OC**:5G; **SK**:20

217. Norwegian Dunkerhound

    HB:1B; **OC**:25

218. Norwegian Elkhound

    EN:5B; **IN**:37,63; **OC**:5H,15,20,23D,23F,29C,41A,44B; **RS**:6; **SK**:9B,13L,20,31,43,45B,64; **UR**:4,5,11

219. Norwich Terrier

    AL:19B; **EN**:5B; **HV**:4; **IM**:1; **IN**:37; **LP**:2B; **MU**:17; **OC**:5H,11E,29C; **SK**:7,20,31,45B,64

220. Nova Scotia Duck-Tolling Retriever

    EN:4,5B,8; **IM**:9; **IN**:63; **OC**:5H,15,41B; **RP**:2; **SK**:9B,20,31

221. Old Danish Bird Dog

222. Old English Sheepdog

    AL:13,16; **BE**:1; **EN**:5B,8; **HL**:21,28; **HV**:1,18,20; **IM**:2,6, 7,8,15; **IN**:49,53B,64, **LP**:3B,5,7; **MU**:6,13,14; **OC**:5A,15,20, 23C,32,33B,38,40,41B,44B,45,52; **RP**:1,2; **RS**:6; **SK**:5,20,41A, 41B,41D,49,53,65B; **UR**:2,13B

223. Olde English Bull Dogge (*Olde English Bulldogge*)

    RS:6

224. Otterhound

    EN:5B; **HL**:11,38,40; **IM**:1; **NE**:19B; **OC**:27, **RP**:2; **SK**:20, 41A,45B,64

225. Owczarek Podalanski (*Owczarek Podhalanski*)

    SK:20

226. Papillon

    EN:5B; **HB**:1C,41C; **IN**:8,12,37; **LP**:6B; **NE**:19B,31; **OC**:5H, 11E,20,41B,50; **RP**:2; **SK**:9B,23,31

227. Pekingese

AL:2,10,23; **EN**:5B; **IN**:22,37,38,49,60,63; **LP**:6B; **NE**:4, 19B,27D,31,50,56; **OC**:5H,12,14,15,16,20,22,26,27,28,29C,30, 33B,35,36,39,41B,42,48,50; **RP**:2,8; **RS**:1,7,9; **SK**:9B,13S,19B, 20,23,25,28,30,31,36,37,38,41D,45B,55,58,65B; **UR**:12,13A,22C

228. Perdiguero de Burgos

229. Perdiguero Navarro

230. Peruvian Inca Orchid (*Inca Hairless Dog*)

IN:5B,63

231. Petit Basset Griffon Vendéen

EN:5B; **IM**:1; **NE**:19B; **OC**:11E,38,44B,45; **SK**:20,31,41A

232. Petit Bleu de Gascogne

233. Petit Gascon-Saintongeois

234. Petit Griffon Bleu de Gascogne

SK:6

235. Pharaoh Hound

EN:5B; **IN**:47; **OC**:22,28; **SK**:20

236. Plott Hound,

EN:5B; **IM**:6; **NE**:19B,42A; **RS**:4; **SK**:31,32

Pointer (see **English Pointer**)

237. Poitevin

238. Polish Hound

239. Polish Owczarek Nizinny (*Polish Sheepdog-Polaski, Owczarek Nizziny*)

EN:5B; **HV**:13; **IN**:22; **NE**:11; **OC**:20; **SK**:20,41A

240. Pomeranian

EN:1,5B; **HB**:1C; **HL**:8,30; **HV**:7,13,16,21; **IN**:22,32,37, 53B,63; **NE**:19B,25,27D,31; **OC**:3,5H,15,20,26,27,41B,50; **RP**:2; **RS**:8; **SK**:19B,23,25,28,30,31,32,37,38,40

241. Poodle (*Barbone*)

 AL:2,9,10,13,16,23,25; **BE**:1; **CA**:1B; **EN**:3,4,5B,6,8; **HB**:1C; **HL**:8,15,20,22,28,30,33,36,41C; **HV**:7,8,13,16,18,19,21; **IM**:1,2,6,8,9,12,15; **IN**:6B,6D,6E,6F,15,17,22,32,37,44,47,48, 51B,53A,58,63,66B; **LP**:1,3B,4,5,6B,7; **MU**:5; **NE**:4,7J,9,14,15, 19B,21,27D,31,39,45,47,55,56,60; **OC**:5B,5H,8A,11A,12,15,18, 20,23D,23F,24,26,27,29C,31,32,33B,35,36,37B,38,40,41A,41B, 42,45,47,50,51; **RP**:1,2,5,6,8,10; **RS**:6,8; **SK**:7,9B,13K,16,20, 23,25,27,28,30,31,32,35B,37,38,41C,41D,41E,43,45B,50,58,59, 64,65B; **UR**:1B,2,7,13B,22C

242. Porcclainc

243. Portuguese Pointer

244. Portuguese Water Dog

 EN:5B,8, **HV**:4; **IN**:6C,6D,8,12,32; **NE**:23A; **OC**:5H,15,33B, 38,41A; **SK**:20,41A; **UR**:3

245. Presa Canario

 SK:20

246. Pudelpointer

 SK:20

247. Pug

 AL:10; **BE**:1; **CA**:2B; **EN**:5B; **HV**:1C,3,5,17,18; **IM**:1,2,6; **IN**:37,38,40,63; **LP**:6B; **NE**:31,49,57G; **OC**:5H,11E,12,14,15,16, 17,20,22,27,28,36,39,41B,50; **RP**:2,4,10; **RS**:7; **SK**:9B,19B,20, 25,30,31,35B,41A,41D,45B,49,64

248. Puli

 EN:5B; **IN**:44,46; **LP**:6B; **OC**:5H,41B,44B; **SK**:6,20,35B

249. Pumi

 SK:41E

250. Redbone Coonhound

 EN:5B; **HL**:31; **IN**:63; **NE**:38; **OC:**6C,17,20,41B; **SK**:10,20

251. Rhodesian Ridgeback

 AL:19B; **BE**:1; **EN**:5B; **HB**:1C; **IN**:6F,21,44; **MU**:16; **NE**:4, 51; **OC**:5H,20,21B,36,38,41B; **SK**:7,19B,20,41A,41D,41F,59,63, 65B; **UR**:13B

252. Rottweiler

    AL:13,18; **BE**:1; **CA**:1B; **EN**:5B,8; **HB**:1C; **HL**:41C; **HV**:11, 18; **IM**:5,6; **IN**:2,6C,15,33B,37,44,64; **LP**:3B,4,6B; **MU**:15,19; **NE**:16,36,38,40,45,46,52,56,57D; **OC**:5H,9,12,15,17,20,30,31, 33B,38,40,41B,42,44B,45; **RP**:2; **RS**:4,6; **SK**:1,7,9B,19B,20,21, 24,28,31,35B,41A,41B,41C,41D,41E,41F,45B,46,49,54,64,65B; **UR**:1B,10G

253. Russo-European Laika

254. Saint Bernard

    AL:13,15,27; **BE**:1; **EN**:5B,6; **HB**:1C; **HL**:20,21,25,29; **HV**:4,5,6; **IM**:6; **IN**:3,24,28,38,53B,63, **LP**:3B,5; **MU**:11; **NE**:16, 19B,45,57E,57G; **OC**:2,5H,8A,9,14,15,17,19,20,21A,21B,23C,30, 32,33B,35,38,42,52: **RS**:4; **SK**:7,20,21,24,31,38,41A,41B,41D, 41E,46,49,50,54,63,65B; **UR**:2

255. Saluki

    BE:1; **EN**:5B; **HL**:41C; **HV**:13; **IN**:6B,8,12,46,63; **NE**:10, 58A; **OC**:5H,11E,14,20,23C,27,38,41B,44B,45; **RP**:2; **SK**:20, 45B,64

256. Samoyed

    AL:20,21; **EN**:1,5B,8; **HB**:1A; **HL**:20,31; **HV**:1,16,18; **IN**:11,22,32,45A,53B,66B; **LP**:3B,6B,7; **MU**:12,15,16,19; **NE**:7K, 12,35E,56,58A,60; **OC**:5H,11E,12,15,20,23B,27,31,33B,35,38, 41B,44B,45,52; **RP**:2; **SK**:7,9B,13O,20,31,35B,41A,41D,41E,46, 50,58,65B; **UR**:10H

257. Sarplaninac

    SK:20

258. Schapendoes

    EN:5B

259. Schipperke

    EN:5B; **IM**:1; **IN**:6B,8,12,15,47,52,63; **LP**:3B; **OC:**3,5H,15, 38,41B; **RS**:5; **SK:**1,6,9B,20,25,28,64

260. Scottish Deerhound

    AL:13,15; **EN**:5B; **LP**:5; **OC**:5H; **RP**:2; **SK**:13P,13Q,20, 41A,49

261. Scottish Terrier

BE:1; **EN**:5B,6,8; **HB**:1C; **HL**:21,39,41B; **HV**:13,18,21; **IM**:1,2,6,8,15; **IN**:6F,17,37,43,51B,53B,63; **LP**:2B,3B,6B; **MU**:17; **NE**:7K,9,12,19B,21,50,53; **OC**:5H,23C,29C,38,41B; **RP**:2,3; **SK**:9B,10,12,13S,20,23,25,31,35B,41A,41D,45B,46,64; **UR**:1A,2,11

262. Sealyham Terrier

EN:5B; **HB**:1A; **HV**:19; **IM**:1; **OC**:5H,23D,26,27,29B,33B,38, 41B,44A,45; **SK**:7,23,45B,64

263. Shetland Sheepdog

AL:2,6,19B; **BE**:1; **EN**:5B; **HB**:1B,2B; **HL**:20,21,41B,41C; **HV**:6,13,21; **IM**:1,6,7,9,11,15; **IN**:6B,9,20,26,36,37,46,47,63; **LP**:6B; **MU**:19; **NE**:19B,46; **OC**:3,5H,6C,8A,11E,15,16,20,25,26, 27,33B,35,38,41B,44B,50,52; **RP**:2; **SK**:7,9B,10,13S,20,25,30, 31,33,34,36,41A,41D,48,49,50; **UR**:2,5,9C,12

264. Shiba Inu

EN:5B; **HL**:41C; **OC**:52; **SK**:20,31,35B,41A,41D,56

265. Shih Tzu

AL:23; **EN**:5B,6,8; **HV**:20; **IM**:1,2; **IN**:21,22,53B; **LP**:6B; **OC**:5H,12,14,15,16,20,22,27,28,30,36,38,39,40,41B,42,50,51; **NE**:31; **RP**:5; **SK**:9B,13S,20,23,28,31,37,40; **UR**:13A,22A

266. Shiloh Shepherd

SK:20

267. Shropshire Terrier

HB:1C

268. Siberian Husky

BE:1; **EN**:5B; **HB**:1C; **HL**:20; **HV**:2,21; **IM**:6,7,15; **IN**:6C,9, 11,22,32,44,46,47,48,55,56,68B; **LP**:7; **MU**:5; **NE**:2,14,19B,53, 54B,56; **OC**:5D,11A,17,18,20,23D,25,29C,33B,36,38,41B,44A,52; **RP**:2; **RS**:4; **SK**:7,9B,20,31,58; **UR**:2

269. Silky Terrier

AL:25; **EN**:5B; **IN**:6B,6G; **LP**:3B,6B; **NE**:2,7K,19B,26,31, 58A; **OC**:5H,38,41B; **RP**:2; **RS**:3,8; **SK**:17,20,23,25,28,31,38, 41A,45B,60

270. Skye Terrier

AL:19B; **BE**:1; **EN**:5B; **IM**:1; **LP**:2B,8; **OC**:15,23C,29C; **RS**:3,8; **SK**:10,12,17,20,35B,45B,49,50,64; **UR**:2

271. Sloughi

272. Slovak Cuvak

SK:20

273. Small Münsterländer

274. Small Spanish Hound

275. Soft Coated Wheaten Terrier

AL:18,22; **BE**:1; **EN**:5B,8; **HL**:41C; **HV**:11,13,16; **IM**:1,10; **IN**:22,25,33B,49; **LP**:6B; **NE**:19B; **OC**:5H,22,35,36,38,41B; **RS**:4, 8; **SK**:10,20,31,35B,45B,64; **UR**:2,10I,13B

276. South Russian Ovcharka

EN:5B

277. Southern Blackmouth Cur

278. Spanish Mastiff

279. Spinone Italiano

EN:5B; **LP**:7; **OC**:17,20; **RP**:13; **SK**:20,24,41A

280. Stabyhoun

SK:60

281. Staffordshire Bull Terrier

AL:23; **BE**:1; **CA**:2B; **HB**:1C; **IM**:1,6; **IN**:6C,16,22; **LP**:6B; **MU**:16; **OC**:5B,20,29C,37A,41B; **SK**:9B,10,20,31,41A,41E

282. Standard Schnauzer

BE:1; **EN**:5B; **HV**:16; **IM**:1; **IN**:6F,13; **OC**:5H,37B,44B; **SK**:20,45B,64; **UR**:5,22C

283. Stumpy-Tail Cattle Dog

OC:36

284. Sussex Spaniel

EN:5B; **HV**:4,16,19; **MU**:13; **OC**:5H,15,20,44B; **SK**:20,23,64

285. Swedish Lapphund

NE:7K,27A,57F

286. Swedish Vallhund

 SK:20

287. Thai Ridgeback

288. Tibetan Mastiff

 EN:5B; **HL**:20; **LP**:4; **NE**:33,35G; **SK**:20,41A

289. Tibetan Spaniel

 EN:5B; **HV**:13,16; **IM**:1; **IN**:63; **NE**:19B; **OC**:11E,15,16,20,22,33B,35,38,41B,42,45; **SK**:20,31,45B

290. Tibetan Terrier

 EN:5B,8; **HB**:2B; **HL**:41C; **HV**:11; **IM**:1,9; **NE**:10,19B; **OC**:5H,6C,15,23C,27,29A,38,41A,45,47; **RP**:2; **SK**:19B,20,23,31,35B,45B,50,51,64

291. Tosa-Ken

 SK:20

292. Toy Fox Terrier

 EN:5B; **IM**:15; **OC**:23D,29C,38,50; **SK**:28

293. Treeing Cur

294. Treeing Feist

295. Treeing Tennessee Brindle

296. Treeing Walker Coonhound

 EN:5B; **HB**:1C,2B; **IN**:63; **NE**:38,59; **OC**:20; **SK**:20; **UR**:16

297. Vizsla

 EN:5B; **HL**:20,25,41C; **IM**:1,8; **IN**:47,53B; **NE**:36; **OC**:5H,20,41B; **SK**:7,10,20,41A,41D

298. Weimaraner

 AL:13; **CA**:1B,2B; **EN**:5B,8; **HL**:5,14,19,20; **HV**:15,20; **IM**:6,13,16; **IN**:2,24,39,48,53B,63; **MU**:19; **NE**:4,8,35H,56; **OC**:5H,11E,12,14,15,19,20,21B,31,41B; **RP**:2,4; **SK**:7,10,13N,13R,20,21,28,31,41B,58,65B; **UR:**10J

299. Welsh Corgi, Cardigan

 BE:1; **EN**:5B; **HL**: 30,41C; **HV**:6; **IN**:9,24,44,48,49; **LP**:5; **NE**:10,19B,53; **OC**:5H,6C,12,14,20,23C,29C,38,41A,44B,45; **SK**:9B,20,23,31,50; **UR**:1B,2

300. Welsh Corgi, Pembroke

BE:1; **EN**:5B; **HL**:30,41C; **HV**:6; **IM**:1; **IN**:9,20,24,44,48, 49,63; **LP**:5; **MU**:15; **NE**:10,19B,36,45,53; **OC**:5H,11E,12,14,20, 23C,29C,38,41B,44B,45; **RP**:2; **SK**:6,20,23,31,41A,41D,45B,64, 65B; **UR**:1B,2,15

301. Welsh Springer Spaniel

EN:5B; **IM**:1; **NE**:19B; **OC**:5A,20,23A,38,41B,44B; **RP**:2; **SK**:20,64

302. Welsh Terrier

AL:19B; **EN**:5B; **HL**:41C; **IM**:2; **IN**:44; **LP**:6B; **NE**:19B; **OC**:5H,15,23C,23D,29C,41B; **RP**:2; **SK**:20,25,31

303. West Highland White Terrier

AL:3,16; **BE**:1; **EN**:5B,8; **HB**:1C; **HL**:36; **HV**:16,21,36; **IM**:1,6,12; **IN**:17,22,27,33A,37,39,51A,63; **LP**:2B,3B;6B; **MU**:16, 17; **NE**:19B,25,31,60; **OC**:5A,12,20,23C,27,29C,33B,38,39,41B, 44B; **RP**:2; **SK**:9A,9B,10,19B,20,22,25,31,40; **UR**:2

304. West Siberian Laika

305. Whippet

AL:13; **EN**:5B; **HB**:1C; **HL**:41C; **IM**:6; **IN**:6B,6C,6D,6E,15, 35,44; **LP**:3B; **NE**:19B,53; **OC**:5H,11E,14,23D,25,27,29C,41B; **RP**:2; **SK**:20,41D,45B,50,64

306. Wire-Haired Pointing Griffon

NE:45; **OC**:17,20; **SK**:20

307. Xoloitzcuintli (*Mexican Hairless*)

IN:5C; **SK**:35B

308. Yorkshire Terrier

AL:18; **BE**:1; **CA**:1B; **EN**:4,5B; **HL**:1,8; **HV**:1,13; **IM**:1; **IN**:6B,6C,6G,15,21,33B,37,42,52,63; **LP**:1,3B,6B;7; **NE**:6,19B, 23B,31,60; **OC**:5H,11E,15,20,27,38,41B,44B,45; **RP**:1,2,6; **RS**:8; **SK**:12,19B,20,23,25,28,30,31,36,37,38; **UR**:1B,2,5,13B,22C

APPENDIX 2

Brief Definitions of Canine Genetic Disorders with Affected Breeds

Numbers following description of the disease indicate affected breeds. See Appendix 1.

Key to abbreviations: R = Recessive, D = Dominant, Und = Undetermined, X = Sex-linked, Inc-D = Incomplete Dominance, < = Under a given age, > = Over a given age.

ALIMENTARY DISEASES (AL)

		Mode of Inheritance/ Age at Onset
1.	Achlorhydria: Inadequate production of stomach acid, causing poor digestion & vomiting. 60	Und/ < 6mo
2.	Acute Hemorrhagic Enteropathy (Hemorrhagic Gastroenteritis: HGE): Clinical signs are acute onset of bloody diarrhea, dehydration & hemoconcentration. 83,104,209,227,241,263	Und/ > 4yr
3.	Adenomatous Polygeniceps: Benign neoplasm of the rectum, although sometimes found on the colon. Symptoms are diarrhea & chronic debilitation. 100,303	Und/ < 7yr
4.	Basenji Enteropathy (Lymphocytic-Plasmacytic Enteritis): Clinical signs tend to be variable at the start & include small-intestinal diarrhea, which may become untreatable, vomiting & weight loss. Death within 2 to 3 years from diagnosis. 29,95,145,201	Und/ < 4yr
5.	Canine Histiocytic Ulcerative Colitis: Bloody mucoid diarrhea, resulting in weight loss & continued diarrhea in some dogs. Prognosis is guarded & euthanasia is sometimes required. 62,99,141	Und/ < 2yr
6.	Canine Sprue: Clinically, this is chronic diarrhea that may be very severe. The diarrhea is generally accompanied by weight loss. 145,263	Und/ < 9yr
7.	Chronic Non-Specific Gastritis: Chronic vomiting at varying intervals, which can be brought on by eating or drinking. 29,111,201	Und/ < 1yr
8.	Cobalamin Malabsorption of Giant Schnauzers (Vitamin B_{12}): Symptoms include poor weight gain, lethargy, loss of appetite, weight loss, recurrent pulmonary infections, cyanosis & persistent coughing. 149	Und/ ≤ 7mo
9.	Cricopharyngeal Dysphagia (Achalasia): Clinical signs are immediate regurgitation & nasal reflux after eating, coughing, continued attempts to swallow & gagging. Aspiration pneumonia is common. 12,99,124,241	Und/ Birth

	Mode of Inheritance/ Age at Onset
10. Elongated Soft Palate: The soft palate extends into the laryngeal area, causing breathing difficulties. 1,33,35,60,61,62,83,97,99,102,117, 141,170,227,241,247	Und/ Birth
11. Enteropathy of the Chinese Shar-Pei: Symptoms include diarrhea, weight loss or poor weight gain & enteritis. 95	Und/ ≤ 7mo
12. Esophageal Hypomobility: Regurgitation, weight loss, recurrent respiratory infections & retarded growth rate because the esophagus fails to push food into the stomach. 95,102,140,145,158,162,174,194,209,213	Und/ < 10wk
13. Gastric Dilatation-Volvulus (Bloat & Gastric Torsion): Distention & twisting of the stomach, resulting in discomfort, vomiting & ineffectual retching. Death is common. 2,4,6,8,33,41,47,50,54,55,59,61,62,70, 75,87,97,100,102,104,109,117,121,124, 145,146,151,152,158,160,162,174,177, 189,192,194,206,213,222,241,252,254, 260,298,305 & any other large, giant, deep-chested breeds	Und/ < 7yr
14. Hiatal Hernia: Regurgitation, hypersalivation, dyspnea & vomiting soon after swallowing. 61,70,95,102,117	Und/ > 1yr
15. Hypersialism (Drooling, Ptyalism): Overproduction & oversecretion of saliva by one or more salivary glands. 33,47,54,95,97,102,117,158,159,160, 174,206,213,254,260	Und/ < 6mo
16. Idiopathic Canine Colitis: Clinically, there is a semiformed-to-liquid stool that may contain mucus &/or blood. There may be weight loss & vomiting. 57,100,102,105,122,145,151,174,194, 209,222,241,303	Und/ < 8yr
17. Immunoproliferative Enteropathy of Basenjis (Lymphangiectasia): Intermittent diarrhea, weight loss &/or swollen oral lymph nodes. 29	Und/ ≤ 6mo
18. Intestinal Lymphangiectasia: Lack of appetite, fluid in abdominal cavity, swelling of extremities & diarrhea. 29,104,151,201,252,275,308	R/ ≤ 6mo
19. Megaesophagus (Esophageal Achalasia): Regurgitation of undigested food occurs due to failure of esophageal muscles to force swallowed food through to the stomach. A. R – 140,209. B. Und – 2,8,11,26,35,47,60,61,62,83,95,99,102,104,105,119,138,139,145, 158,162,174,178,194,213,215,219,251,263,270,302	R Und/ < 6mo
20. Perianal Fistula (Anal Furunculosis): Chronic infiltrating infection in the perianal tissues. There may be excessive licking & scooting on the floor, with mild to severe fecal incontinence. Chronic cases may show weight loss due to anorexia, & there may be severe pain & bleeding with defecation. 100,102,122,145,174,194,256	Und/ < 8yr
21. Perianal Gland Adenomas: Benign growths in perianal area that may hemorrhage & ulcerate. Dog may excessively lick the area. 35,99,117,256	Und/ < 9yr
22. Protein-Losing Enteropathy: Clinical signs may include vomiting, diarrhea, weight loss & dehydration. 29,201,275	Und/ < 2yr
23. Pyloric Stenosis (Hypertrophic Pyloric Gastropathy): Abnormally small opening between the stomach & the duodenum that prevents food from passing & causes sharp projectile vomiting, anorexia & weight loss. 60,62,102,117,199,203,227,241,265,281	Und/ < 12wk
24. Small Intestinal Bacterial Overgrowth Syndrome (SIBO): Clinically, there is intermittent diarrhea that tends to be chronic. There may or may not be a loss of body weight. The exocrine pancreas appears to function normally. 145	Und/ < 1yr
25. Sialoceles (Ranula): Clinically, there is swelling of the ventral cervical/ submandibular region, which is generally not painful on palpation. There may or may not be respiratory problems. 104,145,162,241,269	Und/ < 6yr

		Mode of Inheritance/ Age at Onset
26.	Wheat Sensitive Enteropathy of Irish Setters (Gluten-Sensitive Enteropathy): Weight loss, intermittent diarrhea & intermittent periods of hyperphagia or inappetence. 174	Und/ ≤ 8mo
27.	Vitamin D-Dependent Rickets: Clinically, the dog has a foreleg deformity & may be depressed & dyspneic. 254	Und/ < 12wk

BEHAVIORAL DISEASES (BE)

1.	Aggressiveness (Excessive): Extremely assertive or forceful with other dogs & people, may attack or bite without reasonable provocation. 2,4,8,11,23,25,26,33,35,47,48,56,59,62,74,76,99,100,102,104,105,109,121,124, 140,145,158,159,160,174,178,188,194,195,208,209,213,222,241,247,251,252, 254,255,261,263,268,270,275,281,282,299,300,303,308	Und/ ≤ 3yr
2.	Nervous (Fearful) Pointer: Although experimentally developed, a line of Pointers showing fearful reactions was produced. These dogs show severe fearful behavior toward people, other dogs & new situations. The tail-wagging behavior is depressed, & defensive aggressiveness is demonstrated. 121	Und/ < 6mo
3.	Springer Rage (Episodic Dyscontrol Syndrome): This disorder is characterized by unprovoked attacks or minimally provoked attacks, most commonly by males. 47,87,99,124,151,213	Und/ < 3yr

CANCER (CA)

1.	Histiocytosis (Malignant Histiocytosis, Systemic Histiocytosis): There may be multiple cutaneous nodules or ulcers on any part of the body, with metastatic lesions in the lungs & other organs of the body. Anorexia, weight loss & lethargy is common. A. Polygenic – 47 B. Und –109,124,140,151,187,241,252,298,308	Polygenic Und/ ≤ 7yr
2.	Mastosarcoma: Clinically, there may be masses palpable in the skin & subcutaneous tissue. These lesions may ulcerate or spread & metastasize to other parts of the body. There is generally anorexia, weight loss & lethargy late in the development of this tumor. A. Polygenic – 47 B. Und – 8,15,25,26,33,35,38,50,60,62,74,102,104,117,140,151,194,247,281,298	Polygenic Und/ < 7yr

ENDOCRINE DISEASES (EN)

1.	Congenital Adrenal Hyperplasia-like Syndrome: Symptoms include hair loss in the neck, tail & medial thigh area. Primary hairs are lost first, so the coat develops a puppy-like appearance. Exposed skin may become hyper-pigmented. 26,33,97,187,240,256	Und/ < 2yr
2.	Goiter: Enlarged thyroid gland due to an inability to obtain or metabolize iodine. 58,140	D/ < 1yr
3.	Growth Hormone Deficiency: Lack of production of or inability to use growth hormone may cause dwarfism. 4,241	Und/ Birth

		Mode of Inheritance/ Age at Onset
4.	Hyperadrenocorticism: Abdominal distention, hepatomegaly, polygenicgenicdipsia, polygenicgenicuria, weakness, lethargy & alopecia. 60,62,83,102,103,104,106, 187,198,199, 220,241,308	Und/ < 8yr
5.	Hypothyroidism (Autoimmune Thyroiditis, Hashimoto's Disease, Lymphocytic Thyroiditis): Destruction of the thyroid gland due to an attack from the animal's own immune system. Causes rough, scaly skin; hair loss & weight gain. A. R – 59 B. Und – 1,2,4,5,6,8,10,11,12,14,15,17,21,23,24,25,26,27,29,33,35,36,37, 38,40, 41,42,43,46,47,48,50,54,55,57,58,59,60, 61,62,70,72,73,74,75,76,77,78,79,81 83,85,87,92,93,95,96,97,98,99,100,101,102,103,104,105,106,109,110,117,118, 120,121,122,123,124,125,134,135,138,139,140,141,144,145,146,148,149,150,151, 152,154,158,159,162,167,168,170,174,175,176,177,178,179,181,185,187,188,189, 192,193,194,195,198,199,200,203,204,206,207,208,209,211,212,213,215,216,218, 219,220,222,224,226,227,231,235,236,239,240,241,244,247,248,250,251,252,254, 255,256,258,259,260,261,262,263,264,265,268,269,270,275,276,279,282,284,288, 289,290,292,296,297,298,299,300,301,302,303,305,308	R Und/ < 2yr
6.	Idiopathic Hypoparathyroidism: Clinical signs include anorexia, behavioral changes, tetany, muscle tremors, seizures & respiratory signs. 102,177,194,209,241,254,261,265	Und/ < 5yr
7.	Primary Hyperparathyroidism: Clinical signs include muscle weakness, polygenicgenicuria/polygenicgenicdipsia & slow growth. Puppies may be lame and have difficulty walking. 145	Und/ < 4wk
8.	Primary Hypoadrenocorticism (Addison's Disease): Clinically, dogs show poor appetite, vomiting & lethargy. There may be shaking, weight loss & diarrhea. This disorder tends to come & go. Hypothermia, weakness and collapse may occur. 4,33,36,47,48,92,97,102,106,121,138,145,146,151,158,174,194,198, 203,220,222,241,244,252,256,261,265,275,290,298,303	Und/ < 5yr

HEARING, BALANCE (HB)

1.	Deafness: Inability to hear may be unilateral or bilateral.	
	A. Piebald or Extreme Piebald Gene Deafness < 3mo – R or Und –35,74, 102,105,117,122,159,162,203,256,262	R or Und/ < 3mo
	B. Deafness due to effects of dominant Merle gene < 3mo – D – 12,23,24, 25,57,100,104,118,120,158,217,222,263	D/ < 3mo
	C. Deafness not further defined R/ < 3mo – R –6,76,99,109,121,140,252 D/ < 6mo – D – 62 Und/ < 6mo – Und – 2,12,15,21,48,60,61,81,97,102, 104,113,124,141,145,170,178,179,186,192,194,208,226,240,241,247,251, 254,261,267,268,281,296,303,305	R D Und/ < 6mo
2.	Vestibular Disease: Head tilt, loss of balance, circling, rolling & staggering gait. A. R – 6,35,109 B. Und – 99,100,102,118,122,140,145,263,290,296	R Und/ < 3mo

HEMATOPOIETIC & LYMPHATIC DISEASES (HL)

1.	Anasarca (Congenital Lethal Edema): A generalized subcutaneous collection of fluid affecting all parts of the body. 1,11,60,75,76,99,102,117,141,151,308	R/ Birth
2.	Basset Hound Thrombopathy: Platelet aggregation is impaired, resulting in a severe bleeding tendency. 33	R/ Birth

		Mode of Inheritance/ Age at Onset
3.	Border Collie Neutropenia: Clinically, there is slow growth. Dogs are depressed & dull. They can not or will not walk. Repeated infections occur. 57	R/ < 4wk
4.	Canine Cyclic Neutropenia (Grey Collie Syndrome): Coat color is silver to beige. Increased susceptibility to bacterial infections at 10-12–day intervals; usually death by 1 year of age. 100	R/ Birth
5.	Canine Granulocytopathy (Leukocyte Adhesion Protein Deficiency): Affected dogs show increased susceptibility to bacterial infections & a persistent leukocytosis.109,174,298	R/ Birth
6.	Cavalier King Charles Thrombocytopenia (Macrothrombocytosis): About one-third of Cavalier King Charles Spaniels examined had platelet counts averaging about 56% of normal platelet counts in this breed. In addition, platelet size was larger than that found in 18 dogs of other breeds. No clinical signs were associated with this defect. 83	Und/ ≤ 6yr
7.	Citrullinemia (Argininosuccinic Acid Synthetase, Uric Cycle Enzyme Deficiency): Mental retardation, vomiting & seizures.35,151	R/ Birth
8.	Constitutional Hypoglycemia (Idiopathic Hypoglycemia): Clinically, signs are lethargy, dullness, muscle fasciculation, muscle weakness, seizures, coma & perhaps death. May be provoked by fasting. 92,102,240,241,308	Und/ < 6mo
9.	Dysbetalipoproteinemia (Idiopathic Canine Hyperchylomicronemia): Pancreatitis, atherosclerosis & seizures are seen. There may be abdominal pain, vomiting, diarrhea & abdominal distention. 122,209	R/ < 6mo
10.	Dysfibrinogenemia (Factor I Deficiency): Mild bleeding or life-threatening bleeding if trauma or surgery is experienced. 35,47,59,100	R/ < 6mo
11.	Factor II Deficiency: Puppies show gingival bleeding, becoming milder as they age. Easy bruising occurs in adults. 62,118,224	R/ Birth
12.	Factor VII Deficiency: A missing component in the blood causing slow coagulation. You may see mild subcutaneous bleeding (bruising). 8,35,62,102,117,209	Inc-D/ Birth
13.	Factor X Deficiency: Homozygotic individuals are stillborn or die by 3 weeks of age, due to massive hemorrhage. Heterozygotic individuals show mild to severe bleeding characteristics. 99,179	Inc-D/ < 6mo
14.	Factor XI Deficiency: A missing component in the blood causing mild bleeding, which can be severe after trauma or surgery & can cause death, but usually doesn't. 124,146,159,188,298	Inc-D/ <3mo
15.	Factor XII Deficiency (Hageman's Disease): There is no bleeding tendency with this trait. Individuals may show a higher than normal tendency for thrombosis & infection. 95,146,241	Und/ Birth
16.	Familial Microcytosis: Red cells that are generally smaller in size than those normally found in dogs. This is either common or normal in this breed. 6	Und/ <1yr
17.	Familial Stomatocytosis: Abnormal structure of red blood cells causing hemolytic anemia. 8,111,209	R/ <6mo
18.	Glanzmann's Thrombasthenia (Type I): Clinically, while the deciduous teeth are being shed, there is excessive gingival bleeding. Epistaxis is a common occurrence. 12,159	Und/ <3mo
19.	Glucose-6-Phosphate Dehydrogenase Deficiency: Clinical signs are not associated with this trait. 298	R/ Birth
20.	Hemophilia A: Absence of factor VIII in the blood causing prolonged & excessive bleeding due to failure to form a clot. Affected dogs may die. 8,35,72,76,92,100,102,117,118,122, 124,141,145,146,162,174,194,209,241, 254,256,263,268,288,297,298	X-R/ Birth

		Mode of Inheritance/ Age at Onset
21.	Hemophilia B (Christmas Disease): Absence of factor IX in the blood causing prolonged & excessive bleeding due to failure to form a clot. Affected dogs may die. 4,8,48,50,76,99,102,118,141,145,146,188,194,222,254,261,263	X-R/ Birth
22.	Hereditary Nonspherocytic Hemolytic Anemia: Macrocytic, hypochromic anemia is present, resulting in typical signs of anemia, such as weakness, pale mucous membranes, & tachycardia. May be fatal by 3 years. 241	Und/ < 1yr
23.	Hereditary Platelet Storage Pool Defect (Platelet Delta Storage Disease): Impaired platelet aggregation occurs, resulting in severe bleeding. 99	Und/ < 1yr
24.	Hyperlipoproteinemia: Increased serum high-density lipoproteins, resulting in abdominal distress, pain & seizures of varying intensity. 4,35,72,102,209	Und/ < 6mo
25.	Hypofibrinogenemia (Factor I Deficiency): Severe bleeding if trauma or surgery is experienced. 59,100,199,254,297	R/ Birth
26.	Idiopathic Chylothorax: Severe respiratory distress due to an accumulation of a thick, fatty, gray fluid (chyle) in the thorax. There may be dyspnea, coughing, anorexia & weight loss. 2	Und/ < 3yr
27.	Leukocyte Adhesion Defect (Granulocytopathy Syndrome): Beginning in puppyhood, there are recurring bacterial infections. Pyrexia, lymphadenopathy, anemia, gingivitis, dermatitis & osteomyelitis may occur. 174	R/ Birth
28.	Lymphedema: A pitting edema of the extremities & ventral trunk, effusions of the abdominal or pleural cavities may occur. 43,59,62,102,117,137,146,158, 194,222,241	D/ < 1yr
29.	Macrocytosis: Extra large erythrocytes develop, which may be congenital in some dogs. 254	Und/ Birth
30.	Methemoglobinemia: Clinically, there is lethargy, weakness, tachypnea & cyanosis. 11,59,92,102,122,240,241,299,300	R/ < 6mo
31.	Pelger-Huet Anomaly: In the heterozygotic state, the neutrophils function properly. In the homozygotic state, the pups tend to be stillborn. 12,23,25,29,55,60,99,102,120,145,250,256	D/ < 6mo
32.	Phosphofructokinase Deficiency (PFK): There is usually weakness, lethargy, anorexia, weight loss & fever. There may be darkening of the urine. 99,124	R/ < 1yr
33.	Prekallikrein Deficiency: Clinical bleeding is not a common result of the disorder; it is most often diagnosed as a result of a routine coagulation screening test. 241	Und/ < 14yr
34.	Prothrombin Deficiency: There is a severe hemorrhagic tendency due to the absence of this clotting factor. 62,99	Und/ Birth
35.	Pseudohyperkalemia: No clinical signs are related to this trait. However, based on this anomaly, it is suggested that Akitas not be used as blood donors. 6	Und/ < 6mo
36.	Pyruvate Kinase Deficiency (PK): Absence or low levels of an enzyme (pyruvate kinase) essential for the production of red blood cells; causes anemia. 11,29,35,76,102,241,303	R/ ≤ 1yr
37.	Spitz Thrombopathia: Clinically, there is chronic intermittent bleeding, including epistaxis & spontaneous subcutaneous hematomas. The gums bleed upon mild digital pressure. 138	Und/ < 1yr
38.	Thrombasthenia, Thrombopathia: Abnormality in the structure of blood platelets, causing clotting problems & minor bleeding. 58,120,224	D/ < 3mo
39.	Thrombopathia: Abnormality in the structure of blood platelets (giant platelets), causing clotting problems & minor bleeding. 146,261	Inc-D/ < 3mo
40.	Vitamin K-Dependent Prothrombin Defect: Clinically, a low-grade bleeding defect due to poor clotting. 62,224	R/ < 6mo

	Mode of Inheritance/ Age at Onset
41. Von Willebrand's Disease: Reduced factor VIII in the blood, resulting in a prolonged bleeding time; may be mild, moderate, or severe & can cause death. A. Type I von Willebrand's R – 109,204 B. Type III von Willebrand's R – 261,263 C. von Willebrand's Disease not defined by DNA typing R – 64,145 Inc-D – 2,4,33,36,48,62,76,83,87,102,103,104,124,146,148,149,151,158,160,162,174,177,187,192,194,195,199,209,213,226,241,252,255,263,264,275,290,297,299,300,302,305	R Inc-D/ < 1yr

HEART & VASCULAR DISEASES (HV)

1. Atrial Septal Defect: A right ventricle failure, excessive fluid in the chest cavity, an irregular heartbeat & a hole between the right & left atria. 4,43,62,83,102,109,222,256,308	Polygenic/ < 3mo
2. Canine Essential Hypertension (Canine Primary Hypertension, Canine Systemic Hypertension): Clinically, diagnostic signs are sparse. There may be uni- or bilateral flame hemorrhage in the eyes, or stroke may occur. Diastolic blood pressures are/ > 110 mmHg, & systolic pressures range up to 200 mmHg. No other consistent clinical signs are observed. 102,194,268	Polygenic/ < 3mo
3. Cardiac Standstill: Slow heart rate, heart misses a few beats, dog becomes weak &/or faints. 247	Und/ < 3mo
4. Cardiomyopathy: Abnormality of the heart muscle may cause edema of the lung, weakness at exercise & sudden death. 4,58,62,75,102,118,120,170,177,215,219,244,254,284,303	Polygenic/ < 2yr
5. Degeneration of the Bundle of His: Clinically, sudden, unexpected death due to interference with the cardiac conduction system. 109,247,254	Und/ < 2yr
6. Dilated Cardiomyopathy (DCM): Clinical signs include dyspnea, exercise intolerance, syncope, cough, anorexia, weight loss & lethargy. Heart sounds are muffled. 33,35,62,88,102,105,109,118,145,151,166,168,181,213,261,263,299,300	Und/ < 6yr
7. Endocardiosis: This disease may produce few or no clinical signs. With age, affected dogs may show signs of cardiomyopathy, including syncope & death. 36,60,62,92,99,102,109,124,140,162,209,240,241	Und/ 18mo
8. Heart Valve Incompetence: Failure of the heart valves to function properly; usually, the tricuspid or mitral valves are involved, causing poor circulation & all its effects. 76,138,241	Und/ < 1yr
9. Inherited Ventricular Tachycardia (German Shepherd Dog Ventricular Arrhythmia): Few clinical signs are associated with this disease, except sudden death. Death usually occurs following periods of excitement or exercise &/or during presumed sleep. 145	Polygenic/ < 6mo
10. Klippel-Trenaunay Syndrome: Clinically, reddish-blue hemangiomas are present at or near birth. These lesions can occur anywhere on the body & may bleed if subjected to trauma. 57	Und/ < 2wk
11. Mitral Valve Defect (MVD, Mitral Stenosis): An excess of valvular tissue that limits proper valve movement. Symptoms include coughing, lethargy, weakness & sudden death. 47,55,74,83,92,99,102,109,117,145,151,158,174,181,187,203,252,275,290	Und/ < 1yr
12. Myocardial L-Carnitine Deficient Cardiomyopathy: Clinically, signs of heart failure demonstrated by ascites, pleural effusion, exercise intolerance & syncope. 62	Und/ < 6mo

		Mode of Inheritance/ Age at Onset
13.	Patent Ductus Arteriosus (PDA): Failure of the fetal vessel between the aorta & pulmonary artery to close around the time of birth; causes heart murmurs, exercise weakness & may cause death. 1,8,11,15,25,26,36,47,48,57,60,62,72, 83,92,99,100,102,124,125,145,158,187,194,203,211,213,239,240,241,255,261, 263,275,289,308	Polygenic/ Birth
14.	Persistent Atrial Standstill: Clinically, the heart rate is very slow & the dog shows weakness on exercise. 58,124	Und/ < 1yr
15.	Persistent Right Aortic Arch (Vascular Ring Anomaly, VRA): Failure of one of the fetal aortic vessels to degenerate normally, causing a blockage of the esophagus. 25,33,60,62,99,102,104,109,117,140,145,158,162,174,178,298	Polygenic/ Birth
16.	Pulmonic Stenosis (PS): Narrowing of the pulmonic artery where it attaches to the heart, causing murmurs & enlargement of the right side of the heart. 2,4,8,25,33,35,55,58,62,63,75,83,92,97,99,102,117,118,138,140,141,145, 149,151,187,206,209,213,240,241,256,275,282,284,289,303	Polygenic/ < 1yr
17.	Sick Sinus Syndrome (Sinoatrial Syncope, Sinoatrial Arrest): Interference with the sinus node in the heart causes arrhythmias, fainting & death. 99,104,105, 209,247	Und/ < 1yr
18.	Subaortic Stenosis: A narrowing at the base of the aorta as a result of a fibrous band, causing murmurs,weakness & sudden death. 4,8,15,33, 36,42,47,57,60,61,62,74,92,95,99,100,102,104,105,117,121,122,124,140,145, 146,149,151,158,159,169,187,194,206,209,213,222,241,247,252,256,261	Polygenic/ < 1yr
19.	Tetralogy of Fallot: A disarrangement of vessels in the heart, causing murmurs, heart failure & death. 2,8,33,35,62,102,117,140,145,187,209, 241,262,284	Polygenic/ < 3mo
20.	Tricuspid Valve Dysplasia: There may be anorexia, weight loss, lethargy, ascites & a heart murmur. 4,33,47,59,60,62,83,102,109,145,149,158, 159,174,194,199,203,213,222,265,298	Und/ < 1yr
21.	Ventricular Septal Defect (VSD): A hole in the heart wall that divides the right & left sides, causing poor circulation & possible death. 4,8,33, 35,48,58,62,100,102,117,124,139,140,145,187,206,213,240,241,261, 263,268,303	Polygenic/ Birth

IMMUNE SYSTEM DISEASES (IM)

1.	Atopic Dermatitis: Roughened, itchy, oozing skin caused by immune reactions to various allergens, such as fleas or pollen. 1,4,6,8,14,21,25,26,30,33,35,36,37,38, 43,47,48,50,55,60,61,62,74,76,83,95,97,99,102,104,105,109,117,118,121,122,134, 138,140,141,145,146,149,151,174,176,178,187,188,189,193,194,199,206,208, 209,213,215,219,224,231,241,247,259,261,262,263,265,270,275,281,282,289, 290,297,300,301,303,308	Und/ < 1yr
2.	Autoimmune Hemolytic Anemia: The immune system attacks its own red blood cells, causing severe anemia & possibly death. 4,8,24,25,26,35,47,48, 99,102,109,145,174,188,194,199,222,241,247,261,265,302	Und/ < 4yr
3.	Combined Immunodeficiency (CID): Clinically, the dog is afflicted with cutaneous & oral acute bacterial infections particularly associated with the mycobacterium complex of organisms. It usually dies at about 16 weeks of age from generalized viral infections. 33	X-R/ < 4mo
4.	Complement Deficiency: A clinical absence of C-3, resulting in increased susceptibility to infection, especially in the skin. 72	R/ Birth

		Mode of Inheritance/ Age at Onset
5.	Cutaneous Vasculitis: Cutaneous necrotic foci or ulcers develop on the distal extremities, including the footpads, mucocutaneous junctions & ear tips. 104,252	Und/ < 2yr
6.	Demodicosis: A localized Demodex infection that usually results in a mild erythema & may develop into some form of alopecia. Pruritus may or may not be present. These are most commonly seen on the face, & usually there is spontaneous recovery within 6–8 weeks. This is not considered to be hereditary. A generalized demodicosis usually develops as a chronic dermatitis with crusting, scaling & hyperpigmentation. There may be intense pruritus & a secondary pyoderma. Folliculitis, cellulitis, furunculosis & seborrhea may occur. A susceptibility & predisposition to Demodex canis is thought to be based on a T-cell disturbance. Generalized demodicosis is considered to be inherited. 2,4,8,11,25,33,35,50,60,62,74,76,92,95,99,100, 102,104,105,109,117,121,122,124,145,146,151,152,158,174,194,206,209,222, 236,241,247,252,254,261,263,268,281,298,303,305	Und/ < 1yr
7.	Discoid Lupus Erythematosus (DLE): Typically, a benign skin disorder with no general involvement. Changes include scaling, erythema & loss of pigment of the nose. Erosions, ulceration & crusting may occur. Lesions may also develop in the eye & ear area. 8,25,26,72,100,102,135,138,145,146,222, 263,268	Und/ Varies
8.	Idiopathic Thrombocytopenic Purpura (Primary Immune-Mediated Thrombocytopenia): Clinically, there are cutaneous mucosal, petechial, & ecchymotic hemorrhages. There may be epistaxis, bruising, anorexia, hematochezia, lethargy & weakness. 4,8,11,33,47,83,99,102,104,145,222, 241,261,297	Und/ < 10yr
9.	Immune Mediated Polygenicarthritis: Dog may be febrile & show variable degrees of lameness or arthropathy. There is generally nonseptic inflammation of the joints. Steroid therapy usually relieves the signs, at least temporarily. 6,35,99,100,102,109,145,151,174,194,220,241,263,290	Und/ < 6yr
10.	Polygenicarteritis Nodosa (Beagle Pain Syndrome, Meningitis-Vasculitis, Steroid-Responsive Meningitis- Arteritis, SRMA): Immune mediated vascular lesions in the meningeal & coronary arteries lead to typical neurologic & cardiac signs, such as chronic fever, anorexia, stiff neck & para- or tetraplegia. 35,47,102,146,275	Und/ < 2yr
11.	Rheumatoid Arthritis: Clinically, a stiff gait with soft tissue swelling & joint pain. There may be crepitus, laxity & subluxation. Complete luxation & angular deformities may occur. 4,36,48,76,102,263	Und/ < 4yr
12.	Selective IgA Deficiency: A lack of IgA immunoproteins that defend against infections, allowing repeated lesions to occur on the skin & in the lungs. 4,6,35,95,97,99,102,104,105,109,145, 151,209,241,303	Und/ Birth
13.	Selective IgG Deficiency: Repeated bacterial infections in any part of the body due to neutrophil dysfunction & absence of IgG. 298	Und/ < 6mo
14.	Selective IgM Deficiency: Low IgM levels, resulting in increased susceptibility to infection, especially in the skin. 4,8,11,35,47,50,83,102, 109,138,168,211	Und/ Birth
15.	Systemic Lupus Erythematosus (SLE): Signs shown are positive ANA, LE cell or Coombs' tests, polygenicgenicarthritis, alopecia, anemia, proteinuria, lymph-gland enlargement, anorexia, diarrhea & fever. 25,35,36,38,42,47,48,62, 99,100,102,104,121,140,145,222,241,261,263,268,292	Und/ < 9yr
16.	T-Cell Mediated Defect: Increased susceptibility to infection, particularly of a viral nature. Dwarfism is a constant feature of this disorder. 74,298	Und/ Birth

INTEGUMENTARY DISEASES (IN)

		Mode of Inheritance/ Age at Onset
1.	Acanthosis Nigricans: Hyperpigmentation in the skin over the forelegs, with skin roughening & hair loss. 104	Und/ < 1yr
2.	Acne (Muzzle Folliculitis & Furunculosis): Follicular papules of various sizes, which are generally hairless. Papules may ulcerate & produce a purulent exudate. 62,102,109,117,146,158,206,252,298	Und/ Varies
3.	Acral Mutilation Syndrome (Idiopathic Self-Mutilation, Psychogenic Alopecia & Dermatitis): If the dog is left alone too often & has no positive energy outlet, it may lead to the dog obsessively licking &/or chewing the skin of the distal extremities. 102,109,121,138,145,146,151,158,174,194,254	Und/ Varies
4	Acrodermatitis of Bull Terriers: Rough, cracking, oozing skin caused by an inability to metabolize zinc. 74	R/ < 6wk
5.	Alopecic Breeds (Hairlessness): Dogs that are bred to have little or no hair on the body. A. R – 13 B. D – 93,172,230 C. Und – 307	R D Und/ < Birth
6.	Alopecic Syndromes: Clinically, hair tends to thin & be lost with little or no scaling or any inflammatory changes. Distribution of loss varies. Hyperpigmentation may occur. A. Alopecia Universalis R/ Birth 35 B. Color Dilution Alopecia: Loss of hair & excessive thickening of the skin seen in dilute colors of blacks & fawns. R/ < 6mo 33,47,60,83,92,97,102,104, 109,158,162,174,178,208,213,241,255,259,263,269,305,308 C. Follicular Dysplasia Und/ Varies 4,8,6,62,87,97,102,103,104,109,117,124, 134,141,146,148,158,174,176,178,209, 244,252,268,281,305,308 D. Pattern Baldness Und/ < 2yr 16,33,60,92,102,104,162,178,204,208,241,244,305 E. Pinnal Alopecia Und/ < 2yr 60,92,102,104,178,241,305 F. Seasonal Flank Alopecia (Idiopathic Flank Alopecia or Cyclical Flank Alopecia) Und/ < 5yr 1,4,11,61,62,102,104,109,141,150,209,241,251,261,282 G. Silky Short-Haired Syndrome Und/ < 5yr 269,308	
7.	Aurotrichia: Hairs over the abdominal & thoracic areas develop a golden color. Areas around eyes & ears may be affected. There may be a loss of secondary hairs in these sections. 209	Und/ < 3yr
8.	Black Hair Follicular Dysplasia: Bi- or tricolored coats are affected by hair loss in black areas only. 33,35,36,57,58,87,92,99,102,103,104, 121,152,176,179,209,226,244,255,259	R/ < 9mo
9.	Bullous Pemphigoid: Clinical signs include the development of vesicular & bullous ulcers. These may affect the skin or the oral cavity & mucocutaneous junctions. Lesions commonly occur on the groin, axillae & footpads. 99,100,102, 109,145,158,263,268,299,300	Und/ Varies
10.	Canine Benign Familial Pemphigus: Lesions appear on the ears & on areas where pressure occurs on the limbs. Erythema, alopecia, scaling & crusting develop. 102,109,122	D/ < 7mo
11.	Castration Responsive Dermatosis: Clinically, alopecia of the medial thigh, neck, flank & shoulder. There may be varying degrees of seborrhea, & hyperpigmentation commonly occurs. 8,97,102,187,256,268	Und/ < 3yr
12.	Collagen Disorder of the Footpads: Fistulous tracts occur on the central plantar surface of the metatarsus. Both rear legs are involved, & one or both metacarpal pads may be affected. 33,35,36,99,102,104,121,152,226,244, 255,259	Und/ < 4yr

		Mode of Inheritance/ Age at Onset
13.	Comedo Syndrome: Crusty bumps on the skin caused by plugged hair follicles. 209,282	Und/ < 1yr
14.	Congenital Anonychia: An absence of claws at birth. 162	Und/ Birth
15.	Congenital Hypotrichosis (Congenital Ectodermal Defect): Many affected pups are born with focal hair loss; some pups have normal hair at birth, then lose hair shortly after birth. Hair loss is on ears, dorsal & entire ventral trunk area. 33,35, 42,48,99,102,141,176,194,199,241,252,259,305,308	Und/ < 6wk
16.	Conjoined Footpads: One or more footpads grow together or fail to separate into individual pads. 74,117,281	Und/ Birth
17.	Contact Dermatitis: Contact hypersensitivity causes dermatitis of varying intensity. Usually found in hairless or sparsely-haired areas. Lesions include macules, papules & erythema. Skin might be hypo- or hyperpigmented. Pruritus may be mild to intense. Various allergens may be involved. 102,140,145,151,194, 241,261,303	Und/ < 2yr
18.	Cutaneous Mucinosis (Idiopathic Mucinosis): Exaggerated folding of the skin, particularly on the head, distal extremities & ventrum. Excessive dermal mucin is present in these folds. 95	Und/ < 4mo
19.	Dalmatian Bronzing Syndrome: Clinically, a red to brown coat color change, pruritus & focally distributed folliculitis with secondary pyoderma. 105	Und/ < 2yr
20.	Dermatomyositis: Skin lesions develop in areas susceptible to mechanical trauma. Vesicles develop, followed by erythema, crusting & scaling. Alopecia generally develops, & ulcers may occur in severe cases. 23,100,102,263,300	Inc-D/ < 6mo
21.	Dermoid Sinus (Dermoid Cyst): A high frequency of infection extending from the cyst to the spinal cord; meningitis & myelitis may be present. 62,99,188,251,265,308	R/ < 3mo
22.	Dudley Nose (Nasal Depigmentation): The black pigment of the nose fades to a whitish or chocolate-brown color. The dog is normal at birth. 2,11,60,73,83, 102,109,121,145,151,174,194,199,203,208,227,239,240,241,256,265,269,275, 281,303	Und/ < 1yr
23.	Ear Margin Dermatosis of Dachshunds: The inflammatory lesions are typically mild, with loosely adherent keratin layers. They are restricted to the margin of the ear. As the disease progresses, there may be alopecia & a greasy accumulation of scale. 104	Und/ < 2yr
24.	Ehlers Danlos Syndrome (Cutaneous Asthenia, Dermatosparaxis): Excessively loose, fragile & hyperelastic skin; tears easily. 24,35,62,83,102,104,105,122,124, 145,151,162,180,187,204,254,275,298, 299,300	D/ < 10wk
25.	Eosinophilic Granuloma: Clinically, eosinophilic masses that can occur in the skin or oral cavities of several breeds. These plaque-like lesions may ulcerate & become infected with various bacteria & fungi. 35,83,268	Und/ < 3yr
26.	Epidermolysis Bullosa: Trauma causes cutaneous blistering of the skin, no matter what causes the trauma. Lesions can occur anywhere, especially on the footpads. 35,100,263	Und/ < 16wk
27.	Epidermal Dysplasia (Armadillo Westie Syndrome): Oily coat seen initially, followed by itching, especially in facial area. Itching becomes more intense, skin becomes moss-like & darker in color. 303	R/ < 12mo
28.	Facial-Fold Blindness: Excessively large folds of skin above & below the eye completely cover the eye. These folds cause trauma to the eye & can cause blindness. 95,99,254	Und/ Birth
29.	Familial Footpad Hyperkeratosis: Clinically, severe hyperkeratosis with fissuring & secondary infection involving the entire surface of the pad & all pads on all feet. 102,110,151,175,188,194	Und/ ≤ 6mo

	Mode of Inheritance/ Age at Onset
30. German Shepherd Dog Pyoderma (German Shepherd Dog Folliculitis): Severe pruritus caused by papules, pustules & erosions of the skin, followed by ulcers, hair loss & hyperpigmentation. There may be poor appetite, weight loss & fever. 145	Und/ < 8yr
31. German Shepherd Footpad Syndrome (Familial Vasculopathy of German Shepherds): Depigmentation, swelling or ulceration on one or more footpads due to very tender footpads on all feet. 145	Und/ < 11mo
32. Growth Hormone Responsive Dermatosis: Clinical signs include alopecia, dry hair coat, seborrhea sicca, dermal thinning & hyperkeratosis. 4,8,16,62,97,102, 104,117,148,187,199,240,241,244,256,268	Und/ < 2yr
33. Ichthyosis: Thickening of any or all footpads. Skin is rough & scaly, with severe hyperkeratosis. There may be thickening of the nasal epidermis. These changes cause pain & discomfort.	
A. Lamellar ichthyosis R – 83,303	R Und/ Birth
B. Breeds not further defined Und – 14,15,60,74,76,99,100,102,109,124,151,174, 179,194,252,275,308	
34. Idiopathic Cutaneous & Renal Vasculopathy (Alabama Rot, Cutaneous & Renal Glomerular Vasculopathy): Redness & ulceration of the skin, with fluid accumulation in the distal limbs. Renal glomerulopathy develops, resulting in death of the dog. 162	Und/ < 4yr
35. Idiopathic Onychomadesis: Usually affects the nails of the dog on multiple paws. There is generally ecchymosis & petechiae within the claw. There is often onychalgia & eventual sloughing of the nail. 124,145,305	Und/ Birth
36. Idiopathic Ulcerative Dermatosis: Clinically, there may be lesions at the mucocutaneous junctions of the mouth, genitals, anus & eyes. The lesions are vesicobullous eruptions that result in ulcerations that tend to coalesce. 100,263	Und/ ≤ 3yr
37. Inguinal Hernia: An outpouching of skin in the area of the inguinal ring, which may contain viscera; a scrotal hernia is a type of inguinal hernia. 4,16,25,29,33,35, 48,50,60,62,72,74,76,87,92,95,99,100,102,104,105,118,122,140,151,158,159,167,199, 204,208,209,215,218,219,226,227,240,241,247,252,261,263,303,308	R or Und/ < 6mo
38. Intertrigo: A frictional dermatitis caused by excessive & pronounced skin folding. Inflammatory lesions occur when sebum, moisture & glandular secretions appear in these folds. Folds can occur on the body, head or face. 33,95,99,102,117,124,141,227, 247,254	Und/ Varies
39. Juvenile Pyoderma (Juvenile Cellulitis, Puppy Strangles): Puppies may develop an acutely swollen face & severe lymphadenopathy in the neck region & the lower jaw. 26,76,104,121,146,151,152,194,298,303	Und/ < 1yr
40. Lentiginosis Profusa (Lentigo): An intensely black melanosis occurring as multiple lesions, most commonly on the stomach & chest. 247	D/ < 4yr
41. Lichenoid – Psoriasiform Dermatosis: Erythematosus lichenoid plaques that become increasingly hyperkeratotic & usually involve the face, perineal area & trunk 109,124,134	Und/ < 6mo
42. Melanoderma & Alopecia: Hyperpigmentation & alopecia, with a symmetric pattern over the bridge of the nose, ears & sometimes feet & tail. The skin is shiny, with no evidence of itching. 308	Und/ < 3yr
43. Nasal Vasculitis of Scottish Terriers: Clinically, a nasal discharge at 3 to 4 days of age, or ulcerative destruction of the nasal philtrum. Both the discharge & the ulcerative lesions are bilateral. 261	Und/ < 6mo
44. Onychodystrophy: A loss of nails on multiple paws, resulting in secondary bacterial infection. 97,99,102,104,124,145,241,248,251,252,268,299,300,302,305	Und/ < 5yr

	Mode of Inheritance/ Age at Onset
45. Partial Albinism (Albinoid Syndrome): Affected animals lack normal pigmentation in sites that are normally pigmented. These may include hair, footpads, lips, nose & eye rims. A. R – 256 B. Und – 109	R Und/ Birth
46. Pemphigus Erythematosus: Clinical signs include alopecia & erosion of the skin. Scaling; wet, crusty lesions; pain & pruritus are variable. 4,11,100,102,104,105, 248,255,263,268	Und/ ≤ 4yr
47. Pemphigus Foliaceus: Clinical signs usually start on the ears or face & involve the footpads. There may be erythematous macules that progress to crusty, brown areas. The skin is scaly, & hair loss is present. 6,35,36,47,48,97,99,100,102,104,109, 138,145,179,194,213,235,241,259,263, 268,297	Und/ ≤ 4yr
48. Pemphigus Vulgaris: Clinically, vesiculobullous lesions. The groin, axillae & mucocutaneous junctions demonstrate erosive to ulcerative areas. 62,99, 100,102,104,109,145,158,209,213,241,268,298,299,300	Und/ < 2yr
49. Perineal Hernia: Difficulty in defecation & swelling lateral to the anus, usually on the right side. 2,24,25,35,48,50,60,62,70,100,102,104,222,227,275,299,300	Und/ < 8yr
50. Powder-Puff: The animals are born a normal tricolor & lose pigment at 6 to 8 months of age so that the black areas turn a gray-like color. The hair generally returns to normal color at 1–2 years of age. 100	R/ < 8mo
51. Primary Seborrhea: Excessive production of sebum, causing flaking of the skin, which is greasy & malodorous. There may be multiple crusty, scaly, pruritic areas. A. R – 303 B. Und – 2,4,25,26,33,35,47,95,99,102,104,109,120,124,145,151,174,194,241,261	R Und/ < 1yr
52. Schistosomus Reflexus: Skin & subcutaneous layers of muscle fail to close over the abdomen, leaving the organs exposed. 1,33,36,102,117,259,308	Und/ Birth
53. Sebaceous Adenitis (SA): Symptoms vary but tend to be bilaterally symmetric & can appear anywhere on the body. Hairs are dull, brittle & tend to be matted. There is severe hyperkeratosis. Skin tends to be greasy, & there can be severe alopecia in affected areas. A. R – 241 B. Und – 4,6,11,36,47,97,99,100,102,104,105,109,124,140,145,151,169,174, 194,199,203,208,222,240,254,256,261,265,297,298	R Und/ < 1yr
54. Shar-Pei Syndrome: Clinically, hair loss on the undersurface of the dog, with inflammation & erythema. In long-standing cases, affected areas may be hyperpigmented. There are generally negative or normal results when diagnostic tests are applied. 95	Und/ < 1yr
55. Siberian Husky Follicular Dysplasia: Clinically, hair loss beginning at about 6 months of age. The greatest loss is among guard hairs, resulting in a woolly, often reddish inner coat. 268	R/ < 6mo
56. Snow Nose (Nasal Hypopigmentation): A decrease in pigmentation of the nose, usually during the winter. 47,151,194,268	Und/ < 1yr
57. Spiculosis: Multiple, brittle, follicular spicules occur. They can be found on any hair surface but are more frequent in the lateral hock region. Dogs tend to chew or lick them.188	Und/ < 8mo
58. Subcorneal Pustular Dermatosis: Clinically, lesions generally occur on the trunk & head, with alopecia, crusting & subcorneal pustules. Acantholysis may be present. The lesions are variably pruritic. 100,102,109,145,199,209,241	Und/ < 2yr
59. Symmetric Lupoid Onychodystrophy: Clinically, there may be sloughing of one or more claws, leading to a loss of all claws on all four paws. Secondary infections are common. 145	Und/ < 8yr

	Mode of Inheritance/ Age at Onset
60. True Albinism: An inherited lack of the enzyme tyrosinase, with a resultant lack of ability to produce melanin pigment. 227	R/ Birth
61. Tyrosinase Deficiency: A deficiency of the enzyme tyrosinase, causing the tongue and portions of the hair shafts to depigment. 97	R/ Birth
62. Tyrosinemia: Cloudy corneas, conjunctivitis & cataracts occur. Ulcerations of the tongue, nose & footpads may be present. The nasal planum may be reddened with focal ulcerations. 145	R/ < 3mo
63. Umbilical Hernia: An outpouching of the skin over the "belly button." It may contain abdominal viscera & sometimes regresses spontaneously. 2,4,8,15,16, 25,29,33,35,36,47,48,50,60,61,62,72,74,76,83,87,92,95,99,100,102,104,105,117, 121,122,124,125,140,145,146,149,151,158,159,174,179,187,189,194,199,203, 204,209,213,218,220,227,230,240,241,247,250,254,255,259,261,263,289,296, 298,300,303,300	R or Polygenic/ < 6mo
64. Vitiligo: A depigmentation that is somewhat symmetric occurs in the areas of the lips, nose, buccal mucosa & facial skin. Footpads & hair coat may be affected. 42,43,48,75,97,100,102,104,109,145,149,151,213,222,252	Und/ ≤ 3yr
65. Vitamin A Responsive Dermatosis: Clinically, a seborrheic skin disease with marked plugging of follicles & hyperkeratotic plaques. A rough, dry & dull hair coat is present with some pruritus. 95,99,194,209	Und/ < 3yr
66. Zinc-Responsive Dermatosis: Rough, cracking & oozing skin caused by the inability to metabolize zinc. This disorder can be corrected by zinc supplementation. A. R – 8,14 B. Und – 35,102,109,145,146,158,194,241,256,268	R Und/ < 6wk

LIVER-PANCREAS (LP)

1. Chronic Active Hepatitis: At the start, mild intermittent clinical signs that generally progress & present severe signs of liver disease. There may be anorexia, vomiting, weight loss, ascites, bleeding tendencies & hepatic encephalopathy. Copper commonly accumulates in the liver. Cirrhosis may occur. 47,99,102,104, 109,118,120,121,124, 145,151,188,194,241,308	Und/ < 5yr
2. Copper Toxicosis (CT): Abnormal deposition or accumulation of copper in the liver causes cirrhosis & may be relatively mild or severe enough to cause death. A. R – 38 B. Und – 4,58,74,76,102,140,170, 215,219,261,270,303	R Und/ < 1yr
3. Diabetes Mellitus: Excessive sugar accumulates in the blood & urine due to a lack of or inability to use insulin. A. R – 187 B. Und – 8,25,26,35,76,81,83,97,102,104,105,109,124,125,138,145,194,204,208, 209,222,241,252,254,256,259,261,269,303, 305,308	R Und/ < 3yr
4. Lobular Dissecting Hepatitis: Clinically, the dogs present with anorexia, weight loss, abdominal distension, apathy, polygenicgenicdipsia, & vomiting. Ascites is generally present. 42,57,99,102,151,196,241,252,288	Und/ 11mo
5. Pancreatic Hypoplasia (Exocrine Pancreatic Insufficiency, Pancreatic Acinar Atrophy, PAA): Weight loss & chronic diarrhea; generally correctable with pancreatic enzyme supplementation. 2,4,35,83,97,100,102,109,122,145,158,174, 194,222,241,254,260,299,300	R/ < 1yr

	Mode of Inheritance/ Age at Onset
6. Portosystemic Shunt (Extrahepatic): The animals are born with extra vessels, which allows blood to bypass the liver. A. Polygenic – 76 B. Und – 4,6,23,25,26,42,43,48,57,61,72,83,93,99,100,102,104,106,109,115, 118,122,145,151,169,174,175,177,194,203,209,215,226,227,241,247,248, 252,256,261,263,265,269,275,281,302,303,308	Polygenic Und/ < 1yr
7. Portosystemic Shunt (Intrahepatic): Abnormal blood vessels within the liver, which prevents normal circulation & metabolism within the liver. 8,23,33,35,47, 55,57,76,99,102,104,109,145,151,168,174,177,194,209,222,241,256,268,279,308	Und/ < 1yr
8. Skye Hepatitis: Clinically, the dogs show inappetence, abdominal swelling & lethargy. The disease is often fatal. 270	Und/ < 6mo

MUSCLE DISEASES (MU)

1. Biceps Brachii Tendon Displacement: Clinically, varying degrees of lameness which may progress to severe weight-bearing lameness after exercise. There is muscle atrophy & pain when the shoulder muscles are manipulated. 2,57,102, 145,162	Und/ < 4mo
2. Bouvier des Flanders Myopathy: Clinically, a paddling gait that appears to be due to an overextension of the paws. There is muscle atrophy, weakness & exercise intolerance. High levels of serum creatinine kinase are present. Dysphagia & regurgitation are common in affected dogs. 61	Und/ ≤ 2yr
3. Core Myopathy: A disorder with generalized myopathic signs & apparent central cores in skeletal muscle fibers. 158	Und/ < 1yr
4. Dancing Doberman Disease (Distal Polygenicneuropathy): The disorder begins with flexing of one rear limb progressing to alternate flexing of both rear limbs in sort of a dance-like motion that progresses over several years. Apparently, no pain is associated with the trait. 109	Und/ > 8mo
5. Eosinophilic Myositis: Clinically, inflammatory lesions in the muscle in various parts of the body. These are generally firm to the touch & painful. Depending on the location, there may be lameness. 36,102,109,188,189,241,268	Und/ < 1yr
6. Exertional Myopathy: Clinically, stiffness & hyperextension, particularly in the rear limbs, caused by firm, painful muscles. Pyrexia may occur. 162,222	Und/ > 1yr
7. Familial Reflex Myoclonus: Clinically, puppies are laterally recumbent with opisthotonos & rigidity on stimulation. 105,194	Und/ < 3mo
8. Fibrotic Myopathy: Clinically, this may occur in various muscles that influence the gait. Affected dogs are lame, & there is rotation of the hock & stifle as the limb is moved forward. 145	Und/ > 1yr
9. Generalized Myopathy: Degeneration of multiple muscles occurs, leading to movement & gait abnormalities. 174	X-R/ < 1yr
10. Hereditary Myopathy (Labrador Retriever Myopathy, Type II Muscle Fiber Deficiency): Muscle stiffness, the dog has difficulty raising its head & megaesophagus may develop. Signs can improve with rest. Dogs are acceptable as pets if signs are mild. 145,175,194	R/ < 6mo
11. Malignant Hyperthermia: Signs include exposure to anesthetics, particularly halothane. Hyperthermia, tachycardia, limb rigidity, respiratory & cardiac arrest can occur. 57,87,102,109,121,124,162,194,254	D/ Varies

		Mode of Inheritance/ Age at Onset
12.	Masticatory Myositis (Atrophic Myositis): There can be pain & visible swelling in the temporal & masseter muscles. The dog might not like to open its mouth & may be reluctant to eat. There may be decreased appetite, which can cause weight loss. In chronic cases, the muscles of the head may be atrophied. 109,145,256	Und/ > 1yr
13.	Mitochondrial Myopathy: The dogs are weak during exercise & may collapse. Panting & a rapid heartbeat often occur. 62,83,98,100,179,222,284	Und/ < 6mo
14.	Muscle Cramping: Muscle restriction leading to difficulty in movement. Severe problems may occur. 83,222	Und/ < 6mo
15.	Muscular Dystrophy: Weakness & hypertrophy of limb muscles. Slow growth & dysphagia may be present. 102,151,175,252,256,300	Und/ < 6mo
16	Myotonia: Muscles continue to contract after voluntary movement ceases, causing a stiff gait. 83,97,102,104,158,175,194,251,256, 281,303	R/ < 6mo
17.	Scottie Cramp: Muscle cramps occur triggered by excitement or exercise; may show a rabbit-like, hopping gait. 76,99,105,140,179,219,261,303	R/ < 10wk
18.	Type II Fiber Hypotrophy of German Shepherd Dogs: Clinically, the disorder presents as an abnormality of the gait caused by muscle pathology. 145	Und/ Birth
19.	X-linked Myopathy (Irish Terrier): Muscle degeneration characterized by a stiff gait. Difficulty in swallowing, inability to jump & an enlarged tongue are present. 1,42,175,209,252,256,263,298	X-R/ < 10w
20.	X-linked Myopathy (Golden Retriever): Stiff gait, muscle atrophy, dysphagia & severe cardiac muscle disease occurs. Death may follow. 8,105,151	X-R/ < 2wk

NEUROLOGIC DISEASES (NE)

1.	Afghan Hound Myelopathy (Myelopathy): Signs include ataxia, bunny-hopping, para- or tetraplegia, respiratory failure & death. No treatment is available. 2,114	R/ < 1yr
2.	Agenesis Vermis Cerebellum: Failure of the ridges of the cerebellum to develop, causing incoordination & ataxia. 268,269	Und/ Birth
3.	Alaskan Malamutes Polygenicneuropathy: Clinically, vomiting, coughing, progressive weakness & exercise intolerance. 8	R/ < 18mo
4.	Arachnoid Cyst (Meningeal Cysts): Cavities or cysts may develop within the meninges separated from the spinal cord by the pia mater. They may compress the cord. 35,58,97,102,109,227,241,251,298	Und/ < 1yr
5.	Boxer Neuropathy (Progressive Axonopathy): Axonal swellings that result in progressive ataxia & finally death. 62,159	R/ > 3mo
6.	Cauda Equina Polygenicradiculoneuritis: Clinically, paresis of the pelvic limbs. Muscle atrophy & loss of the patellar reflexes are common. 145,194,308	Und/ < 9yr
7.	Cerebellar Degeneration (Cerebellar Abiotrophies, Progressive Neuronal Abiotrophy): Degenerative diseases of the cerebellum that tend to be breed-specific, resulting in progressive neurologic signs—including incoordination, ataxia, paralysis &, generally, death. There is no treatment. A. Australian Kelpie R/ < 12wk 24 B. Beagle R/ < 6wk 35 C. Border Collie R/ < 8wk 57 D. Brittany R 7–13yr 72 E. Bullmastiff Terrier R/ < 9wk 75 F. Collie R/ < 2mo100 G. Gordon Setter R/ < 30mo 152	

	Mode of Inheritance/ Age at Onset
H. Kerry Blue Terrier R/ < 16wk I. Labrador Retriever R/ < 16wk 194 J. Miniature Poodle R/ < 6wk 241 K. Other Breeds R/ < 20wk 4,47,60,74,76,87,97,99,102,124,140,141,145,151,158, 167,174,179,256,261, 269,285	
8. Cerebellar Vermian Hypoplasia: Failure of development of the ridges of the cerebellum, causing a staggering, uncoordinated gait. 4,25,60,74,75,97,102,104,140, 151,174, 194,204,298	R/ < 6wk
9. Cerebrospinal Demyelination: Progressive loss of the fatty sheath covering the nerves, causing incoordination, ataxia & spastic paraplegia at 3–4 months of age. 4,60,102,179,241,261	R/ < 4mo
10. Ceroid-Lipofuscinosis (ATP Subunit C Storage): Causes night blindness, confusion, unpredictable aggressiveness & ataxia late in the course of the disease. 23,57, 92,99,102,104,105,118,122,151,183,255,290,299,300	R/ > 1yr
11. Ceroid-Lipofuscinosis: Results in visual impairment, confusion, erratic temperament & apparent loss of memory for previously learned tasks. 99,209,239	R/ > 1yr
12. Congenital Myasthenia Gravis: Severe muscle weakness that may cause megaesophagus, fatigue & collapse due to a failure of neuromuscular transmission of nerve impulses. 4,6,102,104,124,140,145,151,179,194,256,261	R/ < 6mo
13. Dalmatian Polygenicneuropathy-Laryngeal Paralysis Complex: Clinical signs include laryngeal paralysis, severe respiratory signs, hyporeflexia, muscle atrophy, paresis & hyperextension of the limbs. Megaesophagus may occur. 105	R/ < 6mo
14. Degenerative Myelopathy (German Shepherd Myelopathy): This slowly progressive disease begins with rear limb ataxia & knuckling of the paws, which progresses to rear limb & structural paresis. 87,100,102,145,188,241,268	Und/ > 1yr
15. Demyelinating Myelopathy: Loss of myelin in all columns of the spinal cord, resulting in pelvic limb paresis, which progresses to tetraplegia. 241	Und/ < 5mo
16. Distal Neuropathy: Pelvic limb ataxia & paresis, which later involves the forelimbs. Atrophy of distal limbs & masticatory muscles is present. 87,100,102,104,210, 252,254	Und/ > 1yr
17. Doberman Pinscher Lower Motor Neuron Disease: Clinically, puppies showed weakness in the rear limbs. Later, 4-limb involvement prevented the pups from walking, & they were in lateral recumbency. The forelimbs were in rigid extension while recumbent. 109	Und/ < 8wk
18. Dysautonomia: Clinically, urinary incontinence & difficulty in defecation. Difficulty in swallowing liquidized food. Signs associated with autonomic nervous system are evident. 23,57,60,102,109,117,145,194	Und/ < 2yr
19. Epilepsy: Seizures occur that are commonly called fits; they recur generally closer together. A. R – 187 B. Und – 4,5,8,11,16,25,29,33,35,36,38,41,42,43,47,48,50,54,55,57,60,61,62,72,75, 76,77,83,87,97,98,99,100,102,104,121,124,134,138,139,140,141,145,149,151,152, 158,170,174,178,179,187,194,199,203,204,206,207,209,224,226,227,231,236,240, 241,254,261,263,268,269,275,289,290,299,300,301,302,303,305,308	R Und/ > 1yr
20. Episodic Falling: A stiff-limbed gait, bunny-hopping & flailing legs in extensor rigidity. May be induced by excitement or stress. 83	Und/ < 4mo
21. Fibrinoid Leukodystrophy (Fibrinoid Encephalomyelopathy): Tremors, pelvic limb ataxia & falling are commonly seen. Personality changes & tetraparesis may occur. 194,241,261	Und/ < 1yr
22. Fucosidosis: A deficiency of L-fucosidase leads to mental & motor deterioration with ataxia, severe incoordination & perhaps death. 124	R/ < 1yr

	Mode of Inheritance/ Age at Onset
23. Gangliosidosis (Storage Diseases): Ataxia, head tremors, blindness & generalized seizures involving all 4 limbs may occur. Dogs can become paraplegic or tetraplegic. A. GM_1 (Portuguese Water Dog Storage Disease, Beta-Galactosidase Deficiency) R/ < 6mo 35,102,124,244 B. GM_2 (Hexamininidase A+B Deficiency) R/ < 6mo 102,122,146,182,184,308	
24. Giant Axonal Neuropathy: Signs include rear limb paresis with atrophy of the distal musculature; ataxia may be present. No treatment is available. 145	R/ > 1yr
25. Globoid Cell Leukodystrophy (Beta-Galactocerebrosidase Deficiency): The collection of fatty material in brain cells due to lack of an enzyme leads to ataxia. 33,35,55,76,105,240,241,303	R/ < 5mo
26. Glucocerebrosidosis (Gaucher's Disease, Glucocerebrosidase Deficiency): Storage of a fatty material in brain cells due to lack of an enzyme leads to ataxia. 26,102,269	R/ < 1yr
27. Glycogenosis (Glycogen Storage Disease): A group of disorders caused by deficiencies of an enzyme involved in the degradation of glycogen. Clinical signs vary with each disease but generally include progressive muscle weakness, cardiac abnormalities, hemoglobinuria, neurologic signs & death. There is no treatment. A. Type II (Pompe's Disease) R/ < 8mo 145,285 B. Type III (Cori's Disease) R/ < 6mo 6, 145 C. Type VII (Phosphofructokinase Deficiency) R/ < 12mo 29,35,42,46,99,124 D. Not further defined R/ < 12mo 92,102,199,203,227,240,241	
28. Hepatocerebellar Degeneration of Bernese Mountain Dogs: Clinical signs start with a mild ataxia & head tremors. Incoordination & stumbling are apparent. Puppies are unable to walk without falling backward or sideways. 47	R/ < 12wk
29. Hereditary Ataxia: A rear-limb ataxia that progresses to complete paralysis. 140,159,179	R/ < 6mo
30. Hound Ataxia: Rear-leg ataxia that progresses; forelimbs are not affected. 35,120,139,167	Und/ > 7yr
31. Hydrocephalus: An accumulation of fluid in the brain, causing severe pressure & degeneration of the brain. 11,47,48,50,60,73,76,83,92,97,99,102, 117,199,203,204,226,227,240,241,247, 265,269,303,308	Polygenic/ < 3mo
32. Hyperkinesis: Stiffness of muscles caused by increased nerve activity. 74	Und/ < 6mo
33. Hypertrophic Neuropathy: A generalized weakness occurs, & puppies severely affected cannot rise. Muscle wasting may occur. 102,288	R/ < 6mo
34. Hypomyelinating Polygenicneuropathy: Begins with a pelvic limb weakness that later includes the forelegs. Limb reflexes are depressed. There is no cure. 151	Und/ < 2mo
35. Hypomyelination: Affects the CNS; signs vary somewhat by breed, but generally cause tremors, incoordination, rear-limb dancing & perhaps nystagmus. A. Bernese Mountain Dog R/ < 10wk 47 B. Chow Chow Und/ < 6wk 97 C. Dalmatian Und/ < 6wk 105 D. English Springer Spaniel X-R/ > 6mo 124 E. Lurcher Und/ < 6wk 202 F. Samoyed Und/ < 5wk 256 G. Tibetan Mastiff R/ < 10wk 288 H. Weimaraner Und/ < 5wk 298	
36. Idiopathic Facial Paralysis: A weakness or paralysis of facial muscles with drooping of the ears & lips & inability to close the eyes. The disease tends to be unilateral but may occur bilaterally. 62,99,102,122,252,297,300	Und/ < 5yr
37. Idiopathic Meningitis: Lethargy, stiffness & cervical pain may be present. There can be atrophy of the musculature of the head & neck, possible decreased appetite & intermittent weakness, fever, & blindness. 57,62,121	Und/ < 2yr

		Mode of Inheritance/ Age at Onset
38.	Idiopathic Polygenicradiculoneuritis (Coonhound Paralysis, CHP): Clinically, weakness in the rear legs, which rapidly progresses toward the hip, resulting in a limp-symmetric paresis. 50,55,102,119,250,252,296	Und/ < 6yr
39.	Lafora's Disease: Progressive myoclonic epileptic seizures that can often be induced by touch or excitement. PAS-positive neuronal inclusions are present. 33,35,102,241	R/ < 6mo
40.	Leukoencephalomyelopathy (Rottweiler Leukoencephalomyelopathy): This progressive disease may first be observed in the forelimbs. Difficulty in getting up, ataxia & tetraparesis may be present. No treatment is available. 33,252	R/ < 4yr
41.	Lissencephaly: A lack of normal convolutions in the cerebrum causes abnormal mental development. 35,140,174,199	Und/ < 1yr
42.	Mucopolygenicgenicsaccharidosis: Signs vary, depending on the specific disease & may include any of the following: mental retardation, abnormal facies, retarded growth, abnormal gait & limb paresis. A. MPS-I L-Iduronidase Deficiency R/ < 6mo 102,236 B. MPS-VI Arylsulfatase B Deficiency R/ < 6mo 208	
43.	Multisystemic Chromatolytic Neuronal Degeneration (MCND, Progressive Neuronopathy): Rear-limb weakness, incoordination, hypermetria, head tremor & tetraparesis may occur. 76,174	R/ < 6mo
44.	Multisystem Neuronal Degeneration (MND): Signs include ataxia, behavioral changes & dysmetria, with normal spinal reflexes present. 99	R/ < 1yr
45.	Narcolepsy (Cataplexy): Excitement, emotional stimulation or eating may cause the animal to suddenly fall asleep; muscle atonia may occur, & the dog may collapse. Frequency of attacks varies greatly. 2,4,8,35,99,102,104,105,109,124, 149,174,194,241,252,254,300,306	R/ < 1yr
46.	Neuroaxonal Dystrophy (NAD): Ataxia, difficulty in maintaining balance & intention tremor occur; all signs tend to progress. The condition does not respond to treatment. 57,92,100,102,179,252,263	R/ < 6mo
47.	Polygenicmicrogyria & Hydrocephalus: All affected dogs are blind, had shallow sulci & irregular small gyri over the cerebral cortex. 151,241	Und/ < 10mo
48.	Progressive Axonopathy: Swelling of the axons of the brain. Signs start with rear-leg ataxia, progressing to paraplegia. 58,62	R/ < 6mo
49.	Pug Encephalitis: Affected develop a mild temperature, pain in head, staggering & paralysis. The disease is fatal. 203,247	Und/ > 6mo
50.	Quadriplegia with amblyopia: Paralysis in all four limbs, with partial loss of vision. 174,227,261	R/ < 6wk
51.	Rhodesian Ridgeback Cerebellar Degeneration & Color Dilution Syndrome: All affected puppies show coat color dilution & cerebellar signs, including growth retardation, ataxia, inability to stand & tremors. 251	R/ < 4wk
52.	Rottweiler Familial Lower Motor Neuron Disease: Affected pups have a slow slow growth rate & are clumsier than normal littermates. They may be para- or quadriplegic. There is muscle wasting. The animals are recumbent, & megaesophagus may occur. 252	Und/ < 8wk
53.	Sensory Gangliorадiculitis: Clinical signs progress over several years, including ataxia, absence of reflexes, head tilt, voice & hearing loss, dysphagia & perhaps self-mutilation. 72,100,109,151,261,268,299,300,305	Und/ < 7yr
54.	Sensory Neuropathy: Brain degeneration that decreases pain sensation; you may see self-mutilation or trauma without apparent pain, particularly of the paws. A. R – 104,121 B. Und – 57,62,100,109,146,159,179,268	R Und/ > 6mo

	Mode of Inheritance Age at Onset
55. Sphingomyelinosis (Niemann-Pick Disease, Phosphocholine Hydrolase Deficiency): Ataxia, tremors, splaying of legs & tetraplegia are common signs, culminating in death. 241	R/ < 6mo
56. Spinal Dysraphism (Spinal Dysplasia, Syringomyelia): Clinically, a bunny-hopping gait, wide-based stance & scoliosis; a normal life is possible. 92,100,102,105,117,151,194,227,241,252,256,268,298	Und/ < 3mo
57. Spinal Muscular Atrophy: This group of disorders appears to be a series of abiotrophies involving the neurons of the spinal cord. Signs vary but tend to progress & generally include weakness of all 4 limbs, tetraparesis, muscle wasting of the limbs & perhaps the trunk. Recovery is rare. No treatment is available. A. Brittany D/ < 8wk 72 Accelerated Dd/ < 12mo Intermediate Dd/ < 7yr Chronic B. English Pointer R/ < 5mo 121 C. German Shepherd Und/ < 13mo 145 D. Rottweiler Und/ < 6wk 252 E. Stockard's Paralysis D/ < 4mo 54,102, 158,254 F. Swedish Lapland Dogs Und/ < 8wk 285 G. Other Breeds Und/ < 8mo 76,100,102,104,140,247,254	
58. Spongiform Degeneration (Spongiform Encephalopathy): Signs may include tremors (rear limb or generalized), progressive ataxia, wide-based stance, spontaneous intermittent contractures & muscle atrophy. A. 41,102, 255,256,269 With Leucoencephalomalacia B. 105,194	Und/ < 6mo
59. Walker Hound Mononeuropathy: Clinical signs include rear-limb paresis, muscle atrophy & missing or slow postural reflexes that may progress to severe self-mutilation & paralysis. 296	Und/ < 4wk
60. White Shaker Dog Syndrome: Tremors can occur in all 4 limbs & the head. Hypermetria & swaying may be present. Tremors can be mild to severe, & the gait may be ataxic. 35,48,102,104,138,203,241,256,303,308	Und/ < 2yr

OCULAR DISEASES (OC)

1. Anterior Uveal Cysts: Uveal cysts do not usually interfere with vision or function. 60,151	Und/ < 3mo
2. Aphakia: Absence of the lens of the eye. 254	R/ Birth
3. Blepharophimosis (Narrow Palpebral Fissure): Palpebral fissure is too narrow when the puppy is born. This can be corrected by surgery at the lateral canthus. 74,97,100,102,188,240,259,263	Und/ < 8wk
4. Borzoi Retinal Degeneration: A degeneration of the retina. Can be bi- or unilateral & can result in blindness. 59	Und/ < 2yr
5. Cataracts: Vary by breed & age of onset. As a generality, any lens opacity that obscures vision & may cause blindness is considered a cataract. A. Congenital Cataracts R/ Birth 6,35,60,97,99,118,151,209,222,301,303	
Early Onset & Progressive Cataracts	R Und/ < 3yr
B. R – 2,138,145,241,281 C. D – Und/ < 3yr D – 83	
Posterior Polar Suture Line Cataracts	D Polygenic/ <3yr
D. Polygenic D/ <3yr – 87,151,194,196 E. Polygenic R –268	
Cataracts with Variable Onset & Apperarance	R Und/ Varies
F. R – 99	

	Mode of Inheritance *Age at Onset*
G. Und – 60,216	
H. Und Cataracts Not Further Defined 1,4,6,11,16,23,25,26,29,33,35,36,38, 41,42,43,47,48,50,55,57,58,59,61,62,70,71,71,73,76,81,83,97,100,102,104,106, 109,117,118,121,122,124,134,139,141,146,148,149,152,158,159,162,168,170,174, 176,177,178,181,187,188,192,195,199,200,214,208,209,213,215,218,219,220, 226,227,240,241,247,248251,252,254,255,256,259,260,261,262,263,265,269, 275,282,284,290,297,298,299,300,302,305,308	Und/ Varies
6. Central Progressive Retinal Atrophy (CPRA): An optical defect due to retinal pigment degeneration, resulting in secondary degeneration of the rods & cones. Central vision loss, but peripheral vision may last to old age. Some dogs may not lose vision. A. R – 70,124,151,174 B. D – 57,194 C. Und – 35,50,62,87,99,100,102,118,121,122,139,145,146,187,250,263,290,299	R D Und/ < 2yr
7. Choroidal Hypoplasia: An incomplete development of the vascular layer between the sclera & the retina in the rear of the eye. 25	Und/ < 3mo
8. Collie Eye Anomaly: Causes variable defects in the choroid, retina & optic nerve; can cause retinal detachment & blindness. A. R – 25,35,57,100,102,104,138,145,209,241,254,263 B. D – 29	R D/ < 1yr
9. Coloboma of the Eyelid: A cleft-like defect of the eyelid or iris. 25,252,254	Und/ Birth
10. Congenital Cataract & Microphthalmia: Cataracts associated with a small eye globe. 209	R/ < 2wk
11. Corneal Dystrophy: Clinically, a corneal opacity without inflammation (gray to white) that interferes with vision. Usually starts with lipid deposits in the corneal stroma. Onset varies by breed. A. R – 241,268 B. D – 99 C. X-R – 4 D. Polygenic – 83,100 E. Und – 2,8,29,33,35,36,48,57,60,62,73,92,100,102,104,121,124,125,139,140, 145, 146,151,162,174,178,179,199,206,208,209,219,226,231,247,255,256,263, 289,298,300,305,308	R D X-R Polygenic Und/ Varies
12. Corneal Erosion Syndrome (Boxer Ulcers): Lacrimation, photophobia & sudden ocular pain due to corneal ulcers commonly occur. 1,8,60,62,73,99,102, 104,106,140,151,174,181,199,227,241,247,252,256,265,298,299, 300,303	Und/ ≤ 6yr
13. Corneal Leukoma: Whitish patches that develop on the surface of the cornea. 29,60	R/ < 2yr
14. Dermoid: A small patch of skin generally on the cornea, often causing irritation. 1,33,35,49,50,58,83,99,100,102,104,105,109,117,122,134,145,151, 199,211,213,227,247,254,255,265,298,299,300,305	R? Und/ < 1yr
15. Distichiasis: Abnormal location of eyelashes on the margin of the eyelid, causing irritation. 2,4,8,11,15,17,25,29,35,38,60,62,73,75,83,87,95,98,99,100, 102,103,104,105,117,118,124,134,138,140,141,145,147,151,158,160,162,168,174, 179,181,188,194,195,199,203,209,218,220,222,227,240,241,244,247,252,254,256, 259,263,265,270,284,289,290,298,302,308	Und/ < 6mo
16. Ectopic Cilia (Aberrant Cilia): Eyelashes are abnormally placed on the conjunctiva (inner surface) of the eyelid (most often upper eyelid). 35,47,60,62,73,76,99,102,104,117,124,139,151,179,187,194,199,227,247, 263,265,289	Und/ Birth

	Mode of Inheritance/ Age at Onse
17. Ectropion: Turning out of the eyelids, causing excessive exposure of the eyeball. 4,33,35,47,48,50,54,62,72,74,75,97,98,99,102,103,105,110,117,118, 121,122,124,134,139,145,151,158,159,174,188,194,206,211,213,247,250,252, 254,268,279,306	Und/ < 6mo
18. Endothelial Dystrophy: A loss of the inner lining of the cornea, causing edema. keratitis, & decreased vision. 60,62,92,99,104,124,241,268	Und/ < 1yr
19. Enophthalmos: The eyeball is recessed into the socket (sunken eyeball). 8,100,102,109,151,158,174,194,254,298	Und/ < 1yr
20. Entropion: Turning in of the eyelids, causing the eyelashes to rub the eyeball. 4,6,8,11,15,17,29,33,35,36,38,47,48,50,54,55,61,62,74,75,76,83,87,92,95, 97,98,99,100,102,103,104,105,106,109,110,117,118,121,122,124,134,135,138, 139,140,141,145,146,148,150,151,152,158,159,174,176,177,188,192,194,199, 206,207,208,209,211,213,218,222,226,227,239,240,241,247,250,251,252,254, 255,256,263,265,268,279,281,284,289,296,297,298,299,300,301,303,306,308	Und/ < 1yr
21. Eversion of the Nictitating Membrane (Eversion of the Third Eyelid): The cartilage in the third eyelid is abnormal, causing the third eyelid to roll away from or toward the globe. A. R – 60,74,146,254 B. Und – 33,35,54,75,87,102,109,121,122,145,146,158,174,177,211,213, 251,254,298	R Und/ < 3mo
22. Exophthalmos: Clinically, the globe protrudes from the skull. This trait is normal conformationally in many brachycephalic breeds. But it may vary strikingly in the degree of protrusion. If it protrudes excessively, it may allow trauma to damage the eye. 60,102,117,138,199,227,235,247,265,275,289	Und/ < 6mo
23. Glaucoma: Increased pressure in the globe, which can be a result of various causes. Without treatment, the pressure damages the eye, causing pain & often blindness. A. Angle-Closure Glaucoma D/ < 10yr 301 B. Congenital Glaucoma Und/ Birth 33,61,99,118,149,256 C. Glaucoma Not Further Defined Und/ < 3yr 2,11,21,23,25,48,50,57,60,75,97, 102,139,145,178,195,204,215,222,254,255,261, 270,290,299,300,302,303 D. Narrow-Angle Glaucoma Und/ < 9yr 6,8,33,38,62,72,92,97,99,102,104,105, 106,118,124,137,138,140,151,158,179,194,195,203,209,218,241,262,268,292, 302,305 R	
Open-Angle Glaucoma E. R – 35 F. Und – 187,208,218,241 G. Pigmentary Glaucoma R/ < 1yr 76	R Und/ < 3yr
24. Hemeralopia: Day blindness due to progressive degeneration of the cone photo receptors. Sight returns when the dog is returned to dim lighting. 8,158,241	R/ < 1yr
25. Heterochromia Iridis (Wall Eye): Odd or different colors of the iris or a portion of the iris. 12,100,102,104,105,146,158,217,263,268,305	Und/ Birth
26. Imperforate Lacrimal Punctum (Epiphora): Failure of development of the nasolacrimal drainage system, causing tears to spill onto the face. 2,11,21,35, 38,48,60,72,95,99,102,104,118,122,145,146,151,174,203,209,227,240,241,262,263	Und/ < 1yr
27. Keratoconjunctivitis Sicca (KCS): Inadequate tear production, causing irritation of the conjunctiva & cornea. 1,8,33,35,36,38,48,54,57,60,62,74,76,83,92,97,98,99, 100,102,103,104,106,117,118,122,124,138,145,151,152,168,179,188,194,199,208, 209,224,227,240,241,247,255,256,262,263,265,290,303,305,308	Und/ < 1yr
28. Lagophthalmos: Inability to completely close the eyelids. 199,227,247,265	Und/ < 1yr

	Mode of Inheritance/ Age at Onset
29. Lens Luxation: Dislocation of the lens from its normal site behind the cornea (partial or complete). A. R – 57,290 B. D – 140,179,262 C. Und – 13,23,25,33,35,50,60,72,74,76,92,99,102,104,106,118,140,141,145, 162,174,194,195,204,207,209,215,218,219,227,241,261,268,270,281,292 299,300,302,303,305	R D Und/ < 1yr
30. Macropalpebral Fissure (Macroblepharon, Diamond Eye): Excessively large palpebral fissures, resulting in exposure of the sclera & cornea. 54,95,98,99,102, 118,122,124,145,188,199,206,211,213,227,252,254,265	Und/ Birth
31. Medial Canthal Pocket Syndrome: Clinically, chronic conjunctivitis, caused by deep orbits, slight entropion & poor drainage of tears. 2,102,109,151,152,158,159, 170,194,213,241,252,256,298	Und/ < 6mo
32. Microcornea: Abnormally small cornea. 25,100,209,222,241,254	Und/ Birth
33. Microphthalmia: An anomaly in development, causing the eyeball to be abnormally small. A. R – 209 B. Und – 6,11,25,35,38,50,59,61,83,99,100,102,104,105,109,118,121,124,145,158, 174,175,194,195,206,222,227,241,244,252,254,256,262,263,268,289,303	R Und/ Birth
34. Multifocal Retinal Dysplasia: Multiple linear or branching retinal folds. Apparent visual deficits have not resulted in affected animals. 35,99	R/ < 6mo
35. Optic Nerve Hypoplasia: Visual impairment or blindness occurs. Pupil of the affected eye may be dilated. 8,25,35,43,47,59,99,100,102,104,118,124,145,151, 159,162,174,178,187,209,215,227,235,241,254,256,263,275,289	Und/ < 3mo
36. Pannus (Superficial Stromal Keratitis): An epithelial growth over the cornea, causing a grayish haze that may obscure vision. 4,23,24,25,41,42,43,57,95,102, 104,105,121,124,145,162,199,208,227,241,247,251,265,268,275,283	Und/ ≤ 1yr
37. Persistent Hyperplastic Primary Vitreous (PHPV): A defect in the regression of the hyaloid artery, which influences the retina & interferes with vision. A. D – 109,281 B. Und – 4,15,35,61,62,83,102,145,162,174,177,194,209,241,282	D Und/ < 3mo
38. Persistent Pupillary Membranes (PPM, Mesodermal Dysgenesis): A failure of blood vessels in the anterior chamber to regress normally; there may be impaired vision or blindness. 2,8,23,25,29,33,35,54,57,59,61,62,75,83,97,99,100,102,103, 104,106,109,117,118,119,122,124,139,140,145,151,158,159,162,168,174,176,194, 195,206,209,211,213,222,231,241,244,251,252,254,255,256,259,261,262,263,265, 268,269,275,289,290,292,299,300,301,303,308	Und/ < 3mo
39. Pigmentary Keratitis: Clinically, deposition of melanin in or on the cornea; may be uni- or bilateral. 76,227,247,265,303	Und/ < 2yr
40. Primary Retinal Detachment: If unilateral, vision may be normal in the unaffected eye; if bilateral, there may be total blindness. 8,102,104,124,168,222,241,252,265	Und/ Varies
41. Progressive Retinal Atrophy (PRA): Degeneration of the retinal vision cells, which progresses to blindness. A. R – 99,100,118,124,151,152,174,175,194,209,218,241,244,290,299 B. Und – 1,2,4,6,8,11,15,16,23,24,25,26,29,33,35,36,38,39,41,42,43,47, 48,50,57,58,59,60,62,70,72,73,74,75,76,77,83,87,92,95,97,102,103,104, 105,109,121,122,134,138,139,140,145,146,149,158,159,162,168,176,177, 178,181,187,188,195,199,200,203,204,206,208,211,220,222,226,227,240, 241,247,248,250,251,252,255,256,259,261,262,263,265,268,269,275,281, 289,297,298,300,301,302,303,305,308	R Und/ Varies

		Mode of Inheritance/ Age at Onset
42.	Prolapse of the Gland of the Third Eyelid (Cherry Eye): Clinically, the gland protrudes into the medial canthus of the eye. This tissue becomes swollen & reddened, resulting in the term cherry eye. 33,35,48,54,60,62,74,92,95,99,102, 117,118,122,199,211,227,241,252, 254,265,289	Und/ < 1yr
43.	Protrusion of the Third Eyelid(s): The third eyelid extends over the globe with no obvious pathology. It may or may not interfere with vision. 25,109,158,209	Und/ < 3mo
44.	Retinal Dysplasia (Folds): Abnormal folds in the retina due to faulty development. A. R – 38,59,124,194,262,268 B. Und – 16,25,26,35,57,58,75,76,83,87,99,100,102,109,117,118,125,134,145,148, 149,151,152,158,162,170,194,203,206,209,218,222,231,248,252,255,256,263, 282,284,299,300,301,303,308	R Und/ < 1yr
45.	Retinal Dysplasia (Geographic Detachment): Large areas of abnormal development of the retina may occur, along with detachment of the retina, causing blindness. 2,4,6,25,35,36,38,57,83,87,99,102,109,124,134,145,151,177, 194,222,231,241,252,255,256,262,289,290,299,300,308	R/ < 1yr
46.	Retinopathy: An early onset of partial loss of vision in dim & bright light. The disease appears to be progressive. 42	R/ < 12wk
47.	Stationary Night Blindness: Inability to see in the dark, with residual sight in bright light. The dog's eyes will rapidly move back & forth (nystagmus). 70,194,241,290	R/ < 6mo
48.	Divergent Strabismus (Exotropia): An outward turning of the eyes (the opposite of cross-eye). 60,146,227	Und/ Birth
49.	Tapetal Hypoplasia: Tapetal cells are disarrayed, resulting in an absence of the normal tapetal reflex. 35	R/ Birth
50.	Trichiasis: Abnormal placement of the eyelashes on the eyelid. 60,62,92,99, 100,102,104,117,140,188,199,203,226,227,240,241,247,263,265,292	Und/ < 3mo
51.	Trichomegaly: Abnormally long eyelashes. 99,102,199,241,265	Und/ Birth
52.	Uveodermatologic Syndrome (UDS, Vogt-Koyanagi-Harada Syndrome, VKH): Loss of pigment around the eyes, nose, pads (vitiligo) & hair (poliosis), with ocular pain due to uveitis. 6,25,29,47,97,104,145,151,174,222,254,256,263,264,268	Und/ < 3yr
53.	Vitreoretinal Dysplasia: Blindness resulting from failure of the retina to attach. 38	R/ Birth

REPRODUCTIVE DISEASES (RP)

1.	Anasarca: A subcutaneous collection of fluid, usually over the whole puppy. The pup may be 4–5 times normal size at birth. 42,43,60,76,102,117,145,158,222, 241,308	R/ Birth
2.	Cryptorchidism: An absence of testicles due to retention in the abdomen or inguinal region; can be one- or both- sided, or may slide in & out of the scrotum. 1,4,8,11,12,15,16,25,26,29,33,35,36,47,48,50,54,55,57,58,60,62,72,76,77,83,92, 99,102,104,117,118,138,140,141,145,146,149,151,158,159,162,169,170,175,178, 181,188,192,194,195,198,203,209,213,220,222,224,226,227,240,241,247,252,255, 256,260,261,263,268,269,290,298,300,301,302,303,305,308	R Und/ < 3mo
3.	Dystocia: The bitch has great difficulty in whelping puppies, due to a variety of reasons. 104,117,261	Und/ Giving Birth
4.	Hermaphrodite: (True) presence of gonadal tissue for both sexes, due to the presence of a full complement of both male & female chromosomes. 11,16,35, 99,188,247,298	XX-XXY/ < 3mo
5.	Hypospadia: The penis & sheath develop abnormally. 35,60,102,140,241,265	Und/ < 3mo

		Mode of Inheritance/ Age at Onset
6.	Immature Gonadocism: Clinically, a failure of males to show interest in a bitch or failure to exhibit leg-lifting behavior. There is hypoplasia of external genitalia. Hair loss occurs early in life. 2,241,308	Und/ < 2yr
7.	Os Penis Deformity: The bone forming the os penis is twisted, leading to difficult urination & copulation. 102,151	Und/ < 6mo
8.	Persistent Penile Frenulum (Prepuce Anomaly): The prepuce & the penis fail to separate at puberty. 99,102,151,227,241	Und/ < 10wk
9.	Preputial Stenosis (Phimosis): The preputial opening is too small to allow the penis to protrude. 145,151,194	Und/ < 10wk
10.	Pseudohermaphrodite (Male, Female): The male has male organs with some female characteristics, & the female has female organs with some male characteristics. 35,99,109,118,145,146,188,209,241,247	XX-XXY/ Birth
11.	Testicular Hypoplasia: The testicles are smaller than normally expected for the breed. 102,166	Und/ < 10wk
12.	Triple XXX Syndrome (Female): The presence of an extra X-chromosome, producing the so-called "super female." 4	XXX/ Birth
13.	Vaginal Prolapse: Clinically, complete or partial extrusion of the vaginal tissue through the vulvar labia. This tissue appears to be doughnut-shaped in most cases. 60,62,102,135,279	Und/ < 2yr
14.	XO Syndrome (Turner's Syndrome): Affected dogs have a normal female phenotype but do not cycle. 109	XO/ ≤2yr

RESPIRATORY DISEASES (RS)

1.	Bronchial Cartilage Hypoplasia (Bronchial Collapse): Severe respiratory distress as a result of blockage of the airways due to collapsed bronchi. 97,227	Und/ < 6mo
2.	Congenital Diaphragmatic Hernia: Clinically, severe respiratory dyspnea due to abdominal organs in the thoracic cavity. Puppies are extremely weak, cyanotic & gasping for air. Death ensues soon after. 11,12,35,102,138,151,189,194	R/ < 4wk
3.	Laryngeal Hypoplasia: Failure of the larynx (voice box) to develop, causing breathing difficulties. 74,269,270	R/ < 1yr
4.	Laryngeal Paralysis: Predominate signs include noisy (stridor), difficult (dyspnea) breathing & a blue tint to the lips & mouth due to lack of oxygen. 2,4,11,50,55, 61,74,87,102,105,117,118,124,151,174,194,198,236,252,254,268,275	D/ < 1yr
5.	Lung Lobe Torsion (LLT): Torsion or twisting of the accessory lung lobe, which generally presents with lethargy, dyspnea, anorexia & coughing. These signs develop acutely. 2,33,59,259	Und/ < 4yr
6.	Primary Ciliary Dyskinesia (Immotile Cilia Syndrome): Leads to a chronic nasal discharge, cough & recurrent bronchopneumonia. 48,57,92,95,97,105,109,121, 122,124, 151,218,223,222,241,252	R/ < 12wk
7.	Stenotic Nares: Smaller than normal nostrils, causing difficult breathing. 60,95, 102,117,141,227,247	Und/ < 3mo
8.	Tracheal Collapse: Improper formation of the cartilaginous rings of the trachea, causing mild to severe breathing problems. 1,11,35,92,117,138,203,209,240,241, 269,270,275,308	Und/ < 1yr
9.	Tracheal Hypoplasia: A small trachea due to improper development causes mild to severe breathing difficulties. 60,62,102,117,207,227	Und/ < 3mo

SKELETAL DISEASES (SK)

		Mode of Inheritance/ Age at Onset
1.	Anury: Lack of or very short tail. 76,99,102,109,117,211,252,259	R/ < 3mo
2.	Akita Arthritis: Marked stiffening of the joints with arthritic signs. Anorexia & pyrexia may occur. Prognosis is poor. 6	Und/ < 1yr
3.	Australian Shepherd Lethal Skeletal Defect Syndrome: Clinically, cleft-palate, polygenicgenicdactyly, brachygnathism & scoliosis. 25	Und/ < 3mo
4.	Basset Hound Cervical Deformity: An abnormality of the third cervical vertebrae, resulting in paralysis. 33	Und/ < 6mo
5.	Bone Cysts: Clinically, animals may have no signs or a history of swelling, lameness, pain & joint stiffness. Pathological fractures are common. Radiographs of the affected limb reveal the cysts. 102,109,145,151,194,222	Und/ < 1yr
6.	Brachury: A tail that is shorter than what is considered normal for the breed. 35,58, 75,97,99,118,141,174,195,234,248,259,300	R/ < 6mo
7.	Calcinosis Circumscripta: Abnormal deposits of calcium in the skin & subcutaneaous tissue. 2,6,29,35,47,54,59,62,72,74,87,99,100,102,109,121,124,140,145, 148,151,158,162,174,177,194,215-219,241,251,252,254,256,262,263,268,297,298	Und/ < 1yr
8.	Carpal Flexion Syndrome: Affected dogs have a flexed carpal position when standing. Paws tend to turn inward. When the puppies walk, they tend to walk on the outside aspect of the digits & forepaws. 95,109	Und/ < 16wk
9.	Cleft Lip/Cleft Palate: A fissure or cleft in the roof of the mouth & upper lip; may be present together or separately. This allows food &/or fluid to enter the nasal respiratory pathway. A. Polygenic – 303 B. Und – 1,14,15,16,25,26,33,35,36,47,48,60,61,62,73,74,75,76,83,92,99,102,104, 117,121,125,138,140,141,145,149,151,159,174,178,194,203,204,206,208,209, 218,220,226,227,241,247,252,256,259,261,263,265,269,281,299	Polygenic Und/ Birth
10.	Craniomandibular Osteopathy (CMO): Abnormal growth of bone involving the lower jaw, the back angle of the lower jaw, the head or the extremities. Any or all sites may be affected. 15,57,58,60,62,74,75,76,81,102,106,109,117,122,145,148,151,158, 174,188,194,206,250,261,263,270,275,281,297,298,303	R/ < 6mo
11.	Cranioschisis: A midline opening in the head through which the meninges may protrude. 99,117	R/ Birth
12.	Crooked Tails: Abnormal bend or crook in the tail. 47,48,76,102,146,158, 158,213,261,270,308	Und/ < 3mo
13.	Dwarfism (Osteochondrodysplasia, Chondrodysplasia, Achondrodysplasia, Pseudoachondroplasia, Primary Metabolic Skeletal Abnormality, Enchondrodystrophy): The skeletal dysplasias are a varied group of inherited disorders that are not well-defined. When breeds are compared, it is difficult to determine which diseases have the same etiology & which are different, although it is possible with some of them. In this listing, breeds are individually categorized & grouped only where there is direct information that they are the same or when there is a lack of information that would allow us to categorize them. Dwarfish is defined here as a disorder that reduces the size of a dog below that which is reasonably established as expected for a given breed. It may or may not include physical deformities, & they may be proportionate or disproportionate. A. Alaskan Malamute Dwarfism R/ < 7wk 8 B. Australian Shepherd Dwarfism X-R Birth 25 C. Beagle Dwarfism (Multiple Epiphyseal Dysplasia) R/ < 3wk 35 D. Cocker Spaniel Dwarfism R/ < 4wk 99 E. Dachshund Dwarfism Und/ < 4wk 104 F. English Pointer Dwarfism R/ < 3mo 121	

		Mode of Inheritance/ Age at Onset
	G. French Bulldog Dwarfism Und/ < 4wk 141	
	H. Giant Schnauzer Congenital Hypothyroid Dwarfism R/ < 2wk 149	
	I. Great Pyrenees Dwarfism R/ < 4wk 159	
	J. Labrador Retriever Dwarfism Und/ < 4wk 194	
	K. Miniature Poodle Dwarfism R/ < 4wk 241	
	L. Norwegian Elkhound Dwarfism R/ < 4wk 218	
	M. Ocular & Skeletal Dysplasia of Labrador Retrievers: Since both the ocular Rlesion & skeletal lesion have been reported independently in this breed, it is possible that these 2 traits are not linked but are 2 separate traits that happen to occur in the same animal. 194	R – Skeletal/ < 2mo D – Ocular/ < 2mo
	N. Pituitary Dwarfism (Cystic Rathke's Cleft)R< 3mo 4,79,138,145,149,186,208,298	
	O. Samoyed Dwarfism R/ < 4wk 256	
	P. Scottish Deerhound Congenital Hypothyroid Dwarfism R/ < 2wk 260	
	Q. Scottish Deerhound Pseudoachondroplasia R/ < 4wk 260	
	R. Weimaraner Immunodeficient Dwarfism Und/ < 4wk 298	
	S. Not Further Defined Und/ < 6mo 16,25,29,60,62,93,100,102,151,181,227, 261, 263,265	
14.	Ectromelia: Absence of one or more limbs at birth. 121	R/ Birth
15.	Elbow Joint Deformity: Abnormal development of the elbow causes front limb lameness. 2,106	Und/ < 3mo
16.	Epiphyseal Dysplasia (Stippled Epiphysis): Clinically, a swaying hind-limb gate, poor growth & sagging hocks. Lameness may occur at various intervals. 35,241	Und/ ≤ 3mo
17.	Foramen Magnum Dysplasia: Abnormal formation of the bone that attaches to the vertebral column; may put pressure on the brain stem & can cause hydrocephalus. 92,99,102,269,270	Und/ < 1yr
18.	Fused Teeth: What are generally considered to be 2 separate teeth are fused together by enamel. 195	Und/ < 5mo
19.	Hemivertebra: Abnormal formation of the body of the vertebrae, which can cause posterior ataxia & paralysis. Causes twisted tail in the screw-tailed breeds. A. R – 146 B. Und – 8,11,33,58,60,102,104,109,117,141,145,174,181,213,227,240,247, 251,252, 290,303,308	R Und/ < 1yr
20.	Hip Dysplasia: Abnormal formation of the hip socket; causes rear-limb lameness. 1,2,4,5,6,8,10,11,12,14,15,16,17,21,23, 24,25,26,29,33,35,36,37,38,40, 41,42,43,47,48,50,54,55,57,58,59,60,61,62,63,65,66,70,72,73,74,75,76,77,79,81 83,84,87,95,96,97,98,99,100,102,103,104,105,106,109,110,117,118,120,121,122, 123,124,125,126,134,135,137,138,139,140,141,142,143,145,146,148,149,150,151, 152,158,159,160,162,167,169,170,173,174,176,177,179,181,186,187,188,189,192, 194,195,198,199,203,204,205,206,208,209,211,213,215,219,216,218,220,222,224, 225,227,231,235,239,241,244,245,246,247,248,250,251,252,254,255,256,257,259, 260,261,263,264,265,266,268,269,270,272,275,279,281,282,284,286,288,289,290, 291,296,297,298,299,300,301,302,303,305,306,308	Polygenic/ < 2yr
21.	Hypertrophic Osteodystrophy: There is a variable presentation, from mild to severe lameness. There may be depression, fever, dehydration & anorexia. 5,33,47,59,62,100,102,105,109,121,139,145,146,151,152,158,162,174,177, 192,194,213,252,254,298	Und/ < 8mo
22.	Infantile Cortical Hyperostosis: Generalized joint pain, resulting from periosteal new bone growth involving the long bones, pelvis & scapula. 303	Und/ < 1yr
23.	Intervertebral Disc Disease (IDD): Dorsal rupture of the discs between the vertebral bodies; causes back pain, rear-end ataxia & paralysis. 2,4,8,11, 16,33,35,38,47,48,62,92,98,99,102,104,106,124,141,145,195,199,208,226, 227,240,241,261,262,265,269,284,290,299,300,308	Und/ > 1yr

	Mode of Inheritance/ Age at Onset
24. Lateral Torsion of the Hind Feet: Clinically, the anterior surface of the foot is directed to the side to varying degrees. It produces no clinical problem, except as a show fault. 47,158,252,254,279	Und/ < 1yr
25. Legg-Perthes: Aseptic necrosis of the head & neck of the femur, causes rear-leg lameness. 1,26,48,58,60,76,92,99,104,140,179,195,200,204,208, 209,227,240,241,247,259, 261,263,269,302,303,308	Polygenic/ < 1yr
26. Lumbosacral Malarticulation: Rear-leg gait abnormalities; lower urinary tract, tail & anus may have neurologic deficits. Pain may occur. 145	Und/ < 1yr
27. Lumbosacral Stenosis (Spinal Stenosis): Clinically, palpation of the lumboscaral area causes pain. There may be pelvic lameness, tail paresis & fecal & urinary incontinence. 35,99,102,109,145,151,194,199,241	Und/ Birth
28. Luxation of the Atlantoaxial Joint: A result of a dislocation or separation of the spinal column at the joint between the atlas & the axis. 26,33,48,75, 83,92,102,109,145,181,209,227,240,241,252,259,265,269,292,298,308,184	Und/ < 1yr
29. Luxation of the Carpus: A dislocation of the carporadial joint that is bilateral. Affecteds limp or tend to walk on their knees. 174,194	X-R/ < 6mo
30. Luxation of the Elbow: Clinically, the ulna rotates laterally & the antebrachium rotates internally. The radiohumeral joint is relatively unaffected & the ulna remains in a nearly normal position; or the radial head is displaced caudolaterally & the ulna remains in a nearly normal position. 2,17,33,48,60,92,97,99,100,102,104, 106,117,181,184,208,213,227,240,241,247,263,308	Und/ < 6mo
31. Luxation of the Patella: Poor development of the structures holding the kneecap in place. The patella usually rotates medially (inward) in small breeds.1,2,6,8, 11,1314,16,23,25,26,33,35,36,47,48,50,58,60,62,63,72,73,76,83,87,92,95,97, 99,100,102,104,106,109,117,118,122,125,138,139,140,141,146,151,159,163, 168,178,179,181,184,187,188,193,194,199,200,203,204,205,209,213,215, 218,219,220,226,227,231,236,240,241,247,252,254,256,261,263,264,265,268, 269,275,281,289,290,298,299,300,302, 303,308	Polygenic/ < 1yr
32. Luxation of the Shoulder: Shoulder slips out of place, usually medially (toward the body). 73,83,92,102,106,140,194,208,236,240,241	Und/ < 1yr
33. Luxation of the Superficial Digital Flexor Tendon: Clinically, a rear-leg lameness of varying severity. Affected legs may be carried periodically. There is distention of the calcanean bursa, which can be readily palpated. 100,151,263	Und/ < 5yr
34. Luxation of the Tarsal, Metatarsal, & Intertarsal Joints (Luxation of the Hock): A separation of the various bones making up the hock joint. 55,100,102,109,145, 151,263	Und/ < 10yr
35. Missing Teeth: One or more teeth are absent in breeds with normal dentition. In brachycephalic breeds, dentition is most often imperfect. A. R – 109 B. Und – 36,48,59,72,76,92,93,98,102,145,146,151,170,179,189,194,196,199, 203,204,209,241,247,248,252,256,261,264,270,275,290,307	R Und/ < 5mo
36. Multiple Cartilaginous Exostoses (Enchondromatosis): Clinically, most often, this disease is silent. It may produce pain on occasion if pressure is put on the protuberances. There may be lameness intermittently. Bony nodules can be felt on the ends of the long bones or ribs, but they may be found anywhere on the body. 8,57,62,102,145,154,158,174,194,227,263,308	Und/ < 18mo
37. Occipital Dysplasia: A defect of the foramen magnum. There is incomplete formation of the occipital bone. Clinical signs as a result of this disease may be minimal. 35,92,199,203,227,240,241,265,308	Und/ > 3mo
38. Odontoid Process Dysplasia: Abnormal connection or articulation between the first & second neck vertebrae causes pain & may progress to paralysis. 92,102, 227,240,241,254,269,308	Und/ < 1yr

	Mode of Inheritance/ Age at Onset
39. Oligodontia: Absence of most if not all teeth. 1,140	R/ < 6mo
40. Open Cranial Fontanelle (Patent Molera): The foramen on the dorsum of the skull may remain open, closing weeks later than expected for a given breed. The foramen in some animals may not close at all. There are no clinical signs associated with this trait unless trauma is involved. 29,48,92,102,117,125,203,240,265,303	Und/ Birth
41. Osteochondritis Dissecans (OCD): Aseptic necrosis of bone under joint cartilage; causes lameness.	
Elbow Joint (Elbow Dysplasia): OCD of the medial humeral condyle, fractured coronoid process & nonfusion of the anconeal process. A. FCP – OCD Polygenic/ ≤ 1yr 2,4,6,8,15,20,23,25,36,40,41,42,43,47,48,57, 59,61,63,72,74,76,77,82,87,95,97,102,109,115,117,122,124,126,135,139, 145,148,149,151,152,158,160,176,187,189,192,194,198,211,213,222,224, 231,234,239,247,251,252,254,256,260,261,263,264,269,279,281,288,297, 300,63 B. Nonfusion of the Anconeus Und/ ≤ 1yr 2,33,54,75,99,102,104,121,141,145, 158,159,174,177,188,192,194,195,206,213,222,252,254,298 C. Hock Joint Und/ ≤ 1yr 23,74,105,151,174,194,206,241,252 D. Shoulder Joint Und/ ≤ 1yr 2,6,8,47,57,62,72,74,81,87,92,95,99,102,104,105, 109,117,121,122,124,145,146,148,151,158,159,160,162,174,177,187,194, 198,203,206,213,222,227,241,247,251,252,254,256,261,263,264,297,300,305 E. Stifle Joint Und/ ≤ 1yr 6,57,59,62,74,97,100,102,109,121,145,158,162,177, 194,206,241,249,252,254,256, 281 F. Tarsocrural Joint Und/ ≤ 1yr 23,74,87,151,174,194,251,252	Und/ < 1yr
42. Osteochondrosis of the Spine: A shortening of the vertebral body & deformity of the end plate. There may be bony erosion of the end plate, resulting in neurological abnormalities & pain. 12,140	Und/ < 2yr
43. Osteogenesis Imperfecta: Abnormal development of bones, particularly of the limbs. 4,38,218,241	Und/ < 1yr
44. Otocephalic Syndrome: Clinically, there is abnormal formation of the head, which includes hydrocephaly, parietal fontanelle & a shortened lower jaw. 35,104	R/ < 1yr
45. Overshot: Upper jaw extends beyond the lower jaw. A. R – 146 B. Und – 36,48,118,120,122,140,145,149,151,158,159,170,174,178,187,192, 195,199,203,209,213,215,218,219,224,227,241,247,252,255,261,262,269, 270,275,282,289,290,300,305	R Und/ < 1yr
46. Panosteitis (Enostosis, Eosinophilic Panosteitis): Usually, sudden onset of a mild, shifting lameness. Fever, anorexia & lethargy may be present. The disease may be serious enough that the animal may not bear weight on the affected limb. This disease is self-limiting. 4,5,8,25,33,35,36,47,76,81,102,109,121,145,146,151,158, 159,160,174,192,194,209,252, 254,256,261	Und/ < 18mo
47. Polygenicostotic Fibrous Dysplasia: Clinically, swelling & lameness in the forelegs. Cyst formation in the long bones & osteolysis in the ulna. 109	Und/ < 1yr
48. Premature Closure of the Tibia: A lateral angulation of the tarsometatarsus & tibial bowing that may be uni- or bilateral. 100,263	Und/ < 1yr
49. Premature Closure of the Ulna: Ulna stops growing sooner than the radius; causes wrists to turn in & front feet to turn out. 2,33,62,83,92,102,109,140,145,158,174, 177,213,222,247,252,254,260,263,270	R/ < 1yr
50. Premature Closure of the Radius (Radial Dysgenesis): Radius stops growing sooner than the ulna, causing bowed front legs. 33,57,62,102,140,145,194,211, 241,254,256,263,270,290,299,305	Und/ < 1yr
51. Retained Deciduous Teeth: One or more deciduous or puppy teeth fail to fall out to allow the permanent teeth to erupt normally. 1,8,290	Und/ < 1yr

		Mode of Inheritance/ Age at Onset
52.	Retrognathia of the Mandible (Pig Jaw): Clinically, a condition in which the maxilla develops normally & the mandible fails to grow to normal length. The mandible may end up being 1/4 its normal length. 99	Polygenic/ < 3mo
53.	Sacrocaudal Agenesis: Urinary & fecal incontinence, occasionally, a weakness of caudal limbs, absence of a tail & sacral vertebrae are all symptoms. 60,117,222	Und/ Birth
54.	Sesamoid Disease: Clinically, lameness in the early stages of the disease that can involve the forelimbs or hindlimbs. In the chronic stages, lameness may be mild or absent & crepitation may occur on manipulation. 62,100,162,194,252,254	Und/ < 12mo
55.	Short Skull: Skull is shorter than expected for the breed. 73,117,141,227	Und/ < Birth
56.	Short Spine: The spinal column, as a whole, is shorter than it should be, leading to a baboon-like appearance. 162,264	R/ < 6mo
57.	Short Toe Anomaly: Affecteds have short or missing toes; one or more toes may be affected.118	Und/ Birth
58.	Spina Bifida: Clinical signs may include rear-limb weakness, urinary & fecal incontinence & perineal analgesia. There may be missing skin, muscle & dorsal spinal processes generally in the lumbosacral area. 4,35,60,62,92,100, 102,105,109,117,141,145,146,162,209,227,241,256,268,298	Und/ Birth
59.	Spondylosis Deformans: Abnormal fusion or bridging between vertebrae; may cause pain &/or paralysis. 4,54,62,99,102,104,139,141,145,159,174,194,241,251	Polygenic/ > 1yr
60.	Teeth (Extra Incisors): Typically, four incisors are present in the affected half of the jaw instead of three, which is normal for dogs. 62,75,117,170,280	Und/ 15wk
61.	Temporomandibular Joint Dysplasia: The coronoid process of the mandible is locked outside of the zygoma. It is difficult for the dog to close its mouth. There may be a spontaneous correction of this locking process. 30,102,174	Und/ < 2yr
62.	Temporal Mandibular Dysplasia: Malformation of the joint between the mandible & the temporal bone of the skull. May be bi- or unilateral. 33,99,174	Und/ < 4mo
63.	Transitional Vertebral Segments (Lumbosacral): Clinical signs associated with this disorder relate to damage to the cauda equina & include paresis, paralysis, denervation atrophy & atonia. 145,159,194,251,254	Polygenic/ Varies
64.	Undershot: Lower jaw extends beyond upper jaw. 4,36,43,48,57,58,60,61,62,72, 76,83,87,92,93,95,98,99,100,102,104,105,109,118,120,121,122,125,140,145,146, 149,151,158,159,160,167,170,174,176,178,179,187,189,192,195,199,203,209,213, 215,218,219,224,241,247,252,255,259,261,262,270,275,282,284,290,300,301,305	Polygenic/ < 1yr
65.	Wobbler Syndrome (Cervical Spondylolisthesis, Vertebral Instability): Abnormality of the neck vertebrae, causing rear-leg ataxia that may progress to paralysis. The main vertebrae affected are 5, 6 & 7. A. R – 59,109,158 B. Polygenic – 2,4,15,33,35,60,62,75,97,99,102,104,105,140,145,151,158, 159,174,177, 194,213,222,227,241,251,252,254,256,298,300	Polygenic/ ≤ 1yr

URINARY SYSTEM DISEASES (UR)

1.	Cystinuria (Renal Tubular Transport Defect): Excessive amounts of the amino acid cystine are excreted in the urine, which may cause urinary calculi or stones. A. R – 213,261 B. X-R – 10,33,62,76,92,102,104,117,137,145,158,174,175,194,196,241,252, 299,300, 308	R X-R/ < 1yr

		Mode of Inheritance/ Age at Onset
2.	Ectopic Ureters: The ureters do not properly attach to the bladder, causing urine dribbling, usually from birth. 35,38,57,61,70,76,100,102,105,117,124,140,151, 157,167,174,177,179,194,195,199,213,222,241,254,261,263,268,270,275,299, 300,303,308	Und/ Birth
3.	Familial Kidney Disease (Type Undetermined): Clinical signs are not distinctive but are typical of uremia & renal failure. 8,38,187,209,244	Und/ < 8mo
4.	Familial Renal Disease of Norwegian Elkhounds: Symptoms of chronic renal failure occur without other distinguishing characteristics. Dwarfing may occur in some cases. 218	Und/ < 6mo
5.	Fanconi's Syndrome: Polygenicdipsia & polygenicgenicuria, muscle & joint pain & marked proteinuria. 2,29,102,194,209,218,263,282,308	Und/ < 6mo
6.	Hereditary Renal Cystadenocarcinomas & Nodular Dermatofibrosis (Multiple Fibrous Nodular Dermatofibrosis): Malignant tumors in the kidney with nodules in the skin. Loss of appetite, weakness, weight loss, vomiting with numerous firm skin nodules & renal carcinomas at autopsy. 145	D/ < 11yr
7.	Hypospadias: Urinary incontinence & secondary bacterial infections are common. 60,72,102,145,241	Und/ Birth
8.	Polygeniccystic Kidneys (Cystic Livers): Cysts occur in the kidneys & liver, causing malfunction & death. 76	Und/ < 6mo
9.	Polygeniccystic Kidney (Normal Livers): Large cysts occur only in the kidney, causing malfunction & death. A. R – 35 B. D – 74 C. Und – 4,263	R D Und/ < 1yr
10.	Primary Glomerulopathies: Signs are those of chronic renal failure & uremia, & they vary somewhat by breed. Onset may be insidious. Lethargy, halitosis, oral ulcers, weight loss, polygenicgenicdipsia, polygenicgenicuria & reduced appetite may be noted. Vomiting & hyperproteinuria may be present. A. Bernese Mountain Dog Familial Glomerulonephropathy R/ < 7yr 47 B. Bull Terrier Hereditary Glomerulonephropathy Und/ < 5yr D – 74 Und – 207 C. Cavalier King Charles Spaniel Glomerulonephropathy Und/ < 1yr 83 D. English Cocker Spaniel Glomerulonephropathy R/ < 2yr 118 E. Doberman Pinscher Glomerulonephropathy Und/ < 6yr 109 F. Newfoundland Glomerulonephropathy Und/ < 2yr 213 G. Rottweiler Atrophic Glomerulopathy Und/ < 1yr 252 H. Samoyed Hereditary Glomerulopathy X-R/ < 9mo 256 I. Soft-Coated Wheaten Terrier Glomerulonephropathy Und/ < 3yr 275 J. Weimaraner Glomerulonephropathy Und/ < 2yr 298	
11.	Primary Renal Glucosuria: The dogs are clinically asymptomatic but have a persistent glucosuria in the absence of concurrent hyperglycemia. 29,102, 218,261	Und/ < 1yr
12.	Renal Aplasia (Renal Agenesis): Unilateral or bilateral absence of the kidney or renal tissue, leading to uremia & death if bilateral. 35,70,102,109,227,263	Und/ < 1yr
13.	Renal Dysplasia: Failure of normal development of the renal parenchyma, causing malfunction & death. Clinical signs are those of renal failure. A. R – 99,199,227,265 B. Und – 4,6,8,17,35,38,62,70,97,100,102,104,117,145,151,158,159,177,187, 194,205,209,222,241,251,275,308	R Und/ < 1yr
14.	Renal Ectopia: Improperly located kidneys at birth. 102	Und/ Birth
15.	Renal Telangiectasia: Clinical signs are hematuria &, on occasion, renal pain. Severe anemia may occur, resulting in death. 300	Und/ < 7yr

	Mode of Inheritance/ Age at Onset
16. Systemic Reactive Amyloidosis: Renal amyloid deposits lead to uremia & chronic renal failure. 2,4,35,95,138,145,296	Und/ < 6yr
17. Urethral Prolapse: Portions of the ureteral mucosa prolapse & extend beyond the tip of the penis. 60,117	Und/ < 1yr
18. Urethrorectal Fistulas: Urine is simultaneously passed from the anus & the penis or vulva during micturition. 117	Und/ Birth
19. Uric Acid Excretion (Hyperuricuria): Usually, a clinically silent disease, except for stone formation from elevated uric acid in the urine. 105,145	R/ < 3mo
20. Urinary Bladder Agenesis: Congenital absence of the urinary bladder. absence of the urinary bladder. 102	Und/ Birth
21. Urinary Bladder Anomalies: Lifelong urinary incontinence caused by hypoplasia or other defects of the bladder. 102,109,117	Und/ Birth
22. Uroliths: Collection of calculi (kidney or bladder stones) in any part of the urinary system. The stones may be composed of varying minerals. Breeds are listed by the major mineral component that accumulates in the stone. A. Calcium Oxalate Und/ < 9yr 199,209,265 B. Cystine See Cystinuria Und/ < 9yr C. Struvite Und/ < 9yr 48,62,97,99,102,104,117,145,227,241,282,308 D. Urate Und/ < 9yr 105,117	

References

ACVO. *Ocular Disorders Proven or Suspected to be Hereditary in Dogs.* W. Lafayette, Indiana: Purdue University, 1992.

Anderson, N. V. *Veterinary Gastroenterology,* 2nd ed. Philadelphia: Lea and Febiger, 1992.

Bojrab, M. J. *Current Techniques in Small Animal Surgery,* 3rd ed. Philadelphia: Lea and Febiger, 1990.

Bonagura, J. D. *Kirk's Current Veterinary Therapy XII.* Small Animal Practice. Philadelphia: W. B. Saunders Co., 1995.

Braund, K. G. *Clinical Syndromes in Veterinary Neurology,* 2nd ed. St. Louis: Mosby-Year Book Inc., 1994.

Chandler, E. A., D. J. Thompson, J.B. Sutton, and C. J. Price. *Canine Medicine and Therapeutics,* 3rd ed. Oxford: Blackwell Scientific Publications, 1991.

Chrisman, C. L. *Problems in Small Animal Neurology,* 2nd ed. Philadelphia: Lea and Febiger, 1991.

Clark, R. D. and J.R. Stainer. *Medical and Genetic Aspects of Purebred Dogs.* Fairway, Kansas: Forum Publications Inc., 1994.

Drazner, F. H. *Small Animal Endocrinology.* New York: Churchill Livingstone, 1987.

Ettinger, S. J. and E. C. Feldman. *Textbook of Veterinary Internal Medicine,* 4th ed. 2 vols. Philadelphia: W. B. Saunders Co., 1995.

Fisher, T. M. *Genetic Counseling.* Med. Vet. Pract., 1982, 63:37–42.

Gelatt, K. N. *Veterinary Ophthalmology,* 2nd ed. Philadelphia: Lea and Febiger Co., 1991.

Grant, G. M. *A Method to Predict the Probabilities of Homozygous Recessive and of Heterozygotes.* J. Hered., 1976, 67:393–396.

Guilford, W. G., S. A. Center, D. R. Strombeck, D. A. Williams, and D. J. Meyers. *Strombeck's Small Animal Gastroenterology,* 3rd ed. Philadelphia: W.B. Saunders Co., 1996.

Harvey, C. E. and P. B. Emily. *Small Animal Dentistry.* St. Louis: Mosby-Year Book Inc., 1993.

Hoskins, J. D. *Veterinary Pediatrics: Dogs and Cats from Birth to Six Months of Age,* 2nd ed. Philadelphia: W.B. Saunders Co., 1995.

Hutt, R. B. *Genetics for Dog Breeders.* San Francisco: W. H. Freeman Co., 1979.

Johansson, I. and J. Rendel. *Genetics and Animal Breeding.* San Francisco: W.H. Freeman Co., 1968.

Leib, M. S. and W. E. Monroe. *Practical Small Animal Internal Medicine.* Philadelphia: W.B. Saunders Co., 1997.

Locke, P. H., R. G. Harvey, and I. S. Mason. *Manual of Small Animal Dermatology.* Shurdington, Cheltenham, Glaucestershire: British Small Animal Veterinary Assn., 1993.

Lorenz, M. D. and L. M. Cornelius. *Small Animal Medical Diagnosis,* 2nd ed. Philadelphia: J. B. Lippencott Co., 1993.

Martin, M. and B. Corcoran. *Cardiorespiratory Diseases of the Dog and Cat.* Oxford: Blackwell Science Ltd., 1997.

Merck and Co. Inc. *Merck Veterinary Manual, The,* 7th ed. Whitehouse Station, N.J.: Merck and Co. Inc., 1991.

Morgan, R. V. *Handbook of Small Animal Practice,* 2nd ed. Philadelphia: W. B. Saunders Co., 1992.

Murphy, E. A. and G. S. Mutalik. *The Application of Bayesian Methods in Genetic Counseling.* Hum. Hered., 1969, 19:126–151.

Nicholas, F. W. *Veterinary Genetics.* Oxford: Clarendon Press, 1987.

Oliver, J. E. and M. D. Lorenz. *Handbook of Veterinary Neurology.* Philadelphia: W. B. Saunders Co., 1993.

Osborne, C. A. and D. R. Finco. *Canine and Feline Nephrology and Urology.* Baltimore: Williams and Wilkins, 1995.

Petersen-Jones, S. M. and S. M. Crispin. *Manual of Small Animal Ophthalmology.* Shurdington, Cheltenham, Glaucestershire: British Small Animal Veterinary Assn., 1993.

Robinson, R. *Genetics for Dog Breeders.* Oxford: Pergamon Press, 1982.

Rubin, L. F. *Inherited Eye Diseases in Purebred Dogs.* Baltimore: Williams and Wilkins, 1989.

Sanders, Anne. Personal communication, 1987.

Scott, D. W., W. H. Miller, and C. E. Griffen. *Small Animal Dermatology,* 5th ed. Philadelphia: W.B. Saunders Co., 1995.

Searle, A. G. *Comparative Genetics of Coat Colour in Mammals.* London: Logos Press Ltd., 1968.

Slattor, D. *Textbook of Small Animal Surgery,* 2nd ed. 2 vols. Philadelphia: W. B. Saunders Co., 1993.

Summers, B. A., J. F. Cummings, and A. de Lahunta. *Veterinary Neuropathology.* St. Louis: Mosby-Year Book Inc., 1995.

Tams, T. R. *Handbook of Small Animal Gastroenterology.* Philadelphia: W. B. Saunders Co., 1996.

Thomson, R. G. *Special Veterinary Pathology.* Burlington, Ont.: B. C. Decker Inc., 1988.

Walkowicz, C. and B. Wilcox. *Successful Dog Breeding,* 2nd ed. New York: Howell Book House, 1994.

Warwick, B.L. *Probability Tables for Mendelian Ratios with Small Numbers.* Texas Agric. Exper. Stu. Bull., 1932.

Wheeler, S. J. *Manual of Small Animal Neurology.* Shurdington, Cheltenham, Glaucestershire: British Small Animal Veterinary Assn., 1995.

Wheeler, S. J. and N. J. H. Sharp. *Small Animal Spinal Disorders: Diagnosis and Surgery.* London: Mosby-Wolfe, 1994.

Willemse, T. *Clinical Dermatology of Dogs and Cats.* Philadelphia: Lea and Febiger, 1991.

Willis, M. B. *Genetics of the Dog.* New York: Howell Book House, 1989.

Wright, S. *The Results of Crosses Between Inbred Strains of Guinea Pigs Differing in Number of Digits.* 1934, Genetics 19:537–551.

Yager, J. A. and B. P. Wilcock. *Color Atlas and Text of Surgical Pathology of the Dog and Cat.* London: Mosby-Year Book Europe Ltd., 1994.

Index